THE ENTREPRENEUR'S GUIDE TO FINANCE AND BUSINESS

Wealth Creation Techniques for Growing a Business

Steven Rogers

Gordon and Llura Gund Family Professor of Entrepreneurship
Clinical Professor of Management and Finance
J. L. Kellogg School of Management, Northwestern University

with Roza Makonnen

Boston, Massachusetts   Burr Ridge, Illinois
Dubuque, Iowa   Madison, Wisconsin   New York, New York
San Francisco, California   St. Louis, Missouri

The **McGraw-Hill** Companies

Library of Congress Cataloging-in-Publication Data

Rogers, Steven.
  The entrepreneur's guide to finance and business / by Steven Rogers, Roza Makonnen.
    p. cm.
  ISBN 0-07-138081-7 (hardcover : alk. paper)
  1. Business enterprises—Finance. 2. Business planning. I. Makonnen, Roza.
  II. Title.
  HG4026 .R65 2002
  658.15—dc21

2002010639

5 6 7 8 9 BKM BKM   0 9 8 7 6

ISBN 0-07-138081-7

McGraw-Hill books are available at special quantity discounts to use as premiums and sales promotions, or for use in corporate training programs. For more information, please write to the Director of Special Sales, Professional Publishing, McGraw-Hill, Two Penn Plaza, New York, NY 10121-2298. Or contact your local bookstore.

This publication is designed to provide accurate and authoritative information in regard to the subject matter covered. It is sold with the understanding that neither the author nor the publisher is engaged in rendering legal, accounting, or other professional service. If legal advice or other expert assistance is required, the services of a competent professional person should be sought.
> —*From a Declaration of Principles jointly adopted by a Committee of the American Bar Association and a Committee of Publishers.*

 This book is printed on recycled, acid-free paper containing a minimum of 50 percent recycled, de-inked fiber.

CONTENTS

Chapter 4

Chapter 5

Chapter 6

Chapter 7

Chapter 8

Raising Capital   223

Chapter 9

Debt Financing   231

Chapter 10

Equity Financing   265

Chapter 11

Financing for Minorities and Women   303

Glossary   313

Appendixes

Index   335

Preface

It is morning at Opryland in Nashville, Tennessee, a place where young crooners from Charlie Pride and Johnny Cash to Garth Brooks and the Dixie Chicks have realized their dreams. Not far away is the Grand Ole Opry—country music's equivalent of the Broadway stage—and a full day of work is about to begin. But this morning, visitors have business, not music, on their minds. This is a conference for future entrepreneurs from around the country. Their schedules are packed with seminars on financing, marketing, and operations. Here is a sample: Business Start-Up Essentials, How to Find Money-Making Ideas, and Designing Products.

Of course, none of this would be particularly noteworthy except when you consider that these conventioneers are ages 7 to 10—and they are not the youngest group here. There is another set of entrepreneur seminars for kids ages 4 to 6. It's called the "Kidprenuers Konference," sponsored by *Black Enterprise* magazine and Wendy's, and this sixth annual event is a sellout. Nearby, the kids' parents, all entrepreneurs or future entrepreneurs themselves, are packed into their own seminars. If there was ever a doubt that this is the glory age of the entrepreneur, a few days with these "titans of tomorrow" should put that notion to bed.

I write this book, this story of opportunities, because I have been blessed with so many of my own. It's said that a good entrepreneur always sees sun in the clouds and a glass half full. My wife, Michele, and daughters Akilah and Ariel laugh at me when I tell them that I have gone through life always believing that when I walk through a door, the light will shine on me no matter who else is in the room. Like every good entrepreneur, I believe in myself, but I also have enough humility to know that one does not go from the welfare rolls on Chicago's Southside to owning three successful companies, sitting on the boards of three *Fortune* 500 companies (SC Johnson Wax, SuperValu, DQE), and teaching at the finest business school in America without a healthy supply of luck—and a handful of caring people.

The first entrepreneur I ever met was a woman named Ollie Mae Rogers—the oldest daughter in a family of 10 kids, and the only one among them who never graduated high school, let alone college. Fiercely independent, she left home at the age of 17 and got married. The marriage, I believe, was simply an excuse to leave home. Leaving home meant she got her independence, and if she was nothing else, my mother, Ollie Mae, was a fireball of independence. When my older brother, my two sisters, and I buried her this past year, the eulogy fell to me. I described my mother as a renaissance woman filled with paradoxes. She was a tough and gutsy woman whose extensive vocabulary flowed eloquently although she barely finished the tenth grade.

I like to think of my mother as an eccentric "mom and pop" entrepreneur. Growing up, we were like the old *Sanford and Son* television series—selling used furniture at the weekend flea markets on Maxwell Street on Chicago's Southside. Nearly every Saturday and Sunday morning, my older brother, John, and I were up at 4 a.m. loading my mother's beat-up jalopy of a station wagon until we could fit no more "merchandise" on the seats, in the trunk, and on the roof. When I talk to prospective entrepreneurs, I tell them go sell something at a flea market. You need to really live, breathe, and feel the rejection of hustling for "sells." When I think back on it now, I realize that my mother just loved the art of the deal, and this among other things became part of my being. It was common for my mother to leave our space at the market and go shopping, leaving the operations to my brother and me—the savvy and sophisticated 5-year-old business maverick. That is how I learned to sell, negotiate, and schmooze a customer. I started my first little business venture in that very same market: a shoeshine stand. People would stroll by, and I'd lure them in with the oh-so-memorable pitch line: "Shine your shoes, comb your hair, and make you feel like a millionaire."

As far back as I can remember, I always held a job. When we weren't working the flea markets, my brother and I found other jobs: From helping the local milkman make his deliveries to working as a stock boy at the neighborhood grocery store, we did what we needed to do. By the time I reached high school, I was plucked out of the Chicago public schools by a nonprofit organization called A Better Chance—a private national program that identifies academically gifted minority kids from low-income communities and sends them to schools where their potential can be realized. I was sent to Radnor High School in Wayne, Pennsylvania. I played on the football team, and when the season was over, I worked as a janitor's assistant to help send some money home to my mother.

My mother started running a small used-furniture storefront, and when I came home for the summer breaks, she stopped working and turned the operation over to me. So by the age of 15, I had to manage a few employees, open and close the business, negotiate with our customers, and run the daily operations. My mother, unbeknownst to her, was nurturing a budding entrepreneur. She truly is the reason that my brother, my sisters, and I have all gravitated to leadership positions in our professional lives. My brother is a supervisor of probation officers, my older sister, Deniece, owns her own delivery business, and my youngest sister, Laura, is manager of a McDonald's restaurant.

I went on to attend Williams College, where, for the first time, the money I made was all mine. It's where I met my future wife, Michele, and between the two of us, we must have had every job on the darn campus. Williams is a liberal arts school, and at the time there were no finance courses or any other business classes to be found on campus. I majored in history. During my senior year at Williams, I took an accounting class at nearby North Adams State College. After graduating from Williams, I worked for Cummins Engine Company. At Cummins, I worked as a purchasing agent with a start-up venture in Rocky Mount, North Carolina, called Consolidated Diesel Company (CDC). At CDC, I was responsible for developing a new supplier organization, and it was there that I got my first taste of finance. It was a position that put me smack-dab in the middle of the expense line item—"cost of goods sold"—because I was ultimately responsible for buying several engine components. The greatest benefit of this experience was the negotiating skills that I continued to develop.

After 4 years, I left and was accepted at the Harvard Business School, where I received my first formal education in finance. That was the main reason that I attended business school: I knew that I wanted to be an entrepreneur, and I knew that if I was going to be successful, I needed to understand finance. My introductory finance class was taught by Professor Bill Sahlman. When I told him about my meager background in the subject, he told me to relax and that any novice can understand the subject with a little common sense. Though he never told me, I quickly realized that the subject was made easier by having an outstanding professor, like Sahlman, who could teach a user-friendly finance course that combined academic theory and real practices into a powerful lesson.

While at Harvard, I recognized what many entrepreneurs find out the hard way: Being a successful entrepreneur is not easy. I knew about the failure rate, and I was never really interested in starting a company from scratch. I wanted to buy an existing business. It's funny when I think back about all the jobs that I had as a kid. My older brother always had the same job first, so even back then, I was taking over an existing enterprise. I decided that going the franchise route was the smartest thing for me to do, and I applied for the franchisee program with McDonald's. My plan was to eventually buy a large number of the stores and become a fast-food mogul. Out of 30,000 applicants for the franchisee program that year, McDonald's accepted 50, and I was one of them. The program would require future franchisees to work 15 to 20 hours a week (for free, of course) over a 2-year period. I actually did my fast-food tour of duty with the McDonald's right around the corner from Harvard. So during my second year at Harvard Business School, my classmates would come in and see this hulking second-year MBA student, decked out in the official McDonald's pants and shirt, dropping their fries into the grease and cleaning the stalls of the bathroom. Of course they were thinking, "What the hell are you doing?" But I learned a valuable lesson over the years: You're making an investment in yourself, and why should you care what someone else thinks? I believe this is an important lesson for everyone. There's a certain level of humility that all entrepreneurs must have. You want to talk about risks? Taking risks is not just about taking risks with your money; it is about risking your reputation by being willing to be the janitor. If you don't have that mindset, and you can't handle that, then entrepreneurship is not for you.

After graduating from HBS, I still had a year to go with the McDonald's ownership program. In order to earn money, I accepted a consulting job with Bain and Company. During the week, I would fly all over the United States on my consulting assignments, and on the weekends, I would return to the Soldiers Field Avenue McDonald's in Boston and put in the hours required. Once I had completed the program and it was time for me to buy my own McDonald's, I could not come to terms with the corporation on a price for the store it wanted to sell. We went around and around, and finally I decided that maybe franchising was not for me after all. Like my mother, I am not very good at taking orders, living my life in a template designed by someone else, and doing what someone else believes I should do. My experience with McDonald's was phenomenal, and I have nothing but respect for the company, but it was time to purchase my own business.

Eventually, after working with a business broker, I settled on purchasing a manufacturing business. Before I sold the company and left for my dream job of teaching at Kellogg, I had purchased an additional manufacturing firm and a retail business. Being your own boss and running your own business is both an exhilarating and a frightening prospect for most people. This is a club for hard workers. If you want an 8-to-5 job, do not join. This is a club whose members flourish on chaos, uncertainty, and ambiguity. These are people who thrive on solving problems. By picking up this book, you have singled yourself out as someone who wants to learn. This book is designed for existing and future entrepreneurs who are not financial managers but want a simple and practical approach to understanding entrepreneurial finance. This is not a traditional, boring, "comprehensive," how-to book, because that is not what most prospective or existing entrepreneurs need, nor is it the way I teach. Most academicians have never worked in business, and the "real-world-practices" component is conspicuously missing from their teaching arsenal. My approach is to combine legitimate and important academic theory with real-world lessons. In my class, I call this "putting meat on the carcass."

But this is not just a book of war stories. Just as I do in my classes, every effort has been made to ensure that the reader gets tangible tools that can be used to improve the potential for entrepreneurial success. The entrepreneur needs to know financial formulas *and* how to use them to spot problems or seize opportunities.

Like Professor Sahlman, I subscribe to the "this is not brain surgery" approach to finance, and stress the fact that everyone can, and more importantly *must*, learn finance! I believe that the baseball always finds a weak outfielder, and the same principle holds true of entrepreneurs—if finance is a weakness, the entrepreneur will be haunted by it. This book is intended for individuals who have little background in financial management, people who have taken entrepreneurship courses, and those who already have practical experience in business. These groups include MBA students, prospective entrepreneurs, and existing entrepreneurs.

A year after purchasing my first business, I vividly remember returning from an early appointment and driving beside Lake Michigan on Lakeshore Drive. It was a gorgeous warm and sunny day, and I pulled off the road and got out of my car. There was no boss to call and no need to conjure up a story for not returning to work. There was no manager to ask for an extended lunch break. I removed my socks and shoes, put my toes in the sand, and stayed there at the beach for the rest of the afternoon. Being an entrepreneur never felt so good.

Entrepreneurship is about getting your hands dirty *and* putting your toes in the sand. This book aims to help you get there. As Irving Berlin once advised a young songwriter by the name of George Gershwin, "Why the hell do you want to work for somebody else? Work for yourself!"

ACKNOWLEDGMENTS

The old african proverb that "it takes a village" to raise a child also applies to writing a book. A village of good people assisted me in completing this book: Stephen Allison, Derrick Collins, Jim Davis, Leslie Davis, Frederick Jordan, Roza Makonnen, Barry Merkin, Gilbert Palmer, Roger Steinharter, Michele and Donna Robinson, Charlene Thomas, David Wildermuth, and Greg White.

CHAPTER 1

The Entrepreneurial Spectrum

INTRODUCTION

The 1990s could be called the "entrepreneurship generation."[1] Never before had the entrepreneurial spirit been as strong, in America and abroad, as it had been during that decade. More than 600,000 new businesses were created at the beginning of the 1990s, with each subsequent year breaking the record of the previous one for start-ups.[2] By 1997, entrepreneurs were starting a record 885,000 new businesses a year—that's more than 2400 a day. This astonishing increase in new companies was over 4 times the number of firms created in the 1960s, and over 16 times as many during the 1950s when 200,000 and 50,000 were being created per year, respectively.[3] The unprecedented growth in entrepreneurial activity was evidenced across all industries, including manufacturing, retail, real estate, and various technology industries. This decade was also an "equal opportunity" time. The entrepreneurial euphoria of the 1990s was shared across genders as well as all ethnicities and races.

ENTREPRENEURIAL FINANCE

In a recent survey of business owners, the functional area they cited in which they had the weakest skill was the area of financial management—accounting, bookkeeping, the raising of capital, and the daily management of cashflow. Interestingly, these business owners also indicated that they spent most of their time on finance-related activities. Unfortunately, the findings of this survey are an accurate portrayal of most entrepreneurs—they are comfortable with the day-to-day operations of their businesses and with the marketing and sales of their products or services, but are very uncomfortable with the financial management of their companies. Entrepreneurs cannot afford this discomfort. They must realize that financial management is not as difficult as it is made out to be. It must be used and embraced because it is one of the key factors for entrepreneurial success.

This book targets prospective and existing "high-growth" entrepreneurs who are not financial managers. Its objective is to be a user-friendly book that will provide these entrepreneurs with an understanding of the fundamentals of financial management and analysis that will enable them to better manage the financial resources of their business. However, the book will not be a course in corporate finance. Rather, entrepreneurial finance is more inte-grative, including the analysis of qualitative issues such as market-ing, sales, personnel management, and strategic planning. The questions that will be answered will include: What financial tools can be used to efficiently manage the cashflow of the business? Why is valuation important? What is the value of the company? Finally, how, where, and when can financial resources be acquired to finance the business?

Before we immerse ourselves in the financial aspects of entre-preneurship, let us look at the general subject of entrepreneurship.

TYPES OF ENTREPRENEURS

There are essentially two kinds of entrepreneurs: the "mom and pop"—a.k.a. the "lifestyle" entrepreneur—and the "high growth" entrepreneur.[4]

The Lifestyle Entrepreneur

The lifestyle entrepreneur includes those entrepreneurs who are primarily looking for their business to provide a decent standard of living. They are not focused on growth; rather, they run their busi-ness almost haphazardly with minimal or no systems in place.

They do not necessarily have any strategic plans regarding the growth and future of their business and gladly accept whatever the business produces. Their objective is to manage the business so that it remains small and provides them with enough income to live a certain, typically middle-class, lifestyle. For example, Sue Yellin, a small-business consultant, says she is determined to remain a one-person show earning just enough money to live comfortably and "feed my cat Fancy Feasts."[5]

While some owners start off as lifestyle entrepreneurs, several ultimately become, voluntarily or involuntarily, high-growth entrepreneurs because the business grows despite their original intention. For example, the *Inc.* magazine 500 is composed of 500 successful high-growth entrepreneurs. When a survey was taken of these entrepreneurs, their answers for the completion of the statement "My original goals when I started the company . . . " suggests that almost 20 percent were originally lifestyle entrepreneurs, given the following responses:

- 50.9 percent. Company to grow as fast as possible
- 29.4 percent. Company to grow slowly
- 5.8 percent. Start small and stay small
- 13.8 percent. No plan at all.[6]

Finally, one of the most prominent stories of a lifestyle entrepreneur turned high-growth entrepreneur is that of Ewing Marion Kauffman, who started his pharmaceutical company, Marion Laboratories, in 1957 with the objective of "just making a living" for his family. He ultimately grew the firm to over $5 billion in annual revenues by 1986, creating wealth for himself (he sold the company in 1989 for over $5 billion) and 300 employees, who became millionaires.[7]

The High-Growth Entrepreneur

The high-growth entrepreneur, on the other hand, is proactively looking to grow annual revenues and profits exponentially. This type of entrepreneur has a plan that is reviewed and revised regularly, and the business is run according to this plan. Unlike the lifestyle entrepreneur, the high-growth entrepreneur runs the business with the expectation of creating wealth and not simply as a means of achieving a comfortable lifestyle. The high-growth entrepreneur understands that a successful business is one that has basic business systems—financial management, cashflow planning, strategic planning, marketing, etc.—in place. *Inc.* magazine surveyed a group of entrepreneurs who were identified as "changing the face of American Business" and found that these entrepreneurs were high-growth entrepreneurs, demonstrated by the fact that not only were they millionaires, but they grew their firms from median sales of $146,000 with 4.5 employees to median sales of $11 million with 219 employees. These data also show that they grew their companies efficiently since their sales per employee increased from $32,444 to $50,228, a 55 percent improvement.

Wilson Harrell, a former entrepreneur and current *Inc.* magazine columnist, did a fantastic job of describing the difference between these two types of entrepreneurs. The first description is that of a lifestyle entrepreneur:

> Let's say a man buys a dry cleaning shop. He goes to work at 7 a.m. At 7 p.m. he comes home, kisses the wife, grabs the kids, and goes off to a school play. At his office you'll see plaques all over the walls: Chamber of Commerce, Rotary Club, the local Republican or Democratic club. He's a pillar of the community, and everybody loves him, even the bankers.

> Change the scenario. After the man buys the dry cleaning shop, he goes home and tells his wife, "Dear, we're going to mortgage this house, borrow money from everyone we can, including your mother and maybe even your brother, and hock everything else, because I'm about to buy another dry cleaner. Then I'll hock the first to buy another, and then another, because I'm going to be the biggest dry cleaner in this city, this state, this nation!"[8]

The second scenario obviously describes the life of a high-growth entrepreneur who has the long-term plan of dominating the national cleaners industry by acquiring competitors first locally and then nationally. His financing plan is to leverage the assets of the cleaners to obtain commercial debt from traditional sources such as banks, combined with "angel" financing from relatives.

But, unfortunately, not all entrepreneurs who seek high growth can attain it. Sometimes circumstances outside of their control can hamper their growth plans. For example, one entrepreneur in Maine complained that he could not grow his business due to common labor shortages in the region. He said, "I'm disgusted by the labor situation around here. People don't want to get ahead. It adds up to businesses staying small."[9]

THE ENTREPRENEURIAL SPECTRUM

When most people think of the term *entrepreneur*, they only envision someone who starts a company from scratch. This is a major misconception. As the entrepreneurial spectrum in Exhibit 1-1 shows, the tent of entrepreneurship is broader and more inclusive. It includes not only those who start companies from scratch (i.e., the start-up entrepreneur), but also those people who own a business through the acquisition of an established company via an inheritance or a buyout (i.e., the acquirer). The entrepreneurship tent also includes the franchiser as well as the franchisee. But be it via acquisition or start-up, each entrepreneurial process, involves differing levels of business risk, as highlighted in Exhibit 1-1.

E X H I B I T   1-1

The Entrepreneurial Spectrum

Low risk				High risk
	Corporation	Franchise	Acquisition	Start-up
	IBM	Dunkin' Donuts	Microsoft	Amazon.com
	McKinsey & Co.	Mailboxes Etc.	Starbucks	Dell
	General Motors	Ace Hardware	Blockbuster	Apple

The Corporation

While the major *Fortune* 500 corporations, such as IBM, are not entrepreneurial ventures, IBM and others are included on the spectrum simply as a business point of reference. Until the early 1980s, IBM epitomized corporate America: a huge, bureaucratic, and conservative multibillion-dollar company where employees were practically guaranteed life employment. Although IBM became less conservative under the leadership of Louis Gerstner, the first non-IBM-trained CEO of the company, it has always represented the antithesis of entrepreneurship with its "Hail to IBM" corporate anthem, white shirts, dark suits, and policies forbidding smoking and drinking on the job and strongly discouraging it off the job.[10] As can be seen, the business risk associated with an established company like IBM is low. Such companies have a long history of profitable success and, more importantly, have extremely large cash reserves on hand.

The Franchise

Franchising is said to account for 40 percent of all retail sales in the United States. Like a big sturdy tree that continues to grow branches, a well-run franchise can spawn hundreds of entrepreneurs. The founder of a franchise—the franchiser—is a start-up entrepreneur, such as Bill Rosenberg, who founded Dunkin' Donuts in the 1950s and now has approximately 5000 stores in 40 countries. These guys sell enough donuts in a year to circle the globe . . . twice! Rosenberg's franchisees, more than 1400 in the United States alone, who own and operate individual franchises, are also entrepreneurs. They take risks, operate their businesses expecting to gain a profit, and, like other entrepreneurs, can have cashflow problems. The country's first franchisees were a network of salesmen who in the 1850s paid the Singer Sewing Machine Company for the right to sell the newly patented machine in different regions of the country.[11] The franchise system ultimately became popular as franchisees began operating in the auto, oil, and food industries. Today, it's estimated that a new franchise outlet opens somewhere in the United States every 8 minutes.[12]

Franchisees are business owners who put capital at risk and who can go out of business if they do not generate enough profits to remain solvent.[13] There are 1 million entrepreneurs in America who are franchisees; 10,000 are home-based. They employ 8 million people and generate annual revenues of approximately $1 trillion, operating in 75 different industries.[14] Examples include Mel Farr, the owner of five auto dealerships. Farr's auto group is just 1 of 15 subsidiaries in his business empire—valued at more than $573 million. Another such entrepreneur is Valerie Daniels-Carter, the founder of a holding company that manages 61 Pizza Hut and 37 Burger King restaurants, with an estimated net worth of $15 million. As Table 1-1 shows, the number of franchised establishments is continually and rapidly growing.

T A B L E   1-1

Growth in Franchises in the United States (Selected Years)

Year	Number of Franchises	Annual Revenues $ Billion
1970	396,000	120
1980	442,000	336
1990	533,000	716
1992	558,000	803

Source: U.S. Department of Commerce, International Franchise Association, 1992.

In terms of business risk, because a franchise is typically a turnkey operation, its business risk is significantly lower than that of a start-up. The success rate of franchisees is between 80 and 97 percent, according to research by Arthur Andersen and Co., which found that only three percent of franchises had gone out of business 5 years after starting their business.[15] Another study undertaken by Arthur Andersen found that of all franchises opened between 1987 and 1997, 85 percent still operated with their original owner; 11 percent had new owners, and 4 percent had closed. The International Franchise Association reports that 70 percent of franchisers charge an initial fee of $30,000 or less.[16]

Max Cooper is one of the largest McDonald's franchisees, with 47 restaurants in Alabama. He stated his reasoning for becoming a franchisee entrepreneur as follows:

> You buy into a franchise because it's successful. The basics have been developed and you're buying the reputation. As with any company, to be a success in franchising, you have to have that burning desire. If you don't have it, don't do it. It isn't easy.[17]

The Acquisition

The acquirer is the entrepreneur who inherits or buys an existing business. This list includes Howard Shultz, who acquired Starbucks Coffee in 1987 for approximately $4 million when it had only 6 stores. Today, more than 12 million customers a week line up for their caffe mochas, cappuccinos, and caramel machiatos in 3500 Starbucks locations in 17 countries. Annual revenues top $2 billion, and according to the company's SEC filings, the ownership team opened 1035 new Starbucks outlets in the year 2000 alone![18]

The list of successful "acquirers" also includes folks like Jim McCann, who purchased the almost bankrupt 1-800-Flowers in 1983, turned it around, and grew annual revenues to $442 million by 2001.[19] Another successful entrepreneur who falls in this category is Cathy Hughes, who over the past 18 years has purchased 51 radio stations that presently generate $240 million in annual revenues, making her broadcasting company the 22nd largest in the nation. The 51 stations have a combined value of $2 billion.[20]

One of the most prominent entrepreneurs who fall into this category is Wayne Huizenga, *Inc.* magazine's 1996 Entrepreneur of the Year. His reputation as a great entrepreneur partially comes from the fact that he is one of the few people in the United States to have ever owned three multibillion-dollar businesses. Like Richard Dreyfuss's character in the movie *Down and Out in Beverly Hills*, a millionaire who owned a clothes hanger–manufacturing company, Wayne Huizenga is living proof that an entrepreneur does not have to be in a glamorous industry to be successful. His success came from buying businesses in the low- or no-tech, unglamorous industries of garbage, burglar alarms, videos, and used cars.

He has never started a business from scratch. His strategy has been to dominate an industry by buying as many of the companies in the industry as quickly as possible and consolidating them. This strategy is known as the "roll-up," "platform," or "poof" strategy—starting and growing a company through industry consolidation. While the term *roll-up* is self-explanatory, the other two may need brief explanations. The *platform* term comes from the act of buying a large company in an industry to serve as the platform for adding other companies. The *poof* term comes from the idea that as an acquirer, one day the entrepreneur has no businesses and the next, "poof"—like magic—he or she purchases a company and is in business. Then "poof" again, and the company grows exponentially via additional acquisitions. As Jim Blosser, one of Huizenga's executives, noted, "Wayne doesn't like start-ups. Let someone else do the R&D. He'd prefer to pay a little more for a concept that has demonstrated some success and may just need help in capital and management."[21]

Huizenga's entrepreneurial career began in 1961 when he purchased his first company, Southern Sanitation Company, in Florida. The company's assets were a garbage truck and a $500-a-month truck route, which he personally worked, rising at 2:30 a.m. every day. This company ultimately became the multibillion-dollar Waste Management Inc., which Huizenga had grown nationally through aggressive acquisitions. In one 9-month period, Waste Management bought 100 smaller companies across the country. In 10 years the company grew from $5 million a year to annual profits of $106.5 million on nearly $1 billion in revenues. In 4 more years, revenue doubled again.[22] He exited this business and went into the video rental business by purchasing the entire Blockbuster Video franchise for $32 million in 1984, after being unable to purchase the Blockbuster franchise for the state of Florida because the state's territorial rights had already been sold to other entrepreneurs before Huizenga made his offer. When he acquired Blockbuster Video, it had 8 corporate and 11 franchise stores nationally. The franchisor was generating $7 million annually through direct rentals from the 8 stores, plus franchise fees and royalties from the 11 franchised stores.[23] Under Huizenga, who didn't even own a VCR at the time, Blockbuster flourished. For the next 7 years, through internal growth and acquisitions, Blockbuster averaged a new store opening every 17 hours, resulting in it becoming larger than its next 550 competitors combined. Over this period of time, the price of its stock increased 4100 percent: Someone who had invested $25,000 in Blockbuster stock in 1984 would have found that 7 years later that investment would be worth $1.1 million, and an investment of $1 million in 1984 would have turned into $41 million during this time period. In January 1994, Huizenga sold Blockbuster Video, which had grown to 4300 stores in 23 countries, to Viacom for $8.5 billion.

Huizenga has pursued the same roll-up strategy in the auto business by rapidly buying as many dealerships as he possibly can and bundling them together under the AutoNation brand. By 2001, AutoNation was the largest automobile retailer in the United States. By the way, if you ever find yourself behind the wheel of a National or Alamo rental car, you're also driving one of Wayne's vehicles—both companies are among his holdings. Eventually what Huizenga hopes to do is have an entire life cycle for a car. In other words, he buys cars from the manufacturer, sells some of them as new, leases or rents the balance, and later sells the rented cars as used.

Huizenga also owns or previously owned practically every professional sports franchise in Florida including the National Football League's Miami Dolphins, National Hockey League's Florida Panthers, and Major League baseball's Florida Marlins. He never owned the National Basketball League's Miami Heat; his cousin did.

Now, here's your bonus points question—the one I always ask my Kellogg students. What's the common theme among all of his various businesses—videos, waste, sports, and automobiles? Each one of them involves the rental of products, generating significant, predictable, and, perhaps most importantly, *recurring* revenues. The video business rents the same video over and over again, as does the car rental business rent the same car a multitude of times. In waste management, he rented the trash containers. But what's being rented in the sports business? He rents the seats in the stadiums and the arenas that he owns. Other businesses in the seat rental business are airlines, movie theaters, public transportation, and universities!

Another example of an acquirer is Bill Gates, the founder of Microsoft. The company's initial success came from an operating system called MS-DOS, which was originally owned by a company called Seattle Computer Products. In 1980, IBM was looking for an operating system. After hearing about Bill Gates, who dropped out of Harvard to start Microsoft in 1975 with his friend Paul Allen, the IBM representatives went to Albuquerque, New Mexico, where Gates and Allen were, to see if Bill Gates could provide them with the operating system they needed. At the time, Microsoft's product was a version of the programming language BASIC for the Altair

8800, arguably the world's first personal computer. BASIC had been invented in 1964 by John Kenney and Thomas Kurtz.[24] As he did not have an operating system, Gates recommended that IBM contact another company called Digital Research. Gary Kildall, the owner of Digital Research, was absent when the IBM representatives visited, and his staff refused to sign a nondisclosure statement with IBM without his consent, so the representatives went back to Gates to see if he could recommend someone else. The true opportunistic entrepreneur that he is, he told them he had an operating system to provide to them and finalized a deal with IBM. Once he had done so, he went out and bought the operating system, Q-DOS, from Seattle Computer Products for $50,000 and customized it for IBM's first PC, which was introduced in August 1981. The rest is entrepreneurial history. So Bill Gates, the world's wealthiest person, with a personal net worth in excess of $50 billion, achieved his initial entrepreneurial success as an acquirer and has continued on this path ever since. Despite its court battles, Microsoft continues to grow—investing hundreds of millions of dollars each year to acquire technologies and companies. Over the last 3 years, Microsoft has spent over $3 billion on acquisitions.[25] Don't worry, however—there's still some spare change in the Microsoft couch. In late 2001, Microsoft had $31.6 billion in cash on its books.[26]

The Start-Up

Creating a company from nothing other than an idea, product, or service is the most difficult and risky way to be a successful entrepreneur. Two great examples of start-up entrepreneurs are Steve Wozniak, a college dropout, and Steven Jobs of Apple Computer. As an engineer at Hewlett-Packard, Wozniak approached the company with an idea for a small personal computer. The company did not take him seriously and rejected his idea; this decision turned out to be one of the greatest "intrapraneurial" blunders in history. With $1300 of his own money, Wozniak and his friend Steve Jobs, launched Apple Computer from his parents' garage.

The Apple Computer company start-up is a great example of a start-up that was successful because of its revolutionary technological innovation created by the technology genius Wozniak. Other entrepreneurial firms that were successful as a result of technological innovations include Intuit with Scott Cook, Netscape with James H. Clark and Marc Andreessen, and Sun with Andy Bechtolsheim and Bill Joy.

But an entrepreneurial start-up opportunity in the technology industry does not have to be limited to those who create new technology. For example, Dell Computer, the largest computer systems company in the world with $32 billion in annual revenues, is not now, nor has ever been, a research and development-driven company, unlike the companies mentioned above. Michael Dell, the founder, got his entrepreneurial opportunity from the implementation of the simple idea that he could "out-execute" his competitors. He has always built computers to customer orders and sold them directly to consumers at prices lower than that of his competitors. As he explained, "I saw that you'd buy a PC for about $3000 and inside that PC was about $600 worth of parts. IBM would buy most of these parts from other companies, assemble them, and sell the computer to a dealer for $2000. Then the dealer, who knew very little about selling or supporting computers, would sell it for $3000, which was even more outrageous."[27]

Michael Dell, who dropped out of the University of Texas and founded his company in 1984 with a $1000 loan from his parents, went on to become in 1992, at age 27, the youngest CEO of a *Fortune* 500 company. Less than 10 years later, Dell had revenues of more than $15 billion in just the first 6 months of 2001, and its founder topped the *Forbes* "40 richest under 40" list with a net worth a few bucks north of $16 billion.

Entrepreneurial start-ups have not been limited to technology companies. In 1993, Kate Spade quit her job as the accessories editor for *Mademoiselle* and, with her husband, Andy, started their own women's handbag company called Kate Spade, Inc. Her bags, a combination of whimsy and function, have scored big returns on the initial $35,000 investment from Andy's 401(k). In 1999, sales had doubled to $50 million. Neiman Marcus purchased a 56 percent stake in February 1999 for $33.6 million.[28]

Finally, there are also numerous successful start-ups that began from an idea other than the entrepreneur's. For example, Mario and Cheryl Tricoci are the owners of a $40 million international day spa company headquartered in Chicago called Mario Tricoci's. In 1986, after returning from a vacation at a premiere spa outside the United States, they noticed there were virtually no day spas in the country, only those with weeklong stay requirements. Therefore, they started their day spa company, based on the ideas and styles they had seen during their international travels.[29]

NOTES

1. Slaughter, Michie P., *Entrepreneurship: Economic Impact and Public Policy Implications*, Center for Entrepreneurial Leadership Inc., Ewing Marion Kauffman Foundation, March 1996; Mike Hermann, Kauffman Foundation, 1997.
2. Beech, Wendy M., "Business Profiles: And the Winners Are . . . . ," Black Enterprise; Brown, Carolyn M., Tonia L. Shakespeare, "A Call to Arms for Black Business," *Black Enterprise*, November 1996, pp. 79–80.
3. Small Business Administration Office of Economic Research.
4. Smilor, Raymond W., *Vital Speeches and Articles of Interest, Entrepreneurship and Philanthropy*, prepared for the Fifth Annual Kellogg-Kauffman Aspen Seminar on Philanthropy, September 1996.
5. *New York Times*, September 23, 1998.
6. "1995 Inc. 500 Almanac," *Inc.*, 1995.
7. Morgan, Anne, *Prescription for Success: The Life and Values of Ewing Marion Kauffman*, 1995.
8. *Inc.*
9. Freedman, David H., "The Money Trail," *Inc.*, December 1998.
10. Greenwald, John, "Master of the Mainframe: Thomas Watson J.R.," *Time*, December 7, 1998.
11. Ibid.
12. "Answers to the 21 Most Commonly Asked Questions about Franchising." International Franchise Association Home Page, October 22, 2001, http://www.franchise.org/resourcectr/faq/faq.asp.
13. Ibid.
14. *Chicago Tribune*, July 27, 1997.
15. Gallop, Gerda D., "15 Franchises You Can Run from Home," *Black Enterprise*, September 9, 1998.
16. "The Profile of Franchising," IFA Educational Foundation Inc., 2001.
17. Godsey, Kristen Dunlop, "Market like Mad: How One Man Built a McDonald's Franchise Empire," *Success*, February 1997.

18. Starbucks 2000 Annual Report, Starbucks Home Page, http://www.starbucks.com/aboutus/ar_financial.pdf.
19. 1-800-Flowers. Com Inc. (FLWS) Annual Report (SEC form 10K), October 1, 2001, http://biz.yahoo.com/e/011001/flws.html.
20. Jones, Charisse, "Owning the Airwaves," *Essence*, October 1998.
21. Andersen, Duncan Maxwell, Michael Warshaw, with Mari-Alyssa Mulvihill, "The #1 Entrepreneur in America: Blockbuster Video's Wayne Huizenga," *Success*, March 1995, p. 36.
22. Ibid.
23. "Wayne Huizenga," video, University of Southern California.
24. Gelernter, David, "Software Strongman: Bill Gates," *Time*, December 7, 1998, p. 131.
25. *BusinessWeek*, January 1997.
26. Vicente, J. P. "Here's How Microsoft Should Spend Its Huge Pile of Cash," *Red Herring*, September 15, 2001.
27. Murphy, Richard, "Michael Dell," *Success*, January 1999.
28. "Top Entrepreneurs of 1999," January 2000, http://www.businessweek.co/smallbiz/content/jan2000/ep3663075.htm.
29. Roberson, Terri, "The Partners behind the Day Spa Explosion," *Today's Chicago Woman*, December 1998.

CHAPTER 2

The Entrepreneur

INTRODUCTION

Faced with a white-knuckle crisis on the Apollo 13 mission, legendary NASA flight director Gene Kranz rallied his troops with the now famous and stirring battle cry, "Failure is not an option." Unfortunately, a few million entrepreneurs beg to differ.

SUCCESS RATES OF ENTREPRENEURS

It takes a certain amount of guts, nerves, chutzpah—whatever you want to call it—to cut the safety net and go out on your own and start a business. No one who does it, including myself, has an end goal of burning through a life savings, failing miserably, and dying alone and penniless! In reality, the deck is stacked against the entrepreneur. The failure rate of companies, particularly start-ups, is staggering. A study by the Small Business Administration (SBA) showed the following failure rates for small businesses:

- 23.7 percent within 2 years after starting up
- 51.7 percent after 4 years
- 62.7 percent after 6 years
- 80 percent after 10 years.[1]

Table 2-1 provides data on the average number of monthly business failures during 1984–1997. While the data show that the number of failed businesses declined substantially in 1994 from a peak of 8000 companies per month in 1992, on average approximately 7000 firms failed every month during 1997; that's a total of more than 83,000 businesses for the year.

T A B L E 2-1

Measures of Business Failure, 1984–1997

Year	Failures	Percent Change
1997	83,384	15.9%
1996	71,931	1.0%
1995	71,194	−0.5%
1994	71,558	−16.8%
1993	85,982	−11.4%
1992	97,069	10.1%
1991	88,140	45.8%
1990	60,432	20.0%
1989	50,361	−11.8%
1988	57,099	−6.8%
1987	61,236	−0.6%
1986	61,601	7.6%
1985	57,253	9.9%
1984	52,078	

Sources: Small Business Administration, Office of Advocacy, Dun & Bradstreet.

Those failure rates began to climb again in 2001, as the "dot-bomb" era claimed thousands of casualties, turned NASDAQ darlings into duds, and foreshadowed a broader economic slowdown. True entrepreneurs have remarkable resilience, however; and the statistics suggest they need it. The average entrepreneur fails 3.8 times before succeeding.[2] One such entrepreneur is Steve Perlman, the cofounder of Web TV Networks, which he sold to Microsoft in 1997 for $425 million. Before his success with Web TV, he had been involved in three start-up failures in a 10-year period. Despite these odds, people are still pursuing the entrepreneurial dream. And this is taking place not only in the United States but overseas as well. For example, in Taiwan 1373 electronic companies were started in 1997. By the end of the year, 1147 of these companies, or 84 percent, had gone out of business. Despite this high failure rate, the entrepreneurial spirit is alive and well in Taiwan as evidenced by the fact that the venture capital industry, which was virtually nonexistent 10 years ago, now consists of 97 firms that have invested approximately $10 billion in entrepreneurial firms.[3]

One of the obvious reasons for the high rate of entrepreneurial failure is that it is tough to have a successful product, let alone an entire company. In 1999, an Ernst and Young study found that about 65 percent of new products fail within 12 months of introduction.[4] Another reason for failure is that people are starting companies and then learning about cashflow management, marketing, and human resource development, etc., on the job. Too many people are learning about what to do when you have cashflow problems when they actually have those problems, rather than in a classroom setting or as an intern with an entrepreneurial firm. This type of training is costly, because the mistakes that are made have an impact on the sustainability of a company. A study of unsuccessful entrepreneurs found that most attributed their lack of success to inadequate training.[5] The area in which they lacked the most training was cashflow management.[6]

T A B L E   2-2

Retail Bankruptcies

Year	Number of Bankruptcies
1990	13,000
1991	17,000
1992	19,000
1993	18,500
1994	17,750

Source: SBA.

Now let's look at Table 2-2, which shows the number of bankruptcies in the retail industry from 1990 to 1994.

What we see in the table is that business failure trends in the retail industry, followed the general trends cited in Table 2-1. Specifically, we see that the number of failures increased for the first 3 years of the 1990s. Why? The country was mired in a recession. Thus, during tough economic times the number of business failures will increase because owners cannot pay the bills. At the same time the number of entrepreneurial start-ups will also increase because people get downsized.

On average, more than 17,000 retailers also go belly-up every year—filing for bankruptcy. Again, it's often a case of an entrepreneur who lacks the expertise to manage inventory and cashflow. There's an important lesson here. All entrepreneurs, prospective and existing, should easily and readily be able to answer the question, What happens to my business during a recession? Businesses respond to recessions differently. For example, a few businesses that do well during recessions are auto parts and service because people tend to repair old cars rather than buy new ones. The alcoholic beverages industry also does well during recessions because people tend to drink more when depressed or unhappy. Businesses that do not fare as well include restaurants (people eat at home more), the vacation industry, and any businesses that sell luxury items, such as boats.

But just because a business does not fare well during a recession does not mean that a business should not be started at the beginning of or during a recession. It simply means that the entrepreneur should plan wisely, keeping costs under control and maintaining adequate working capital through lines of credit and fast collection of receivables. About a year after I bought my first business, a lampshade-manufacturing firm, the country went into a recession. The Gulf War started, and people stopped shopping and sat home in front of their televisions watching events unfold. I needed them in department stores buying my lampshades! I remember sitting at my desk at work, holding my head in my hands, when my secretary Angela interrupted the silence with a gentle knock on my door. "Are you crying?" she asked. "No," I answered. "But I should be! I've had this business less than a year, I've got all this debt, and I've got to figure out how to pay it off." Prior to purchasing the business, I had laid out a specific plan for dealing with a downturn, and we did manage to make it through.

But in the spirit of candor, I have to admit that I underestimated how tight business would be. It was ugly! Years ago, former heavyweight champion Mike Tyson was preparing to fight Michael Spinks. A reporter doing a prefight interview with Tyson told him that Spinks had a carefully laid-out a plan for beating the champ. Tyson replied, "Everyone's got a plan until they get smacked upside the head." I couldn't say it better myself. Do yourself a huge favor; be brutally honest with yourself and any investors, and paint the ugliest damn picture you can imagine. Imagine how the economy, competitors, or other conditions could "smack you upside the head." Now, tell everyone how your business is going to survive, thrive, and live to ring the cash register another day.

Finally, before starting a business and preparing for a recession, the prospective entrepreneur should be able to answer the question, Where is the recession? Is it yet to come, has it passed, or are we currently in one? The year 2001 saw mass layoffs and an economy slipping into a recession that officially began in the first quarter of 2002. The last recession in the United States ended in 1992, and the country's economy typically goes through a recession every 5 to 7 years. During the Reagan administration, the country went 92 consecutive months, 7.7 years, before going through a recession. The second longest period that the country has gone without a recession was during the Vietnam War at 106 consecutive months (8.8 years).[7] And the entrepreneurship decade of the 1990s holds the record for the longest period that the country has not been in a recession. As of September 2001, the country had gone through 139 consecutive months (i.e., 11+ years) without a recession.

But as noted earlier, failing does not exclude one from becoming an entrepreneur. There are many notable examples of entrepreneurs who have succeeded despite initial failures. For example, Fred Smith had an unsuccessful company before succeeding with Federal Express. Berry Gordy, the founder of Motown Records, started a jazz record shop that went bankrupt. Following this bankruptcy, he went to work for Ford Motor Company on the assembly line to get his personal finances in order and then left that job to start Motown Records. Henry Ford went bankrupt twice before Ford Motor Company succeeded. And as Henry Ford said, "Failure is the chance to begin again more intelligently. It is just a resting place."[8]

Therefore, all prospective entrepreneurs should take heed of the fact that entrepreneurial success is more the exception than the rule. In all likelihood, one will not succeed. But one must simply realize that failure is merely an entrepreneurial rite of passage. It happens to almost everyone, and financiers will typically give the entrepreneur another chance as long as the failure did not come from lying, cheating, stealing, or laziness. They would rather invest in someone who has failed and learned from the experience than an inexperienced person. Venture capitalists in Silicon Valley deem failure not only inevitable but also valuable. Michael Moritz, a partner at Sequoia Capital, who invested $500,000 in Apple Computer in 1978 and turned that investment into a $120 million investment 3 years later when the company went public, noted that entrepreneurs who have suffered a setback could be better bets than those who have only enjoyed success.[9]

Warren Packard, managing director at the Silicon Valley venture capital firm Draper Fisher Jurvetson, is quoted as saying:

> Failure is just a word for learning experience. When we meet an entrepreneur who has not been successful, we ask ourselves, "Did he learn from past mistakes or is he just crazy?" As long as an entrepreneur is honest about his abilities, his past doesn't matter. He has learned some very important lessons on someone else's dollar."[10]

Renowned venture capitalist John Doerr of Kleiner Perkins Caufield & Byers (KPCB), the Silicon Valley fund that successfully invested in dozens of Internet-related companies including Netscape and Amazon.com, said:

> Great people are so hard to find that even if one particular start-up fails, you're not tainted for life."[11]

And finally, Thomas G. Stemberg, founder and CEO of Staples, Inc., noted:

> How you recover is more important than the mistakes you make."[12]

WHY BECOME AN ENTREPRENEUR?

A Gallup study found that 50 percent of the adult population in the United States wanted to own their own business. Now, why do people want to become entrepreneurs? Why has entrepreneurship become so popular? Everyone has a different reason for wanting to start a business.

Inc. magazine surveyed the owners listed on the *Inc.* magazine 500 and found that the number one reason these entrepreneurs gave for starting their own company was to gain the independence to be able to control their schedule and workload. In fact, 40 percent of the respondents indicated that they started their own companies to "be my own boss."[13]

Many people become entrepreneurs because they loathe working for others. As one person said, he became an entrepreneur because having a job was worse than being in prison:

In prison: You spend the majority of your time in an 8 × 10 cell.
At work: You spend most of your time in a 6 × 8 cubicle.

In prison: You get three free meals a day.
At work: You only get a break for one meal and you have to pay for it.

In prison: You can watch TV and play games.
At work: You get fired for watching TV and playing games.

In prison: You get your own toilet.
At work: You have to share.

In prison: You spend most of your life looking through bars from the inside wanting to get out.
At work: You spend most of your time wanting to get out and go inside bars!

In prison: There are wardens who are often sadistic.
At work: They are called MANAGERS!"[14]

The second most cited reason is the sense of accomplishment achieved when they proved they could start or own a successful company. Interestingly, most people, young or old, do not become entrepreneurs to become rich. For example, in a survey of high school teens undertaken by the Gallup Organization, 70 percent of the respondents said they were interested in starting their own businesses. However, only 18 percent cited earning a lot of money as their primary motivation for starting a business.[15] In the *Inc.* magazine survey mentioned above, "making a lot of money" was only the third most popular reason why entrepreneurs started their own companies.

What is evident is that for most people, making a lot of money is not necessarily the driving force for becoming an entrepreneur. However, despite this fact, the majority of wealthy people in the United States became rich as a result of being an entrepreneur. The by-product of entrepreneurship is wealth creation. In the United States there are approximately 170 billionaires, 250,000 deca-millionaires, and over 5 million millionaires.[16] In fact, recent estimates show there are 6.3 million millionaires, down from the historical record of 7.1 million in 1999.[17] In *The Millionaire Next Door*, the authors found that 80 percent of these people gained their wealth by becoming entrepreneurs or as a result of being part of an entrepreneurial venture. For example, the country's wealthiest person, Bill Gates, achieved his wealth by founding Microsoft. Besides Gates, Microsoft has produced an additional 6000 millionaires.[18] Many of these wealthy people are young men and women who were very ambitious, smart, and talented. Today, for the first time in the country's history, there are more millionaires in America age 50 and younger than those 50 years old and older.[19]

To further support the wealth-creation–entrepreneurship relationship, *Forbes* reported that in 1984, 63 percent of the *Forbes* 400 richest Americans were first-generation entrepreneurs. By the late 1990s, the number had increased to 72 percent. But this wealth-creation–entrepreneurship relationship is not new. John D. Rockefeller cofounded Standard Oil, the first major U.S. multinational corporation, in 1870. In 1913, his personal net worth was $900 million, which was equivalent to more than 2 percent of the country's gross national product. Today, 2 percent of the country's gross national product would be approximately $190 billion, more than 3 times Bill Gates's net worth.[20]

As mentioned earlier, for some people, becoming an entrepreneur was not a choice; rather they took this route when they were laid off from their jobs. Others started companies with the objective of creating jobs for others. One entrepreneur who has been selected by *Inc.* magazine as one of the company builders who is "changing the face of American businesses" is quoted as saying, "I have a business that has the highest integrity in town. . . . People respect me and I support 72 families."[21] For some entrepreneurs, their business is an outlet for their creative talent. Others feel the need to leave behind a legacy that embodies their values. Still others have community or societal concerns that they feel can best be addressed through their company.[22]

For some, becoming an entrepreneur is the natural thing to do. They either are the offspring of an entrepreneur or have developed an interest in it because they were exposed to the business world at an early age. Successful high-growth entrepreneurs who were offspring of entrepreneurs include Berry Gordy of Motown Records; Wayne Huizenga of Waste Management, Blockbuster Video, and AutoNation; Josephine Esther Mentzer of Estée Lauder; Ted Turner of TBS and CNN television stations; and Akio Morit, who left the sake business that his family owned for 14 generations to start Sony. Donald Trump is also included in this group; ironically, in contrast to Donald and his high-income real estate clients, his father owned real estate that he rented to low-income and working-class families in New York. Another high-growth entrepreneur who belongs in this category is John Rogers, Jr., the founder of Ariel Capital—a financial management firm that manages billions of dollars. Financial management is in Rogers's blood. To encourage his son's interest in business, every birthday and Christmas, John's father gave his young son stocks as gifts. John's parents, grandparents, and great-grandparents have always owned their own businesses. In fact, his great-grandfather, C. J. Stafford, was an attorney by training but also owned a hotel in Florida. It burned down in the early 1900s when he was falsely accused of starting a race riot. Instead of giving up, Stafford fled Florida and came to Chicago, where he started his own law firm.

Other entrepreneurs start companies to develop a new idea or invention. For example, as discussed earlier, Steve Wozniak, the cofounder of Apple Computer, became an entrepreneur by default. If Hewlett-Packard had not rejected his idea for a user-friendly small personal computer, he probably would not have resigned from the company to start his own business and launch a dramatic change in the computer hardware industry.

Another reason why people want to become entrepreneurs is because of the emergence of role models. Until approximately 10 years ago, the main business role models were corporate executives such as Robert Goizueta, the legendary CEO of the Coca-Cola Corporation who died of cancer in 1997, and the recently retired Jack Welch of General Electric. In the entrepreneurship decade of the 1990s, entrepreneurs became primary business role models, the people that everyone wanted to emulate. For example, Christian and Timbers, a consulting firm, identified the top CEOs who were mentioned the most often in major business publications in 1997. As Exhibit 2-1 shows, three of the CEOs who received the most mentions were founders of their companies [those names with an asterisk (*)].[23]

E X H I B I T   2-1

The Most Mentioned CEOs

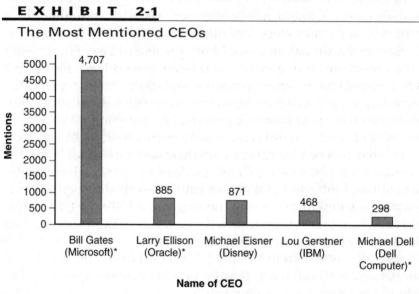

Source: *Inc.* magazine.

In 1997, *Inc.* magazine conducted a study aimed at assessing the impact of entrepreneurs and their companies on American businesses. A total of 500 entrepreneurs who had founded their companies between 1982 and 1996 as well as 200 upper- and middle-level *Fortune* 500 executives (vice presidents, directors, and managers) were surveyed and asked the same questions. When asked whether they agreed with the statement "Entrepreneurs are the heroes of American business," 95 percent of the entrepreneurs and 68 percent of the corporate executives agreed. These results were starkly different from the responses given by these two groups 10 years earlier, when 74 percent of entrepreneurs and

49 percent of executives had agreed with this statement. Interestingly, 37 percent of the corporate executives noted that if they could live their lives over, they would choose to run their own companies.[24]

Surprisingly, corporations are encouraging their employees to pursue entrepreneurial ventures. Several companies have, in fact, demonstrated this support by creating programs that encourage and assist employees who want to become entrepreneurs. For example, AT&T offers up to $10,000 in start-up capital to employees who are starting a new business.[25] Xerox Corporation has a program for employees opening new Xerox sales agencies. Lockheed-Martin has an official Entrepreneurial Leave of Absence Program where an employee can take an unpaid leave for up to 2 years to pursue an entrepreneurial endeavor. After 2 years, the employee must make the decision to come back to the company or to stay with the new business venture. The company makes equity investments and strikes licensing agreements with those entrepreneurs who choose to continue with their new businesses.[26] On the international scale, Acer, Taiwan's leading personal computer maker, has a program that allows employees to start new companies while still working at the company on a full-time basis. Over 120 companies have been founded as a result of this program, and Acer has equity in more than 100 of them.

Finally, as shown in Exhibit 2-2, a recent Coca-Cola Company announcement to all its employees provides an example of corporations supporting entrepreneurship.

E X H I B I T   2-2

Coca-Cola Corporation's Fizzion Announcement

To: All Employees Worldwide

Subject: Fizzion, L.L.C.

We recently renewed our company's commitment to benefit and refresh everyone who is touched by our business. Today, I am proud to announce a new endeavor to help The Coca-Cola Company gain access to innovations that will spur our growth as we press forward into a new century. Reflecting the creative energy that it will generate, this new initiative is called "Fizzion," a wholly owned subsidiary of The Coca-Cola Company where new ideas and technologies can grow into successful businesses. Located

continued on next page

E X H I B I T   2-2

E X H I B I T   2-2

Coca-Cola Corporation's Fizzion Announcement (continued)

across the street from our main complex in The Learning Center, Fizzion will provide a host of powerful benefits to entrepreneurs from around the world. Entrepreneurs who become a member and reside at Fizzion will have access to world-class sales and marketing expertise, business management experience, office space and other basic infrastructure. In return, Fizzion member companies will be chosen based on their ability to positively impact the company's volume, revenues or profits when their applications are used in our business.

Fizzion is just one of the projects we are implementing to spur innovation in our business. Fizzion will augment our other partnerships with Ideas.com, Ideashare, and our new Think Tank, which are already underway. In making services available to Fizzion entrepreneurs, opportunities will be created for employees to work with startups in various functional areas. I encourage you to avail yourself of these opportunities as they present themselves in the future.

Source: Coca-Cola Corporation.

Corporate Downsizing

While the 1990s will be known as the entrepreneurship decade, the past 10 years will also be noted for corporate America's continuous downsizing. This corporate downsizing was so pervasive that it became an intrinsic part of the story line for Bill Cosby's television sitcom *Cosby*, which debuted in 1996. In the show, Hilton Lucas, played by Cosby, deals with the travails of being laid off from his job at a major airline. It accurately characterizes the plight of many who have lost their jobs. When laid off, Lucas had hoped to be called back, but 3 years later he was still waiting to hear from his former company.[27] Ironically, CBS eventually downsized the show itself—canceling it.

Since January 1995, over 68 percent of all insurance companies, 66 percent of manufacturing companies, and 69 percent of banking and financial institutions had laid off employees. Layoffs have become a fact of life for American workers, and in 2001, the corporate carnage set new records. The numbers were so significant that *Forbes* magazine began to post a daily body count on its web site. As of October 2001, the "layoff tracker" reported that 876,073 workers had been laid off. Major corporations trimming their ranks included Lucent (40,000 workers), Ford (5000 white-collar workers), Agilent (4000 workers), and Gateway (5000 workers). By September 2001, more than 1.1 million employees had gotten the ax—an 83 percent jump from the previous year's tally and far above any annual total in the last 12 years.[28] The terrorist attack on the World Trade Center in September 2001 added even more casualties, with virtually all of the nation's airlines announcing major layoffs, more than 100,000 workers, in the weeks that followed. Others in the travel industry followed suit, with Starwood Hotel and Resorts laying off 10,000 workers. American workers have plenty of company overseas. More than 2 million workers in Japan and Southeast Asia lost their jobs in 2001.[29]

While many furloughed workers will eventually return to other corporate jobs, it's likely that others will follow in the footsteps of previous pink-slip recipients. Many workers who lost their jobs during the corporate cutbacks of the 1980s and 1990s have either chosen or been forced to pursue the entrepreneurial route rather than employment in the corporate arena. A survey of the founders of the 1996 *Inc.* 500—a list of the 500 fastest-growing small companies—found that 40 percent of these founders started their businesses after a company reshuffling.[30]

An example of an entrepreneur who chose to start his own business after being downsized is Patrick Kelly, who started a company called Physicians Sales and Services, which now has over $600 million in revenue and employs more than 1800 people. When asked why he became an entrepreneur, he said, "I didn't choose to become an entrepreneur. I got fired and started a company in order to earn a living. I had to learn to be a CEO. I'll tell you right now, I stole every idea I have. There is not an original thought in my head. I stole everything and you should too." Another happy story regarding a downsized employee is the story of Bill Rasmussen, who was laid off from his public relations job in 1979. He went on to start the Entertainment Sports Programming Network (ESPN) in Connecticut, which is now jointly owned by Disney (80 percent) and the Hearst Family (20 percent), and had $2 billion in annual revenues and more than $600 million in annual operating profit in the late 1990s—more than ABC, CBS, and NBC made at their national networks combined.[31]

The increasing number of bank mergers in the 1990s has resulted in the downsizing of many CEOs, a number of whom have started their own banks. In fact, more new banks have been started in Illinois in the last 4 years, a total of 46, than in the entire previous decade.[32]

Academic Training

In 1970, only 16 American universities provided training in entrepreneurship. Today more than 600 universities throughout the country have at least one class; many more classes are being taught in universities all over the world. In 1980, there were 18 entrepreneurship-endowed chairs at business schools; today there are more than 200.[33] In fact, entrepreneurship has become an academic discipline in virtually all of the top business schools across the country. Another indicator of academia's commitment to this field is the fact that business schools offer not only classes, but also minors and majors of concentration in the field of entrepreneurship. Jerome Katz of St. Louis University undertook a study that showed that in 1991, out of 300 accredited business schools in the country, only 24 offered some course work in entrepreneurial studies.[34] Today, approximately 120 business schools offer entrepreneurship as a major, including such graduate schools as the University of California at Los Angeles, University of Texas, Wharton, and Kellogg.

Future entrepreneurs are being provided formal training in the field of entrepreneurship in an academic setting, which in some instances, includes internships for academic credit at entrepreneurial firms, instead of learning through costly mistakes on the job. For example, since 1995, over 60 schools throughout the country have placed more than 1500 students in internships at entrepreneurial firms through the Kauffman Foundation's Kauffman Entrepreneurial Internship Program (KEIP).

Finally, the growth in entrepreneurship will be forever matched with America's technological revolution, which began in the early 1980s. Companies such as Microsoft, Apple, Lotus, and Dell (which was the best-performing publicly owned stock of the decade, up 26,000 percent since 1990), to name a few, gave birth to the present $600 billion technology industry. Advances in technology have led to the proliferation of new products and services fostering the creation of companies in new areas such as the Internet.

For example, in 1999, a new computer product was developed every 7 seconds, and a new Internet-related company was established every 48 hours.[35] 1995 and 1996 were heady times for Internet pioneers. Table 2-3 shows the growth of Internet services companies as the new sector's growth began to explode.

T A B L E   2-3

Fastest-Growing Businesses, 1995–1996

Business	Number of Firms in 1995	Number of Firms in 1996	Growth
Internet services	24	2298	9475%
PC networking services	4539	6573	45%
Pager services	1636	2148	31%
Bagel shops	2522	3291	31%
Cellular phone services	4037	5253	30%
Tattoo parlors	2156	2569	19%

Source: *USA Today*, March 26, 1997.

This spur in entrepreneurial activity resulted in unprecedented job and wealth creation. In 1997, for example, in Silicon Valley (which is 50 miles long, crossing 30 different city lines), 11 new companies were created each week, resulting in the creation of 62 new millionaires every day.[36] Of course, many of those millionaires saw their "paper fortunes" disappear in the coming years. One of the most prominent entrepreneurial technology firms of the 1990s was Yahoo! It was started in 1995 and went public in 1996 at an astonishing valuation of $850 million, despite the fact that its profits in 1996 were only $81,000 on revenues of $400,000. In 2001, the company lost 90 percent of its market capitalization, forced out its CEO, announced not one but two series of layoffs, and was struggling to regain its footing.

Technological advances have also facilitated the emergence of entrepreneurship. Improved access to information and communication has allowed individuals to pursue entrepreneurial ventures outside the traditional corporate setting, such as from home or "virtual" office settings. According to IDC/Link Resources, a research firm, 37 million people worked from home in 1994 using e-mail, faxes, and the Internet. Over 8000 home-based businesses are being started each week. By the end of 1998, it was estimated that there were 60 million home-based workers, and the numbers continue to grow every year.[37]

New technologies have leveled the playing field, allowing entrepreneurs to compete effectively and successfully with larger companies. Technological advances have also lowered the cost of starting a business—the average entrepreneurial start-up in 1997 was a surprisingly low $25,000.[38] Technology has also had a positive impact on entrepreneurship in another way. An Arthur Andersen survey of 1000 small and medium-sized companies showed that companies using computers in 1997 saw a 5 percent profit increase compared with those that did not use a computer, which saw a 1 percent decrease in profits over the previous year. The good news is that small businesses are increasingly gravitating toward using computers; thus profits should increase. A survey by the New England Business Service of 300 business owners showed that only 21 percent reported they do not use a computer, which compares favorably to 31 percent in 1996.[39] The study also showed that companies that used the Internet saw an average annual revenue increase of 57 percent over the previous year, compared with 4.5 percent for all 1000 businesses surveyed.

Further, the Internet is providing entrepreneurs with better and quicker access to information and also creating new marketing and distribution channels, oftentimes at less cost. By 2000, more than 40 million homes in the United States had personal computers and Internet access, representing about 43 percent of all households. Online business-to-consumer (B2C) sales, which were $6.1 billion by the end of 1998, increased to approximately $20 billion worth of goods and services by the year 2000. Online commerce between companies, or business to business (B2B), which totaled approximately $15.6 billion in 1998, reached $175 billion by the year 2000.

The Internet is growing faster than all previous technologies. It took radio 38 years to reach 50 million listeners, and television 13 years to reach the same number of households. With the number of Internet users doubling every 100 days, it took only 4 years to reach 50 million users.[40] According to the Internet usage tracking company, Nielsen/NetRatings, 165.2 million Americans had home-based Internet access in mid 2001. There were 459 million users with home-based access worldwide in 2001. This technology is here to stay, and it provides entrepreneurs with new, and as yet unexplored, ways to market and distribute their goods and services. Every year, Dun & Bradstreet surveys small-business owners about interests, concerns, and expectations for the coming year. In the 2000 survey, small-business owners were asked how the Internet was used at their company. The results in Table 2-4 suggest that entrepreneurs are only in the early stages of tapping into the power of the Internet.

T A B L E   2-4

Small-Business Owners and Internet Usage

E-mail	74%
Business purchases	44%
Personal purchases	31%
Business research	69%
Personal research	47%
Find new customers and markets	28%
Sell goods and services	27%
Phone calls (Internet voice)	5%
Video conferencing	4%

Source: Dun & Bradstreet, *20th Annual Small Business Survey.*

The Internet IPO boom began in August 1995 with the initial public offering (IPO) of Netscape, which turned a company with sales of $20 million and no profits into one with a market capitalization of $2 billion.[41] In 1996, 39 Internet companies went public—an all-time record. Between 1996 and 1998, the Internet industry sector of the NASDAQ stock exchange had outperformed not only the S&P 500, but also the entire technology stock category.[42] As we would see later, many of the absurd valuations in tech stocks on the NASDAQ would come crumbling down—and take much of the economy with it. In the fall of 2001, the NASDAQ had dropped more than 60 percent from the same date 1 year earlier, while the S&P 500 had dropped 30 percent.

With regard to the computer revolution, the public markets have interestingly favored the entrepreneurial firms, which evolved with the personal computer, rather than the big, staid firms. The big technology companies of the 1980s were IBM, Digital Equipment, Wang, and Unisys. Between 1987 and 1997, these four companies experienced market value growth from $93 billion to $113.5 billion, a 22 percent increase. During the same 10-year period, the value of Microsoft, Intel, Compaq, Dell, 3Com, and Cisco, all companies whose success came from the explosion of the PC market, increased from $11.8 billion to $588 billion, an astounding 4883 percent appreciation![43]

Small high-tech firms have proved to be more productive, efficient, and innovative than large corporations. Since World War II, they are responsible for:

- 95 percent of the radical innovations that have occurred.
- 50 percent of *all* innovations.

In relation to companies with more than 500 employees, small high-tech firms have:

- Twice as many innovations per R&D dollar.
- Twice as many innovations per scientist.
- 24 times as many innovations per R&D dollar versus firms with greater than 10,000 employees.[44]

However, as is now evident, simply being a technology company did not guarantee it success. For example, in 1997, only 20 percent of all software makers had revenues of $10 million or more.[45] In the multibillion-dollar CD-ROM industry, only 6 percent of the titles are profitable.[46]

TRAITS OF AN ENTREPRENEUR

Building a successful, sustainable business requires courage, patience, and resilience. It demands a level of commitment that few people are capable of making. Membership in the "entrepreneurs club," while not exclusive, does seem to attract a certain type of individual. What, if any, are the common attributes of successful high-growth entrepreneurs?

While it is impossible to identify all the traits that are common to all entrepreneurs, it is possible to describe certain characteristics that are exhibited by most successful entrepreneurs. A survey of 400 entrepreneurs undertaken by an executive development consultant, Richard Hagberg, identified the top 10 characteristics that define entrepreneurs. These characteristics include:

- Focused, steadfast, and undeviating
- Positive outlook
- Opinionated and judges quickly
- Impatient
- Prefers simple solutions
- Autonomous and independent
- Aggressive
- Risk taker
- Acts without deliberation and reactive
- Emotionally aloof[47]

While this list is thorough, the addition of a few more traits would make it more complete.

- Opportunist
- Sacrificer
- Visionary
- Problem solver
- Comfortable with ambiguity or uncertainty.

Some of these traits are worth discussing in more detail.

Focused, Steadfast, and Undeviating

Successful entrepreneurs are focused on their mission and committed to getting it accomplished despite the enormous odds against them. They are tenacious in nature—they persevere. They are not quitters. If you want to join the club of entrepreneurship and you have never done anything to its completion in your life, this may not be the club for you because it is one where you will be required to hang tough even when times get rough. And in all likelihood, especially in the first 3 to 5 years of a new business, there will be more bad times than good, no matter how successful a venture.

An example of an entrepreneur who was focused on her goals is Josephine Esther Mentzer, the founder of the Estée Lauder Cosmetic Company, who is described as a person who "simply outworked everyone else in the cosmetics industry. She stalked the bosses of New York City department stores until she got some counter space at Saks Fifth Avenue in 1948."[48] Her company, which presently controls 45 percent of the cosmetics market in U.S. department stores and had $3.6 billion in revenues in 1997 from 118 countries throughout the world, pioneered the practice, which is common today, of giving a free gift to customers with a purchase.

Positive Outlook and Optimist

Entrepreneurs are confident optimists, especially when it comes to their ideas and their abilities to successfully achieve their goals. They are people who view the future in a positive light, seeing obstacles as challenges to be overcome, not as stumbling blocks. They visualize themselves as owners of businesses, employers, and change agents. The rough-and-tumble world of entrepreneurship is not a good fit for someone who is not an optimist.

Bryant Gumbel, the former *Today* show host and CBS morning show anchor, once told a story that best illustrates this point:

> It is Christmas morning and two kids—one a pessimist, the other an optimist—open their presents. The pessimist gets a brand new bike decked out with details and accessories in the latest style. "It looks great," he says. "But it will probably break soon." The second kid, an optimist and future entrepreneur, opens a huge package, finds it filled with horse manure and jumps with glee, exclaiming, "There must be a pony in there somewhere!"[49]

Prefers Simple Solutions

Ross Perot, the founder of EDS, and Ted Turner, the founder of CNN, are two successful entrepreneurs who have a prototypical knack for always describing the simplicity of their entrepreneurial endeavors. One of their favorite quotes, stated with their respective, comforting southern accents, is "It's real simple." One can easily envision one of them being the entrepreneur described in the following story of a chemist, a physicist, an engineer, and an entrepreneur: Each of them was asked how he or she would measure the height of a light tower with the use of a barometer. The chemist explained that she would measure the barometric pressure at the base of the tower and at the top of the tower. Because barometric pressure is related to altitude, she would determine from the difference in pressures the height of the tower. The physicist said that he would drop the barometer from the top of the tower and time how long it took to fall to the ground. From this time and the law of gravity he could determine the tower's height. The engineer said she would lower the barometer from the top of the tower on a string and then measure the length of the string. Finally, the entrepreneur said that he would go to the keeper of the tower, who probably knows every detail about the tower, and say, "Look, if you tell me the height of the tower, I'll give you this new shiny barometer."[50]

Autonomous and Independent

Entrepreneurs are known to be primarily driven by the desire to be independent of bosses and bureaucratic rules. Essentially, they march to their own beat. As one observer who was experienced with training entrepreneurs noted, "Entrepreneurs don't march left, right, left. They march left, left, right, right, left, hop, and skip."[51]

Risk Taker

The most common misconception people have of entrepreneurs is that they are blind risk takers. Most people think that entrepreneurs are no more than wild gamblers who start businesses with the same attitude and preparation they would undertake if they were going to Las Vegas to roll the dice, hoping for something positive to happen. This perception could not be further from the truth. Successful entrepreneurs are, without doubt, risk takers— they have to be if they are going to seize upon new opportunities and act decisively in ambiguous situations—but for the most part they are "educated" risk takers. They weigh the opportunity and its associated risks before they take action. They research the market or business opportunity, prepare solid business plans prior to taking action, and afterwards diligently "work" the plan. They also recognize that risk taking does not—despite the fact that it is a calculated risk—always guarantee success. There are always exceptions to the rule, however. Fred Smith, the founder and CEO of Federal Express delivery companies, did roll the dice, so to speak, 20 years ago when his start-up was low on capital. Despondent after being unsuccessful at raising capital during a trip to Chicago, he boarded a plane to Las Vegas at O'Hare Airport instead of to his home in Memphis and played blackjack, winning $30,000, which he used to save his company. Entrepreneurs are risk takers because failure in trying does not scare them. As John Henry Peterman, the founder of the Kentucky-based J. Peterman Catalog, an 11-year-old company with over $65 million in annual revenues, and more importantly, the company that employed Elaine Benis on the hit television series *Seinfeld*, said, "There is a great fear of failure in most people. I never had that. If failing at something destroys you, then you really have failed. But if failing leads you to a new understanding, new knowledge, you have not. If you don't make any mistakes, you're not doing it right."[52]

Opportunist

Entrepreneurs are proactive by nature. The difference between an entrepreneur and a nonentrepreneur is that the former does not hesitate to seize upon opportunities. When entrepreneurs see an opportunity, they execute a plan to take advantage of it. That disposition is in stark contrast to nonentrepreneurs' who may see something glittering at the bottom of a stream and say, isn't that gold? But instead of stopping and mining the gold, they simply keep paddling their boat.[53] An example of this type of opportunism is the story of Henry Kwahar, who owned a hot dog stand on the south side of Chicago in the early 1970s. During one of the hottest days of August 1973, a refrigerated truck filled with frozen fish broke down in front of Henry's stand. Rather than let the fish spoil, Henry, who had never sold fish before, offered to buy the entire stock at a very sharp discount. The truck driver agreed, and that is how Dock's Great Fish Fast Food Restaurant began. Henry named the restaurants after his father, Dock. There are presently 20 Dock's restaurants in Chicago and Cleveland.

Sacrificer

Every successful entrepreneur will acknowledge that success does not come without sacrifice. The most common sacrifice that an entrepreneur makes is in terms of personal income, particularly during the initial stages of a company. Almost all entrepreneurs must be willing to give up some amount of personal income to get a business started, either by committing their own resources or by taking a cut in pay. One of Jeff Bezos's early investors said that the most convincing factor was that Bezos had given up an annual seven-figure salary job at D. E. Shaw to start Amazon.com. The investor quoted, "The fact that Bezos had left that kind of situation overwhelmed me. It gave me a very, very powerful urge to get involved with this guy."[54] In fact, capital providers, such as bankers and venture capitalists, want to see an entrepreneur earning a salary that is enough to live comfortably, but not too comfortably, during the buildup stage of the business. Specifically, the entrepreneur's expected salary should be enough to cover personal bills (e.g., home mortgage, car payment, etc.) but not enough to provide for personal savings of any significant magnitude. This would indicate to potential financial backers the entrepreneur's level of commitment to the venture as well as his or her realism about the challenges that lie ahead.

A case in point: In 1996, a venture capitalist received a business plan from a team of three prospective entrepreneurs who wanted to start a national, daily newspaper targeting middle-class minorities. The idea seemed sound—such a newspaper did not exist to meet the demands of a rapidly growing segment of the U.S. population. The request for start-up capital was rejected, however, as it was evident to the venture capitalist, upon reading the business plan, that the team did not understand this key notion of sacrificing personal income. They included in their projections starting salaries in excess of $300,000 each, comparable to the corporate salaries they were earning at the time! Such salaries put them in the top 1 percent of the highest salaried people in the country. The venture capitalist viewed this as a sure sign that these three businesspeople were not sincere entrepreneurs. Business owners in general earn much less than what these three prospective entrepreneurs expected. Executive recruitment firm Christian and Timbers found that the average compensation for small-business owners in 1997 was $70,000. For the entrepreneurs backed by venture capital it was $206,000.[55] According to the SEC, Bill Gates's 2001 annual salary, excluding bonuses, was only $639,401.[56] In 2000, the chief executives of the top 200 U.S. companies received a record average of $10.89 million, according to a survey by Pearl Meyer & Partners, a New York–based executive-compensation consulting firm.[57] Table 2-5 provides data on the average salary plus bonus for CEOs of companies with revenues up to $200 million.

T A B L E 2-5

Average Salary and Bonus for CEOs of Companies with Revenues up to $200 Million

Region	Average Salary
Northwest	$324,000
Southeast	$318,000
South	$304,000
West	$288,000
Midwest	$264,000
Mid-Atlantic	$246,000

Source: *USA Today*, January 21, 1999.

Another difficult sacrifice that successful entrepreneurs have to make is spending less time with their families. For example, entrepreneur Alan Robbins, the owner of a 50-employee firm called Plastic Lumber Company, once said that he regretted not spending more time with his children during the beginning of his business, but considered it a trade-off he had to make. He argued that "when you start a business like this . . . you have to deny your family a certain level of attention."[58] The demands of owning or building a business put considerable strains on the time of an entrepreneur. However, this doesn't mean that the entrepreneur must *completely* neglect family or friends in order to run a successful business. To do so in the name of entrepreneurship is called "entremanureship!" When I owned my businesses, I didn't miss the nightly dinner with my family. I didn't miss my kids' birthday parties or baseball games—I worked around them. My two daughters are older now—one in college, one in high school—but when I started my businesses they were ages 8 and 4. I coached my youngest daughter's little league baseball team and her flag football team. I would have coached the oldest one too, but she'd decided that perhaps it would be best for me to simply cheer from the stands. I've seen more of my kids' games and events than any other parent I know. *Of course* you're going to work long hours to get your business going in the first couple of years. But one of the beautiful things about being your own boss is that, by and large, you're the one who determines *which* hours to work. In addition to sitting on several boards of billion-dollar companies, I'm also a director for several start-ups. I tell these entrepreneurs, "Go home, have dinner with the family, and read the kids a bedtime story. Then get your butt back to work." When Dun & Bradstreet surveyed small-business owners for its 20th annual Small Business Survey, nearly two-thirds of the respondents said they worked more than 40 hours per week.[59] When *Inc.* magazine surveyed the CEOs of its 500 fastest-growing companies, 66 percent of them remember working at least 70 hours a week when they started their companies. And 40 percent reported working more than 80 hours per week.[60] Ken Ryan, CEO of Airmax, told *Inc.*, "There were times when I slept on the floor by the phone so as not to miss a call." The good news is that only 13 percent say they now log more than 70 hours. Trust me, it gets better. You *can* make time to take your kids to the park, but nobody said starting a business was a walk in one.

Visionary

Webster's Collegiate Dictionary defines a visionary as someone who is "marked by foresight." This is an appropriate characterization of most successful entrepreneurs. They are able to anticipate future trends, identify opportunities, and visualize the actions needed to accomplish a desired goal. They must sell this vision to potential customers, financiers, and employees. A couple of entrepreneurs who were great visionaries and made an impact on almost everyone's daily lives include:

Ray Kroc, Founder—McDonald's Corporation

Ray Kroc was an acquirer, who purchased McDonald's restaurants in 1961 for $2.7 million from two brothers who founded it, Dick and Mac McDonald. After concluding that Americans were becoming people who increasingly liked to "eat and run" versus the traditional dining at a restaurant or eating at home, his vision was to build the quick service, limited menu restaurant throughout the country. McDonald's, with operations in 120 countries, is now the largest restaurant company in the world. By the way, for the graying dreamers reading this book, Kroc was a 52-year-old salesman when he bought McDonald's.

Akio Morita, Cofounder—Sony Corporation

Akio Morita cofounded Sony—the company that a Harris survey ranked as the number one consumer brand in America. The company, which was started in 1942 under the name Tokyo Telecommunications Engineering Inc. and went on to become the first Japanese firm on the NYSE in 1970, succeeded using Akio's vision to market the company throughout the world so that the name would immediately communicate high product quality. While this is a marketing concept commonly used today, it was not so 40 years ago, especially in Japan. In fact, most Japanese manufacturers produced products under somebody else's name including Pentax for Honeywell, Ricoh for Savin, and Sanyo for Sears. Sony successfully introduced the small pocket-sized transistor radio in 1957. Six years later, in 1963, with the vision of making Sony an international company, Morita moved his entire family to New York so that he could personally get to know the interests, needs, and culture of Americans and the American market.[61]

All successful entrepreneurs are visionaries at one time or another. They have to constantly reinvent their strategy, look for new opportunities, and go after new products and new ideas if they are to survive. However, this does not mean they have this ability all the time. Visionaries can become nonvisionaries. In fact, as Cognetics Consulting points out, sometimes "the most astute masters of the present are often the least able to see the future."[62] Examples of some famous nonvisionaries include:

Heavier than air flying machines are impossible.

—Lord Kelvin
President of the Royal Society in 1895[63]

Everything that can be invented has been invented.
—Charles H. Duell
Commissioner, U.S. Office of Patents, in 1899[64]

I think there is a world market for maybe five computers.
—Thomas Watson
Chairman, IBM, in 1943[65]

We don't like their music, we don't like their sound, and guitar music is on the way out.
—Decca Recording Company
rejecting the Beatles in 1962[66]

There is no reason anyone would want a computer in their home.
—Ken Olsen
Founder and Chairman,
Digital Equipment Corp., in 1977[67]

Problem Solver

Anyone working in today's competitive and ever-changing business environment knows that the survival of a company, be it large or small, depends on its ability to quickly identify problems and find solutions. Successful entrepreneurs are comfortable with and adept at identifying and solving problems facing their businesses. Risk takers by nature, they are willing to try new ways to solve the problems facing their companies and are capable of learning from their own and other's mistakes or failures. The successful entrepreneur is one who says, "I failed here, but this is what I learned." Successful entrepreneurs are always capable of extracting some positive lesson from any experience.

An example of someone who exhibits this characteristic is Norm Brodsky, a former owner of six companies and presently a writer for *Inc.* magazine. In an article, he says, "I prefer chaos. Deep down I like having problems. It's hard to admit it, but I enjoy the excitement of working in a crisis atmosphere. That's one of the reasons I get so much pleasure out of starting businesses. You have nothing but problems when you are starting out."[68]

Comfort with Ambiguity or Uncertainty

The ability to function in an environment of continual uncertainty is a common trait found among successful entrepreneurs. Often, they will be required to make decisions, such as determining market demand for a newly developed product or service, without having adequate or complete information. Other important traits that successful entrepreneurs have in common are that they are hardworking people who possess numerous skills, as they are required to play multiple roles as owners of businesses. They are good leaders. They have the ability to sell, whether it is a product, an idea, or a vision. One of the most infamous sales pitches used by an entrepreneur was when Steven Jobs, the cofounder of Apple Computer, was closing his recruiting speech to Pepsi Co.'s John Sculley, whom he wanted to become Apple's CEO. To sell John on the opportunity, Jobs asked him, "Do you want to spend the rest of your life selling sugared water or do you want a chance to change the world?"[69]

IMPACT ON THE ECONOMY

Entrepreneurs with small and medium height growth businesses are playing an increasingly crucial role in the success of the U.S. economy.[70] Not only are they providing economic opportunities to a diverse segment of the population, but they are also providing employment to an increasing segment of the U.S. population. The *Fortune* 500 companies are no longer the major source of employment; rather, entrepreneurs are creating jobs and therefore are doing "good for society by doing well." As one employee of a 400-employee firm said about his company's owner, "To everybody else she's an entrepreneur. But to me she is a Godsend."[71]

In the 1960s, 1 out of every 4 persons in the United States worked for a *Fortune* 500 company. Today, only 1 out of every 14 people works for these companies. Employment at *Fortune* 500 companies peaked at 16.5 million people in 1979 and has steadily declined every year to approximately 10.5 million people today. During this same period, small and medium-size companies created more than 30 million new jobs.[72] Most of the 122.5 million American workers are employed at small and medium-size businesses. Companies with fewer than 500 workers employ 57 percent of all employees.[73] Approximately 10 million people work at companies with 20 to 49 employees, a work force second only to companies with at least 5000 employees.[74]

Finally, entrepreneurial firms are also important participants in U.S. international trade. Data from the Department of Commerce show that in 1992, companies with fewer than 500 employees represented 95.7 percent of all U.S. exporters and contributed approximately 30 percent of the $349 billion in exports that year.[75]

As the data in Table 2-6 show, entrepreneurial firms created almost all of the net new jobs from 1992 through 1996. In 1998, 2.9 million new jobs were created, with entrepreneurial firms contributing over 60 percent of this job growth.[76]

TABLE 2-6

Job Creation by Industry and Size of Firm, 1992–1996

Industry	Firm Size (by Number of Employees)								
	1–19	%	20–99	%	100–499	%	500+	%	Total
All industries	8,080,404	72	1,417,267	13	2,326,038	21	−642,791	−6	11,181,024
Manufacturing	406,831		181,309		363,680		−1,055,132		−103,312
Retail trade	1,226,906		250,746		243,845		−423,376		1,298,121
Services	4,191,452		799,525		1,377,706		1,130,633		7,499,316
Other	2,255,213		185,684		340,801		−294,912		2,486,786

Source: Small Business Administration, Small Business Profile, 1998.

The findings of a study undertaken by Cognetics Consulting Firm, a company specializing in small businesses, reinforces the data provided in Table 2-6. As you can see in Table 2-7, from 1991 through 1996, employment increased mainly in small companies, while it decreased in larger ones.

TABLE 2-7

Employment Growth by Firm Size, 1991–1996

Number of Employees	Employment Growth, 1991–1996
1–19	9.0%
20–99	1.2%
100–4999	0.2%
Over 5000	(2.4)%

Source: Cognetics Consulting Firm, April 1997.

Contrary to popular belief, small businesses are not the exception in the American economy; they are the norm. This fact was highlighted when *Crain's Chicago Business* weekly business newspaper advertised its new small-business publication by taking out a full-page advertisement that read:

THERE WAS A

TIME WHEN 90% OF

CHICAGO AREA

BUSINESSES HAD

REVENUES OF

UNDER $5 MILLION.

(YESTERDAY).[77]

On the national level, the same holds true. Out of the approximately 22.5 million businesses in the United States, only about 4 percent have annual revenues greater than $1 million, and less than 1500 companies have sales of $100 million or more.[78] Exhibit 2-3 provides data on the ownership category of all businesses in 2000.[79]

E X H I B I T   2-3

Business Ownership 2000

5.8 million non-farm employer firms

9.9 million self-employed

17.9 million sole proprietorships

2 million partnerships

5.5 million corporations

Source: SBA Office of Advocacy, August 2001.

In terms of firm size, again Chicago is an excellent example of the national situation. As the *Chicago Tribune* reported, in "Metropolitan Chicago," 97.7 percent of businesses have fewer than 100 employees.[80] As stated earlier, the national situation is the same, where only 70,000 companies have more than 100 employees and only 14,000 employ more than 500 employees. In fact, of the 5.7

million companies with at least 1 employee, more than 50 percent employ fewer than 5 people, while 90 percent employ fewer than 20.[81] Clearly, large companies are the exception.

The dominance of small businesses as major employers holds true on the international level as well, particularly in Asia. In Japan, for example, 78 percent of the work force is employed at companies with 300 or fewer workers; in South Korea 69 percent of the work force is employed in such companies. In Taiwan, 80 percent of the labor force is employed by companies with fewer than 200 employees.[82] Small companies are also very dominant in the United Kingdom, where only 100,000 of the 3.5 million businesses in the country have revenues of $3 million or more.

Thus, small-business owners should not be ashamed or embarrassed by their size, but rather be proud that they are major contributors to the success of the U.S. and the global economy. They are, in fact, economic "heroes and sheroes."

IMPACT ON GENDER AND RACE

The entrepreneurial phenomenon has been widespread and inclusive, affecting genders as well as all races and nationalities in the United States. One group that has benefited is female entrepreneurs. In the 1960s there were fewer than 1 million women-owned businesses employing less than 1 million people. By the 1970s, women owned less than 5 percent of all businesses in the United States. In the 1980s, they owned about 3 million businesses, approximately 20 percent of all businesses, generating $40 billion in annual revenues. Census Bureau statistics always lag several years behind. In April 2001, the bureau released its latest statistics—for 1997. In that year, privately held women-owned businesses in the United States totaled 5.4 million, employed 7.1 million people, and generated $818.7 billion in revenues. The 1997 economic census defines women-owned businesses as privately held firms in which women own 51 percent or more of the firm. The bureau noted that there were an additional 2 million firms in which women owned 50 percent of the company.[83] Between 1992 and 1997, women-owned firms increased 16 percent—almost triple the rate of all other firms (excluding publicly held companies). Revenues for these firms increased 33 percent, compared with a 24 percent increase for all firms. In addition, these companies seem to have a better chance of staying in business. Nearly 75 percent of women-owned companies started in 1991 were still in business in 1994, 3 years after starting up, compared with 66 percent for all other businesses started the same year.[84]

The entrepreneurship revolution over the past decade has also included virtually all of the country's minority groups. Minority firms grew 4 times faster than the national average between 1992 and 1997, increasing from 2.1 million to about 2.8 million firms. The 33 percent growth exceeded the 6 percent increase for all firms. Revenues of minority-owned firms (excluding C corporations) rose 60 percent to $335.3 billion in 1997, compared with a 40 percent increase for all U.S firms over the same period.[85] The number of African-American businesses jumped 94 percent to 823,500 from 1987 to 1997, according to census data. The number of Asian-owned businesses jumped 180 percent to 832,000 in the same 10-year period. Hispanic enterprises increased 184 percent to 1.2 million.[86] Exhibit 2-4 shows the diverse characteristics of the small-business owner in 1996.

E X H I B I T   2-4

Characteristics of the Small-Business Owner, 1996–1997

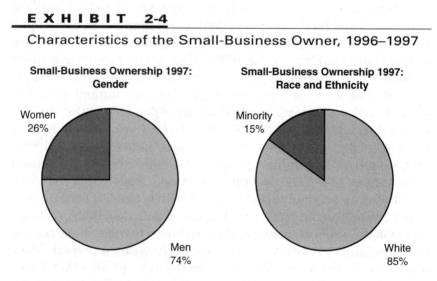

Small-Business Ownership 1997: Gender

Women 26%

Men 74%

Small-Business Ownership 1997: Race and Ethnicity

Minority 15%

White 85%

Source: 1997 Economic Census—Minority and Women Owned Business.

Characteristics of the Small-Business Owner, 1996–1997 (continued)

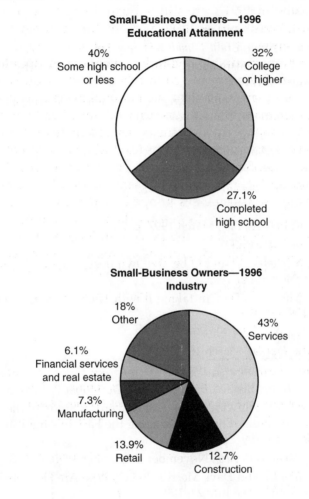

Small-Business Owners—1996
Educational Attainment

40%
Some high school
or less

32%
College
or higher

27.1%
Completed
high school

Small-Business Owners—1996
Industry

18%
Other

6.1%
Financial services
and real estate

7.3%
Manufacturing

13.9%
Retail

43%
Services

12.7%
Construction

N O T E S

1. Small Business Administration, 1992. *Note:* This study includes companies which have gone out of business voluntarily or in which the owner retired. *Crain's*, November 16, 1992.

2. *Black Enterprise*, December 1997.

3. Moore, Jonathan, Pete Engardio, and Moon Ihlwan, "The Taiwan Touch," *BusinessWeek*, May 25, 1998.
4. "Failure Rate of New Products Is 65%," *International Manufacturing Review*, July 1, 1999.
5. Hisrish and Brush survey, 1988.
6. Dun & Bradstreet, *Crain's Small Business*, February 1997.
7. Jones, Del, "Optimism about Economy Astounds Experts," *USA Today*, March 24, 1998.
8. Mariotti, Steve, *The Young Entrepreneur's Guide to Starting and Running a Business*, Times Books, 2000.
9. Port, Otis, "Starting Up Again—and Again and Again," *BusinessWeek*, August 25, 1997.
10. *New York Times*, September 23, 1998.
11. *Fast Company*, February–March 1998.
12. *Success*, May 27, 1998.
13. Mamis, Robert A., *Inc.*, March 1997, p. 73.
14. Bishop, Jack, Jr., Ph.D.
15. Donley, Michele, "I Want to Be My Own Boss," *Crain's Small Business*, November 1995.
16. Arnold, Michael, "They're Taking It with Them," *Chicago Sun-Times*, June 5, 1998, p. 48.
17. *USA Today*, April 23, 2001, p. 28.
18. *Wall Street Journal*, March 16, 1998.
19. *USA Today*, December 2, 1998.
20. Chernow, Ron, "Blessed Barons," *Time*, December 7, 1998, p. 29.
21. Roper Starch Worldwide, "Risk and Reward: A Study of the Company Builders Who Are Changing the Face of American Business," *Inc.*, 1997, p. 5.
22. *Harvard Business Review*, November–December 1996, p. 122.
23. Carey, Anne R., and Dave Merrill, "CEOs Who Are Household Names," *USA Today*, July 22, 1998.
24. Roper Starch Worldwide, "Risk and Reward: A Study of Company Builders Who Are Changing the Face of American Business," *Inc.*, 1997, p. 5.
25. Ho, Rodney, "AT&T's Offer of $10,000 May Test Entrepreneurship of Laid Off Employees," *Wall Street Journal*, March 12, 1997.
26. Hise, Phaedia, "New Recruitment Strategy: Ask Your Best Employees to Leave," *Inc.*, July 1997, p. 28.

27. *USA Today*, December 7, 1998.
28. Koretz, Gene, "Downsized in a Down Economy," *BusinessWeek*, September 17, 2001.
29. "Layoff Tracker," Forbes.com, September 25, 1001, http://www.forbes.com/2001/01/30/layoffs.html.
30. *Inc.*, March 1997.
31. Lieberman, Dave, "Disney's Kingdom Counts on Bounty from Sports," *USA Today*, October 7, 1998.
32. *USA Today*, April 14, 1998, p. 14.A.
33. Bronner, Ethan, "Students at B-Schools Flock to the E-Courses," *New York Times*, September 23, 1998, p. 6.
34. Ibid.
35. Hanson, Cynthia, "Working Smart," *Chicago Tribune*, October 8, 1995.
36. *Forbes*, November 15, 1998.
37. *Black Enterprise*, September 1998.
38. *Forbes*, June 15, 1998.
39. Langdon, Jerry, "Small Businesses Shun Technology," *USA Today*, September 21, 1998.
40. Nee, Eric, "Surf's Up," *Forbes*, July 27, 1998.
41. Hof, Robert D., "Netspeed at Netscape," *BusinessWeek*, February 10, 1997, p. 79.
42. *Forbes*, July 27, 1998.
43. Ibid.
44. Herman, Mike, Kauffman Foundation, 1997.
45. "Former Producer Found Niche with Games," *Chicago Tribune*, September 14, 1998.
46. Kirk, Jim, "In World of Computer Games, Software Maker Plays to Win," *Chicago Sun-Times*, January 14, 1996.
47. Dugan, I. Jeanne, ed., "Portrait of an Entrepreneur," *BusinessWeek/Enterprise*.
48. Mirabella, Grace, "Beauty Queen: Estee Lauder," *Time*, December 7, 1998.
49. Stemberg, Tom, *Staples for Success*.
50. Kamien, Morton I., "Entrepreneurship: What Is It?" *BusinessWeek Executive Briefing Service*, 1994.
51. Verrochi, Paul, "The Quotable Entrepreneur," *Inc.*, December 1998.
52. *USA Today*, April, 23, 1997.
53. *Inc.*, December 1998.

54. *Business 2.0*, April 2000, p. 261.

55. "How Many Bucks Stop with You?" *BusinessWeek Enterprise*, May 25, 1998.

56. *USA Today*, January 21, 1999.

57. Day, Kathleen, "CEO's Compensation at Record Highs Despite Plunging Stock Prices," *Washington Post*, April 1, 2001.

58. Aeppel, Timothy, "Losing Faith: Personnel Disorders Sap a Factory Owner of His Early Idealism," *Wall Street Journal*, September 27, 1996, p. A13.

59. Dun & Bradstreet, "*20th Annual Small Business Survey*," 2000.

60. Murphy, Anne, "Analysis of the 2000 Inc 500," Inc.com, http://www.inc.com/articles/details/1,3532,CID20477_REG3,00.html.

61. Ottmae, Kenichi, "Guru of Gadgets: Akio Morita," *Time*, December 7, 1998.

62. Cognetics Consulting, October 17, 1997.

63. Ibid.

64. Ibid.

65. Ibid.

66. Ibid.

67. Ibid.

68. Brodsky, Norm, with Bo Burhingham, "Necessary Losses," *Inc.*, December 1997, p. 120.

69. Elmer DeWitt, Philip, "Steve Jobs: Apple's Anti-Gates," *Time*, December 7, 1998, p. 133.

70. *Note:* Unless otherwise stated, small businesses are defined as firms with fewer than 500 employees.

71. "Owning the Airwaves," *Essence*, October, 1998.

72. *Chicago Tribune*, May 25, 1997.

73. *Chicago Sun-Times*, June 8, 1998; Small Business Administration, "Exporting by Small Firms: A Report by Firm Size," Office of Economic Research of the U.S. Office of Advocacy, April 1998.

74. Ibid.

75. Iritani, Evelyn, "Small Companies Hit by Asia Fiscal Crisis," *Chicago Sun-Times*, June 8, 1998; Small Business Administration, "Exporting by Small Firms: A Report by Firm Size," Office of Economic Research of the U.S. Office of Advocacy, April 1998.

76. Small Business Administration, Small Business Profile, 1998.

77. *Crain's Chicago Business*, January 24, 1994.

78. Small Business Administration, Small Business Profile, 1998.

79. "The State of Small Business 1995," *Nation's Business*, 1996.

80. *Chicago Tribune*, August 8, 1997.

81. *Nation's Business*, 1996.

82. Kim, James, "Made in Taiwan: Entrepreneurs, Self Starters Help Rev Up Economy," *USA Today*, June 23, 1998, B1–B2.

83. 1997 Economic Census Report, "Minority and Women Owned Businesses in the United States."

84. Ibid.

85. U.S Department of Commerce, July 12, 2001, news release.

86. *LA Times*, June 2, 2001.

CHAPTER 3

The Business Plan

INTRODUCTION

Starting a new business or growing an already established one requires careful planning. An entrepreneur is faced with the challenge of making decisions in an ever-changing business environment, which is impacted by external factors, many beyond his or her direct control. The emergence of new competitors, technological advancements, and changes in the macroeconomic and regulatory environments are just a few of the factors with which an entrepreneur needs to deal. In order to build a successful and sustainable business, entrepreneurs must be forward-looking and determine what lies ahead for their company, what their future objectives and strategies are, and how they plan to achieve their goals and manage risks. This is done through a business plan, which, unfortunately, many entrepreneurs never write. As Thomas Doherty, the senior vice president of Chicago's La Salle Bank, said, "Most small business owners have the plan in their head, but we would like to see a larger number who actually put it down on paper and think through some of the details—financing, competition, strengths and weaknesses, the whole strategic plan."[1] Essentially, the business plan is the evidence that the entrepreneur respects the "seven p's of business": proper prior preparation prevents piss-poor performance.[2]

THE DUAL-PURPOSE DOCUMENT

For the entrepreneur, the business plan serves a dual purpose. First, it should be used as an internal document to help define a company's strategies and objectives and provide a plan for the future growth of the company. It is basically the company's "road map," which lays out the planned entrepreneurial journey. The plan should not be written and filed away. It must become a living, breathing document. To be successful and experience high growth, the entrepreneur must "work the plan" by using it as a proactive tool. The business plan is an evolving, rather than an immutable, document. The entrepreneur should update and revise it at least once a year, preferably at the end of each year in preparation for the next year's operations.

Alternatively, an entrepreneur must always present it to a potential investor(s) when raising capital. It should be noted that all business plans are not always automatically capital-raising documents. Some entrepreneurs mistakenly believe the business plan is synonymous with raising capital. There are an endless number of stories about business plans sent to potential investors that never provide key information, such as how much capital the entrepreneur wants, what the capital is going to be used for, and what the investor will get in terms of targeted returns. A well-articulated business plan—one in which a company's vision, strategies, financing needs, and goals are clearly outlined—will not only help an entrepreneur keep his or her business on track but also make it easier to raise capital.

Investors are inundated with business plans but are willing to finance only a few. The old axiom "You only get one chance to make a good first impression" is especially true when procuring capital for your business. Typically, that one chance is through the business plan. For example, Frontenac, a Chicago venture capital firm with over $300 million under management, receives 3000 business plans a year but only invests in approximately 15 companies. John Doerr, of the venture capital firm of Kleiner, Perkins, Caufield & Byers (KPCB), said, "We receive 2,500 plans per year, meet with at least 100 of those who submitted the plans and invest in about 25."[3] To the investor, the business plan in most cases is the first, and oftentimes only, representation of an entrepreneur. Therefore, it is important to have a well-written, original, and thorough business plan. A well-written business plan is one that is free of grammatical errors, concise, and simple to understand; it clearly describes the company's product or service and tells the reader the amount of capital being sought and the way it will be repaid. A business plan consisting of all of these elements will be well received by the potential investor.

BUSINESS PLAN DEVELOPMENT AND ADVICE

One venture capitalist suggests that the business plan be written or edited by the entrepreneurial team member who is the best writer and most articulate.[4] The result should be that the document is understood by the average 14-year-old. In fact, after writing the plan the entrepreneur should give it to a teenager and ask him or her to read it and verbally explain what the proposed product or service is, how it is going to be made available to the marketplace, how much capital is being requested, and if the management team is experienced, inexperienced, old, or young. There is nothing more frustrating for a potential investor than to expend valuable time reading a plan that is difficult to understand due to complicated and/or vague descriptions, poor writing, misspellings, and grammatical errors. In response to criticism that the business plan could not be understood, many entrepreneurs will say, "I know. Let me meet with you to explain it." No! The business plan should be a viable and adequate communication tool on its own, in the absence of the entrepreneur.

Another option available to the entrepreneur for getting the business plan written is to approach a graduate business school. Many of these schools allow their students to get academic credit for working on business projects, including writing business plans for local entrepreneurs, under the supervision of an entrepreneurship professor. Such graduate schools include New York University's Stern School of Business and Northwestern University's Kellogg School of Management. There are also numerous web sites (e.g., Garage.com) and books (e.g., *Business Plans for*

Dummies) that can help with basic templates. More sources are noted at the end of this chapter, in Exhibit 3-1.

Investors are primarily interested in knowing what they will get in return for risking their capital and whether the entrepreneur has the ability to successfully execute the plan that will deliver this return. A well-written plan provides all the necessary information about the company and the business opportunity to enable investors to assess if the venture is worth financing. What is the proper length of a business plan? While there is no "right" length, the shorter plans tend to be better received. At the maximum, a business plan should be no longer than 30 pages.

The information contained in a business plan will vary depending on the investor(s) being solicited for financing as well as the type of company seeking funding. Is the financing for an acquisition or a start-up? For instance, a start-up company with a new product or service should provide data that substantiates the existence of market demand for the product or service. Also, priority should be placed on ensuring that investors are convinced that the management team has the experience and skills necessary to launch and manage a new business venture. Bill Sutter, former general partner at Mesirow Capital, says that the three most important things he looks for in a business plan are (1) management, (2) management, and (3) cashflow.[5]

Concerning the targeted audience, if the business plan is to be presented to someone who is familiar with the industry, the company, or the management team, it may not be necessary to provide as much detailed information as it would if it were presented to potential investors who had no such knowledge.

The greatest examples of this fact are the plans submitted by Intel and Sun Microsystems to Kleiner, Perkins, Caufield & Byers venture fund. The Intel business plan was one page and the Sun Microsystems business plan was three pages. KPCB financed both companies.

THE BUSINESS PLAN

The development of a business plan can be a difficult, time-consuming process, but it must be done. While the general format of a business plan is standard, it should be written in a way that highlights the uniqueness of the company. The business plan should:

- Tell a complete story about the company, its management team, product or service, financing needs, strategies, and the financial and nonfinancial goals the company expects to achieve.
- Be a balanced document highlighting both the positive and negative aspects of the business opportunity.
- Be a forward-looking document with a time frame of at least 3 years.
- Be clear, concise, and organized.
- Be simple to understand.
- Provide realistic data to substantiate claims.
- Propose the deal to the investors—what are the expected returns on their investments, what are the exit or liquidation options available to investors.
- Provide historical and projected financial statements.

The contents of the business plan will vary depending on the type of business. For example, a research and development section should be included if the company's product is in the research and development stage or if the company has undertaken substantial research and development to get the product to market, e.g., a new drug or new technology. On the other hand, this section would not be required in a plan for a restaurant, for example. The research and development section should include a summary of the major findings, while the details should be included in the appendices. In general, a business plan contains the following sections:

Executive Summary

In most instances, given the large number of business plans that they receive, potential investors will only thoroughly read the executive summary. This section may be the only opportunity for an entrepreneur to make a good first impression on a potential financier. Therefore, it is *the* most important section of the business plan. It has to capture all the main issues contained in the detailed business plan. It should be concise (i.e., no longer than two pages), be clear and simple to understand, and present a good summation of the most relevant information needed by potential investors.

In support of the point stated above, Barbara Kamm, senior vice president at Silicon Valley Bank, said, "When bankers review a business plan, they want to see a well-written executive summary. The executive summary is the key—it's where you distill the essence of your business."[6] A good executive summary should include:

- Return on investment (ROI). The amount earned on a company's total capital, expressed as a percentage
- Internal rate of return (IRR). The return on investment with consideration to the length of the investment
- The current and potential risks

The Company

The objective of this section is to provide information on the background of the company. The following questions should be answered:

- When was the company established and by whom?
- Is it a start-up or an ongoing concern?
- What type of industry is it in? Service, retail, manufacturing?
- What market area(s) does it serve or intend to serve?
- What is the business's legal structure? Sole proprietorship, corporation, limited partnership?
- Who are the company's principals, and what are their ownership stakes? What experience and skills do they bring, and what is their involvement in the day-to-day operations of the company?
- What is the total number of employees?
- What is the revenue size of the company?
- What is the historical growth rate of the company?

Information related to the legal structure of the company should also be provided. There are advantages and disadvantages of different legal structures as detailed below:

Sole Proprietorship

Advantages:

- No legal expense of setting formal structure.
- Easy to set up—therefore most typical way small businesses start.
- All income reported on Schedule C on personal income tax return.
- All legitimate expenses can be deducted from business income or income you earned at another job.

Disadvantages:

- Unlimited personal liability for business debts.
- Can't have employees unless you get employer ID number to file payroll tax returns.
- Unable to take certain kinds of business deductions.

General and Limited Partnerships

Advantages:

- Save money on accounting and legal fees.
- Business income or losses go to partners, who report it on personal income returns.
- Business expenses and other deductions flow to partners.
- Limited partners are not personally liable and only in some instances are they liable to the amount of their original investment.
- Despite ownership percentage, all operational decisions are made only by the general partners.

Disadvantages:

- General partners are personally liable for business obligations and can be personally sued.
- Limited partners cannot participate in any decisions or they will jeopardize their liability status.

C Corporation

Advantages:

- Protection from personal liability.
- Unlimited number of shareholders with no limit on stock classes or voting arrangements.
- Can provide qualified stock option and employee stock purchase plans to employees as incentives.
- No need to restructure prior to an IPO.

Disadvantages:

- Costs can be significant to incorporate.
- Taxed as a separate entity.
- Dividend income is taxed at corporate and shareholder level (double taxation).
- Corporate tax rate may be higher than personal tax rate.

S Corporation

Advantages:

- Same limited liability as C corporation has.
- Profits are passed through to shareholders and taxed on individual's return similar to partnership.
- Deduction of losses on personal return is allowed up to the amount of individual's cost of the company's stock, plus any loans made to the company.

Disadvantages:

- Can't have more than 35 shareholders.
- Can only have one class of stock, limiting flexibility to add future investors and restrict their share of profits.
- Can't have foreigners, trust, or other corporations as shareholders.
- Can't offer some benefits that a C corporation can, such as medical reimbursement plans.

LLC (Limited Liability Corporation)

Advantages:

- Ownership flexibility of C corporation.
- No limit to number of shareholders.
- Can create several classes of shareholders (founders can be entitled to greater share of profits or of stock's future value if sold to public.)
- No double taxation because profits are only taxed at the shareholder level.
- No limit to deductibility of losses for shareholder.

Disadvantages:

- If you convert a current corporation to an LLC, you might have to liquidate first and owe a big tax.
- You cannot transfer the business of your old corporation to a new LLC.

The Industry

It is necessary to provide the context in which the business will operate. Macroeconomic as well as industry-specific data should be presented to provide a better understanding of the overall environment in which the company will operate. This information should include:

- Macroeconomic data such as unemployment rate, inflation, interest rates, etc., that have or will have an impact on the industry, and more specifically, on the company's operations.
- Information on regulatory changes that might have an impact on the industry or the company.
- A description of the industry—e.g., major participants, competition, etc.
- Size of the industry—e.g., historical, current, and future trends, etc.
- Characteristics of the industry—e.g., seasonal, cyclical, countercyclical.

- Trends taking place in the industry that have an impact on the business—i.e., consolidation, deregulation.
- The key drivers in the industry—e.g., R&D, marketing, price, quick delivery, relationships.
- Industry growth rates—past and future.
- Customer payment practices—for example, are there slow payers, such as the government or insurance companies?

The Market

This section should provide a description of the target market(s)—primary as well as secondary. It's important to be specific when identifying the markets to be targeted. If the product or service is new, market research data should be included to provide information on initial and future markets. Research can be done by paying a consulting firm or getting it free, or at a substantially lower cost, by going to a local business school and asking the marketing department to assign students to do it as a project for academic credit. Questions to be answered include.

- What are the key customer market segments? What is their size?
- Where are they located? Are they regional, national, international?
- What are the past growth rates in market and anticipated trends?
- What are the market characteristics—seasonal, cyclical, etc.?
- Are there any anticipated changes within the primary market?
- How will each customer market segment be reached?
- How are purchasing decisions made? By whom? What are the factors that influence purchasing decisions?
- How do customers buy products—through competitive bidding, contracts, unit purchases, etc.?
- Is there a possibility to create new customer bases? If so, how?

Product or Service Description

Investors need to know the type of product or service the company will offer to customers. They will need the following information:

- A detailed description of the product or service to be developed and marketed including:
  - Benefits of product or service
  - Stage of product or service—is it an idea, prototype, etc.?
- Key product characteristics—performance, quality, durability, price, service, etc.
- What is your differentiation strategy?
- What is your positioning strategy?
- What is your pricing strategy? Why?
- Chances of product obsolescence.
- Legal issues relating to the product or service that provide legal protection, e.g., obtained or pending patents, copyrights, trademarks, royalties, etc.
- Other legal and regulatory issues that relate to the product or service.

Competition

Competition is a reality for every business. One should not underestimate a competitor's capabilities and overestimate one's capacity to deal with them. Investors prefer to go with entrepreneurs who have a realistic assessment of their competitors, and accordingly, realistically plan to deal with this competition. In this section, key competitors—direct and indirect—should be identified and an explanation provided about how the company will successfully compete. Questions to be answered include:

- Who are the key competitors, both direct and indirect? Are they mom and pop or high-growth entrepreneurs? What are their strengths and weaknesses?
- Where do they operate? Are they local or national players?
- What is their market share?
- What are the key competitive factors—pricing, quality, performance, etc.? How does the company fare in this regard?

- Present market share? Expected market share? How will market share be gained?
- Are there any barriers to entry into the market—i.e., is it a capital-intensive industry?
- What do you plan to do to mitigate this competition?

Marketing and Sales

The main question to answer here is how the product or service is going to be made available in the marketplace.

- What is your marketing strategy?
- How is the product or service going to be advertised and promoted?
- How important is marketing to the industry?
- What is the expected return on resources spent on marketing?
- What is the sales growth? Historical, current, expected in 3 years?
- What is the sales strategy to achieve these sales levels? At a regional or national level?
- What is the product distribution strategy? In-house sales force, outside manufacturer's representatives? What is the sales compensation plan?
- What are the sales per employee? Historically, present, future, and for the industry as a whole?

Facilities

Information provided in this section should include:

- Description of plants and their operations—size, location (e.g., rural or urban), age, and condition of plants
- Ownership or lease
- Cost estimates to run facilities
- Capital equipment requirement
- Condition of equipment and property
- Sales per square foot

- Insurance—coverage and name of provider(s)
- Access to public transportation
- Utilities
- Available parking for customers and employees

Operating Plan

Information should be provided to explain the day-to-day operations of the company, including:

Business Operations
- Days of operation and hours
- Shutdown period
- Number of shifts

Production
- Production plans
- Key quality control issues
- Capacity
- Utilization
- Bottlenecks
- Automation: technology versus manual
- Build to order versus build to inventory

Purchasing
- Purchasing plans
- Material resource systems
- Inventory plan
- Suppliers—local or national, proximity, single or multiple
- Product delivery
- Office: invoicing, payables, collecting
- Receiving and shipping

Labor Force
- Number of employees

- Skill levels
- Gender
- Age range
- Union versus nonunion status
- Years of service
- Compensation and salary plan
- Hourly versus exempt
- Payroll—weekly versus monthly
- Benefits
- Safety concerns
- Insurance
- Source of labor
- Productivity per employee
- Projections for labor force changes in the future

Management Team

One of the most important elements that investors look for when assessing the viability of a business venture is the strength of the management team. In this section it is important to provide background information on the personnel who will be involved in the day-to-day operations of the company. From this information the investor will try to determine if the management team can successfully implement the plan. The ideal management team has complementary skills and expertise. Information should include:

- Names and titles of the key management personnel
- Experience, skill levels, and functional responsibilities of the key management personnel
- Anticipated changes in the management team
- Names of the principal owners
- Names of the members of board of directors
- Names and affiliation(s) of advisers—external as well as internal
- Compensation plan for key management team members

- Life insurance policy for the CEO or president of the company
- Succession plan
- Investments

Appendices and Tables

Information in this section may include:

- Résumés and biographies
- Union contracts
- Leases
- Customer contracts
- Research findings

References

References should include financial (i.e., personal and business) as well as character references. The idea is to make the investor as comfortable and knowledgeable as possible about the company and the entrepreneurial team. For example, when seeking bank financing, Tom and Cherry Householder, the founders of Staffing Resources, a $10 million temporary staffing company, submitted more than 15 letters of reference from their local police chief, from politicians, and even from competitors of their bank. It worked. They got the $135,000 line of credit they needed to start their business.[7]

Potential Risks

An assessment of risks currently facing the company, as well as future risks and how the company intends to mitigate these risks, needs to be presented. Some risks, such as "acts of God" (e.g., weather, major disasters, unexpected death, etc.), may not be exclusive to the company and therefore cannot be dealt with by the company. The objective is to assure the investor that the entrepreneur (1) has a realistic view of the business opportunities and the risks associated with pursuing the opportunities and (2) has proactively thought through how to manage and mitigate those risks that can be dealt with by the company. Potential risks to consider include:

- The advent of a recession.
- The unanticipated demise or removal of the CEO.
- Unanticipated changes in key management personnel.
- Insurance.
- The loss of a major customer(s). This issue is particularly relevant if the company's revenues are dependent on one or a few major customers.
- Problems with suppliers.
- A potential strike or labor stoppage.
- A capital or financing shortfall.

Financial Statements and Pro Formas

Projecting the future is challenging, but it must be done. Debt and equity investors know that financial projections that go out 3 to 5 years in the future are at best guesstimates—they have to be, as no one can predict the future, unless of course guaranteed future contracts have been signed. Potential investors are looking for projections grounded in defensible logic. When asked how financiers knew when pro formas were correct, a venture capitalist responded, "We don't know. In all likelihood, they will be ultimately wrong. In a start-up, it is rare for pro formas to ever match reality. We are looking for logical, defensible reasoning behind the numbers versus B.S.—'Blue Sky'—projections simply pulled out of the air."

DEVELOPMENT OF PRO FORMAS

Pro formas should be developed by entrepreneurs for a start-up as well as an existing company being purchased. Any pro forma should have figures for at least 3 years and three scenarios—a best-case, worst-case, and most-likely-case scenario. If only one scenario is provided, then the automatic assumption is that it is the "best case" because most people always put their best, not worst, foot forward. The historical performance of a company drives the financial projections for the future of the company, unless there is other information that indicates that past performance is not a good indicator of future performance.

For example, if a new contract from a new customer has been signed, then this could be used to adjust the financial projections. Otherwise, historical numbers must be used. For instance, Livent Inc. created major musicals such as *Joseph and the Amazing Technicolor Dreamcoat* and *Ragtime*. In 1998, the company added Chicago's Oriental Theatre to the three other company-owned theaters in New York, Toronto, and Vancouver. Livent's pro formas for the newly renovated Oriental Theatre were allegedly based on its success with *Joseph*, which it staged 2 years earlier at the Chicago theater and in similar venues throughout the country. Livent's projections were as follows:

Oriental Theatre
- 80 percent capacity
- 52 weeks per year
- $40 million annual gross revenues

Before the end of 1998, Livent Inc. experienced major financial difficulties and filed for Chapter 11 bankruptcy. In bankruptcy court, an attorney for the city of Chicago, who filed a condemnation case, challenged the legitimacy of the pro formas. He argued that the $40 million annual projected gross revenues were out of line with reality and intentionally fraudulent, given the fact that "in a recent year, a similar theater located in downtown Chicago and similar in size, reported an annual gross of just $20,455,000!"[8]

When there are no historical data, financial projections for a start-up company can be determined in one of the following ways:

- Conduct an industry analysis and select a company within the same industry. This company can be used as a comparable. Where possible, review the sales figures of this company to determine its sales history from year 1 as well as sales growth in the past few years. Extrapolate from these figures and use data to determine sales growth for your company. Cost figures may be determined from cost data obtained through research of, for example, a publicly owned company in the same industry.
- If sales commitments have already been secured, use these commitments to calculate the worst-case scenario. Use

larger amounts to calculate the best-case and most-likely-case scenarios.

- If the product or service is completely new, market research can be undertaken to determine the overall market demand for this new product or service. Identify the size of the market and assume the company will get a specific percentage of the total market depending on the total number of competitors. Also, identify the potential customers and estimate the number of units that can be sold to each.

- Alternatively, you can determine to use specific figures for your projections, based on your own assumptions or expectations. It is important to state what these assumptions are and to justify why you believe them to be realistic.

An important issue to consider for a start-up company is to make sure that all the necessary equipment financing needs are included.

Before closing this section on pro forma development, a major warning must be given. It is important that the worst-case-scenario pro formas show that the cashflow can service the company's debt. Otherwise procuring financing, particularly debt, may prove to be virtually impossible. This does not mean that the pro formas should be developed by working backward and "plugging" numbers. For example, if the debt obligations for principal payments are $7000 per month, it would be wrong to forecast the monthly revenue size, gross margins, etc., such that at least $7000 would be generated in after-tax cashflow to service this obligation.

No, pro formas should be developed from the top down; forecasting defensible revenues against legitimate variable costs, including labor and materials, and against market-rate fixed costs such as rent. If, after developing the pro formas in this manner, it is shown that debt cannot be serviced, the action that needs to be taken is not to plug numbers but rather:

- Reduce the amount of the debt
- Lower the interest rates on the debt
- Extend the terms of your loan

All of the above actions are designed to free up cashflow to service short-term debt.

Even if the entrepreneur is successful in raising capital off pro formas filled with plugged numbers, he or she will ultimately experience difficulties when the company's performance is lower than projections and cashflow cannot meet debt obligations. Finally, experienced business investors such as bankers and venture capitalists can easily detect pro formas filled with plugged numbers because typically the projections are such that all the company's debt can be serviced with maybe a little cash left over. Therefore, do not plug numbers. A pro forma development case study, titled "Clark Company," is included at the end of Chapter 5.

CHECKLIST OF FINANCIAL INFORMATION

For investors to better understand the information presented in this section, it is best to provide a summary of financial data and then present the detailed financial tables. Data should include:

- Historical financial statements (i.e., 3–5 years):
  - Cashflow
  - Income statement
  - Balance sheet
- Pro formas (i.e., 3–5 years). Financial projections (as described above) should be provided in three scenarios— best, worst, and most likely cases—where each scenario is based upon a different set of assumptions. For example, the worst-case scenario may assume no growth from year 1 to year 2, the best-case scenario may assume a 5 percent growth, and the most-likely-case scenario may assume a 2 percent growth rate. A summary of the assumptions should also be provided.
- Detailed description of banking relationships for business accounts and payroll.
- The terms and rates of loans and their amortization period.
- Proposed financing plan including:
  - Amount being requested.

- Sources and uses of funds. (*Note:* This information is important for several reasons. First, financiers need to know how their funds are going to be used. Second, identifying other investors who are willing to provide you with resources (sources) will encourage potential investors to make a similar commitment—people find it easier to invest once they know that others have already done so. Third, value-added investors may be able to help you find alternative ways of getting resources.)
- Payback and collateral.
- Proposed strategy for the liquidation of investors' positions.

■ Financing plan for the immediate term, short term, and long term.

■ Working capital needs.

■ Line of credit.

■ Cashflow from operations—outside investors, sell debt, or IPO.

MOST IMPORTANT BUSINESS PLAN SECTIONS

By now you realize that your business plan better be compelling if your venture hopes to receive funding. Here's one more review of the "must haves" of any good business plan.

The Executive Summary

As stated earlier, the executive summary is probably the most important section of the business plan. Most potential investors don't have the time to read through a detailed plan, and so therefore they quickly read through the summary to assess whether or not a venture is worth pursuing. It is extremely important to make sure this summary is clear and explicitly highlights the differentiating factors between the company seeking capital and its competitors. For example, the 20-page Amazon.com business plan was very successful at highlighting the fact that the book retailing industry averaged 2.7 inventory turns a year, while Amazon.com planned annual inventory turns of 70.

The Management Team

Jeff Bezos's first investors said, "We didn't invest in Amazon.com, we invested in Jeff."[9] This is a perfect confirmation of the old axiom, "The investment is in the jockey, not the horse." In other words, the investment is in the team, not necessarily in the idea, product, or service. Experience has shown that the right management team can usually be the deciding factor for the success or failure of a business venture. Remember, the venture capitalist Bill Sutter noted management as two of the three most important things that he looks for. The scarcest resource today for venture capitalists is good management. A good management team can take a mediocre idea and make it successful. Conversely, a bad management team can take an outstanding idea and ruin it. One venture capitalist said, "In the world today, there's plenty of technology, plenty of money, plenty of venture capital. What is in short supply are great teams."

Investors look carefully to see who the members of the management team are, particularly if the venture is a start-up company. Do they have complementary skills, or is it a homogeneous group? Do they have relevant industry, market, or product experience? How was the leader selected? Do the team members have experience working with each other? Do they have contacts in the industry that can be leveraged? What are their track records in management, leadership, and execution?

Great teams are made up of smart people with complementary skills and styles—not everyone can deal with "in-your-face" managers—and the commonality of passion for the business, commitment to grow it rapidly and exponentially, and the experience and drive to execute quickly without quitting.

Financial Projections

Investors understand the difficulty of preparing projections of future revenues and profits. They do not expect the financial projections to be "correct"; rather they want to see whether or not the entrepreneur used realistic assumptions in preparing these projections. They look to see whether or not the analysis is logical and defensible given the realities of the marketplace. They not only look to see if the projected cashflow can service debt, but ask whether the cashflow projections justify the value placed on the firm today and in the future, as well as whether the company meets the expected size they are interested in. For example, some financiers only want to do business with companies that will have at least $200 million in revenue by year 3. It is important to make sure that all relevant information is provided in this section and to make all the assumptions used clear.

BUSINESS PLAN DEVELOPMENT SOURCES

Numerous books are available that provide detailed information on the preparation of a business plan; you can find them in the small-business section of most major bookstores. In addition, various companies provide consulting services on business plan development to entrepreneurs, albeit sometimes at a considerable cost. Local small-business development centers are also a good source of information and assistance. In addition, as mentioned earlier, business schools can be good sources of talented, and in most instances, free assistance. Alternatively, Exhibit 3-1 shows several online sources that provide detailed information on business plan development, available for free.

E X H I B I T   3-1

Business Plan Development Sources

The American Express Small Business Services
www.americanexpress.com
   The Small Business Exchange provides a business plan template and other relevant information on small businesses.

Canada/British Columbia Business Service Centre
www.sb.gov.bc.ca
   The Preparing a Business Plan section provides an online small-business workshop with information on business plan preparation.

Small Business Administration
www.sbaonline.sba.gov
   The Business Plan Outline section, in addition to providing a business plan template, provides other relevant information, including financing for small businesses.

continued on next page

E X H I B I T   3-1

Business Plan Development Sources (continued)

Business Plan Preparation Centre

www.bizplanprep.com

Venture Capital Resource Library

www.vfinance.com

This online library features free business plan templates and evaluations of business plans.

AFTER THE BUSINESS PLAN IS WRITTEN

It is very important to choose potential investors carefully—you will be establishing an important long-term relationship with them. Do your research on a potential investor(s) before sending your business plan to ensure a better success rate of acceptance. Find out what types of deals the investor pursues. What is the firm's investment strategy, and what are its selection criteria? What is its success rate? How have the investors reacted during critical situations, a financial crisis, etc.? Do the investors just bail out, or are they in for the long haul? One good source of information in this regard is other companies that have received backing from that particular investor. Will the investors be "value-added" investors, discussed in more detail in Chapter 8, providing useful advice and contacts, or will they only provide financial resources?

It is extremely important to know your audience so that you limit your search to those who have an affinity for doing business with you. If your company is a start-up, then you should send the plan to those who provide "seed" or start-up capital versus later-stage financing. For example, it would be a waste of time to send a business plan for the acquisition of a grocery store to a technology-focused lender, such as the Silicon Valley Bank. This issue will be discussed in more detail in Chapter 8, "Raising Capital."

It is always advisable to get what Bill Sutter calls "an endorsed recommendation," preferably from someone who has had previous business dealings with the investor, before submitting your business plan. John Doerr at KPCB stated, "I can't recall ever having invested in a business on the basis of an unsolicited business plan."[10] This endorsement will guarantee that your business plan will be considered more carefully and seriously. If a recommendation is not possible, then an introduction by someone who knows the investor will be helpful. In most instances, unsolicited business plans submitted to venture capital firms without a referral have a lower chance of getting funding than those submitted with one. If submitting an unsolicited business plan, it is important to write it to be consistent with the investment strategy of the investor.

A good example of someone who did it correctly is Mitch Kapor, the founder of Lotus Development Corporation, who, in 1981, sent his business plan to only one venture capital firm. Recognizing that his business plan was somewhat different—it included a statement that said he wasn't motivated by profit—he knew himself and his company well enough to know that not all venture capitalists would take him seriously. He carefully selected one firm—Sevin and Rosen. Why? Because this firm was used to doing business with his "type"—namely, computer programmers. They knew him personally, and they also knew the industry. It was a good decision. He got the financing he sought even though he had a poorly organized, nontraditional plan. The way to find debt and equity providers who have a proclivity for certain deals will be discussed in Chapter 8.

N O T E S

1. Russis, Martha, "Loans Will Flow, but Less Freely Than during 1998," *Crain's Chicago Business/Small Business Report*, December 14, 1998, p. SB4.
2. *Black Enterprise*.
3. *Fast Company*, February–March 1998.
4. *Fast Company*, February–March 1998.
5. Bill Sutter classroom presentation at Kellogg School of Management, March 10, 1999.

6. *Chicago Sun-Times*, April 4, 1996.
7. *Inc.*, December 1998.
8. Cohen, Laurie, and Andrew Martin, "Theater Plan Not Living Up to Billing," *Chicago Tribune*, January 15, 1999.
9. *Business 2.0*, April 2000, p. 259.
10. *The New Yorker*, August 11, 1997.

CHAPTER 4

Financial Statements

INTRODUCTION

As stated earlier, one of the most important sections of the business plan is the one that details the firm's financial statements. Therefore, the discussion contained in this chapter is intended to be an overview of the main issues of relevance regarding key financial statements. The objective is to teach the purpose of the different statements, their components, and the significance to entrepreneurs who are not financial managers. This is the final step toward making financial statement analysis, which will be the focus of the next chapter, simple and user-friendly.

Financial statements are important because they provide valuable information that is typically used by business managers and investors. However, it is not required that the entrepreneur be able to personally develop financial statements.

In this chapter, we will focus on three financial statements—the income statement, the balance sheet, and the statement of cashflows. Each of these statements, in one way or another, describes a company's financial health. For example, the income statement describes a company's profitability. It is a measurement of the company's financial performance over time. Is the company making or losing money? On the other had, the balance sheet describes the financial condition of a company at a particular time. Does it own more than it owes? Can it remain in business?

THE INCOME STATEMENT

The income statement, also known as the profit and loss (P&L) statement, is a scoreboard for a business and is usually prepared in accordance with the generally accepted accounting principles (GAAP). It records the flow of resources over time by stating the financial condition of a business at the end of a period, usually a month, quarter, or year. It shows the revenues (i.e., sales) achieved by a company during a particular period and the expenses (i.e., costs) associated with generating this revenue. That is the reason why the income statement, in addition to being known as the P&L statement, is also referred to as the statement of revenues and expenses.

The difference between a company's total revenues and total expenses is its net income. When the revenues are greater than the costs, the company has earned profit. When the costs are greater than the revenues gained, then the company has incurred a loss.

The income statement is used to calculate a company's cashflow, which is also known as EBITDA: earnings (i.e., net income or profit after taxes) before interest (i.e., the cost of debt), taxes (i.e., the payment to the government based on a company's profit), depreciation (i.e., a noncash expenditure for the valuation decline of a tangible asset), and amortization (i.e., a noncash expenditure for intangible assets such as patents or goodwill). To determine a company's EBITDA for any period—that is, the cash being generated by the company after paying all the expenses directly related to its operations, and therefore the cash available to pay for nonoperational expenses such as taxes and principal and interest payments on debt—one must utilize the income statement. A sample income statement is provided in Exhibit 4-1.

The income statement is divided into two sections: "Revenues," a measure of the resources generated from the sales of products and services, and "Expenses," a measure of the costs associated with the selling of these products or services. The accounting equation to remember is Formula 4-1.

F O R M U L A   4-1

Net Income

Revenues − expenses = net income

E X H I B I T   4-1

Bruce Company Income Statement YE 12-31-98

Revenues	$8000
Expenses	
Cost of Goods Sold	$2000
Gross profit	**$6000**
Operating expenses	
Wages	$1000
Rent	300
Selling expense	400
Depreciation	500
Amortization	300
Total operating expense	$2500
Operating profit *or* profit before interest and taxes	**$3500**
Interest expense	200
Profit before taxes	**$3300**
Income tax expense	$1320
Net income	**$1980**

Using the information contained in Exhibit 4-1, we can calculate EBITDA at the end of the year for the Bruce Company as shown in Exhibit 4-2. As you can see, we added back "noncash" item expenses, i.e., those where no cash is actually disbursed, such as depreciation and amortization, to determine the company's true cash position—EBITDA.

E X H I B I T   4-2

Sample EBITDA Calculation

Net income	$1980
+ Interest expense	200
+ Taxes	1320
+ Depreciation	500
+ Amortization	300
EBITDA	**$4300**

Let us define and analyze each revenue and expense item on the typical income statement:

Revenues
- The sale of products and services
- Returns on investments such as interest earned on a company's marketable securities, including stocks and bonds
- Franchising fees paid by franchisees
- Rental property income

Expenses
- Cost of goods sold
- Operating expenses
- Financing expenses
- Tax expenses

Cost of Goods Sold

The cost of goods sold (known as the COGS) or the cost of services rendered is the cost of the raw material and direct labor required to produce the product or service that generated the revenue. The COGS does *not* include any overhead such as utilities or management costs. The difference between revenues and the COGS is gross profit, a.k.a. gross margin. The proper way to calculate the gross profit is simply to subtract the COGS, as defined earlier, from the revenues produced by the sales of the company's goods or services. Other income, such as interest earned on investments, should not be included. The reason for this is because in the world of finance, internal comparisons of a company's year-to-year performance, as well as external comparisons of a company's performance relative to another company or an entire industry, are quite common. These kinds of comparisons are called internal and external benchmarking. Therefore, in order to make "apples-to-apples" comparisons that are not skewed because, for example, company A's revenues are stronger than company B's due to the former getting higher interest payments on investments, only the revenues from operations are used. To determine gross profit from total revenues, regardless of the source, would be to ignore the obvious definition of the COGS, which is the cost of *only* the goods sold to generate revenues.

Operating Expenses

Operating expenses, also known as sales, general, and administrative expenses (SG&A), are all of the other tangible and intangible (e.g., depreciation and amortization) expenses required to run the day-to-day activities of a company. Included in this category are fixed costs (i.e., the costs that do not vary with the volume of business) such as insurance, rent, and management salaries, as well as variable costs (i.e., the costs that vary depending upon the volume produced) such as utilities (e.g., electricity and water) and invoice documents. For example, in the Bruce income statement above, the rent is $300 per year—an amount that remains the same whether 200 or 2000 widgets per year were produced.

Another simple way to think about fixed versus variable costs is to determine the expenses that would be affected by, for example, closing the company for a month. Rent would still be due to the landlord, and interest payments on bank loans would still be due to the bank. These are the fixed costs. On the other hand, since the company is closed and not producing or shipping for a month, there would be no need to buy invoice documents, and utility bills would dramatically decrease since electricity and water were not being used.

Excluded from this category are interest expenses, which are not operating expenses, but rather financing expenses. Therefore, revenues minus the sum of the COGS and operating expenses equals operating income, or EBIT (earnings before interest and taxes). The operating income is then used to make any interest payments on debt. The balance is called earnings before taxes (EBT), and these funds are then used to pay taxes on the company's EBT figure.

As stated earlier, "intangible, noncash item" expenses—expenses that do not require actual cash disbursements, such as depreciation and amortization—are also included in the operations category. Every company, under GAAP, is allowed to "write off" (i.e., expense) a portion of its tangible assets each year over the life of the asset. The theory behind this practice is that typically the value of all assets depreciates over time due to natural deterioration and regular use. Therefore, the depreciation of an asset is the same as a cost to the company because its value is declining. As we will see in the discussion of the balance sheet later in this chapter, the depreciated value of the asset is recognized on the balance sheet, and the amount it depreciates each year is presented on the income statement. The amount to be depreciated each year is determined by the accounting method selected by the company to recognize depreciation. The most common methods are straight line (i.e., equal percentage of the asset's cost minus salvage value for the predetermined number of useful years) and accelerated (i.e., double-declining balance or sum of the years' digits).

The method used to calculate depreciation can have a significant impact on the timing of reported income. Using the straight-line depreciation method rather than one of the two accelerated methods, the double declining or sum of the years' digits, will result in a higher net income in the early periods and lower net income in the later years of an asset's estimated useful life. Also, the change in net income from one period to the next is greater under the double-declining balance method than it is under the sum-of-the-years'-digits method. This makes the former method the most extreme form of depreciation. Finally, the two accelerated methods produce low levels of net income in the early periods that increase rapidly over the asset's life.[1]

While depreciation is the expensing of tangible assets, amortization is the expensing of intangible assets. Intangible assets include such items as goodwill (i.e., the surplus paid over an asset's book value), franchise rights, patents, trademarks, exploration rights, copyrights, and noncompete agreements. These items must be amortized, in equal annual amounts, over 15 years.

Financing Expenses

Found on the income statement, financing expenses are basically the interest payments paid on loans to the business. And finally tax expenses are the taxes due on the company's profits. There are also other taxes that a company incurs, including unemployment and real estate taxes, but these fall in the operating expenses category.

If a company has a negative profit before taxes, in other words a loss, then corporate taxes are not due to the government. In fact, not only will taxes not be due, but also the company's losses can be used against future positive profits to reduce tax obligations. This is called a tax-loss carry forward, where a company's previous losses can be carried forward against future profits. Interestingly, a company with a history of annual losses can be more valuable to a prospective buyer than a company that regularly has a breakeven or profitable financial history. Since tax-loss carryforwards are transferable from seller to buyer, they are attractive to a prospective buyer because they are assets for companies trying to shield future profits.

At the end of the year, if a company's net income after taxes is positive, it is retained in the form of retained earnings, reflected on the next year's beginning balance sheet or distributed to investors as dividends, as shown in Formula 4-2.

F O R M U L A   4-2

Retained Earnings and Shareholders' Dividends

Revenues − expenses = net income
→ Retained earnings and shareholders' dividends

Before closing out the discussion on the income statement, it is imperative that we clear up a few terms that are commonly used interchangeably. These include:

- Revenues and sales
- Margins, profits, earnings, and income

The three different kinds of margins, profits, earnings, and income—in the order of appearance on the income statement—are as follows:

- *Gross.* The difference between revenues and COGS
- *Operating.* Revenues − (COGS + operating expenses)
- *Net.* The difference between revenues and *all* of the company's costs

Cash versus Accrual Accounting

A final point to be made about the income statement is that it can
be affected by the accounting method selected by the entrepreneur.
The options for the entrepreneur are cash or accrual accounting.
Typically, a company will select the accounting method that provides the greatest immediate tax benefit. It must also be noted that
a company can, in its lifetime, change from one method to another
only once, but this change must be approved by the Internal
Revenue Service (IRS). The IRS usually approves the requested
switch from cash to accrual and usually rejects the request to
change from accrual to cash. What is the main difference between
cash and accrual accounting? Simply stated, it is the time at which
a company recognizes its revenues and expenses. Exhibit 4-3
clearly shows the difference.

E X H I B I T   4-3

Cash versus Accrual Accounting

Accounting Method	Revenues Recognized	Expenses Recognized
Cash	When actual cash is received from the customer	When actual cash is paid to the supplier
Accrual	When the product is shipped and the invoice is mailed	When the invoice is received from the supplier

The accrual accounting method gives the reader of the income
statement a richer and more complete depiction of the business's
financial condition since all revenues generated by the business
and all expenses incurred are stated, regardless of whether actual
cash has been received or disbursed. Because this method recognizes items immediately, many business owners try to use it to
their advantage. For example, prior to the end of the year, many
owners will increase their inventories dramatically. The result is an
increase in expenses and therefore the reduction of profits and
taxes.

For publicly owned companies where the markets reward revenue and profit growth by increasing stock price, many owners prefer and use the accrual method because it helps them achieve the aforementioned increases. Unlike many privately owned companies that seek to minimize taxes by reducing their reported EBT, public companies seek to show the highest possible EBT, as well as revenue growth. Given this objective, it is not unheard of for a company's owner to get too aggressive and sometimes even unethical relative to growth. For example, Premiere Laser Systems Inc., a spin-off from Pfizer, won FDA approval for a new laser device that promised to make drilling cavities painless. The publicly owned company, trading on the NASDAQ market, shipped and recognized revenues of $2.5 million in products to Henry Schein, Inc., the powerhouse distributor in the dental business, in December 1997. The only problem was that Henry Schein claimed it never ordered the products, refused to pay, and alleged that the products were shipped to it so that Premiere could show an increase in revenues to current and future stockholders. Obviously, the supplier used the accrual method that allowed it to recognize the revenue immediately upon shipment. Had its accounting method been cash, the revenue would have never been recognized because the recipient company had refused to pay.[2] Premiere settled a number of class-action suits; it also cooperated with a securities investigation and replaced its CEO. The company eventually filed for Chapter 11 in March 2000.[3] Another "fishy numbers" case involved Sunbeam Corporation, which conceded that while under the leadership of Al Dunlap, a.k.a. "Chainsaw Al," its "1997 financial statements audited by Arthur Andersen LLP may not be accurate and should not be relied upon."[4] Sunbeam filed for Chapter 11 bankruptcy protection in 2001 after 3 years of trying to turn around its fortunes. The company was saddled with a debt load of $2.6 billion.[5]

Private-practice physicians usually operate some of the most profitable small businesses in the country. Typically, doctors use the cash accounting method, which gives the reader a more limited picture of the company's financial condition. Physicians and others who use this method do so primarily because notoriously slow payers such as insurance companies and the government, also known as third-party payers, pay their revenues. Therefore, instead of recognizing this unpaid revenue and ultimately paying taxes on the profits it helps to generate, the users of the cash method prefer to delay revenue recognition until it is actually received, thereby reducing the company's profit before taxes and consequently the taxes paid. Using this method does not result in tax avoidance or elimination, however; it just simply delays tax payments into future years.

Not all companies are allowed to use the cash method including, the following:

- Companies with average annual revenues of $5 million or more
- Companies where inventories are a heavy part of their business, such as auto dealerships and grocery wholesalers

Let's look at Exhibit 4-4, which shows an end-of-the-year income statement using both methods. The company has sold and invoiced $1 million worth of merchandise and has received payment of $600,000. The merchandise cost was $500,000, an amount for which the company has been billed. The company has paid its suppliers $400,000.

E X H I B I T   4-4

Cash versus Accrual Accounting Example

	Cash Method	Accrual Method
Revenues	$600,000	$1,000,000
Cost	$400,000	$ 500,000
Profit before taxes	$200,000	$ 500,000
Taxes (50% rate)	$100,000	$ 250,000
Profit after taxes	$100,000	$ 250,000

As is obvious from this simple example, the accounting method used by a company can affect not only the taxes owed but also the three profit categories mentioned earlier. All three would be lower as a percentage of revenues under the cash method versus the accrual method. Therefore, it is imperative that when comparing income statement items against those of other companies, the comparison be made with those using the same accounting method.

As mentioned earlier, a company can change its accounting method with the approval of the IRS. To see the impact of these changes, examine Exhibit 4-5.

E X H I B I T   4-5

Income Statement for the Bruce Company

	Cash Business with No Receivables	Business with Receivables
Cash to accrual	▪ Revenues remain the same.	▪ Revenues increase.
	▪ Expenses increase	▪ Expenses increase
	▪ Profit before taxes decreases.	▪ Profit before taxes increases.
	▪ Taxes decrease.	▪ Taxes increase.
	▪ Net income decreases.	▪ Net income increases.
Accrual to cash	▪ Revenues remain the same.	▪ Revenues decrease.
	▪ Expenses decrease.	▪ Expenses decrease.
	▪ Profit before taxes increases.	▪ Profit before taxes decreases.
	▪ Taxes increase.	▪ Taxes decrease.
	▪ Net income increases.	▪ Net income decreases.

Why would someone in a business with receivables want to switch from a cash system to an accrual accounting method when the result can be an increase in taxes? There could be several legitimate business reasons, including:

- For better comparison purposes, the company may want to use the same accounting method used by its competitors.
- The entrepreneur may be preparing the company to go public or to be sold. The accrual method would show the company to be bigger and more profitable than it would appear using the cash method.

Before closing the discussion on accounting methods, it should be pointed out that the IRS, in December 1999, issued new rules regarding this topic. Specifically, the IRS said that companies carrying no inventory and having annual revenues between $1 million and $5 million could no longer choose the cash method. They must use the accrual method. The result of this change will be quite significant to the cashflow of businesses in this revenue range. They will be expected to pay more taxes sooner. The beneficiary will be the U.S. Treasury, which expects to collect an additional $1.8 billion by 2005 due to accelerated tax payments.[6]

THE BALANCE SHEET

An example of a balance sheet is shown in Exhibit 4-6.

E X H I B I T   4-6

Bruce Company Balance Sheet YE 12-31-98

Assets	
Current assets	
Cash	$300
Accounts receivable	300
Less: Uncollectibles	(10)
Inventory	600
Total current assets	**$1,900**
Property, plant, and equipment	
Property	$5,000
Buildings	4,000
Less: Accumulated depreciation	(1,000)
Equipment	3,000
Less: Accumulated depreciation	(1,000)
Total property, plant, and equipment	**$10,000**
Other assets	
Automobiles	$4,500
Patents	1,000
Total other assets	**$5,500**
Total assets	**$16,690**

continued on next page

E X H I B I T   4-6

Bruce Company Balance Sheet YE 12-31-98 (continued)

Liabilities and shareholders' equity	
Current liabilities	
Accounts payable	$500
Wages	700
Short-term debt	900
Total current liabilities	**$2,100**
Long-term liabilities	
Bank loans	$4,000
Mortgages	5,000
Total long-term liabilities	**$7,000**
Shareholders' equity	
Contributed capital	$5,000
Retained earnings	2,590
Total shareholders' equity	**$7,590**
Total liabilities and shareholders' equity	**$16,690**

The information contained on the balance sheet is also often presented in the format shown in Exhibit 4-7. The balance sheet is a financial snapshot of a company's assets, liabilities, and stockholders' equity at a particular time. Bankers have historically relied on the balance sheet to analyze ratios of various assets and liabilities to determine a company's creditworthiness and solvency position.

E X H I B I T   4-7

Balance Sheet Information

Assets	Liabilities
▪ Current	▪ Current
▪ Long-term	▪ Long-term
▪ Tangible	
▪ Intangible	**Equity**
	▪ Stock—common, preferred, etc.
	▪ Retained earnings

A company's assets on the balance sheet are separated into current and long-term categories. Current assets are those items that can be converted into cash within 1 year, including a company's cash balance, dollar amount due to the company from customers (i.e., accounts receivable), inventory, marketable securities, and prepaid expenses.

Long-term assets, tangible and intangible, are the remaining assets. They are recorded at original cost, not present market value, minus the accumulated depreciation from each year's depreciation expense, which is found on the income statement. The assets that fall in this category include buildings, land, equipment, furnaces, automobiles, trucks, and lighting fixtures.

As stated earlier in this chapter, all long-term assets can be depreciated over time. This is permissible under GAAP despite the fact that some assets, in fact, appreciate over time. An example is real estate, which usually tends to appreciate over time, but the balance sheet does not reflect this fact. Therefore, it is commonly known that the balance sheet may give an undervalued estimate of a company's assets, especially when real estate is owned. This fact was highlighted in the mid-1980s during the leveraged-buyout, hostile-takeover craze. Corporate raiders, as the hostile-takeover artists were known, would forcibly buy a company at an exorbitant price because they believed the company had "hidden value" in excess of what the financial statement showed. One of the primary items they were concerned with was the real estate owned by the company, which was recorded on the balance sheet at cost minus accumulated depreciation. The raiders would take over the company, financing it primarily with debt. Then they would sell the real estate at market prices, using the proceeds to reduce their debt obligations, and lease the property from the new owners.

The right side of the balance sheet belongs to the liabilities and shareholders' (stockholders') equity sections. A company's liabilities consist of the amounts owed by the company to creditors, secured and unsecured. The liabilities section of the balance sheet, like the assets section, is divided into current and long term. Current liabilities are those that must be paid within 12 months. Included in this category is the current portion of any principal payments due on loans for which the company is responsible—remember the current interest payments on the loan are on the income statement—and accounts payable, which are very simply money owed to suppliers. Long-term liabilities are all of the company's other obligations. For example, if the company owns real estate and has a mortgage, its total balance due minus the current portion of long-term debt would be reflected in the long-term liabilities category.

Stockholders' equity is the difference between total assets and total liabilities. It is the net worth of the company, including the stock owned by the company and accumulated earnings that the company has retained each year. Remember, the retained earnings are an accumulation of the profits from the income statement. Note the fact that the net worth of the company is not necessarily the company's value or what it would sell for. A company with a negative net worth, where total liabilities exceed total assets, may sell for quite a bit of money without any problems. As we will see in the Chapter 7, the net worth of a company typically has no bearing on its valuation. A few important equations to remember are shown in Formula 4-3.

FORMULA 4-3

Shareholders' Equity

Total assets − total liabilities = shareholders' equity
Net worth = total assets − total liabilities

Therefore Net worth = shareholders' equity

Finally, the items on the balance sheet are also used to compute a company's working capital and working capital needs. Net working capital is simply a measure of the company's ability to pay its bills—in other words, the company's short-term financial strength. A company's net working capital is measured as shown in Formula 4-4.

FORMULA 4-4

Net Working Capital

Net working capital = current assets − current liabilities

The fact that two companies possess the exact same level of working capital does not mean they have equal short-term financial strength. Look, for example, at Exhibit 4-8. While both companies have the same amount of working capital, a banker would prefer to lend to Cheers Company because Cheer has greater financial strength. Specifically, for every dollar that Cheers owes, it has $6 in potentially liquid assets compared with the Hill Company, which has only $2 in assets for every dollar owed.

EXHIBIT 4-8
Working Capital Comparison

	Hill Company	Cheers Company
Current assets	$1,000,000	$600,000
Current liabilities	500,000	100,000
Working capital	$ 500,000	$500,000

Now look at the example in Exhibit 4-9. It shows that a company with greater working capital than another is again not necessarily the strongest. With a 10-to-1 asset-to-liability ratio, Guthrie is obviously financially stronger than Webb with a 2-to-1 ratio, despite the fact that Webb has more working capital.

EXHIBIT 4-9
Working Capital Comparison

	Guthrie Company	Webb Company
Current assets	$10,000,000	$20,000,000
Current liabilities	1,000,000	10,000,000
Working capital	$ 9,000,000	$10,000,000

The entrepreneur must recognize that potential investors use the company's working capital situation to determine if they will provide financing. In addition, loan covenants may establish a working capital level that the company must always maintain or risk technical loan default, resulting in the entire loan being called for immediate payment.

The balance sheet assumes greater importance for manufacturing companies than for service companies, primarily because the former tend to have tangible assets such as machinery and real estate, whereas the latter tend to have people as their primary assets.

THE STATEMENT OF CASHFLOWS

The statement of cashflows uses information from the two other financial statements, the balance sheet (B/S) and the income statement (I/S), to develop a cashflow statement that explains changes in cashflows resulting from operations, investing, and financing activities. Exhibit 4-10 provides an example of a cashflow statement.

E X H I B I T   4-10

Richardson Company Cashflow Statement YE 12-31-98

Cashflow from operations	
Net income	$400,000
Noncash expenditures	
Depreciation	110,000
Amortization	95,000
Net working capital	10,000
Cash available for investing and financing activities	**$615,000**
Cashflow from investing activities	
Equipment purchases	($140,000)
Automobiles	(50,000)
Sale of old equipment	70,000
Cash available for investing activities	**$495,000**
Cashflow from financing activities	
Dividends paid	$30,000
Mortgage payments	100,000
Loan payments	200,000
Sale of stock	65,000
Net cashflow	**$100,000**

The relationship between the sources and uses of cash are shown in Formula 4-5.

FORMULA   4-5

Cashflow

Cash sources − cash uses = net cashflow

→ Fund operations and return to investors

Cashflow Ledgers and Planners

The cashflow ledger, without regard to accounting issues such as cash versus accrual methods or noncash item expenses such as depreciation, provides a summary of the increases (inflow) and decreases (outflow) in actual cash over a period of time. It provides important information primarily to the entrepreneur but also possibly to investors and creditors (such as banks) about the balance of the cash account, enabling them to assess a company's ability to meet its debt payments when they come due. A famous (but unnamed) economist once said, "Cash flow is more important than your mother"—well maybe not more important, but it is essential because it is the lifeline of any business. Cashflow is different from profit and more important, as we will see later in this chapter.

The cashflow at the end of a period (for example, a month) is calculated as shown in Exhibit 4-11. And Exhibit 4-12 provides an example of a monthly cashflow ledger. It indicates, on a transaction basis, all cash received and disbursed during a month's period. As shown, the cash balance at the end of the month is equal to the total cash received less the total cash disbursed for the month.

EXHIBIT   4-11

Sample Cashflow Calculation

	Cash on hand at the beginning of the month
plus	Monthly cash received from customer payments, etc.
equals	Total cash
minus	Monthly cash disbursements for fixed and variable costs
equals	**Cash available at the end of the month**

The successful entrepreneurs are those who know the actual cash position of their company on any given day. Therefore, unlike the comparatively few number of times they need to reread the income statement and balance sheet, it is recommended that entrepreneurs, especially the inexperienced and those in the early stages of their ventures, review the cashflow ledger at least weekly.

E X H I B I T 4-12

Oscar's Business Ledger*

Date	Explanation	To/From	Received	Disbursed	Balance
6/30/95					$1000
7/1/95	Silkscreen start-up supplies	Ace Arts		$ 250	750
7/2/95	Bought 4 doz. T-shirts	Joe		240	510
7/6/95	Monthly registration fee	Flea market		100	410
7/6/95	Business cards	Print shop		20	390
7/6/95	Flyers	Print shop		10	380
7/7/95	4 doz. @ $12	Flea market	$ 576		956
7/10/95	Bought 5 dozen T-shirts	Joe		300	656
7/14/95	4 doz. @ $12, 1 doz. @ $10	Flea market	696		1352
7/16/95	Bought 5 doz. T-shirts	Joe		300	1052
7/16/95	Silkscreen ink	Print shop		50	1002
7/16/95	Flyers	Print shop		10	992
7/21/95	3 doz. @ $12 (rained)	Flea market	432		1424
7/25/95	Bought 2 doz. T-shirts	Joe		120	1304
7/26/95	4 doz. @ $12	Flea market	576		1880
Totals			**$2280**	**$1400**	**$1880**

* Mariotti, Steve, *The Young Entrepreneur's Guide to Starting and Running a Business*, p. 93.

Exhibit 4-13 provides a weekly cashflow projection summary, which every new and inexperienced entrepreneur should prepare immediately upon opening for business and each month thereafter. It indicates the anticipated cash inflow during the month as well as cash payments to be made. In the exhibit, the anticipated cash inflow—59— is less than the expected cash outflows—60—for the month; therefore the cash balance for the month will be negative 1.

E X H I B I T   4-13

Sample Weekly Cashflow Projections

Week of	Oct. 1	Oct. 8	Oct. 15	Oct. 22	Oct. 29	Oct.'s Total Cash Received
(Cash in)						
1. Beginning cash	10					10
2. Receivables						
Customer 1					5	5
Customer 2		3	3	3		9
Customer 3		8				8
Customer 4			12			12
3. Cash payments	5	3	1	1	5	15
	15	14	16	4	10	59
(Cash out)						
1. Payroll	3	3	3	3	3	15
2. Loan payments			6			6
3. Rent	5					5
4. Insurance						
Property	2					2
Health	3					3
5. Vendor payments						
Vendor 1	1	2	3	4	4	14
Vendor 2	1		3			4
Vendor 3		2	6			8
Vendor 4	1		2			3
	16	7	23	7	7	60

Source: Teri Lammers, "The Weekly Cash-Flow Planner," *Inc.*, June 1992, p. 99.

The projection in Exhibit 4-13 was prepared at the end of September for the following month. It anticipates the cash inflow during the month as well as cash payments to be made. The "Cash in" section includes expected payments from specific customers based on the terms of the invoice and aging of the corresponding receivable. The terms were net 30, which means the payment was due 30 days following the invoice date. But the entrepreneur who completed this projection did not simply project October 29 because that was 30 days after invoicing. To do this would be too theoretical and quite frankly naïve on the entrepreneur's part. Instead, she used common sense and factored in the extra 7 days that customer 1 typically takes before paying the bills. Thus, the product was invoiced on September 22, and the entrepreneur is forecasting the actual receipt of payment on October 29. This section also includes the cash payments expected each week throughout the month. These are expected to be actual cash payments that customers make when they pick up their merchandise. In these cases the entrepreneur is not supplying any credit to the customer.

By doing this kind of projection each month the entrepreneur can schedule her payments to suppliers to match her expected cash receipts. This planner allows her to be proactive, as all entrepreneurs should be, with regard to the money owed her suppliers. It enables her to let specific vendors know in advance that her payment will probably be late. The cashflow ledger and planner are simple and very useful tools that the entrepreneur should use to successfully manage cashflow.

NOTES

1. Pratt, Jamie, *Financial Accounting*; South-Western Publishing Co., Cincinnati, Ohio, 2nd ed., 1994, p. 396–397.

2. Morris, Kathleen, "No Laughing Gas Matter—A Dental-Tech Start-up May Have Hyped Its Numbers," *BusinessWeek*, June 9, 1998, p. 44.

3. Premier Lasers Systems Inc. home page, http://www.premierlaser.com/pressreleases/bankruptcyannouncement.htm.

4. Brannigan, Martha, "Sunbeam Concedes 1997 Statements May Be Off," *Wall Street Journal*, July 1, 1998, p. A4.

5. *U.S. Business Journal*, February 2001.

6. *Crain's Chicago Business*, July 10, 2000.

Financial Statement Analysis

INTRODUCTION

Sadly, it is common to hear entrepreneurs say, "I do not know any-thing about finance, because I was never good with numbers. Therefore, I focus on my product and let someone else bother with the numbers." Someone with such an attitude can never achieve successful high-growth entrepreneurship. Financial statement analysis is not brain surgery! Everyone can understand it. In fact, no matter how distasteful or uncomfortable it might be to the high-growth entrepreneur, he or she must learn and use financial state-ment analysis. Finance is like medicine. No one likes it because it usually tastes awful, but everyone knows that it is good for you.

THE PROACTIVE ANALYSIS

The proactive analysis of financial statements must be used by entrepreneurs to better manage their company and influence the business decisions of a company's managers, as well as attract cap-ital from investors and creditors.[1]

Financial statements must be used as tangible management tools and not simply as reporting documents. While it is not required that the entrepreneur be able to personally develop these statements—a job that is completed by the CFO—he or she must be able to completely understand every line item. The entrepreneur who does not will have a much more difficult time growing the company and raising capital.

For example, one of the fundamentals of finance says accounts receivable (A/R) and inventory should not grow at an annual rate faster than revenue growth. If they do, it is a sign that the company's working capital is being depleted because the accounts receivable and inventory represent a drag on a company's cash.

A case in point: The management team at Lucent Technologies failed to do a proactive analysis of this relationship. The result? The stock price declined 30 percent shortly after the company reported its 1999 financial results. The results showed that compared with the previous year, revenues grew an impressive 20 percent. Unfortunately A/R and inventory grew 41 percent and 54 percent, respectively!

Another problem for entrepreneurs who do not proactively analyze their financial statements is that these entrepreneurs will also then risk being taken advantage of or exploited. There are numerous accounts of companies losing money to employees who were stealing products and cash. In many instances, the theft was not immediately identified because the owners excluded themselves from all financial statement analysis. Not surprisingly, many of the thieves are bookkeepers, accountants, accounts receivable and payable clerks, and CFOs. All of the aforementioned are positions intimately involved in the company's financings. There's a lesson here: Thieves do not always look like scumbags! Heck, if that were the case, you would not have hired *that* person in the first place. Automated Equipment Inc. is a family-run manufacturing business in Niles, Illinois. The company's bookkeeper was a friendly 35-year-old woman who was inflating payouts to vendors and then altering the names on the checks and depositing them in accounts under her control. It took the company 4 years to discover the embezzlement, and by then the woman had stolen nearly $610,000, leaving the company in near financial ruin. Among other things, the bookkeeper purchased a Cadillac sport-utility vehicle, expensive clothing, and fine meats. Oh, she also put a $30,000 addition on to her home. The theft forced the company to lay off 4 of its 11 employees, including the owner's wife and a 27-year worker. By the way, the bookkeeper had a separate federal student loan conviction from her *previous* job.

Bette Wildermuth, a longtime business broker in Richmond, Virginia, has 20 years' worth of stories of business owners getting surprised by the people they trust. Often, she's the one who catches the shenanigans when pouring over financials at the time of a sale. "I was asked by the owner of a fabrication company to come talk about the possibility of selling his company. He specifically asked me to come on a Wednesday afternoon because his bookkeeper would not be there. You see he didn't want to cause her any worry over a possible job loss. After all, she'd been with his company for 15 years." Wildermuth was left alone with the books and records to try and determine a valuation. After about 2 hours, she says the owner returned and proudly asked, "Did you notice our sales are up and we're continuing to make a profit?" Wildermuth had noticed and congratulated him. "I also told him that an astute buyer would notice that and more, and that both of us would have the same question. 'Bob,' I asked, 'Why are you paying your home mortgage from the business account?' He told me that that was impossible because his mortgage had been paid off years ago." It turns out that the sweet, Norman Rockwellesque woman who had handled his finances for 15 years was robbing him blind. She was also paying her personal Visa card off from the company books. "When I told him what was going on," Wildermuth remembers, "he looked like he had been punched in the stomach."

Another great example to highlight this point is the story of Rae Puccini, who, by the time she was 55 years old, had been convicted eight times over two decades for stealing money from her employers. In July 2000, while facing another conviction for the same crime, she committed suicide. The final crime was using her position as the office manager to steal $800,000 from her employer Edelman, Combs & Latturner (ECL), a prominent Chicago-based law firm that hired Puccini in 1996. The lawsuit against her stated, "She forged signatures, cut herself 'bonus' checks and transferred money from her bosses' bank account. She used the firm's American Express credit card to pay for a Caribbean cruise and a vacation at the Grand Hotel on Mackinac Island, Michigan. She also used the credit card to pay for a Mexico vacation with her boyfriend as well as groceries, flowers, furniture and liquor. Her 2000 Buick LeSabre was paid for by a $35,000 bonus that she paid herself. Her most expensive gift to herself was the $200,000 house that she purchased in the suburbs, using a $42,000 check that she cut from the firm.[2] How did she pull this incredible crime off? First, she created a fake résumé to hide her prison record. Second, she earned her employers' trust easily. Third, she worked long hours to create an impression that she was very dedicated to the firm. As an attorney at another law firm, where she also stole money, stated, "She ostensibly was very loyal and trusted. She came in early and stayed late."[3] The final reason was because no one in the law firm was involved in the supervision and analysis of its financials. She was practically given carte blanche, without any checks and balances. She was finally caught when ECL partners asked her to show documentation explaining how the company's cash had been spent. After she hedged, the partners looked through her work area and found incriminating evidence.[4] Approximately 1 month before her death, Puccini went to a funeral home, selected flowers, and paid for her body to be cremated. She donated many of her clothes to Goodwill and set up a post-funeral dinner at a Greek restaurant. Her final act was to type a confessional letter that included the statement, "No one knew what I was doing with the finances of ECL."[5] She was absolutely correct.

When the entrepreneur is involved in his or her company's finances, such sordid stories regarding losses of cash to theft can be practically eliminated because the entrepreneur's knowledge and participation serve as a deterrent.

To utilize the financial statements as management tools, the entrepreneur must have them prepared more than once a year. Monthly financial statements developed by an outside accounting firm can be expensive. In addition, monthly statements, by their definition, are short-term-focused, and their analysis may encourage entrepreneurs to micromanage and overreact. The ideal is to produce quarterly statements that should be completed, and be in the entrepreneur's hand for analysis, no later than 30 days following the close of a quarter.

In this chapter, we will learn that the data contained in financial statements can be analyzed to tell an interesting and compelling story about the financial condition of a business. Included in the financial statement analysis discussion will be a case study. We will examine the income statement of the Clark Company to determine what is taking place with its operations, despite the fact that we know nothing about the industry or the company's products or services. Using information provided in this statement, we will then prepare financial projections (i.e., pro formas) for the next year.

CASHFLOW STATEMENT ANALYSIS

In terms of financial analysis, all items, including expenses and the three margins—gross, operating, and net—mentioned in Chapter 4, are analyzed in terms of percentage of revenues. As Exhibit 5-1 shows, the COGS percent *plus* the gross profit percent should equal 100 percent. The COGS percent *plus* total operating expense percent *plus* interest expense percent *plus* tax expense percent *plus* net income percent should also equal 100 percent.

E X H I B I T   5-1

Income Statement Analysis

Total revenues	$8000	100.00%
COGS	2,000	25.00%
Gross margins	**$6000**	**75.00%**
Operating expenses		
Wages	$1000	12.50%
Rent	300	3.75%
Selling expenses	400	5.00%
Depreciation	500	6.25%
Amortization	300	3.75%
Total operating expense	$2500	31.25%
Operating profit	**$3500**	**43.75%**
Interest expense	200	2.50%
Profit before taxes	**$3300**	**41.25%**
Income tax expenses	1320	16.50%
Net income	**$1980**	**24.75%**

RATIO ANALYSIS

A ratio analysis, using two or more financial statement numbers, may be undertaken for several reasons. Entrepreneurs, as well as bankers, creditors, and stockholders, typically use ratio analysis to objectively appraise the financial condition of a company and to identify its vulnerabilities and strengths. As we will discuss later, ratio analysis is probably the most important financial tool that the entrepreneur can use to proactively operate a company. Therefore, the entrepreneur, at least quarterly, should review the various ratios that we discuss in this section, along with the other three key financial reports: income statement, balance sheet, and cashflow statement. There are six key ratio categories:

- Profitability ratios
- Liquidity ratios
- Leverage (capital structure) ratios
- Operating ratios
- Cash ratios
- Valuation ratios

Exhibit 5-2 provides a description of selected financial ratios and the formulas used to calculate them.

E X H I B I T   5-2

Financial Accounting Ratios

Ratio	Description	Formula
Profitability ratios	**Measures earning potential.**	
Gross margin percentage	Measures the gross profit margin the company is achieving on sales—that is, the profit after COGS is deducted from revenues.	Sales − COGS/sales
Return on equity	Measures return on invested capital. Shows how hard management is making equity in business work.	Net income/ stockholders' equity
Net operating income	Measures income generated from operations without regard to the company's financing and taxes.	Sales − expenses (excluding interest)/ sales
Net profit margin	Measures the net profit margin the company is achieving on sales.	Net profit/sales
Liquidity ratios	**Measures a company's ability to meet its short-term payments.**	

continued on next page

E X H I B I T   5-2

Financial Accounting Ratios (continued)

Ratio	Description	Formula
Current ratio	Measures if current bills can be paid. A 2-to-1 ratio minimum should be targeted.	Current assets/current liabilities
Quick ratio acid test	Measures liquidity. Assesses whether current bills can be paid without selling inventory or other illiquid current assets. A 1-to-1 ratio minimum should be targeted.	Current assets − inventory, etc./current liabilities
Leverage ratios	**Evaluates a company's capital structure and long-term potential solvency.**	
Debt/equity ratio	Measures the degree the company has leveraged itself. Ideally, the ratio should be as low as possible, giving greater flexibility to borrow.	Total liabilities/ stockholders' equity
Operating ratios	**Focuses on the use of assets and performance of management.**	
Days payable	Measures the speed at which the company is paying its bills. Ideally one should wait to pay the bills as long as possible without negatively affecting product service or shipments from suppliers.	Accounts payable/ (COGS/365)
Collection ratio "days receivable"	Measures the quality of the accounts receivable. It shows the average number of days it takes to collect receivables. The ideal situation is to get paid as quickly as possible.	Accounts receivable/ (revenues/365)
Inventory turns	Measures the number of times inventory is sold and replenished during a time period. It measures the speed at which inventory is turned into sales.	COGS/average inventory outstanding
Days inventory carried	Measures the average amount of daily inventory being carried.	Inventory/(COGS/365)
Cashflow ratios	**Measures a company's cash position.**	
Cashflow cycle	Measures the number of days it takes to convert inventory and receivables into cash.	Receivables + inventory/COGS
Cashflow debt coverage ratio	Measures if a company can meet its debt service. A 1.25-to-1 ratio minimum should be targeted.	EBITDA/interest + principal due on debt

continued on next page

E X H I B I T 5-2

Financial Accounting Ratios (continued)

Ratio	Description	Formula
Valuation ratios	**Measures returns to investors.**	
Price-to-earnings ratio	Measures the price investors are willing to pay for a company's stock for each dollar of the company's earnings. For example, a P/E ratio of 8 means investors are willing to pay $8 for every dollar of a company's earnings.	Price of stock/earnings per share

The ratios of a company cannot be examined in a vacuum, i.e., looking at 1 year only for one company. To attempt to do so renders the ratios virtually meaningless. The greatest benefit of historical and present-day ratios derived from two analytical measurements—internal and external—is the ability to do annual internal comparisons. This type of analysis will show if there are any trends within a company across time. For example, a comparison can be made of selected income statement line items across a 2-year, 5-year, or 10-year period. This type of analysis will help to assess the soundness of a company's activities as well as identify important trends. Basically, it allows the entrepreneur to answer the question, Is my internal performance better today than last year, 5 years ago, or 10 years ago? If the answer is yes, then the next question is, How did it get better? If the answer is no, then the next question is, Why didn't it get better? Deeper analysis should be undertaken to determine not only why things are getting worse but also what is making things better. If the entrepreneur knows and understands the detailed reasons why ratios improved over time, then he or she can use that information for prescriptive elements of future strategic plans.

The entrepreneur should also do an external comparison of the company's ratios against the industry. This comparison should be against the industry's averages as well as the best and worst performers within the industry. This will allow the entrepreneur to assess the company's operations, financial condition, and activities against comparable companies. The successful entrepreneur knows that respecting and understanding the competition is a basic business requirement, and the first step to take toward that endeavor is to understand how you compare with the competition. Ratio analysis is one of the most objective ways to do such measurements. For example, an analysis of the discount retail industry in 2000 shows Wal-Mart as being the best in inventory turnover ratios (see Exhibit 5-3).

E X H I B I T   5-3

Inventory Turnover Ratios

Store	Turnover
Wal-Mart	7.3
Target	6.3
Kohl's	4.6
Kmart	4.3
J.C. Penny	3.6

Charles Conaway, Kmart's CEO since the beginning of 2000, is well aware of his company's place in this comparison. He told the *New York Times*, "Take Halloween and all of that candy. The day after Halloween, Wal-Mart marks the candy down 75%. They don't want it there. It's like dead fish, and Target will have it for 50–75% off. At these two stores, it will be gone within a week. But at Kmart, it will be marked down at 20% and it will be straggling for God knows how long."[6]

Many banks provide business loans on the condition that the company maintain certain minimum ratios such as debt to equity, net worth, and acid test. These conditions are usually included in the covenant section of the loan agreement, and exceeding the minimum ratios puts the company technically in default of the loan. Other investors such as venture capitalists may use ratio attainment as "milestones," determining if and when they will invest more capital. For example, they may tell the entrepreneur that their next round of financing will occur when the company attains 50 percent gross margins for four consecutive quarters.

In addition to performing historical and present ratio analyses internally and externally, the entrepreneur should also use ratios to drive the future of the business. For example, the entrepreneur's strategic plans may include growing revenues while decreasing inventory. Therefore, the ratio of days of inventory carried must be reduced while the inventory turnover ratio must be increased to some targeted number. Simply stating these objectives is not enough. After determining the respective targeted numbers, a strategic plan must be developed and implemented to actually reduce the amount of inventory carried and to quickly ship to customers new inventory that is received.

Such a relationship between the two ratios would look as shown in Exhibit 5-4.

EXHIBIT 5-4

Inventory Ratio Comparison

	1999	2000	2001	2002	2003
Inventory turns	8	11	11	12	14
Days of inventory carried	43	34	33	30	28

As you can see in the exhibit, the amount of average daily inventory being carried decreases from 43 days' worth of inventory to 28 over a projected 5-year period. Now if the entrepreneur's goal is to also increase revenues over this same period of time, then he or she must turn the smaller volume of daily inventory each year more frequently. And as the exhibit shows, that is in fact what the entrepreneur forecasts: to increase the inventory turns from 8 times a year to 14. The just-in-time inventory model, pioneered and perfected by companies such as Toyota and Dell, only works if a company's vendors and partners are highly synchronized. Events outside the control of the company can also cause big problems. In the wake of the terrorist attacks in New York in September 2001, Cherry Automotive of Waukegan, Illinois, was forced to shut down three production lines while it waited for circuit boards to be flown in from Asia. The delay cost the company $40,000. To ensure it didn't happen again, Cherry started carrying 3 weeks' worth of components inventory, compared with the 2 to 3 days' worth it carried prior to the attacks. Managers described the move as "going from just-in-time to just-in-case." Not that the owners took the decision lightly; by their estimates, that one change will cost the company $250,000 annually.[7] Appendix A offers a listing of national average inventory turnover ratios and amount of sales in ending inventory for selected retail and wholesale industries.

Another proactive way to use ratios is for the entrepreneur to make short-term, midterm, and long-term objectives with regard to internal and external ratios. For example, the short-term plan covers the next 12 months to get the days receivable ratio back down to the best level in the company's 10-year history. And the midterm (i.e., 24 months) plan may be to get the company's days receivable down to at least the industry average. Finally, the long-term (i.e., 36 months) plan may be that the company's days receivable would be the lowest in the industry, making it the market leader. Thus, ratios have immense value to the entrepreneur as analytical and proactive management tools. And successful entrepreneurs regularly compare their performance against historical highs, lows, and trends, as well as against the industry.

What are good and bad ratios? Well, it depends on which ratios are being examined and, more importantly, the specific industry. Regarding the first point, good days receivable are determined by a company's invoice terms. The standard invoice has the following terms: "2-10 net 30 days." This means the payer can take a 2 percent discount if the invoice is paid in 10 days. After 10 days the invoice's gross amount must be paid within the next 20 days. Thus, the customer is being given a total of 30 days following the date of invoice to pay the bill. If the company does business under these terms, then days receivable of 45 days or greater are considered bad. The ideal target is to have days receivable no more than 10 days greater than the invoice.

The second factor that determines what are good and bad ratios is the industry (see Exhibit 5-5 for good and bad key ratios for several industries). For example, if we analyze two different technology industries—computer manufacturing and computer software—we will see two distinctly different ideas of what is considered good operating margins. In the computer manufacturing industry, the company with the strongest operating margin is Dell

Computers at 11 percent.[8] That is significantly lower than that for Microsoft, the computer software industry's leader, which had an operating margin of 45 percent![9] As stated earlier, everything is relative. Both of these companies have significantly better operating margins than Amazon.com, whose operating margin was—5 percent in 2000.

Typically, the financial ratios of successful firms are never lower than the industry's average. For example, companies in the computer-manufacturing industry carry, on average, 80 days of inventory. That dramatically contrasts with Dell, which carries inventory an average of 4 days. This is one of the reasons why Dell has been so financially successful. In its industry, inventory loses 1 percent of its value every week that it sits on the shelf.[10]

There are some instances where a company's ratios are worse than the industry's average and it is perfectly acceptable. This occurs when the below-average ratios are planned as a part of the company's strategic plan.

For example, inventory turns and days inventory carried that are slower and greater, respectively, than the industry average may not be negative signs of performance. It could be that the company's strategic plan requires the company to carry levels of inventory greater than the industry average; as a result, inventory turns would be slower. For example, if a company promises overnight delivery, compared with the competitors who ship in 14 days, the former's inventory carried will be higher and turns will be slower. Ideally, the gross margins should be higher than the industry's because the company should be able to charge a premium for the faster deliveries. Given this fact, it is essential that the entrepreneur perform a comparison of industry averages when writing the business plan, when developing the projections, and, most importantly, before submitting the plan to prospective investors.

How can entrepreneurs find out industry averages for private companies? Exhibit 5-6 lists periodicals and other resources commonly used to compare an existing company's performance against the industry, as well as to determine if the pro formas in a business plan are in line with the industry being entered. As noted previously, you'll also find national averages for turnover ratios in Appendix A.

E X H I B I T   5-5
Key Ratios for Various Industries*

Industry	Ratio	Best	Worst
Lawn and services	Current ratio	3.2x	1.0x
	Inventory turns	107.0x	14.0x
	Days receivable	17.0x	55.0x
Grocery stores	Current ratio	3.8x	1.2x
	Inventory turns	28.0x	13.0x
	Days receivable	1.1x	6.3x
Electronics and computers	Current ratio	3.2x	1.4x
	Inventory turns	17.0x	6.0x
	Days receivable	35.6x	85.5x
Colleges and universities	Current ratio	4.9x	1.1x
	Days receivable	10.2x	43.1x
Airlines	Inventory turns	94.1x	3.9x
	Days receivable	9.0x	37.8x
Apparel manufacturing	Inventory turns	8.9x	3.9x
	Days receivable	15.7x	69.7x
Beverages	Inventory turns	16.4x	6.4x
	Days receivable	21.1x	51.6x

*Industry Norms and Key Ratios, 1995–1996, Desktop Edition; and "Working Capital Survey," CFO, July 1998, p. 40.

E X H I B I T   5-6
Industry Ratio Resources

Annual Statement Studies, Robert Morris Associates.
Almanac of Business and Industrial Financial Ratios, Prentice Hall.
Industry Norms and Key Business Ratios, Dun & Bradstreet.
Robert Morris Associates Guide.
Value Line Investment Survey.

BREAKEVEN ANALYSIS

The analysis of financial statements should also be used to perform a company's breakeven (BE) point. Successful entrepreneurs know how many widgets, meals, or hours of service they have to sell, serve, or provide, respectively, before they can take any real cash out of the company. Formula 5-1 shows the equation for calculating a company's BE point.

F O R M U L A   5-1

Breakeven Point

Fixed expenses ÷ gross margin = total breakeven sales
Total breakeven sales ÷ unit price = number of units to sell

Using information contained in Exhibits 4-1 and 4-5 for the Bruce Company, one can prepare a selected set of financial ratios and BE for the company. Exhibit 5-7 shows the financial ratios, BE, and an explanation of the numbers.

E X H I B I T   5-7

Selected Financial Accounting Ratios for the Bruce Company

Ratio	Amount	Explanation
Gross margin percentage	75%	75 cents of every dollar of sales goes to gross profit. Or the product's labor and material costs were 25 cents.
Return on equity	26%	The company is getting a return of 26% on its capital invested in the company.
Net profit margin	24.75%	24 cents of every dollar of sales goes to the bottom line.
Current ratio	0.57	The ratio is less than 1, which indicates that the company can't meet its short-term financial obligations.
Quick ratio acid test	0.28	The ratio is less than 1, which means that the company can't pay its debt.
Debt/equity ratio	1.2	The company owes $1.2 of debt for every dollar of equity.
Collection ratio	13 days	It takes 13 days on average to collect receivables.
Inventory turns	3.33	Inventory turns 3.33 times.

continued on next page

E X H I B I T   5-7

Selected Financial Accounting Ratios for the Bruce Company (continued)

Ratio	Amount	Explanation
Cashflow cycle	0.45 day	It would take less than a day to convert inventory to cash.
Breakeven point		BE = $700 ÷ 0.75 = $933

MEASURING GROWTH

When measuring the growth of a company, the entrepreneur should be sure to do it completely. Many people use compounded annual growth rate (CAGR) analysis when measuring and discussing growth. In addition to CAGR, another means of measurement is simple growth. Before going any further, let's discuss the two. In finance, both terms are typically used to discuss the rate of growth of money over a certain period of time.

Simple interest is the rate of growth relative to only the initial investment or original revenues. This base number is the present value (PV). Future value (FV) is the sum of the initial investment and the amount earned from the interest calculation. Thus, the simple interest rate or the rate of growth of a company with revenues of $3,885,000 in year 1 and $4,584,300 in year 2 is 18 percent, because $699,300, the difference between revenues in years 1 and 2, is 18 percent of year 1 revenues. Using the simple interest rate of 18 percent, year 3's revenues would be $5,283,600. This was determined by simply adding the $699,300, or 18 percent of the initial number $3,885,000 to year 2's revenue number. Therefore, an 18 percent simple growth rate would add $699,300 to the previous year's revenue to determine the level of revenues for the next year. In conclusion, the formula to determine the simple growth rate is the equation shown in Formula 5-2.

F O R M U L A   5-2

Simple Growth Rate

$$\text{Simple growth rate} = \frac{\text{dollars of growth}}{\text{initial investment} \times \text{time}}$$

Using Formula 5-2, let's input the numbers to answer the question, At what simple interest rate must $3,885,000 grow in 2 years to equal $5,283,600? Or another way to look at this question is, If you received a 2-year loan of $3,885,000 at 18 percent simple interest, what would you owe in total principal and interest? The answer would be $5,283,600, as calculated in Exhibit 5-8.

E X H I B I T   5-8

Components of Dollar of Growth Calculation

Year 1 (present value)	=	$3,885,000
Year 3 (future value)	=	$5,283,600
Dollars of growth (or FV − PV)	=	$1,398,600
Time	=	2 years

The concept of compounding is used commonly by financial institutions such as banks, relative to the money they lend as well as the deposits they receive. CAGR analysis—which is popular among professionals with graduate business school backgrounds, including consultants and commercial and investment bankers—simply shows the interest rate, compounded annually, that must be achieved to grow a company from revenues in year 1 to revenues in a future year. That sounds similar to what we said above about simple interest. But the word *compounded*, which is *not* included in the definition of simple interest, makes a huge difference. Compounding means you earn interest on the initial investment (i.e., PV), as was the case with simple growth, in addition to the interest earned each year, or the actual dollars of growth. Therefore, unlike simple growth, the compounded rate of growth each year reflects the initial investment plus the earnings on reinvested earnings.

Let's use the same numbers from the simple growth rate discussions to illustrate the concept of CAGR. A company with an 18 percent CAGR and year 1 revenues of $3,885,000 will have the future revenues shown in Exhibit 5-9.

E X H I B I T   5-9

CAGR Example

Year 2: $4,584,300 (i.e., $3,885,000 × 1.18)
Year 3: $5,409,474 (i.e., $4,584,300 × 1.18)

In comparing simple annual growth with compounded annual growth, clearly the comparison in Table 5-1 shows the latter to be more advantageous to the investors or entrepreneurs who want rapid growth.

T A B L E   5-1

Simple and Compounded Annual Growth Comparison

Revenues @ 18% Rate	Simple Growth	Compounded Annually
Year 1	$3,885,000	$3,885,000
Year 2	$4,584,300	$4,584,300
Year 3	$5,283,600	$5,409,474
Year 4	$5,982,900	$6,383,179
Year 5	$6,682,200	$7,532,151

As you can see in Table 5-1, the first year growth when compounding is the same as simple growth because the base is the same. The shortcoming with using CAGR is that it only looks at 2 years, the beginning year, and the ending year, completely ignoring the years in between. Therefore, when used alone, this popular growth measurement tells an incomplete story that can be misleading.

For example, a company with year 1 revenues of $3,885,000 and year 5 revenues of $7,532,151, as is the case in Table 5-2, will show the same 18 percent CAGR despite the fact that the revenues in years 2, 3, and 4 looked very different from those shown in Table 5-1.

TABLE 5-2

CAGR Comparison

	Simple Growth	Compounded Annually
Year 1	$3,885,000	$3,885,000
Year 2	$4,584,300	$3,000,000
Year 3	$5,409,474	$2,900,000
Year 4	$6,383,179	$2,700,000
Year 5	$7,532,151	$7,532,151

The reason why both companies have the same CAGR is that both had the same revenues at year 1 and year 5. The formula for CAGR only considers these two data points. It ignores what happens in between because theoretically CAGR means that in any given year throughout the 5-year period, the company's annual compounded growth in revenues was an even 18 percent based on information given about year 1 and year 5 and based on how CAGR is calculated. That is to say, the growth followed a relatively linear progression. But as Table 5-2 shows, that is not always the case. Company 2's revenues declined 3 consecutive years. So the major shortfall in using CAGR is that it does not take into account the actual growth rates from year to year over the 5-year period. Therefore, a more complete analysis using CAGR must include the analysis of real annual growth rates to see if there are any trends.

Finally, if we want to determine the actual revenues in year 5 (i.e., FV) of a company that had revenues of $3,885,000 in year 1 (i.e., PV), growing at a compounded annual rate of 18 percent, the formula shown in Exhibit 5-10 could be used.

EXHIBIT 5-10

Sample Future Value Calculation

Future value = Present value × (1 + year 1 rate) × (1 + year 2 rate) × (1 + year 3 rate) × (1 + year 4 rate)
Future value = $3,885,000 × (1.18) × (1.18) × (1.18) × (1.18)
Future value = $3,885,000 × (1.18)^4
Future value = $7,532,151

Note: 1 is added to each year's interest rate to show that for every dollar invested, 18% will be returned.

CASE STUDY—CLARK COMPANY

Exhibit 5-11 presents an income statement for the Clark Company for 3 years. There is no information regarding the company's industry, products, or services. This information is not needed. Numbers alone can tell a story, and every entrepreneur must get comfortable with being able to review financial statements, understand what is going on with the company, and recognize its strengths, weaknesses, and potential value. As we stated in Chapter 1, a successful entrepreneur must have the ability, willingness, and comfort to make decisions given ambiguous, imperfect, or incomplete information. The analysis of Exhibit 5-11 gives you the opportunity to demonstrate this trait. As you will see, it is an itty bitty, tiny business. Nevertheless, the analysis would be exactly the same as if each line item were multiplied by $1 million. The point being made is that the analysis of a small company's financials is the same as that of a large company. The only difference is the number of zeros to the left of the decimal points. An appropriate analogy can be made to swimming. If you can swim in 4 feet of water, you can also swim in 10 feet and deeper.

By examining the income statement, we will be able to better understand how management is handling the company's overall operations. Using financial ratio analysis, we will assess how well the company's resources are being managed. A good analysis will enable a potential buyer to assess, for example, whether the company is worth acquiring, based on its strengths and weaknesses, and to determine how much to pay for it.

When analyzing the numbers, it is important to 1) look at the numbers and compare them with historical performance or with a benchmark such as an industry average, to assess how the company is performing in the specific area, and 2) highlight any trend. The importance of trends as one looks at financial statements is that they are used to predict the future. One should always ask, Is there a trend in this line item? Is it an upward or downward trend? What is the main reason(s) for this trend? What does the trend mean for the future?

The following assumptions should be made in the analysis of the Clark Company case:

- This company is a cash business; there are no receivables.

- It is owner-operated.
- The numbers provided are correct.

An analysis of every line item could be made, but our analysis will focus on three of the most important items: revenue, gross profit, and net profit.

E X H I B I T   5-11

Clark Company Income Statement (Selected Years)*

	1999	2000	2001
Revenues	137,367	134,352	113,456
Returns and allowances			588
Cost of goods sold	42,925	38,032	40,858
Gross profits	**94,442**	**96,320**	**72,010**
Operating expenses			
Advertising	3,685	3,405	2,904
Bad debts	150	50	130
Automobile expense	1,432	460	732
Depreciation	1,670	1,670	835
Employee benefits programs			
Insurance	2,470	2,914	1,915
Interest			
Mortgage			
Other	153		2,373
Legal and professional services	1,821	1,493	
Office expense	10,424	8,218	8,965
Rent	14,900	20,720	13,360
Repairs and maintenance	1,293	2,025	
Supplies	305	180	195
Taxes and licenses	11,473	5,790	1,062
Travel	730	1,125	
Meals and entertainment	108	220	192
Utilities	2,474	2,945	2,427
Wages	5,722	11,349	12,214
Other			
Freight	1,216	1,645	874
Sales tax			7,842
Total Expenses	**60,026**	**64,209**	**56,020**
Net profit or loss	**34,416**	**32,111**	**15,990**

Note: The cash accounting method was used for 1998 and 1999. The accrual accounting method was used for 2000.

Revenue Analysis

The analysis of a company's historical annual revenue includes answers to the following questions: What are the sales growth rates for the past few years? What is the trend sales growth? Is it declining or increasing? Why are revenues increasing or decreasing? Not only should you be concerned about whether or not revenues are increasing, but you should also ask whether the increase is consistent with what is taking place in the industry. Sales increasing for a short period may not be good enough. You need to compare a company's sales growth with the rate at which you want it to grow. The absolute minimum amount you want sales to grow, at an annual rate, is at the rate of inflation, which since 1956 has averaged approximately 4 percent per year. Some industries have clearly outperformed this benchmark. For example, in the sports industry, since 1991, the average annual percentage increase in ticket prices for the four major sports leagues (i.e., NBA, NFL, NHL, and MLB) has been 7.2 percent.[11] In a 1997 survey of 900 companies, *BusinessWeek* found that, on average, the companies increased their revenues by 9 percent when inflation that year was less than 3 percent.

Revenue for the Clark Company has been declining. Revenues declined by 2 percent between 1999 and 2000 and 16 percent between 2000 and 2001. This downward trend is a cause for concern. Some of the reasons for the decline in revenues may be:

- Price increase due to higher costs.
- The owner is despondent, and he is not managing his business properly. Or he is simply not present at the company.
- Increased competition, due to the high gross margins, could be putting pressure on prices. One way to keep prices high is to have a patent on a product, which would allow the owner to set the price fairly high. This assumes of course that there is a demand for the product or service. When the patent expires, the business will inevitably face competition.
- The product could be becoming obsolete.
- An unanticipated event or an act of God, known in the legal profession as a "force majeure," could be one reason

for the decline in revenue. For example, there could have
been a tornado or severe rainstorm and the storage area
where the entire inventory was kept could have been
flooded, thereby damaging inventory and reducing the
volume that was available for sales.

- Recession.
- Construction outside of a company's place of business,
  which prevents easy access to customers.

So there are, in some instances, legitimate reasons why revenue could be decreasing that have nothing to do with the soundness of the business or management. It is important when
undertaking financial analysis to consider all likely scenarios.

While strong revenue growth is typically viewed positively, it
can also be a sign of bad tidings. The fundamentals of finance asso-
ciate excellent revenue increases with at least corresponding
increases in the company's net income. The best example of this
point is Microsoft. From 1990, when Microsoft introduced its
Windows 3.0 operating system, to 1999, its revenues grew 17 times,
from $1.18 billion to $19.8 billion. During the same time, its net
income grew an astounding 28 times, from $279 million to $7.79
billion!

But if revenues are growing because prices have been lowered, then that means the company is probably growing at the
expense of margins. Therefore, the growth may not in fact be profitable. For example, Hewlett-Packard's revenue for personal computers increased dramatically during the period 1991 to 1997 to
approximately $9 billion in annual revenues. At this time, its mar-
ket share increased from 1 to 4 percent. In 1998, with the support of
price cuts, sales increased 13 percent. Despite all this good news,
HP's personal computer business experienced a loss in excess of
$100 million.[12]

Another issue one should be aware of regarding revenue
growth is that the growth may be occurring because competitors
are conceding the market. Competitors may be leaving the market
because the product will soon be obsolete; or perhaps they are leaving because the ever-increasing cost of doing business—things
such as liability insurance—is driving them out of the market.
Thus, it is just as important for the entrepreneur to know why he

or she is experiencing excellent growth, as it is to know the reasons for low or no growth. The successful entrepreneur knows that revenues should be grown strategically. It is well-managed growth that ultimately improves the profitability of the company.

Sometimes growing too fast can be just as damaging as no growth at all. A few problems common to rapid growth are poor quality, late deliveries, an overworked labor force, and cash shortages. Unmanaged growth is usually never profitable. For example, Michael Dell, the founder of Dell Computers, which grew 87 percent per year for the first 8 years and 55 percent annually since 1992, said, "I've learned from experience that a company can grow too fast. You have to be careful about expanding too quickly because you won't have the experience or the infrastructure to succeed."[13] This comment was made after he experienced a $94 million charge against earnings in 1993 for, among other things, the failure of a line of poor-quality laptops.

The Largest Customer

Inherent in the growth issue is a key question: How large is the company's largest customer? Ideally an entrepreneur's largest customer should account for no more than 10–15 percent of a company's total revenues. The reasoning is that a company should be able to lose its largest customer and still remain in business. For example, Spatial Data Integrations is a $1 million company that generates 85–95 percent of its revenues from the U.S. Department of Defense.[14] The loss of the Defense Department contract would certainly devastate this company. The company should therefore, work hard to acquire new customers, to grow, and to have less dependence on any one customer.

Interestingly, many companies find that losing the customer generating the largest revenue actually results in more company profitability, because the largest customers are rarely the most profitable. The reason is that customers who provide large volumes often are invoiced at lower prices. For example, Morse Industries, a private lamp manufacturer, was ecstatic to get Wal-Mart, the country's largest retailer, as a customer. The addition of Wal-Mart increased its revenue over 50 percent in 1 year. But after 1 year, the company decided to drop Wal-Mart as a customer. Why? The revenues of Morse Industries had grown enormously, but the gross, operating, and net margins had actually declined because the company charged Wal-Mart 25 percent less than its other customers. Another reason for the decline was that Wal-Mart orders were so large that Morse Industries' labor force could barely produce enough. The result was that orders placed by other consumers, who were not receiving a discount and therefore generating higher margins, were being delayed or even canceled. Several of these long-term, excellent, paying customers quietly moved their business from Morse Industries to another supplier.

The founder of Morse solved the company's problem after he performed an analysis of his company's growth and found that it was not profitable. His analysis included using the matrix shown in Exhibit 5-12 to define each customer and the importance of that customer.

E X H I B I T   5-12

Customer Analysis Matrix

High volume Low margin	High volume High margin
Low volume Low margin	Low volume High margin

Source: Susan Greco, "Choose or Lose," *Inc.*, December 1998, p. 58.

He defined the categories as follows:

- *High volume/low margin.* Customers who provided revenues greater than $1 million per year, with gross margins of no more than 35 percent.
- *Low volume/low margin.* Customers who provided revenues of less than $1 million per year, with gross margins of no more than 35 percent.
- *Low volume/high margin.* Customers who provided revenues of less than $1 million per year, with gross margins in excess of 35 percent.

- *High volume/high margin.* Customers who provided revenues greater than $1 million per year, with gross margins in excess of 35 percent.

His immediate initial response was to simply drop only the customers in the low-volume/low-margin section. But on second thought, he decided to analyze even further to determine how profitable each customer was to the company by performing a contribution margin analysis on each customer

Formula 5-3 shows the contribution margin formula.

F O R M U L A   5-3

Contribution Margin

Revenues − variable costs = contribution margin
→ Fixed costs and profits

It is the difference between revenues and all of the variable costs (i.e., the costs that would not be incurred if this customer left) associated with a unit of product. Therefore, it is the profit available, after breakeven, to contribute to the company's fixed costs and profits.

T A B L E   5-3

Customer Analysis Calculation

	High Volume/ Low Margin	Low Margin/ Low Volume	Low Volume/ High Margin	High Volume/ High Margin
Annual revenues	$12,000,000	$800,000	$900,000	$3,000,000
Variable costs	10,000,000	600,000	500,000	1,500,000
Contribution margin	$2,000,000	$200,000	$400,000	$1,500,000
Percentage	17%	25%	44%	50%

The contribution margin analysis is presented in Table 5-3. Clearly, as you can see from the table, the least profitable business was not the low-margin/low-volume business but, in fact, the high-volume/low-margin businesses. Therefore, Morse attempted to raise his prices to customers who fell into these two categories. Several refused to accept the price increase, including Wal-Mart, so he dropped them. His growth strategy for returning the company to profitability included attempting to grow the volume of the remaining customers, who fell in the high-volume/high-margin and low-volume/high-margin categories, without decreasing prices. The second part of the strategy was the implementation of a policy that all new business had to have at least a 40 percent contribution margin. While his revenues in the immediate term went down, his net profits and cashflow dramatically increased. Ultimately, his revenues increased, as a result of his ability to maintain high-quality standards and ship promptly. Most importantly, his profit dollars and percentages also increased.

The lesson: Growth for the sake of growth, without regard to profitability, is both foolish and harmful and will inevitably lead to insolvency. This is what happened to the dot-com companies of the late 1990s. Many businesses are engaged in such growth in the name of gaining market share. But evidence repeatedly shows that the companies with the strongest market share, excluding perhaps Microsoft, rarely are the most profitable. For example, General Motors, in its successful efforts to increase market share from 28 percent to 32 percent, offered 1.9 percent financing, heavy rebates, and almost breakeven lease rates. All three actions helped to sell more cars and thereby increase the overall market share, but at the expense of profits. On the other hand, Ford, the most profitable automobile manufacturer in the world, has a 25 percent market share and earned $978 more in profit per car than General Motors.[15]

The theme of high market share and lower profitability was confirmed by a study of more than 3000 public companies. The study's results showed that more than 70 percent of the time, firms with the greatest market share do not have the highest returns, as the examples in Exhibit 5-13 show.

The study found that the key to success for smaller, more profitable competitors was their absolute vigilance for controlling costs and eliminating customers who returned low margins.

EXHIBIT 5-13

High Market Share versus High Returns

Category	High Market Share	Higher Returns
Discount stores	Wal-Mart	Family Dollar
Office furniture	Steelcase	Hon Industries
Pharmaceuticals	Merck	Pfizer

GROSS MARGINS

One of the initial financial ratios that business financiers examine when reviewing the income statement is the gross margin. What are good gross margins? Well, "good" gross margins, like all the other items we will be analyzing, are relative and depend on the industry in which a company operates. In general, gross margins of 35 percent and above are considered to be very good. Table 5-4 provides comparative gross margins for different companies.[16]

TABLE 5-4

Comparative Gross Margin Percentages

Company/Industry	Gross Margin, %
Amazon.com	13.0
Hewlett-Packard	17.0
Compaq Computer	21.6
Nike	40.0
Starbucks	70.0
eBay	71.0
Yahoo!	88.0
Starbucks-espresso	90.0
Microsoft	92.0

Source: *USA Today*, February–March 2000.

Supermarkets have razor-thin margins ranging between 10 and 15 percent. Computers, which have almost become a commodity product, have gross margins that are also very slim. That is why it is so difficult to compete in the computer hardware industry, because the average price at which a retailer sells a computer is only about 10 percent higher than what it costs to produce it. On the other hand, some computer manufacturers have been able to achieve gross margins that are higher than the industry average. One example, Compaq Computer, the number 2 computer manufacturer in the country before its merger with Hewlett-Packard in 2002, has consistently had gross margins above 20 percent.

There are several industries in which companies make very decent gross margins. For example, Nike's average gross margin is about 40 percent, whereas Starbucks, as indicated in Table 5-4, applies toward its gross profit 70 cents of every dollar it makes selling coffee. Or more profoundly, as Table 5-4 shows, a cup of Starbucks espresso, with a 90 percent gross margin, only costs 10 percent of its selling price![17] Microsoft enjoys a gross margin of 92 percent.

Gross margins are also very high in other businesses, some illegal. University of Chicago economist Steven Leavitt and Harvard sociologist Sudir Venkadisch undertook an analysis of the financial books of a drug gang—a very rare set of financial statements to analyze. Not surprisingly, they found that the gang was able to reap very high gross margins—approximately 80 percent—by selling crack cocaine.[18]

A venture capitalist once stated that "gross margin is the entrepreneur's best friend. It can absorb all manner of adversity with two exceptions, philanthropy or pricing stupidity. Actually, in this case the two are synonymous."[19] Good gross margins provide a novice entrepreneur with breathing space, allowing him or her a chance to make costly mistakes and still be potentially profitable. On the other hand, when operating in a low-gross-margin business—such as grocery stores, for example—management mistakes and waste, as well as theft and pilferage, must be minimized, because the margins are too thin to be able to absorb these costs. A low-gross-margin business must also have volume, whereas a high-gross-margin business may sacrifice unit volume sales, because its ultimate profit comes from the high margins. The ideal business, like Microsoft, dominates its industry relative to units of volume, while at the same time maintaining high gross margins. This is a rarity. High-gross-margin industries inevitably attract competitors who compete on price, thereby reducing gross margins throughout the industry.

For example, independent retailers of books used to enjoy gross margins in excess of 35 percent. Those attractive gross margins were the primary reason major chains such as Barnes and Noble and Amazon.com entered the market and now dominate it. Twenty years ago, independent retailers sold 60 percent of all book titles. Since 1991, the independents' share of the book market has declined from 32 to 17 percent. The big competitors increased because of the attractiveness of the gross margins.[20] I always tell my Kellogg students, "If you leave here, start your own business, and are lucky enough to have good gross margins, for God's sake, don't brag about it." If someone asks you, "How's business?" Your standard reply should be a simple shrug of the shoulders and a polite response of "Not bad; could always be better." It is always tough to maintain high gross margins. One way companies are able to do so is to have a patent or copyright on the product, essentially giving them a legal monopoly for a period of time. That is the case with the product Nutrasweet, an artificial sugar sweetener whose patent expired in 1999.

Ironically, not every entrepreneur is interested in high-gross-margin businesses. One of the primary reasons, as stated earlier, is because heavy competition is inevitable. Therefore, those interested in low-margin businesses are those who view excellent operational execution as their competitive advantage or barrier to entry of competitors. For example, as noted earlier, the computer manufacturing industry is notorious for low gross margins. Despite this fact, Dell Computers is able to prosper as the number 2 manufacturer in the world because of its outstanding operations—it carries 4 days of inventory compared with Compaq's 26 days. This means that Dell can turn its inventory more than 30 times a year compared with the industry's average of 10 to 12. The attitude of an entrepreneur who knows his competitive advantage is best illustrated by Michael Dell, who stated he was not happy with his company's inventory of 4 days—his ultimate goal is to measure Dell's inventory, not in days, but in hours.[21]

Gross margins are a factor that the entrepreneur should focus on very heavily in the business plan as well as in operations. Good, healthy gross margins do not happen by chance. They may happen by luck for the "mom and pop" entrepreneur who haphazardly runs a business. Because the strategy is to sell whatever can be sold at whatever cost, the mom and pop enterprise expects to absorb the costs and take whatever falls to the bottom line.

A high-growth entrepreneur, in contrast, is one who manages with a plan in mind. This entrepreneur expects to grow the company at a certain rate and plans to have a certain level of gross margins. A high-growth entrepreneur is one who looks to have a company for the purpose of wealth creation and therefore is one who is an absolute bulldog when it comes to managing gross margins. The question that logically follows, is, How can gross margins be increased?

Cut Labor and/or Material Costs

The following are ways to reduce labor costs:

- Train the work force so that productivity increases.
- Reduce the labor force and have fewer employees work more efficiently. GE, which in 1997 became the first corporation valued at more than $200 billion, did just this. From 1989 to 1997, GE cut 208,000 jobs worldwide. In one division, it cut 1800 jobs, and profits rose 21 percent.[22]
- Reduce employee absenteeism, which results in increased labor costs due to overtime pay. This is becoming a major problem—just from June 1997 to May 1998, employee absenteeism increased 25 percent.[23]
- Make the work force more productive by using technology. For example, technology has been used in McDonald's franchises to reduce labor costs. The production process has been automated to the point where one person can now do what it used to take four people to do in terms of cooking and food preparation.
- Increase volume. The cost per item produced or cost per service rendered should go down as the volume goes up. Labor costs should go down as employees gain more experience. People learn more and therefore should become more efficient even if it is not through the introduction of new technology.

- Find a cheaper labor force. Company operations can move, for instance, to a different region in the country or abroad where labor is cheaper. For example, Nike manufactures all of its products outside the United States in low-labor-cost countries such as China and Thailand, where unskilled labor can cost as little as $0.25 per hour. Even skilled labor can be significantly cheaper outside the United States. Westbound Consulting, a $1 million software-consulting firm, employs all of its programmers at its location in India, where they make roughly $6000 per year. Compare that with U.S. programmers, who earn between $50,000 and $100,000 per year.[24] One cautionary note here: Using labor outside the country sometimes has its own risks. After the September 11, 2001, terrorist attack in New York, Illinois-based Product Development Technologies Inc. scratched plans to source a client's manufacturing job in Brazil. The company was worried about the reliability of air shipments from abroad. Making the parts at home squeezed profits on the $60,000 dollar order because labor costs were 30 percent higher. But as PDT's owner said, "We can't afford to be even a week late."[25]

- Provide employees with stock options or other incentive programs in lieu of higher salaries. This option is increasingly becoming a common practice, particularly in California with high-tech start-up companies.

- Continually turn over the work force, reducing the number of higher paid, unskilled workers. For example, fast-food restaurants expect and want a certain amount of annual turnover in their unskilled employees because newer workers cost less.

- Implement good management skills. One of the easiest ways to reduce labor costs is simply for entrepreneurs to manage their employees. They need to manage, referring to the good-old way of managing people, which means stating expectations, giving employees the necessary tools, and holding them accountable for their performance.

The following are ways to reduce material costs:

- Obtain competitive bids from suppliers, which may allow for the purchase of materials at lower cost.
- Buy at higher volumes to get volume discounts. The problem here is the inventory carrying cost. Ideally one does not want to increase inventory. Therefore, the entrepreneur should make commitments to its suppliers to buy a certain volume within a period of time. Such a commitment should result in price-volume discounts. The commitment versus buy strategy allows entrepreneurs to keep inventories low, costs down, and cash available for other investments or uses.
- Outsource part of the production. Someone else may be able to produce a piece of a product or render a specific part of a service at a lower cost.
- Use a substitute material in the production process, which can be purchased at a lower cost. Ideally you want to keep the quality of the product the same, but there is a possibility that you can actually get a substitute material that may be less expensive.
- Manage waste, pilferage, and obsolescence. Materials that have been stolen, thrown away, or destroyed, or are just sitting around due to obsolescence, negatively affect material costs.
- Do quality control checks throughout the various stages of the manufacturing process before additional value is added. This is in contrast with the traditional way of checking quality at the end of the process only. Waste and rework costs are always greater using the process of checking quality at the end.
- Let the most experienced and trained person perform the most detail-oriented or labor-intensive work, for example, cutting all patterns, because they should be able to get more cuts per square yard than an inexperienced person. For example:

	Worker 1	Worker 2
Material cost per yard	$10	$10
Units cut per yard	4	2
Cost per unit	$2.50	$5

Thus, the cost per unit for worker 1 is lower because there is less material wasted.

Raise the Price

Raising the price of the product or service will enable the entrepreneur to increase gross margins, assuming, of course, costs do not increase proportionately. However, raising prices may be very difficult in today's "new economy era" business environment. In the past it was almost automatic—when companies wanted to increase revenue, they simply raised their prices. Companies did not focus on managing cost. In today's price-sensitive environment, however, where we have all been "Wal-Martized," consumers do not take price increases favorably. But increasing the price is a way to increase the gross margin, if you can get away with it. An industry that had gotten away with it is the airline industry, which used price increases combined with decreasing fuel costs, their second biggest cost after labor, to generate record profits in the late 1990s. In that period, airline prices for coach class with no restrictions, primarily purchased by business travelers, increased 34 percent while the U.S. consumer price index increased 7 percent over the same period.

The airline industry was an exception. In fact, a government index, which measures the ability of companies to raise their prices each year, was at a 35-year low in 1997.[26] A company's ability to raise its prices is also dependent on what is going on with inflation. Currently, as the inflation rate is less than 3 percent, a company cannot expect to raise prices and be able to sell its product or service. In fact, Brian Wesbury, an economist, noted that "pricing power by companies is non-existent. We are moving into an era of deflation that can last as long as two decades."[27] A great example is Ford Motor Company, the most profitable carmaker in the world, which decreased its prices on 1999 models, the first such reduction in 30 years.[28] Another great example is the technology industry, in which prices on personal computers and related technology have averaged a 15 percent decline per year for the past decade.

Amazingly, there were companies which, for a short time, were successful in challenging the importance of business fundamentals with regard to gross margins. For the most part, this was true in the e-commerce industry, where most companies were primarily focused on growing revenues even when it was at the expense of gross margins. For example, buy.com used to sell merchandise including CDs, books, videos, software, and computer equipment at cost and shockingly even sometimes below cost. The company guaranteed the lowest prices available on the Internet. The result was zero and sometimes negative gross margins! Despite these facts, buy.com, which was founded in 1996, had 1998 revenues of $111 million and a public market valuation in excess of $400 million.[29] But reality set in, and by September 2001, the vultures were circling with stockholder class-action lawsuits. In just over a year, buy.com's stock price had dropped from its opening-day price of just over $30 a share to about $0.08 per share. I hope your kid's college fund was not tied up in that one. All kidding aside, these kinds of infamous cases—where managers "fumble the fundamentals"—play out everyday in far more subtle ways in every business sector. When entrepreneurs ignore the fundamentals of finance or simply trust someone else to stand guard, they invite trouble to the table.

Before we close this section on gross margin, let us analyze the Clark Company. What are the gross margins for the Clark Company? They are as follows:

- 1999: 70 percent
- 2000: 72 percent
- 2001: 64 percent

The company has excellent gross margins—in excess of 60 percent for all 3 years. However, one sees an 8 percent decline in gross margins in 2001, indicating that something has changed.

What are some of the possible reasons for a decline in gross margins?

- There may have been a change in the product mix being sold. A higher percentage of lower-end-margin items may have been sold.
- The cost of the supplies may have gone up.
- The company may have changed its accounting system from a cash system to accrual. This change in accounting system results in no change in the timing of cash receipts; since this is a cash business and it therefore does not have

receivables, the change in the system will not affect the timing of when revenues are recognized. However, the accounting system change forces the company to recognize costs earlier. The result of this change is potentially lower gross margins because you're recognizing costs earlier and therefore lower net profit as well.

- The company may be buying from different suppliers at higher costs and/or selling to different customers.

An examination of the income statement shows that 2001 was the first year that products were returned. Also, and more importantly, as the note at the bottom of the statement shows, there was a change in the accounting method, from cash to accrual. And as we stated earlier in this chapter, the change does not affect revenues because this is a cash business, but it does negatively affect all three margins because more expenses are being recognized. Therefore, as a result of the change, we are not comparing "apples to apples" with the prior year.

NET MARGINS

What are acceptable net margins? We've determined that the Clark Company has outstanding gross margins. But how do its net margins compare? In general, net margins of 5 percent or better are considered very good. In a 1997 survey of 900 U.S. companies, *Business Week* found that the average net margins were 5.5 percent.[30] In that same year, *Fortune* surveyed the top 500 companies in the world and found the average net income to be 3.2 percent. Three of the top four companies relative to net income, throughout the world, were U.S.-based. Coca-Cola was number 4 with a net income of 21.9 percent, Intel was number 3 with 27.7 percent, and Microsoft was number 1 with a net income of 30.4 percent. In fact, Microsoft's net profit increased from 25 percent in 1996 to 35 percent in 1998, while the net profits of all other computer software companies remained 6 percent.[31]

Privately owned companies want to minimize taxes and therefore they reduce operating income, which in turn reduces their net income. The point being made is that the net income is usually a manipulated number that understates the true financial performance. A few exceptions might be companies preparing to go public or be sold. These companies may want to look as financially strong as possible.

In contrast, a publicly owned company aggressively seeks positive net margins, as high as possible, because it affects the stock price. As one money manager remarked, "There is a greater tendency among companies to pull out the stops to generate the kind of positive earnings that Wall Street demands."[32] For example, a few years ago America Online, decided not to recognize some huge marketing expenses in its quest for annual positive earnings. The Securities and Exchange Commission unearthed this fact and forced AOL to take a charge of more than $385 million in 1996, wiping out all the profit the company had made up to that point.

Another example is General Motors, which in 1987 decided to extend the depreciation period of its assets, such as tools and dies. This resulted in a lower annual expense for depreciation and therefore higher earnings. Specifically, the result of this legal change was a 33 percent increase in net income. The pressure for public companies to show strong earnings has become so intense that 12 percent of all CFOs surveyed admitted they had "misrepresented corporate financial results at the request of senior management"; 55 percent said they had been asked to do so, but did not.[33] Therefore, when analyzing the financial statements of a privately or publicly owned company, beware. Things—especially net income—may be significantly different than the statements show.

The problem with looking at just net income for a public or private company is that income does not pay the bills. Cashflow pays the bills. Net income is typically an understatement of the cashflow of the company, because it includes noncash item expenses such as depreciation and amortization. In addition, expenditures that have nothing to do with the operation of the company may also be included, thereby lowering the net income of the company. It is common for owners of private companies to run certain personal expenditures through their income statement because they view it as one of the perks of ownership. Therefore, one must realize that net income can be, and usually is, a manipulated number. For example, Leona Helmsley, the owner of several upscale hotels in New York and known as the "Queen of Mean," made improvements to her personal home and charged them to her company, thereby reducing taxes owed. She was convicted of tax evasion as a result and served time in prison. One of the smoking guns used to convict her was an employee who quoted her as saying, "Only poor people pay taxes."

The reality that net income can be a manipulated number is best illustrated by a controversy regarding the 1995 movie *Forrest Gump*. The movie has grossed over $600 million worldwide, making it one of the highest grossing movies in history. A fellow who agreed to take a percentage of the movie's net income as his compensation wrote the story. Believe it or not, this movie never reported a positive net income and thus the writer was due nothing. The issue is presently being litigated. What's the entrepreneurial moral of the story? As an investor, never agree to take a percentage of the net income because you cannot control the expenses, be they real or make-believe.

Conversely, if you are the entrepreneur, always try to compensate investors based on net income, never on revenues. Basing compensation on revenues has gotten many entrepreneurs in financial trouble, because giving someone a percentage of revenues ("off the top") ignores whether a company has a positive cashflow.

The final problem that must be highlighted, in regard to putting too much importance on net earnings, is that the net earnings figure does not tell you where the earnings came from. Did they come from strong company operations or financial instruments? A fundamentally sound company derives most of its earnings from operations, specifically from product sales or services rendered, not interest earned on invested capital. The primary reliance upon interest earned would force the company to be in the money management business. Yahoo!, which had always been touted as one of the few profitable Internet companies, found itself being justifiably criticized in 1997 and 1998. The criticism came from the observation that "in 1997 and 1998, Yahoo!'s interest income accounted for nearly 40% of its net income. By comparison, Cisco's 1998 interest income was only 12.5% of its earnings and Microsoft's 15.5%."[34] As noted in Chapter 2, Yahoo! began an ugly downward spiral in 2001 and is struggling to recover.

Before we close this section, let us analyze the net income of the Clark Company. The net margins for the Clark Company are 25, 24, and 14 percent for 1999, 2000, and 2001, respectively. This would indicate that the company's net margins are outstanding.

The trend, however, is downward, with the caveat that the final year was negatively affected by the change in accounting method previously discussed.

OTHER ISSUES TO CONSIDER

Is the Owner Managing the Business Full Time?

When evaluating the income statement of the Clark Company, one can find evidence that the owner may not be at the place of business on a full-time basis. First, there is an increase in wages, which may represent the hiring of a new employee to run the business as the owner is taking more time off. An examination of the financial statements of a company requires a thorough analysis of the wages section. It is important to ask, Who are the employees? Do these employees actually exist? In some cities like Chicago, dead men have been known to vote in elections, and they also appear on city payrolls. During the due diligence, if the name of an employee is provided, one should not only look to see if the name of the employee matches the name of the owner. It would also be wise to follow up with the question, "How many employees are relatives, and what are their specific tasks and responsibilities?" Wages may have increased because a relative of the owner has been added to the payroll and is being paid an exorbitant wage for doing nothing or for doing something as simple as opening and locking up the company every day.

Exhibit 5-14 presents financial projections for 2002 for the Clark Company, based on historical information.

E X H I B I T   5-14

Clark Company Pro Forma Income Statement for 2002

	Best Case	Worst Case	Most Likely
Income			
Gross sales	111,187	95,303	103,245
Returns and allowances			
Cost of goods sold	31,132	35,262	33,555
Gross profits	80,055	60,041	69,690

continued on next page

E X H I B I T 5-14

Clark Company Pro Forma Income Statement for 2002 (continued)

	Best Case	Worst Case	Most Likely
Expenses			
Advertising	3,336	2,859	3,097
Bad debts	111	95	103
Automobile expense	1,112	953	1,032
Depreciation	835	835	835
Employee benefits programs			
Insurance	2,224	1,906	2,065
Interest			
Mortgage			
Other			
Professional services			
Office expense	9,200	9,200	9,200
Other business property	13,400	13,400	13,400
Repairs and maintenance			
Supplies	226	226	226
Taxes and licenses	1,112	953	1,032
Travel			
Meals and entertainment	173	173	173
Utilities	2,600	2,600	2,600
Wages	12,200	12,200	12,200
Other			
Freight	1,245	1,245	1,245
Sales tax	7,783	6,671	7,227
Total expenses	55,556	53,317	54,437
Net profit or loss	**24,499**	**6,724**	**15,253**

How can you be sure the numbers are correct? In all likelihood, they will not be. It is rare that the projections meet actual numbers. Pro forma development is simply educated guessing.

Revenues

Historically, if we look back at the Clark Company pro forma income statement shown in Exhibit 5-14, the best case is a decrease in revenue of 2 percent; the worst case is a decrease of 16 percent. And the most-likely-case scenario is taken as an average of these two extremes—a decrease of 9 percent. This is a reasonable, logical argument for preparing the projections for sales revenue.

Gross Margins

In regard to gross margins, there were no clear trends during the 3 years of data that were provided. Gross margins increased between 1998 to 2000 and then declined from 2000 and 2001. The best-case gross margins would be 72 percent, worst-case margins would be 64 percent, and the most-likely-case scenario would be an average of the two—68 percent. Again, there is very logical reasoning behind the development of these projections, which is what financiers hope to find.

NOTES

1. Pratt, Jamie, *Financial Accounting*, South-Western Publishing Co., Cincinnati, Ohio, 2nd ed., 1994, p. 709.
2. *Chicago Tribune*, July 25, 2000, p. 12.
3. Ibid.
4. Ibid.
5. Ibid.
6. "Slow Lane to Kmart's Recovery," *New York Times*, November 8, 2001, p. 61.
7. *Crain's Chicago Business*, October 1, 2001.
8. *Forbes*, December 28, 1998, p. 53.
9. Ibid.
10. Ibid.
11. "Scoreboard," *Sports Illustrated*, July 13, 1998.
12. Nee, Eric, "Defending the Desktop," *Forbes*, December 28, 1998, pp. 53–54.
13. Murphy, Richard, "Michael Dell," *Success*.
14. Gallop, Gerda, "Business Management," *Black Enterprise*, February 1999, p. 186.
15. Miniter, Richard, "The Myth of Market Share," *Wall Street Journal*, June 15, 1998.

16. *BusinessWeek*, September 7, 1998.
17. Horovitz, Bruce, "Big Markups Drive Starbucks' Growth," *USA Today*, April 30, 1998, p. 1B.
18. Woolley, Scott, "Greedy Bosses," *Forbes*, August 24, 1998, p. 53.
19. Mid-Atlantic Venture Partners, 1997.
20. Rea, Shawn, "Buy the Book," *Black Enterprise*, February 1999, p. 176.
21. *Fortune*, May 11, 1998.
22. Sherrill, Robert, "Corporate Cannibalism at GE," *Chicago Sun-Times*, November 22, 1998, p. 20E.
23. Armour, Stephanie, "Workplace Absenteeism Soars 25%, Cost Millions," *USA Today*, August 15, 1998.
24. Rewick, C.J., "Software Firm Taps India Connection," *Crain's Chicago Business*, January 25, 1999, p. 14.
25. Arndorfer, James B., "Attacks Show Risks of Exporting Jobs," *Crain's Chicago Business*, October 1, 2001.
26. *BusinessWeek*, March 2, 1998.
27. *Chicago Tribune*, August 30, 1998.
28. Ibid.
29. Gove, Alex, "Margin of Error," *Red Herring*, February 1999, p. 140.
30. Byrnes, Nanette, "Is This the End of the Glory Days," *BusinessWeek*, March 2, 1998, pp. 110–135.
31. Coco, Christine, "Microsoft Prices Slammed," *Chicago Sun-Times*, January 10, 1999, p. 56A.
32. Valdmanis, Thor, "Cooking the Books, a Common Trick of the Trade," *USA Today*, August 11, 1998.
33. Ibid.
34. *Forbes ASAP*, February 22, 1999, p. 24.

CHAPTER 6

Cashflow
Management

INTRODUCTION

Nothing is as important as positive cashflow to a business. As I often tell my students, "For any business, depending on the entrepreneur's gender, positive cashflow is King or Queen!" Without cash, an entrepreneur will not be able to buy inventory or equipment, make payroll, pay bills and utilities, or repay debt. Cash is necessary not only to keep a business going, but also to grow the business. Seth Godin is the founder of Yoyodyne, an online direct-marketing company that he later sold to Yahoo! for $30 million. As an entrepreneur who bootstrapped his business for the first few years, he notes that happiness for a business owner boils down to one simple thing: positive cashflow.[1] Companies that cannot achieve positive cashflow are essentially nonvoluntary, not-for-profit organizations that eventually become insolvent. That is the reason why so many dot-com companies became dot-bombs.

TYPES OF CASHFLOW

A business cashflow is commonly referred to as EBITDA, which is an acronym for earnings before interest, taxes, depreciation, and amortization. EBITDA is the cash available to service debt (i.e., principal and interest), pay taxes, buy capital equipment, and return to shareholders after paying all of a company's operating expenses. A company's EBITDA is calculated as shown in Formula 6-1.

F O R M U L A   6-1

EBITDA

	Net Earnings
plus	Interest
plus	Taxes
plus	Depreciation
plus	Amortization
equals	**EBIDTA**

It should be noted that the true cash position of a company includes the adding back of depreciation and amortization. While these two items can be expensed on an income statement, they are noncash item expenditures, as was stated in Chapter 5. Their presence on an income statement helps the company's cashflow by reducing its taxable profits. This adding-back practice is the reason why a company with negative net earnings on its income statement can still have a positive cashflow.

While EBITDA and free cashflow or, FCF, are important for the entrepreneur to understand, he or she must also understand that these are simply cashflow descriptions used for cashflow statement purposes. They describe what the cashflow of the company should ideally be. Unfortunately, for entrepreneurs, the ideal and actual are often miles apart. It is common to hear entrepreneurs say, "On paper my cashflow numbers show the company to be rich and making plenty of money, but in reality we are cash-poor and starving." The reason this comment is so often stated is because money owed the company has not been paid. For example, the company could have had an extraordinary month of growth in revenues such that all of the actual cash had to be used to finance it by paying overtime to employees and paying for raw materials used to make the product. About 90 percent of the month's revenues were shipped on the last day of the month, and the terms are net 30. Such a scenario describes a situation where, on the income statement for that month, the cashflow looks strong, but the reality is that the cash will not actually arrive until at least 30 days later. This "paper-rich, cash-poor" situation resulted from taking advantage of the opportunity to increase profitable revenues.

"Paper-rich, cash-poor" as it relates to poor cashflow management occurs when the money from the customer is past due. To succeed, the entrepreneur must be an absolute vigilant bulldog about maximizing the actual day-to-day cashflow of the business.

Ensuring that a company has adequate cash on hand to fund operations as well as pay off obligations is essential. It is important to put in place a system that enables the entrepreneur to properly monitor and manage both expected cash receipts (i.e., cash inflows) and payables (i.e., cash outflows). The lack of an efficient cashflow management system can have severe negative consequences on a company's bottom line. For example, for service companies, whose expenses are heavily front-loaded into labor costs, profits diminish with every additional unnecessary week it takes to get costs reimbursed. For manufacturers this problem is even more severe since they often have to spend large amounts of money up-front on materials, production, and inventory and have long lag times between cash outflows and receipt of money from customers. How does the delay in cash receipts diminish profits?

The importance of accurately managing a company's cash needs is highlighted by the following example: The Gartner Group is a high-tech consulting firm that generated $511 million in revenues in 1997. When founder Michael Fernandez and his cofounders were raising capital for the company, they decided to limit the capital they raised to $30 million, even though they could have raised twice as much. They placed this limit because they wanted to restrict the amount of equity they would have to give up. However, they did not anticipate the problems they would face as they tried to develop a new product for their company, nor did they adequately assess their cash needs during this crucial period. One problem that occurred was that the manufacturer of the disk drives for the company's laptops went out of business. Given that there was only one company equipped to manufacture these drives, Gartner experienced production delays until a second manufacturer could be found. Once this manufacturer was identified, Gartner had to spend several months redesigning the disk drive so that the new manufacturer could produce it. In the meantime, the company ran out of money and was forced to file Chapter 11. The lesson Mr. Fernandez learned, the hard way, is that it is essential to focus on cashflow. As he notes, "We were obsessed with revenues and profits and trying to hold on to the equity," rather than on cashflow.[2] Today he insists that his executives and employees look at cashflow every single day. However, this is an area that few entrepreneurs focus on, particularly when they start their companies.

There are endless examples of entrepreneurs who neglect to pursue prudent cashflow management, particularly when their company is doing well. As Godin noted, "We think about this [cashflow] every day. But there are a lot of people who forget, when times are as good as they have been over the past few years, that the business world is cyclical and that you need money to make money."[3] The stronger the economy is and the faster a company is growing, the easier it can be to overlook cashflow controls, sometimes without suffering immediate negative consequences. But eventually when there is a downturn in the economy, the entrepreneur may face a cash crunch. As a CPA once told me, "The best thing about volatile economic conditions is that they remind managers to refocus their attention on the basics." In fact, during a cashflow crisis, fast growth usually exacerbates problems because companies spend cash on supplies and payroll—often at an accelerated rate because of fast growth—while waiting long periods to collect receivables. A case in point is Douglas Roberson, president of Atlantic Network Systems, a data and voice systems integrator, whose company's revenues quadrupled from $100,000 its first year to $460,000 the next. During this growth period, his staff did not concern themselves with cashflow because sales were growing at such a phenomenal rate. "I actually believed that the more money companies owed us, the better shape we were in," Roberson confessed.[4] It was not until his company went through an extended period in which it was unable to collect its receivables that he realized the importance of managing cash. His company had to use all its existing lines of credit to keep its operations going while waiting for bills to be paid. It was a real-life lesson. He, like most entrepreneurs, learned that managing cashflow was different from just accumulating sales. As he noted "If you don't do serious projections about how much cash you'll need to handle sales—and how long it will take to collect on invoices—you can wind up out of business, no matter how fast you're growing."[5]

CASHFLOW FORECASTS

Preparing a cashflow forecast allows an entrepreneur to determine a business's financing needs. If an entrepreneur finds that the business has a forecasted cash shortage due to rapid growth, then it might be necessary to raise external money to meet the company's financial needs. A good cashflow forecast will allow the entrepreneur to determine the exact amount of cash needed and also the time when it is needed. In general, there are several reasons why businesses raise outside capital. First, seasonal needs, such as a holiday sale, require the purchase of additional materials and the payment of additional production expenses to meet this temporary increase in demand. Second, more capital may be needed to finance long-term sales growth. As a company's sales grow, more inventory must be purchased and additional workers will be needed. All these activities will require additional cash that may not be on hand. A good cashflow forecast will allow an entrepreneur to forecast financing needs for these activities. Third, an entrepreneur may have to purchase expensive capital equipment or make expensive repairs to existing equipment.

Entrepreneurs must know that projected cashflow determines the amount of capital a company needs in the future. The following steps should be taken to make that determination.

- Prepare a 3- to 5-year (i.e., monthly annual projection) cashflow projection.
- To make the projection, use FCF *plus* debt obligations (i.e., interest and principal), which is called net cashflow.
- Choose the largest cumulative negative cashflow number—this is the capital needed.

To better illustrate these steps let's look at the 5-year net cashflow numbers for the Johnson Company shown in Table 6-1.

With the information in Table 6-1, the Johnson Company can now easily determine its capital needs by completing the chart in Table 6-2.

TABLE 6-1

Projected Net Cashflow Calculation

Year	Projected Net Cashflow
1	−100
2	−90
3	−70
4	85
5	100

TABLE 6-2

Cumulative Net Cashflow Calculation

	Year 1	Year 2	Year 3	Year 4	Year 5
Projected NCF	−100	−90	−70	85	100
Cumulative projected NCF	−100	−190	−260	−175	−75

By plugging in the numbers from the cashflow projection, the Johnson Company would determine that $260 is needed because that is the largest cumulative number over the projected time frame.

The obvious question now is, When should you get the cash? There are two schools of thought in response to this question. The first is that you should only get what you need from year to year, or a "series of funding." The second is that you should get the maximum that you will need at once. Both have advantages and disadvantages as shown below:

Obtain Series of Funding

Pros:

- Keeps entrepreneur disciplined and minimizes wasting money.
- Only paying for current expenses.
- New series of capital comes in at higher valuation, thereby allowing less equity to be surrendered.

Cons:

- No certainty that more capital will be available in the future.
- Required to allocate resources to secure additional funding.

Obtain All Funding at One Time

Pros:

- Does not need to allocate resources to raise future funding.
- Avoids risk of capital not being available in the future.

Cons:

- Forecasts may be wrong as a result of incoming cashflows occurring earlier than year 4, requiring less up-front capital. Additionally, in the case of an equity capital investment, too much equity is surrendered, or in the case of a debt capital investment, interest on unnecessary capital will be paid.
- Too much capital at one time spoils the inexperienced entrepreneur and could lead to unnecessary waste of the capital.
- Invested capital comes in at lower valuation.

What is the correct answer? In today's financial climate, where capital is tougher to access, the advice is to get as much up-front as possible.

CASHFLOW MANAGEMENT

Cashflow management can be as simple as preserving future cash by not spending as much today. For example, in order to deal with seasonal sales, a company may choose not to spend as much in October if December—when October's bills come due—is traditionally a poor sales month and won't generate enough receipts to cover those bills.[6] Cashflow management can also involve making somewhat complicated decisions about delaying payments to a supplier in order to use cash resources to temporarily increase production. Or it can involve making decisions about borrowing or using factoring companies to generate cash quickly to meet short-term cash shortages.

The relationship between the sources and uses of cash are shown in Formula 6-2.

F O R M U L A   6-2

Sources and Uses of Cash

Sources of cash − uses of cash = net cashflow

→ Fund operations and return to investors

Sources of Cash or Cash Inflows

- Accounts receivable
- Cash payments
- Other income (i.e., income from investments)
- Borrowing

Uses of Cash or Cash Outflows

- Payroll
- Utilities—heat, electricity, telephone, etc.
- Loan payments—interest plus principal
- Rent
- Insurance—health, property, etc.
- Taxes

Key Cashflow Goals

The goal of good cash management is obvious: to have enough cash on hand when you need it. The major goal of prudent cash-flow management is to ensure there is enough cash on hand to meet the demands for cash at any given time. This is done by getting cash not only from operations (i.e., managing cash inflows including accounts receivable) and disciplined spending (i.e., managing accounts payable), but also through the use of external capital (i.e., borrowing). While this may appear to be a simple concept, in reality it is a process that even the most experienced financial officers and executives find difficult to successfully achieve.

The trick to handling cashflow is in the timing—as an entrepreneur you want your customers to pay as soon as possible (if possible in advance) while you pay your suppliers and vendors as late as possible without jeopardizing your relationship with them or your credit standing. The idea is that money which is collected in receivables today, and which does not have to go out as payables, is, in fact, an important source of internally generated working capital.

While it may not be the most fun thing to do, it is important for an entrepreneur to spend time, at least an hour a day, working on cashflow. It is without a doubt one of the most crucial things an entrepreneur can do for a business. This exercise forces an entrepreneur to think about what he or she is doing in terms of cold, hard cash.

Cashflow Ledgers and Projections

The cashflow ledger provides important information about the balance of the cash account, enabling the entrepreneur to assess the company's ability to fund its operations as well as meet debt payments as they come due. It indicates, on a transaction basis, all cash received and disbursed during a month's period. Successful entrepreneurs are those who know the actual cash position of their company on any given day. Therefore, it is recommended that the entrepreneur, especially the inexperienced and those in the early stages of their ventures, review their cashflow ledger at least weekly.

In addition to the ledger, a weekly cashflow projection summary, as discussed in Chapter 3, should be prepared when opening a business and every month thereafter. This projection indicates the anticipated cash inflow during the month as well as cash payments to be made. By doing this kind of projection each month the entrepreneur can schedule payments to suppliers to match expected cash receipts. This planner allows the entrepreneur to be proactive with regard to the money owed to suppliers and enables the entrepreneur to let specific vendors know in advance that a payment will probably be late. The cashflow ledger and planner are simple and very useful tools that should be used to successfully manage cashflow. It is important to be consistent and work through each line item so that forecasts can be as accurate as possible.

To prepare cashflow forecasts, the entrepreneur should first look at historical cashflow, if this information is available. Construct monthly historical cashflows for at least the past year or, if possible, the past few years. By so doing, it will be easier to forecast many items, for example utility bills, if it is known what has been spent in the past.

Using these historical figures, prepare forecasts for the weekly cashflows for a month at a time. First, determine the cash inflows for each month—usually cash sales and accounts receivable. Then determine the cash outflows—utilities, payroll and other employee-related expenses, inventory, equipment purchases, etc. Compare inflows with outflows to determine the net cash position of the company.

The cashflow forecast allows an entrepreneur to track actual performance against forecasts and plans. Each month an entrepreneur should compare the forecast with actual results and calculate the variance between the actual amount incurred and the forecast line by line. Then calculate the percentage variance (i.e., the actual minus the forecast divided by the forecast). Focus on the areas where overspending occurred, looking at the dollar amount and percentage over the budget. Where the difference is significant, determine if the expenditure was justified, and, if not, how to reduce it. By doing this every month, an entrepreneur will find that he or she can control expenses much more effectively.

ACCOUNTS RECEIVABLE

The major area of vulnerability for many entrepreneurs is accounts receivable. On any given day, it is estimated that 5 million businesses are behind on their bills.[7] As stated earlier, many entrepreneurs, particularly in the early or fast-growth stages of their business, focus more on generating sales than they do on collecting receivables. While this is never a good idea, it can turn into a disastrous situation when the economy slows down and more customers take longer to pay their bills—usually the result is a cash crunch for a company. Every year, Dun & Bradstreet surveys small-business owners. The survey is designed to give an overview of current issues and problems facing these business owners, as well as a brief look at expectations for the coming year. In 2001, for the 20th annual survey, small-business owners were asked about their priorities. For example, in the coming year, would they put more of an emphasis on increasing sales? What about collecting debt? The answers given are shown in Table 6-3, and they suggest that collecting customer debt is a secondary concern.

T A B L E   6-3

Dun & Bradstreet Small-Business Survey

	Sales	Control Costs	Financing	Uncollected Debt
Increase emphasis	67%	53%	16%	21%
Decrease emphasis	3%	4%	10%	7%
Same emphasis	28%	40%	59%	50%
Don't know/not applicable	2%	3%	16%	21%

Source: Dun & Bradstreet 20th Annual Small Business Survey

Alan Burkhard, president of The Placers, Inc., a Wilmington, Delaware–based temporary placement and permanent job search firm, initially did not value the importance of having good financial controls for accounts receivable. He notes, "I always told myself that accounts receivable didn't create sales, so they weren't worth paying attention to."[8] This was his belief until a time when, although his company was generating record sales, he was having difficulty running his company due to cash problems. The root of the problem—an inefficient accounts receivable system.

"None of our customers paid us in any kind of timely fashion. And 60–70% of our delinquent accounts were actually owed by our regular customers. Every single week we had to pay salaries and payroll taxes for every temp we placed on a job. But it was taking us 60 or 90 days or longer to collect our bills from the companies that were hiring those temps."[9] By allowing its customers to take so long to pay, The Placers was actually giving them an interest-free loan to cover their own payroll costs. Unfortunately, it is quite common for entrepreneurs to complain about their need for more working capital when in fact the company already has the money in accounts receivable. When you are an entrepreneur, you better be an absolute vigilant bulldog (as noted at the beginning of this chapter) when it comes to collecting your receivables. This is the lifeblood of the business—collecting your receivables as quickly as possible. Candidly, when I first owned my business, I was a bit of a wimp. I was scared that if I called the customers and said something, well, then they would no longer do business with me. I learned very quickly that if you do not say something, you are not going to be sitting around long saying, "Where's my money?" Instead, you're going to be saying, "Where's my business?" The money simply needs to be collected by whatever means necessary. As one entrepreneur stated, "I get on the phone and beg."[10]

Accounts Receivable Systems

A good accounts receivable collection system is proactive. It also allows the entrepreneur to do business with customers that may not have a credit history or even those who have a bad credit history. The major components of an effective system include these steps:

- Before you go into business, perform an analysis of the industry's payment practice. Is it an industry characterized by historically slow-paying customers such as the government or health insurance companies? Exhibit 5-6 lists periodicals to do an industry analysis. And if an industry is characterized by slow-paying customers, that does not necessarily mean you should not enter it. It simply means you should be even more diligent about developing and maintaining a disciplined system.
- Have all new customers complete a credit report before you provide any services or products. The report should be simple but thorough and should contain the following information:
  - The age of the company.
  - The owner(s) of the company.

- Whether the company has ever declared Chapter 7 or 11 and whether the owner has ever declared Chapter 13.
- The current name of the company and any previous names.
- The maximum credit level desired.
- The telephone numbers and fax numbers and/or addresses of three supplier references. The length and terms of the relationship with these suppliers.
- The name of the company's primary bank, its account number(s), and a contact number for the bank officer responsible for managing the company's accounts.
- Whether or not the company agrees to pay invoices according to your terms.

- Consider the following options if a potential customer does not have a credit history or has a bad one:
  - At the time of order receipt, require an up-front payment equal to the costs of goods sold for the order, with the balance due at the time of shipment. This ensures that costs are covered if the customer cancels the order after production has begun.
  - Obtain a 100 percent payment before work on the order can begin.
  - Require a 100 percent payment before or at the time of delivery (COD).
  - Request a 33 percent payment at order receipt, 33 percent at time of shipment, and the balance due 30 days later.

- Contact all references immediately and inquire about their credit experience with the prospective customer. Questions should include:
  - How many years have they had this customer?
  - What is the maximum amount of credit they have provided this customer? Have there been any increases or decreases in the credit limit? If so, why?
  - What are their invoice terms?
  - Does the customer typically pay within 10, 30, 60, or 90 days?

- Have they ever received any checks from this customer, and have any bounced?
- Do they recommend this company as a good customer?
- Have they had any problems doing business with the company?

If all references are satisfactory, inform your customers that their orders will be processed immediately. Also remind customers of the company's invoice terms and ask if they have any problems adhering to them. Specifically, ask customers how they normally pay their bills. The reason behind this question is that some companies have their own system for paying bills, regardless of the supplier's invoice terms.

Successful entrepreneurs know how their key customers pay their bills. For example:

- Some customers pay their bills once a month, and typically on the 30th or 31st. To be paid on the 30th, the merchandise must be received by the 10th, otherwise the payment will be made on the 30th of the next month.
- Some pay 30 days after receipt of the goods or services. Therefore, the supplier is penalized if the shipment is delayed by the carrier.
- Some pay 30 days after products damaged during delivery have been replaced.

It is also important to ask customers for the name of the accounts payable clerk who will be responsible for paying invoices. When I operated my business, you better believe that I knew every accounts payable clerk at every one of my customers. I knew their names, their kids' names, the flowers they liked. Heck, *their* employers must have wondered why we were so cozy. You know why? Any edge I could gain in getting my bills paid earlier was well worth a few timely cards, a few nice words, and flowers on a birthday.

Other important key steps toward the effective management of accounts receivable include:

- All invoices should be mailed on the same day that the product is shipped or services rendered. Do not hold invoices until the next day or the end of the week, nor should you wait to send invoices once a month. Such a practice will certainly delay payment.

- Make sure that the invoice highlights the payment terms in bold capital letters or in a different color from the rest of the invoice. The terms should be printed at the top of the page of the invoice. The most common invoice terms are "2, 10 net 30." This means if the customer pays within 10 days from the invoice date, he or she is allowed a 2 percent discount. Otherwise the entire invoice amount is due within 30 days of the invoice date.
- Manage the collection of accounts receivable. It is naïve to expect all customers to pay in a timely fashion. In the business of collecting receivables, the squeaky wheel does in fact get the oil.
- The entrepreneur should have a weekly receivables aging report showing the customer accounts that are over 30 days or more.
- For invoices not paid 7 days after the due date, automatic action of some kind should be taken.
- Excellent payment history is no longer than 10 days more than the invoice terms. If the terms are net 30 and payment occurs in 50 days, then no future orders should be sent before receipt of some kind of payment, as mentioned earlier.

The act of collecting accounts receivable can be an intimidating experience, especially for the inexperienced entrepreneur. In many instances the new entrepreneur is afraid to implement a system similar to the one mentioned above because of the fear of losing revenue if the customer gets offended. Such a concern is foolish and naïve. It is also a good idea to have someone other than you send the strong letters and make the tough phone calls. At my company, a woman named Angela—our CFO—was our resident pit bull. We had a system in place where our terms were net 30, and if we weren't paid by the 35th day, an automatic reminder went out to the customer—a neon green sheet of paper in a neon green envelope. It said, "Just a reminder if you've forgotten us." If we hadn't been paid 5 days after that, another notice—this one hot pink—

went out. I had one customer call me to say, "Steve, every time I open one of these doggone notices, I get blinded by the sheets of paper. Why don't you stop sending them to me?" I replied, "Listen, I just own the company. Angela runs everything out there. Now the way that I can get Angela to stop is for you to simply pay on time. It's a simple solution."

But everyone has his or her own system, and occasionally the entrepreneur needs to show a little "tough love." I love the story that a business broker in Richmond, Virginia, Bette Wildermuth tells about one of her clients. "This gentleman owns an excavation company. He always does excellent work, meets the developers' time schedule and makes sure his crews clean up after themselves. Usually he gets paid within ten days of completing the job. But every once in a while, a developer really drags things out. The excavator's solution: He puts on his muddiest contractor boots and goes to the developer's fancy office with the nice oriental rugs. When he arrives he announces in a very loud voice that he has come to pick up the overdue check and plans to sit in the lobby until its ready. Needless to say, this does tend to speed up the process."

For the entrepreneur who just doesn't have the stomach for collections, one option is to get "credit insurance," where the insurer pays the claim within 60 days and then assumes the responsibility for collection. Baltimore, Maryland–based American Credit Indemnity Company, the country's largest issuer of credit insurance, charges 1 percent of the sales insured and will only insure receivables that have historically been from customers who pay within 30 days.[11]

Remember, good customers typically expect to pay their bills within 5 to 10 days following the due date, unless they have a special payables system as was mentioned earlier. Even those customers plan to pay, but according to their system. A bad customer is one who is very cavalier about paying bills. These types of customers will only pay when they are forced to do so, even when they have the money. Ultimately, the experienced entrepreneur sees that the latter are not profitable customers and does not mind losing them.

When such a decision has been made, extreme action should be taken, such as hiring a lawyer, at the cost of approximately $2000, to get a "writ of attachment" within 60 days against the delinquent customer's corporate bank account. This action generally gets the customer's immediate attention for settling the delinquency.[12]

Before leaving the subject of an accounts receivable system, here are a few don'ts:

- Don't be rude to customers. Don't threaten them.
- Don't assume that a slow-paying customer is a thief or a bum. It may be that the customer has fallen on temporary tough economic times.
- Don't take legal action against a customer until the bill is at least 45 days past due and you have personally spoken to the customer and tried to get payment.
- Don't pay independent sales representatives until you receive payment from the customer. Some sales representatives do not care if a customer is a known delinquent payer. Taking an order from such a customer may not bother the salesperson since he or she is not investing in raw materials, etc. Therefore, discourage such action with a policy that specifies that sales representatives will not receive their full commission if payment is received after a certain number of days late. For example, if the payment is 15 days late, the commission is reduced by 15 percent.

To check on the quality of accounts receivable, several ratios can be used. The first step in checking the quality is to determine what the company's collection ratio or "days receivable" or "accounts receivable turnover" is. This ratio measures the quality of the accounts receivable of a company. It shows the average number of days it takes to collect accounts receivable. To look at it another way, this ratio indicates the number of days, on average, it takes a business to convert receivables to cash. Formula 6-3 shows the equation to calculate days receivable.

F O R M U L A   6-3

Days Receivable

Outstanding receivables/annual sales/365 days

The same formula can be restated as Formula 6-4.

FORMULA 6-4

Days Receivable

Outstanding receivables/average daily sales

In this case, average daily sales can be calculated using Formula 6-5.

FORMULA 6-5

Average Daily Sales

Average daily sales = annual sales/365 days

The goal is to get the customers to pay as soon as possible. Therefore, a low number is desirable. At a minimum, a company's days receivable should be equal to the industry's average. Also, it should not exceed the company's days payable ratio, because if it does, this would indicate that bills are being paid faster than payments are being received.

For example, a company with $5 million in annual revenues and $800,000 in accounts receivable has an accounts receivable turnover ratio of 58.4 days calculated as shown in Exhibit 6-1.

EXHIBIT 6-1

Receivables Turnover Ratio Calculation

$5 million in sales/365 days = $13,699 (average daily sales)
$800,000 in receivables/$13,699 = 58.4 days

This number would indicate that, on average, it takes the company approximately 58 days to convert receivables into cash. Is this good or bad? Well, most importantly it depends on the invoice terms.

If the terms are 30 days, this is bad even if the industry average is more. This says that customers are paying almost 1 month later than they should. That is money that could be reinvested and could generate returns if the company received it closer to the invoice terms.

Companies usually do not understand the importance of collecting accounts receivable quickly and consistently. Entrepreneurs usually focus resources on boosting sales, rather than on faster collection of receivables, because the benefits of higher sales are easier to quantify. Entrepreneurs sometimes ignore the costs of inefficient collection systems because they usually do not understand the costs of these inefficiencies to the company's bottom line. However, it is easy to quantify the benefits of faster collection of accounts receivable in terms of dollars saved. Faster collection means that the company will not have to use external financing for current payables. Formula 6-6 is the formula for calculating dollars saved resulting from faster collection of accounts receivable.

F O R M U L A   6-6

Dollars Saved

(Gross annual sales $\times$ annual interest rate) $\times$ days saved/365 days = dollars saved

In calculating dollars saved, use the most recent complete year's sales figures, unless the company is growing rapidly and has a good projection for the current year. For the annual interest rate, include the cost of debt capital. To find the days saved, subtract the company's improved days sales outstanding (DSO) from its original DSO. The equation for DSO is shown in Formula 6-7.

F O R M U L A   6-7

Days Sales Outstanding*

$$\frac{\text{Average accounts receivable balance over past 3 months} \times 90 \text{ days}}{\text{Total sales over past 3 months}}$$

*Fraser, Jill Andresky, "Collection: Days Saved, Thousands Earned," *Inc.*, November 1995.

For example, a $4 million company, borrowing at the prime rate of 6.75 percent plus 2 points (i.e., 2 percent), improves its days sales outstanding by 5 days. The total amount of dollars the company saves by improving its collection of accounts receivable is shown in Exhibit 6-2.

E X H I B I T   6-2

Accounts Receivable Collection Savings

($4,000,000 × 8.75) × 5 days/365 days = $4795 in savings

ACCOUNTS PAYABLE

The ideal situation is to collect all your receivables quickly while paying outstanding bills as late as possible without jeopardizing the service from suppliers. However, delaying payables is not always necessarily a good thing. If you have cash on hand or can borrow at low rates, should you take discounts? Yes. As Jay Gohz, the author of *The Street Smart Entrepreneur*, explains:

> Suppose your supplier terms are 2, 10 net 30—2% discount if you pay in 10 days; the entire balance is due in 30 days. You don't take a discount and pay in 40 days instead of 30. Basically, you have borrowed from your vendor for 30 days, which is essentially one-twelfth of a year. The loan cost equals 2% (i.e., the 10-day discount) of the invoice annualized, which is 24%. If every month you lose a 2% discount, it is like paying 24% over the course of a year.

To determine whether or not the company's accounts payable are what they should be, analyze the accounts payable turnover ratio and compare it with the industry average. This ratio measures the average number of days it takes the company to pay its bills. The ratio can be calculated as shown in Exhibit 6-3.

E X H I B I T   6-3

Accounts Payable Turnover Ratio Calculation

COGS/365 days = average daily costs.
Accounts payable/average daily costs = number of days it takes to pay

Management of Accounts Payable

To improve the accounts payable days, the entrepreneur can take the following actions recommended by several professionals:

- Negotiate better payment terms, such as net 45 or 60—instead of net 30.
- Time payments according to their due dates, such as 30 days following receipt of material, rather than some artificial schedule.
- Plan cashflow realities. For example, to avoid big cash outflows, some companies pay their employees' payroll biweekly and then pay outstanding bills during the other 2 weeks of the month.
- Avoid interest penalty charges. If you have to stretch out your own payables due to temporary cashflow problems, make sure you are not late with those bills that incur additional interest charges.
- Communicate with your suppliers. If you establish a good working relationship with a supplier and make regular payments, you can usually avoid paying late charges by contacting the owner in advance if you expect to make a late payment or if you need to request a payment extension.
- Set scheduling goals. Try to establish a final date at which all payables are to be made. While it is unrealistic to assume that you will always be on schedule, it is important to keep the accounts payable as close to the schedule goal date as possible.
- Be organized. Keep a paper trail and close track of details, especially of the aging of bills. Invest in a good accounts payable system.
- Look for warning signs, including low cash levels which could result in future problems paying vendors and suppliers. Reevaluate your collection controls to ensure that you are collecting cash as soon as possible.
- Prioritize. You can't devote the same amount of time to all payables. Prioritize payables depending on some type of priority rating. For example, fixed expenses such as rent may be paid first, utilities second, and then other bills.

- Identify problems early. Look for accuracy of information on invoices from suppliers.
- Provide supervision from the top.
- Have specialists monitor the accounts payable daily.
- Try to stretch your accounts payable as much as possible without hurting your relationships with vendors and without damaging your credit status.

THE CASH GAP

You now own a business. Whether it's a manufacturing, retail, or services firm, you soon discover a simple truth: First *you* pay for the goods or services, and then eventually someone else—*your* customer—pays you. The spread of days between payment of cash and receipt of cash is called the *cash gap* or *cash conversion cycle*. How long do your goods sit in inventory? How many days before you have to pay your supplier? Finally, how many days does it take your customers to pay you? The answers to those three questions are plugged into the cash gap formula shown in Formula 6-8.

F O R M U L A   6-8

Cash Gap Calculation

	Inventory days
plus	Days receivable
minus	Days payable
equals	Cash gap

That interval between payment of cash and receipt of cash must be financed. The longer the time, the more interest a company must pay on capital loaned from a lender, thereby using working capital. The wise way to reduce the need for working capital is to decrease the gap. The entrepreneur's goal must be to continually shorten the gap, because for each day that it is decreased, the daily interest cost saved goes entirely and directly to pretax profits.

Let's explore this concept in more detail using an example and illustrations. We can make the following assumptions for the Varnadoe Company.

- Days inventory carried*: 40.5
- Days payable*: 40
- Days receivable*: 35
- Annual revenues: $50 million
- Gross profit*: 30 percent
- Cost of debt: 6 percent

Therefore, the cash gap can be calculated as shown in Exhibit 6-4.

E X H I B I T   6-4

Cash Gap Calculation

	Inventory days	40.5
plus	Days receivable	35.0
minus	Days payable	40.0
equals	Cash gap	35.5 days

To determine the savings from reducing the cash gap by 1 day, the calculation shown in Exhibit 6-5 should be made.

E X H I B I T   6-5

Cash Gap Reduction Calculation

Determine the company's daily revenues:
$50 million ÷ 365 = $136,986

Determine the cost of goods sold:
100% − 0.30 (gross profit) = 0.70

Determine the COGS for 1 day of revenue:
0.70 (COGS) × $136,986 (daily revenue) = $95,890

continued on next page

*The formulas for these ratios can be found in Chapter 5.

E X H I B I T   6-5

Cash Gap Reduction Calculation (continued)

The cash gap:
35.5 days

Determine how much Varnadoe Company needs to borrow to cover 35.5 days of COGS:
35.5 × $95,890 (COGS for 1 day's revenue) = $3,404,109

Determine the interest expense to be paid on the borrowed money:
3,404,109 × 0.06 (cost of debt) = $204,246

Determine the savings from reducing the cash gap by 1 day:
$204,246 ÷ 35.5 (cash gap) = $5753

As you can see from the exhibit, for every day that the cash gap is reduced, the savings of $5753 will go directly to profits before taxes, thereby increasing the Varnadoe Company's cashflow. Using the Varnadoe Company's information, Exhibit 6-6 illustrates the cash gap concept.

E X H I B I T   6-6

Cash Gap Illustration—Varnadoe Company

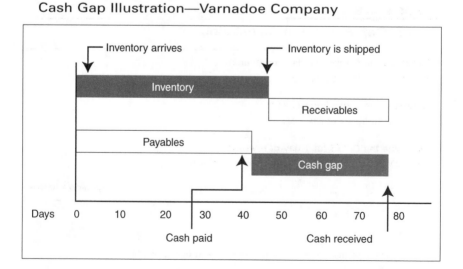

There are only three ways that a company can reduce its cash gap: (1) Increase the number of days it takes to pay for inventory; (2) decrease the number of days it takes to collect receivables; or (3) increase the inventory turns. Let's analyze each.

Increase Days Payable

- Most companies allow their customers up to 2 weeks past the due date before they consider the invoice seriously delinquent. Therefore every entrepreneur should take advantage of these extra days by paying no later than 2 weeks after the due date. This shortens the cash gap because it extends payments that may have been due in 30 days to 44 days. Using the information from the Varnadoe Company, if days payable were increased 4 days to 44, the cash gap would be 31.5 instead of 35.5. Such a decrease would save the company $23,012 in interest payments (4 days × $5753).

Decrease Days Receivable

- This topic has been discussed in great detail in Chapter 4. Some industries historically have lower days receivable than others. For example, manufacturing companies typically expect payment in 30 days, whereas retailers such as Amazon.com get paid immediately upon sale. They have no receivables because payment is required at the time of order. In fact, Amazon.com reported in 1998 zero receivables, 87 days payable, and 23 days of inventory. The result was that Amazon.com's cash gap was a beautiful, negative 64 days $(0 + 23 - 87 = -64)$, which means that it raised interest-free money from its customers for approximately 2 months. Specifically, with average cost of sales, which at the time was $1.3 million, the company raised $83 million ($1.3 million × 64 days), which it used to help pay overhead expenses.[13] Using the Varnadoe Company data again, if the days receivable were reduced from 35 to 29, the effect would be a 6-day reduction in the cash gap and therefore a $34,518 cash savings.

Increase Inventory Turnover

- The faster a company converts inventory into cash, the less cash is needed because the company can reduce its days of inventory carried and decrease its inventory carrying costs, which was discussed in Chapter 4. A company that has successfully increased its inventory turns is Wal-Mart. In 1998 Wal-Mart sold 55 percent of its inventory before payment was required. In 1999 it had increased to 63 percent. Its 2002 goal is to turn 100 percent of the inventory before the bills come due.[14] Another company that has success with improving cashflow by turning inventory faster is Amazon.com. It turns its inventory an amazing 150 times per year, compared with less than 4 times for traditional bookstores.[15]

The hope is, as a result of this rich discussion, that it is now clear that every entrepreneur must know why cash gap analysis is important and how to use it as a proactive tool for operating the company. Every entrepreneur should do the complete analysis explained in this section at least annually and use the information for strategic planning for next year.

What is the ideal cash gap? It varies by industry. An industry comparison should be made annually using the Robert Morris Associates guide. A few of the industries are highlighted in Table 6-4.

T A B L E   6-4

Cash Gaps by Industry, 1998

	Receivables +	Inventory −	Payables =	Cash Gap
Manufacturing				
Bread and bakery	27	19	29	17
Bottled soft drinks	28	25	24	29
Women's dresses	55	37	38	54
Wholesale				
Office supplies	40	28	31	37
Auto	17	63	10	70

continued on next page

T A B L E   6-4

Cash Gaps by Industry, 1998 (continued)

	Receivables +	Inventory −	Payables =	Cash Gap
Toys, hobby goods	49	118	35	131
Retail				
Gasoline stations	6	10	13	2
Drugstores	30	60	35	54
Shoes	2	159	54	107

Source: *Journal of Accountancy*, October 1999, p 29.

WORKING CAPITAL

The procurement, maintenance, and management of working capital seem to be some of the most common and challenging tasks facing entrepreneurs. Therefore, let's devote a little more time to the subject.

As was stated earlier in this chapter, the interval between a company's payment and receipt of cash must be financed. The money for this is called working capital, which consists of funds invested in all current assets including inventory, accounts receivable, and cash. Gross working capital is used to finance only the company's current assets. Net working capital, which is a measurement of a company's solvency, is current assets minus current liabilities. The goal is to have positive net working capital. The greater the net working capital, the stronger the company's cash position relative to its ability to service other expenses including long-term debt.

Very few companies are able to internally finance their working capital needs. Therefore, external financing in the form of debt or equity is inevitable. How much working capital is ideal? One expert, Skip Grandt, a commercial lender with 20 years of experience, says he likes to see a company have net working capital levels at three to six times its annual fixed costs.[16]

FINDING CASH

Entrepeneurs have frequently asked me to help them raise external financing from debt and/or equity investors. Most of the time, after reviewing the financial statements, I have told them that they do not need outside capital. They simply need to reduce their inventory and/or accounts receivable levels. That's right. Cash is often readily available to entrepreneurs who carry excessive amounts of these two assets.

What is the ideal level of inventory that an entrepreneur should carry? The formula to make this determination is shown in Formula 6-9.

FORMULA   6-9

Ideal Inventory Calculation

Ideal inventory = COGS/targeted inventory turns

Let's use the information from the Hoy Company to show how an entrepreneur can raise internal cash by applying the formula. The Hoy Company had the following numbers for 2001:

- Revenues—$30,848,000
- GOGS—$13,989,000
- Inventory—$9,762,000
- Inventory turns—1.43 times
- Average industry inventory turns—2 times
- Accounts receivable—$5,996,000
- Days receivable—71
- Average days receivable for industry—40

If in 2002 the revenues and COGS remained the same as 2001 but the entrepreneur was able to turn inventory 2 times versus 1.43 times, the cash savings would be dramatic. The ideal level of inventory is $6,994,500, determined by $13,989,000/2. The actual savings based on the 2001 inventory level would be $2,767,500 in cold, hard cash!

What is the ideal level of accounts receivable that an entrepreneur should carry? The formula to make this determination can be seen in Formula 6-10.

F O R M U L A   6-10

Ideal Level of Accounts Receivable

Ideal level of accounts receivable = average daily sales × targeted days receivable

Using the same information that was used in the Hoy Company, if days receivable can be reduced from 71 to 40 days, the cash savings would be significant. To compute average daily sales, the annual revenue must be divided by 365. Therefore, $30,848,000/365 generates average daily sales of $84,515. This figure multiplied by 40 days receivable shows that the Hoy Company's ideal level of receivables should be $3,380,600. The actual savings based on the 2001 accounts receivable or $5,996,000 would be $2,615,400 in cold, hard cash!

N O T E S

1. Fraser, Jill Andresky, "Riding the Economic Rollercoaster," *Inc.*, December 1998, p. 126.
2. Fernandez, Michael, "My Big Mistake," *Inc.*, December 1998, p. 123.
3. Fraser, Jill Andresky, "Getting Paid," *Inc.*, June 1990.
4. "Running on Empty," *Inc.*
5. Ibid.
6. Fraser, Jill Andresky, "Riding the Economic Rollercoaster," *Inc.*, December 1998, p. 126.
7. Harrison and Scott, *Collection Techniques for a Small Business*, PSI Research, Oasis Press, 1994.
8. Fraser, Jill Andresky, "Getting Paid," *Inc.*, June 1990.
9. Ibid.
10. *Wall Street Journal*, October 25, 1999, p. 9.
11. *Chicago Sun-Times*, May 25, 1999, p. 48.
12. Ibid.
13. *Journal of Accountancy*, October 1999, p. 29.
14. Merrefield, David. *Supermarket News*, November 22, 1999.
15. *Business 2.0*, April 2000, p. 264.
16. Grandt, Skip, interview with author.

CHAPTER 7

Valuation

INTRODUCTION

When I teach my MBA students about entrepreneurial finance, on day 1 of the classes, I run though an exercise where students attempt to value a company. You should know that many of these students have previously sat through high-level finance classes, know about discounted cashflows, and have a head full of formulas. We look at the numbers. "Tell me what you would pay for the company," I demand. The valuations range from zero to $300,000. Actually, I tell them, when the company sold, it went for $38,000. It sold for the price of its inventory. There is a story behind the valuation that is not quantitative. The owner had to sell the company, because his wife told him if he didn't, she was going to leave him and retire down in Florida by herself. It had nothing to do with a multiple of cashflows, multiple of revenue, or anything other than he simply had to get out of the business.

Here's the lesson: Valuation is very tricky and can never be done in a vacuum. Entrepreneurs must learn the methods used to value companies and become comfortable with the "ambiguity of valuation" and the fact that the valuation process is not a hard-and-fast science. The story of Bain Consulting highlights this fact. In 1973, Bill Bain, a former vice president at Boston Consulting Group, and seven partners founded the consulting firm Bain Consulting. During the mid-1980s through 1993, it was estimated that Bain's revenues had increased from $100 million to $220 million. During this time, the eight partners decided to sell 30 percent of the company for $200 million to a Bain Employee Stock Option Plan (ESOP). This transaction gave the company an implied valuation of $666 million. A few years later the vice presidents of the company took legal action against these partners, which ended in the partners returning $100 million to the company as well as the 70 percent of equity they held in the company. This transaction, where essentially the eight partners sold 100 percent of their equity back to the company, changed the valuation from $666 million to $200 million, a reduction of more than 70 percent! The point of this story is to show that even a world-class organization such as Bain, filled with brilliant MBA graduates from some of the finest business schools in the country, including Kellogg, Harvard, Stanford, and Wharton, could not initially come up with the "correct" valuation.

Let me repeat it again. The valuation of a company, particularly that of a start-up, is not an exact science. As Nick Smith, a venture capitalist in Minnesota, stated, "Valuation in a start-up is an illusion." Therefore, the true value of a company, be it a start-up or a mature business, is established in the marketplace. Very simply, a company's ultimate value is the price agreed to by the seller and the buyer. This fact can be traced back to the first century BC when Publius Syrus stated, "Everything is worth what its purchaser will pay for it."

One of the best examples of this fact is highlighted by the story of Apple Computer and Be, Inc. In October 1996, Apple Computer's CEO Gil Amelio began negotiations to buy Be, Inc., from its CEO Jean-Louis Gassee. Be had developed a new operating system called BeOs that some people in the industry said "put Apple's Macintosh and Microsoft's Windows to shame."[1] Like most opportunistic entrepreneurs, Gassee was more than willing to sell his 6-year-old entrepreneurial venture, which he had financed with $20 million from venture capitalists and other private investors. In 1996, Be, Inc. had 40 employees and approximately $3 million in annual revenues. Amelio offered $100 million for the small company. Gassee thought the value of Be, Inc., was much greater and countered with a $285 million asking price, which amounted to approximately 10 percent of Apple's valuation. Amelio refused to offer anything over the $100 million price. Instead, he bought the more established NeXt Software, Inc., which ironically had been founded by Steven Jobs, Apple Computer's founder and current CEO. Therefore, what was the value of Be, Inc. in 1996? It was an amount that was between $100 million and $285 million. And what happened to Be, Inc.? In September 2001, NAS-DAQ regulators told the company it was delisting it for failing to maintain a minimum bid price of at least a dollar for 30 consecutive days. Be, Inc.'s shares were trading for about 14 cents. That same month, Be, Inc. announced it would sell its remaining assets and technology to Palm Inc. for $11 million.

This overvaluation experience taught Gassee the valuable lesson that all entrepreneurs must learn: "Pigs get fat and hogs get slaughtered." He could have been a nice fat happy pig by accepting the $100 million. Instead, he got greedy, a common trait of hogs, and got nothing.

Despite the fact that business valuation is not an exact science, entrepreneurs should determine a value of their company at least once a year. This process must not intimidate them. As has been repeatedly stated throughout this book, it is not brain surgery. In fact, it can be rather simple, and almost everyone can do it. What is the reason for performing an annual valuation of a company? There are many. If the entrepreneur does not determine the value of his company, then someone else will and the entrepreneur will not be happy with the result. For example, if the entrepreneur is selling his business and relies entirely on a prospective buyer to determine its worth, the buyer will certainly look out for her own interests and price it low. The entrepreneur must, therefore, look out for his own best interests by establishing a price he is comfortable with, using logical and acceptable valuation methods. Which methods are correct? As you will see later in this chapter, all of them!

Valuation involves estimating the worth or price of a company. Different industries use different methods to determine this value. Some industries use complicated quantitative models, while others use relatively simple approaches. Regardless of the methodology used, however, the valuation of a business incorporates not only a financial analysis of the company but also a subjective assessment of other factors that may be difficult to quantify, including:

- Stage of the company
- Management team assessment

- Industry
- Reason the company is being sold
- Other general macroeconomic factors

Ultimately, the value of a company is driven by the present and projected cashflows, which are impacted by all the aforementioned factors. As Bill Sutter, a former venture capitalist with Mesirow Partners, said to a class of MBA students, "Where does value come from? Cashflow. It does not come from assets or revenues. It comes from cashflow."

VALUING THE CLARK COMPANY

At the beginning of this chapter, I shared the story about the owner whose selling price had more to do with his wife's threats than with any fancy formula. The company is called the Clark Company, and it is worth examining in a bit more detail. As we discussed in Chapter 5, Clark had year 2001 revenues of about $113,000. The cashflow that the business generated was an astonishing $45,000, or 39 percent of revenues. This was calculated after scrutinizing the income statement and asking questions of the seller. Remember, the starting point for calculating cashflow is net profit plus depreciation plus any other noncash item expenditures. In this case, we add the $16,000 in net profit to the $835 for depreciation. Cashflow calculations will often also include discretionary expenses, which new owners of the business would not incur if they were to acquire the company. For Clark Company, the additional add-backs include wages, which were in fact wages ($12,215) being paid out to the owner's spouse.

The $8965 allocated for office expenses were in reality personal expenditures that the owner was running through the company for a new car that his wife drove. In addition, as the owner of the business also owned the building that the business was renting, he was in effect renting the building to himself. The company was paying about $7000 more than market value for the rent for this building.

Net income	$16,000
plus Depreciation	$835

plus Excess wages	$12,215
plus Personal expenses	8,965
plus Excess rent	$7,000
	$45,015

This company is really "a little engine that could." To value this company or any other, many different valuation methods could be used. For example, using a conservative multiple of 3x in the multiple of cashflow valuation method, the company's valuation is approximately $135,000 (3 × $45,015). If another valuation method, such as multiple of revenues, was used, then a different value could be determined. For example, if a conservative 0.9x multiple of revenue was used, Clark Company's value would be $101,700. Clark actually sold for $38,000, which was the value of the inventory on hand. Why did it sell for the price of inventory? Again, the answer was because the owner had to sell it. His wife told him if he did not sell, she was going to leave him and retire in Florida by herself. The price was not determined by using a free cashflow, a multiple of cashflow, or a multiple of revenue method, or for that matter, any other valuation method that is usually used in determining the value of a business. Again, this case perfectly highlights two major points. One is that valuation is not a hard-and-fast science. Two is that the valuation of a business can never be done in a vacuum. A myriad of things affect valuation, quantitative as well as qualitative.

Before we proceed further, it is important that we give clarity to two terms commonly used when discussing valuation. Those terms are *premoney valuations* and *postmoney valuations*.

PREMONEY AND POSTMONEY VALUATIONS

Private equity investors routinely ask entrepreneurs, at the beginning of negotiations, for the value of their company. When an answer is given, the usual follow-up question is, Is the valuation a premoney or postmoney valuation? Premoney means the company's value, using whatever method the entrepreneur chooses, before the investment. Postmoney is very simple. It means the premoney valuation plus the amount of the equity investment.

As we will see later in this chapter, there are several ways to determine the value of a company. These methods render a premoney valuation. Therefore, if the multiple of revenue method creates a $12 million valuation and the company is pursuing $3 million of private equity capital, the postmoney valuation will be $15 million if the equity capital is successfully raised.

The significance of the two valuation terms is to ensure that both parties, the entrepreneur and the investor, are viewing the valuation the same way. The other significance is that postmoney valuations determine how much equity the investor gets. This ownership amount is calculated by dividing the investment by the postmoney valuation. Using the example above, if the premoney value is $12 million, then the person who invests $3 million will get 20 percent (i.e., $3 million investment divided by the sum of the $12 million premoney valuation plus the $3 million investment).

The problem arises when the investor thinks the value is postmoney and the entrepreneur considers it premoney. In that instance, if the $12 million valuation is thought to be postmoney, the premoney would be $9 million. The investor thinks his $3 million investment would get him 25 percent of the equity (i.e., $3 million divided by the sum of $9 million + $3 million), while the entrepreneur wants to give up only 20 percent.

This is the reason why it is imperative for both parties to quickly agree to what they mean. Therefore, when asked by investors if the valuation is premoney or postmoney, the entrepreneur's answer should be a resounding "premoney with the equity amount for the investor determined by the postmoney valuation."

Another major point to be made is that the postmoney valuation of the last financing round is usually where the premoney valuation of the next round begins—unless there is an increase in the valuation using another agreed-upon method. In the earlier example, the first round, the "Series A," was financed at a $15 million postmoney valuation. Therefore, the premoney valuation for the next round of financing, the "Series B," will be $15 million, and if a new investor puts in $3 million, the new postmoney valuation will be $18 million. The Series B investor will receive 17 percent of the equity for his or her second round of financing.

Finally, the private equity industry has a rule of thumb that Series B financing should never be done at a valuation more than twice the Series A valuation.[2]

WHY VALUE YOUR COMPANY?

There are numerous reasons why an entrepreneur should know the value of his or her business. These include:

- To determine a sale price for the company
- To determine how much equity to give up for partnership agreements
- To determine how much equity to give up for investor capital

Let us discuss this final point in a little more detail.

How Much Equity to Give Up

It is quite common for entrepreneurs to unknowingly establish the value of their companies when they are raising capital. Many will determine the amount of capital they need and at the same time arbitrarily state the level of ownership they wish to retain. Such an act automatically places an implied value on the company. For example, if an entrepreneur is looking to raise $100,000 and says he wants to retain 90 percent of the company, the postmoney valuation is $1 million.

The most common minimum level of ownership that many start-up entrepreneurs seek is 51 percent. They believe this to be the minimal number to maintain control of the company. Therefore, they are willing to give up 49 percent. The problem with arbitrarily giving up 49 percent for an investment is that it typically gives the company too low of a valuation and little equity to sell to future investors.

Another very simple way to determine the level of equity to give up is by calculating the company's value using the methods that will be cited later in this chapter. This calculation should be done prior to taking any fund-raising action. After the valuation has been logically, versus arbitrarily, calculated, the amount of equity capital needed, as explained in Chapter 10, should be determined. Once these two numbers have been identified, the entrepreneur is prepared to actively pursue investors because he or she can now inform investors what they will get for their capital. For example, if the company has a postmoney value of $2 million and the entrepreneur is raising $200,000, then the investor will get 10 percent of the company.

The entrepreneur should be aware of the fact that sophisticated and experienced investors will want to use a more complex formula to determine their future equity position. Investors may determine the equity stake they want using calculations that factor in the company's present and future valuations as well as time and their desired rate of return. In this instance, four, not two, variables are needed: the future expected value of the company, the amount of capital invested, the desired annual return of the investors, and the number of years that the capital will be invested. This approach is shown in Formula 7-1.

F O R M U L A   7-1

Equity Stake

$$\text{Amount of investment} \times \frac{(1 + \text{year 1 expected return}) \times (1 + \text{year 2 expected return}) \times \cdots}{\text{future expected value of company}}$$

Using this formula, the entrepreneur, who is seeking an equity investment of $400,000 for a company valued at $5 million, can calculate the amount of equity he or she should expect to give up to an investor who wants to cash out in 4 years with an annual return of 30 percent. See for example, the calculation shown in Exhibit 7-1.

E X H I B I T   7-1

Post-Equity Investment Ownership Calculation

$$\frac{\$400,000 \times (1 + 0.30) \times (1 + 0.30) + (1 + 0.30) + (1 + 0.30)}{\$5,000,000}$$

or

$$\frac{\$400,000 \times 2.86}{\$5,000,000} = 0.23$$

It shows that the entrepreneur should expect to give up 23 percent of the company.

The final way to determine the amount of equity to give up requires knowing the equity investment amount, knowing the desired return by the investor, and placing a value on the company before and after the investment. In the example in Exhibit 7-2, the entrepreneur established the company's value at the time of the investment at $10 million, and forecasted that the company's value would be $40 million in 5 years. The entrepreneur also found out, by asking the investor, that the investor expected an internal rate of return (IRR) of 38 percent, which is the same as 5 times the investment in 5 years. The $5 million investment would generate a $25 million return. Therefore, the $25 million return the investor would be entitled to equals 63 percent of the company's future projected value of $40 million.

E X H I B I T   7-2

Equity Amount Calculation

	Today	5 Years Later
Company value	$10 million	$40 million
Investors' equity	$5 million	$25 million
Investors' ownership	50%	63%

Regardless of the reason, however, every entrepreneur who owns a business, or who intends to own one, should have some idea of its worth. Thomas Stemberg, CEO of Staples, Inc., gives excellent advice when he notes that "no one will ever value your business as highly as you do. No one really knows how a new business will fare. A company's valuation is very much a test of your own conviction."[3]

KEY FACTORS INFLUENCING VALUATION

As noted earlier, the value of a business is influenced by a multitude of factors, qualitative as well as quantitative. Before a final value can be determined for any company, these factors must be identified and reviewed by the entrepreneur. This procedure is commonly referred to as completing a "contextual factor analysis." In other words, what is the general context in which the valuation is taking place? A proper valuation of a company does not occur in a vacuum. A solid valuation contextual factor analysis should include the following factors:

- The historical, present, and projected cashflow of the company.
- Who is valuing the company?
- Is it a private or public company?
- The availability of capital.
- Is it a strategic or financial buyer?
- The company's stage of entrepreneurship.
- The state of the economy.
- The reason the company is being valued.
- Tangible and intangible assets.
- The industry.
- The quality of the management team.
- Projected performance.

Let's discuss each factor in more detail.

Cashflow Status

Historically, the value of a company has been largely driven by its present and projected cashflow. Contrary to this historical practice, however, over the last few years, technology companies, particularly Internet and e-commerce businesses, have created immense value without the existence or the projection of positive cashflow in the foreseeable future. Despite this fact, which we will analyze and discuss in more detail later in this chapter, it is the argument of this book that all entrepreneurs should focus on creating and maximizing value by aggressively pursuing positive cashflow.

The idea that value comes from positive cashflow is rather simple and direct. The entrepreneurial pursuit of business opportunities usually comes with one basic goal in mind: Make more money than you spend—also known as positive cashflow. The other issues mentioned in Chapter 1 regarding why people choose to become entrepreneurs, including to create jobs, nurture an idea, and get rich, are simply by-products of the successful attainment of the goal to make more money than you spend.

Thus, the cashflow of the company is where the true value lies. This cashflow can be used to reward employees with special bonuses, reward owners and investors, or reinvest in the company to make it even stronger in the future. It also should be noted that the timing of a company's cashflows could also impact its value depending on who is valuing the company. For example, the entrepreneur who is buying a company should give the greatest importance to the targeted company's present, not future, cashflows. The reason is that future cashflows are uncertain. They are merely projections, with no assurance of achievement. Experienced entrepreneurs like Wayne Huizenga correctly refuse to pay for the unknown. When asked about valuation, Huizenga said, "We pay for what we know, today's cashflow, not tomorrow's."[4]

The other reason that buyers should base their valuation on today's cashflow is because future cashflow comes from the work put in by the new buyer. To pay the seller for the company's future performance would be rewarding the seller for the work the buyer will do. In such an instance, the buyer would essentially be giving away the value that he or she created. The craziness of the practice of valuing a company and paying the seller based on a company's future cashflow is something akin to the following: A prospective home buyer sees a house for sale in Beverly Hills which had been appraised at $10 million in its present condition and needs a lot of repairs. The buyer does due diligence and finds that once the repairs have been completed, the value of the house would be $30 million. With this information, the buyer makes an offer of $30 million, paying the seller for the work he is about to do! Obviously, such a scenario is utterly ridiculous, and the same should hold true with a business. The value of a business for a buyer should be based on the company's most recent cashflow, not the future. The difference between the present and future cashflows belongs to the buyer. On the other hand, if the person valuing the company is the seller, he or she will want the valuation to be based on future cashflow because the future is always projected to be rosier than the present, which would lead to a higher valuation. In the case of a start-up, a valuation based on cashflow projected for the future is acceptable to investors and the entrepreneur because there is no historical or present cashflow.

Finally, the cashflow of a company directly affects its value based on the amount of debt it can service. This can be determined by working backward. The idea is that, for the buyer, the value of a company is primarily based on the amount of debt that can be serviced by the company's cashflow in 5 to 7 years (the typical amortization period for a commercial loan), under the worst-case scenario (the worst-case scenario should be the actual for the most recent year). Most highly leveraged acquisitions have capital structures consisting of 80 percent debt and 20 percent equity. Therefore, if an entrepreneur were able to get a 7-year commercial loan for 80 percent of the value of a company that had a worst-case projected cashflow of $100,000 for the first year, the company's value would be $875,000. This valuation is based on the fact that 80 percent of the company's value equals $700,000 cumulative cashflow projected over 7 years. Thus, each percent ownership of the company is valued at $8.75, or 100 percent equals $875,000.

Who Is Valuing the Company?

Are you the entrepreneur who is selling the business or raising capital? Are you the buyer of the entire company or an equity investor? As Stemberg aptly points out:

> The central tension in a venture capital deal is how much the new company is worth. The company's valuation governs how much of it the entrepreneur will own. Venture capitalists yearn to keep the valuation low and take control. Entrepreneurs want to push the number up to raise the maximum amount of cash and keep control themselves.[5]

His experience with venture capitalists highlights the tension that often exists between financiers (venture capitalists as well as others) and the entrepreneur. He notes:

> I thought Staples was worth $8 million post-money when I went out to raise capital. I wanted to raise $4 million for 50% of the company. Relative to the company's value, are you the insurance company who has to pay a claim, or are you the claimant. The former wants a lower company valuation than the latter. Are you the party in a mar-

riage divorce trying to minimize payments to your spouse as assets are being divided or are you the spouse? The venture capitalists wanted to value the company at $6 million. On January 23, 1986, I struck a deal: The venture capitalists would pay $4.5 million for 56% of the company. Staples was worth $8 million.[6]

The value placed on a business will depend on which side of the table you sit: If you are the entrepreneur, you will want as high a valuation as possible so that you give up as little equity as possible. If you're the investor (e.g., the venture capitalist), you will want a low valuation because you will want to get as much equity as possible for your investment. As Scott Meadow, a professional investor with William Blair, said, "I'm going to pay you as little as possible for as much of your company as I can get."[7] This point is best illustrated by the experience cited above by Stemberg. The venture capitalists initially wanted 66.6 percent of Staples for their investment compared with the 56 percent they received. All investors are not as aggressive as Scott, mentioned above. Another venture capitalist is quoted as saying, "The key to valuing a company is to do it in a way that enables the investor to get his desired return, while keeping the entrepreneur happy and motivated." Obviously, this venture capitalist seeks a valuation that creates a "win-win" situation for the investor and the entrepreneur.

Public versus Private Company

Two companies of similar age, operating in the same industry, producing exactly the same products or services, achieving the same level of revenues, profits, and growth rates, will have significantly different values if one is publicly traded (i.e., listed on the NYSE or NASDAQ stock exchange) and the other privately owned. A publicly owned company will always have a greater value than a private one. Specifically, private companies have historically been valued at 15 to 25 percent lower than similar companies trading publicly.[8] This difference in valuation is explainable by the following factors:

- According to the Securities and Exchange Commission (SEC) rules, all public companies are required to disclose all details regarding a company's financial condition, past and present. These disclosures allow investors in public companies to make their investment decisions with more information. As private companies do not have to adhere to SEC disclosure rules and regulations, investors in private companies do not have access to this type of information.

- Investors in publicly owned companies have a ready market to buy and sell shares of stock. As you will see in more detail in Chapter 8, "Raising Capital," anyone can buy and sell stocks of public companies. That is not the case with the stock of private companies. Legally, private companies are only supposed to sell stock to "sophisticated" investors whom they know directly or indirectly. *Sophisticated* is loosely defined to include individuals with a certain minimum of net worth who understand the risks associated with equity investing. Investors known "directly" means those who are associates, family members, or personal friends. Investors who are known "indirectly" are people known through others, for example, through a banker, lawyer, or accountant.

Therefore, publicly owned companies have greater value because they provide greater and more reliable information regularly to investors than do private companies. This fact supports the axiom "Information is valuable." Publicly owned companies also have greater value because of the liquidity opportunities available to investors.

Availability of Capital

By 2000, more money was available to entrepreneurs today than at any time in this country's history. As we will see in Chapter 8, the amount of capital invested up to the year 2000, debt or equity, from almost all sources, increased every year for 5 years. This huge pool of capital, almost $300 billion in 1998, resulted in higher company valuations, especially for those entrepreneurs seeking equity investments or selling their companies entirely. Up until the middle of 2000, the valuation leverage was on the side of the entrepreneur because, as the saying goes, "There was too much money chasing too few deals." For example, I-drive.com, which allows users to store, organize, and share information online, raised $17 million from venture capitalists in 1999 but was offered $50 million.

Another example comes from an article in the February 26, 1996, *Wall Street Journal*, which reported that "buyers of small concerns are paying an average of 7.8 times past year earnings, 13% higher than a year earlier. By February 1997, the multiple had increased to 8 and by February 1998 it had increased to 9.2."[9]

As stated earlier, entrepreneurs raising equity capital were commanding the same high company valuations as those selling their companies. In 1996, the average value that venture capitalists placed on companies in which they invested was $12.46 million. A year later it increased by 22 percent to $15.2 million."[10]

But the market has changed since approximately June 2000, primarily because the value of companies on the stock market—the NASDAQ in particular—began dramatic declines. One of the results was that venture capitalists began making fewer investments and at lower valuations. In other words, as capital became scarcer, valuations declined. For example, in January 2000, MBA students with business plans were getting equity investments at premoney valuations upward of $7 million. In January 2001, the premoney valuations had gone down to $1 to $2 million.

VentureOne Corp., a Reuters company, tracks venture capital investments. As indicated in Tables 7-1 and 7-2, the premoney valuations vary dramatically by the sector or industry that the firm competes in and also by the round class. Firms in hotter industries get a higher premoney valuation, as do firms that are further along in their evolution.

T A B L E   7-1

Median Premoney Valuation by Industry Group, $ Millions

Industry Group	1999	2000	2001, Q2
Health care	$14.65	$19.80	$17.29
Information technology	$26.00	$28.80	$20.00
Products and services	$20.00	$23.00	$15.60

Source: VentureOne Corp.

T A B L E   7-2

Median PreMoney Valuation by Round Class, $ Millions

Round Class	1999	2000	2001, Q2
Seed	$4.00	$5.15	$3.50
First	$10.00	$12.50	$9.99
Second	$30.00	$39.82	$23.00
Later	$62.90	$93.00	$45.00
Restart	$13.40	$13.40	(No statistics)
Grand median	$21.70	$25.00	$18.30

Source: VentureOne Corp.

Venture capital firms were investing less money in new firms and concentrating more on their existing portfolio companies. In late 2001, the National Venture Capital Association reported that fund-raising activity, while still very strong by historical standards, was down 68 percent from the previous year.[11]

Debt financing also contributed to the decreased valuations. In 1999, one financier said, "You used to be able to get five times cashflow, now the most you can get is four times."[12] As of April 2001 things had changed again. It was reported that lenders were rarely willing to provide more than 3x EBITDA, which compares with 3.5x in 2000."[13]

Strategic or Financial Buyer

The value of a company is also affected by who the buyer is. Corporations, such as those in the *Fortune* 500, have historically valued companies at higher prices than do financial buyers, entrepreneurs with financial backing from leveraged buyout funds (i.e., leveraged buyouts, or LBOs), and other private equity sources. In fact, corporate buyers, which purchase companies for strategic corporate reasons, are willing to pay more than other investors in all sectors—sometimes as much as 23 percent higher in health care.[14] This fact is highlighted in the Table 7-3.

TABLE 7-3

Average EBITDA Multiples by Sector

	Financial Buyers	Strategic Buyers
Manufacturing	6.8	7.0
Services	7.3	7.1
Retail	8.2	8.4
Health care	5.2	6.1
Communications	10.9	11.0
Overall	7.4	7.5

Source: Thomas Financial, 2000.

Speculation

There are some companies that gain all of their value based on future projected performance. This was the case with the vast majority of Internet and e-commerce companies, which we will examine in more detail later in this chapter, that typically had modest revenues and no history of profits.

In response to the question, "Are Internet stocks overvalued?" one business writer responded, "Let's put it this way: They sell more on hype and hope than on real numbers."[15] That is the reason why Amazon.com, at the end of March 1999, had a 27 percent greater market value than Sears, a company with revenues more than 15 times greater—and more importantly, with actual profits compared with losses for Amazon.com, as Exhibit 7-3 shows. After the market crash in 2001, both companies took a huge hit from investors, but Amazon.com was slapped silly. Later that year, Sears's market capitalization was listed at $11.2 billion, while Amazon was valued at just over $2 billion—a 91 percent drop from its value in 1999.

E X H I B I T   7-3

Valuation Comparison

	Sears	Amazon.com
Value	$18.6 billion	$23.6 billion
Revenues	$9.0 billion	$293 million
Net profit (loss)	$144 million	($62 million)

Note: As of the quarter ending March 1999.

Stage of Company Development

The earlier the stage of the company, the lower its value. A company in the early seed stage will have a lower value than a company in the more mature growth stage. The reason is because less risk is associated with the later-stage company. It has a history. Therefore, many entrepreneurs are advised to develop their products and companies as much as possible before they seek outside private equity financing. Unfortunately, many entrepreneurs learn this lesson too late. They procure equity financing in the earliest stages of the company when the valuation is extremely low and the leverage is on the side of the investors.

This problem is further exacerbated by the fact that early-seed-stage entrepreneurs typically need relatively little money to start their company and/or develop prototypes. It is not uncommon for these entrepreneurs to need as little as $25,000 or as much as $200,000. When equity investors come in at this stage, they want to own at least 50 percent of the company for their investment. Their investment of $25,000 to $200,000 for half the company results in a postmoney company valuation of only $50,000 to $400,000. This creates major problems for the entrepreneur later because he or she is left with little stock to sell to future investors.

Another common problem that arises is the "seller's remorse" disposition that entrepreneurs feel once they realize that they gave so much of their company up for so few dollars. This was the feeling that Joseph Freedman had with the company he founded in 1991, Amicus Legal Staffing, Inc. (ALS). He raised $150,000 for 65 percent of the company, thereby giving the company a value of only $230,769. In 1997, Freedman sold ALS to AccuStaff, and his investors received $13 million, or 65 percent of the price, for their initial $150,000 investment.[16]

State of the Economy

The condition of the country's and possibly even the world's economy can dramatically affect the valuation of a company. As stated earlier in this chapter, the value of companies being started up or purchased increased annually for 5 years until 2000. It is not merely a coincidence that this occurred at the same time that the U.S. economy experienced the longest period of continuous economic growth without a recession, as stated in Chapter 2.

A strong economy translates into an increased availability of investor capital, which in turn, as we mentioned earlier in this chapter, translates into leverage for the entrepreneur. Obviously, the converse is true. Typically the value of companies declines as the economy worsens because investors have less money to invest. Therefore, the economy impacts the availability of capital, which in turn affects the value of companies.

This is not just economic theory, but a fact evidenced by, for example, what occurred during the last recession. In the third quarter of 1989, the United States went into a recession. Capital raised (i.e., available for investing) by all private equity firms (i.e., venture capital, LBO, and mezzanine funds) was $14.7 billion. The next year, 1990, was the first full year of the recession. Capital raised for the year plummeted to $7.8 billion, a 47 percent decrease from a year earlier. Every year since 1990, the economy has improved, and correspondingly the private equity available to entrepreneurs has increased, as the data in Tables 7-4 and 7-5 show.

T A B L E   7-4

Commitments to Private Equity Partnerships, $ Millions

Year	Total Funds	$ Raised	Average $ per fund	Median $ per fund
1991	81	7,502.5	92.6	40.0
1992	144	18,233.0	126.6	53.0

continued on next page

T A B L E   7-4

Commitments to Private Equity Partnerships, $ Millions (continued)

Year	Total Funds	$ Raised	Average $ per fund	Median $ per fund
1993	186	23,703.0	127.4	54.5
1994	256	31,751.4	124.0	49.9
1995	291	43,966.0	151.1	50.0
1996	304	52,030.3	171.2	65.0
1997	403	78,878.4	195.7	67.0
1998	495	112,144.2	226.6	80.0
1999	635	139,260.1	219.3	80.0
2000	812	200,299.9	246.7	90.5
2001*	274	57,476.0	209.8	74.5
Total	3,881	765,244.8	197.2	65.0

*2001—as of 6/30/01.

Source: Venture Economics/National Venture Capital Association.

T A B L E   7-5

Private Equity Invested

Year	Invested, $ Millions
1991	19,210
1992	43,058
1993	24,863
1994	21,610
1995	19,310
1996	32,717
1997	52,044
1998	77,212
1999	113,714
2000	168,000

Source: Venture Economics.

Reason for Selling

The value of a company being sold is directly related to the reason behind the sale. A company has its greatest value if the entrepreneur is not selling due to personal or business pressures. For example, the value of a company being sold due to the threat of insolvency brought on by cash shortages will be much less than the value of the exact same kind of company that does not have financial problems.

The same holds true for personal reasons. The value of a company being sold, for example, to settle the estate of divorcing owners will be lower than if that circumstance were not driving the sale. Other personal reasons that may negatively affect the value of a company include, but are not limited to, illness or death of the owner(s) or owner's family members and internal conflict (i.e., business or personally related) among the owners.

Because these personal and business problems can negatively affect the value of a company being sold, it is common for owners to disclose as little as possible about the real reasons for the sale. That is why it is essential that any entrepreneur who is buying a company does thorough due diligence to determine the reason the company is being sold *before* valuing the company and making an offer. The major lesson to be learned from this section is that information is valuable. The same lesson was the highlight in an earlier section in this chapter, which discussed the reason why public companies have greater value than private companies.

Tangible and Intangible Assets

The tangible and intangible assets of a company will also impact value. Most of the value of manufacturing companies typically lies in tangible assets. The age and condition of these assets—such as machinery, equipment, and inventory—will have a direct impact on the company's value. For example, if the equipment is old and in poor condition due to overuse or lack of maintenance, the company will have a lower value than a similar company with newer and better-maintained equipment.

The same holds true for intangible assets, including a company's customer list, patents, and name. For example, if a company's name is damaged, the company will have less value than another company with a strong, reputable name in the same industry. That is the reason why AirTran Airlines changed its name from Value Jet Airlines. The latter's name had been severely damaged as a result of a disastrous plane crash in 1996.

Type of Industry

The industry that a company competes in is also very important to its valuation. It is not uncommon for two separate companies, in different industries but with similar revenues, profits, and growth, to have two significantly different valuations. As we will see later in this chapter, that was most certainly the case a few years ago when comparing Internet and e-commerce companies with companies in almost any other industry. Based on the price-to-earnings ratio (P/E ratio) valuation method, which we will also discuss in more detail later in this chapter, the industries with the highest and lowest valuations were the ones shown in Exhibit 7-4.

E X H I B I T   7-4
Highest and Lowest Industry P/E Ratios

Highest P/E Ratios		Lowest P/E Ratios	
Industry	Ratio	Industry	Ratio
Networking companies	50.3	Automobiles	7.8
Telecommunications	49.7	Airlines	9.2
Entertainment	45.1	Home building	11.4
Paper and forest products	42.0	Electric company	12.0
Computer software	39.1		

Source: *Chicago Tribune*, July 28, 1997.

The reasons why some industries had greater value than others was due to the sexiness of the industry and growth potential. Those companies viewed as being sexier, with high and rapid growth potential, typically were valued greater than those companies in staid, conservative, and moderate-growth industries, despite the fact—that as we saw earlier in this chapter, comparing Sears and Amazon.com—the conservative industries were immensely more profitable.

Quality of Management Team

The quality of the management team, which is primarily measured by the number of years of experience each member of the team has and the individual members' success and failure rates, will impact the value of a company being sold or raising capital from external investors. In the situation where a company is being sold and the existing management requires the new owners to retain them, the value of the company will be negatively affected by the evaluation of the management team. If the new owner views the old management team as poor, then she will be less willing to pay a high price for the company because she will have to pay to further train or replace team members. The chance that the management team may need to be replaced adds risk to the future of the company, which in turn decreases the value of the company.

Private equity investors will give greater value to a company that has experienced management. The reason is exactly the same as that mentioned above: risk. The greater the risk, the lower the valuation. For example, two start-up companies looking for the same amount of investor capital will have significantly different valuations if one company's management is composed of people with start-up experience and the other's has none.

VALUATION METHODS

There are numerous ways to value a company, and seemingly, almost nobody does it the same. Methods may differ from industry to industry, as we will see later in this chapter, as well as from appraiser to appraiser. It is important to know that there is no single valuation methodology that is superior to the other; each has its own benefits and limitations. But ultimately, most business appraisers prefer and use one method over another. Typically, the commitment to one method comes after experimenting with several methods and determining which consistently provides a valuation the person is most comfortable with. Candidly, valuation is part gut and part science, and simply saying that you believe in one valuation method is all well and good. The rubber hits the road when you actually risk your own capital using one or more of these methods to value a business. The point is that an entrepreneur's valuation method is determined by experience; without that valuable experience, it is strongly recommended that the entrepreneur use at least two different valuation methods to determine a company's range of valuations.

Valuation methods basically fall under three categories: (1) asset-based, (2) cashflow capitalization, and (3) multiples. In the world of entrepreneurship, if there is a most popular and commonly used valuation category, it is multiples, and within this category, the most popular method is the multiple of cashflow.

Multiple of Cashflow

The cashflow of a company represents the funds available to meet both its debt obligations and its equity payments. These funds can be used to make interest and/or principal payments on debt, as well as to provide dividend payments, share repurchases, and reinvestments in the company. One way of valuing a company is by determining the level of cash available to undertake these activities. This level of cash is determined by calculating earnings before interest, taxes, depreciation, and amortization—EBITDA.

In this valuation methodology, EBITDA is multiplied by a value (i.e., the multiplier) to determine the value of the company. In general, as shown below, a multiplier between 3 and 10 is used. However, buyers' market or sellers' market, sales growth, industry growth potential, variability in a company's earnings, and exit options available to investors are all factors that impact the level of the multiplier used in valuation. The multiple is not static, but evergreen. It can change for a myriad of reasons.

As venture capitalist Bill Sutter, a graduate of Princeton University and Stanford Business School, stated:

> Virtually every conversation about a company's valuation in the private equity industry starts with a 5 times cashflow multiple discussion. The multiple will go up for qualitative reasons like super management and higher growth and will go down for other types of industries that are recessionary, where risk and volatility is perceived to be higher."[17]

Another means of reducing or improving valuations based on cashflow multiples is to adjust EBITDA. The adjusted EBITDA should be calculated after the entrepreneur's salary has been deducted. The reason is that the entrepreneur is entitled to receive a market-rate salary. This salary should be treated as a legitimate expense on the income statement. If the owner's salary is not recognized, then the company's EBITDA will be artificially inflated, resulting in an overvaluation of the company. This result would not be in the best interest of a buyer, who would pay more for a company, nor would it be in the best interest of an investor, who would get less equity for his or her investment. In the case of a buyer, the proper way to determine EBITDA is to replace the seller's salary with the new salary anticipated by the buyer, as long as it is at a justifiable market-rate level. The calculation is shown in Formula 7-2.

FORMULA 7-2

EBITDA Salary Adjustment

Adjusted EBITDA = EBITDA + seller's salary − buyer's salary

For example, if a company in an industry that commonly uses a 7x multiple had an EBITDA of $500,000, one would assume a valuation of $3.5 million. But further analysis of the seller's financial statements shows he only took a salary of $50,000 when similar-size companies in the same industry paid their owner's $125,000. If the buyer intends to pay himself the market rate of $125,000, then the company's value, using the EBITDA multiple of 7x, should be $2,975,000 (i.e., $500,000 + $50,000 − $125,000 × 7). This $525,000 difference is an 18 percent overvaluation!

Please note that the change in owner's salary would also impact the amount of taxes paid by the company. Since the new salary would decrease the operating profit, the taxes would also decrease.

As stated earlier, multiples of EBITDA up to 10x are not uncommon. But this author discourages acceptance of such multiples unless you are the seller of the entire company or a portion of it. As a buyer, it is suggested that multiples no greater than 5x should be accepted. The reason is because valuation should be such that cashflow, under the worst-case scenario, must be able to completely service the debt obligation in the typical 5 to 7 year amortization period.

At a 5x multiple, if the capital structure is 60 to 80 percent debt, as is common, then it can be serviced within 7 years. For example, if the Grant Company's EBITDA is $1 million, a buyer should pay no more than $5 million. With an 80 percent, or $4 million, loan at 7 percent, if the cashflow over the next 7 years remained the same and no major capital improvements were needed, the total $7 million could comfortably service the debt obligation.

Multiple of Free Cashflow

Finally, for companies requiring major investments in new equipment in order to sustain growth, it is common to use a multiple of the company's free cashflow (FCF) instead of just EBITDA. This is a more conservative cash description that yields a lower valuation. For multiple purposes, FCF is calculated as shown in Formula 7-3.

F O R M U L A   7-3

Free Cashflow

$$FCF = EBITDA - \text{capital expenditures}$$

Manufacturing companies are usually valued based on a multiple of FCF. On the other hand, media companies such as television stations are usually valued based on a multiple of EBITDA. For example, in 1995 Westinghouse and Disney purchased CBS and ABC, respectively. Westinghouse paid 10 times EBITDA, and Disney paid 12. In fact, a quick review of the television broadcasting industry (see Table 7-6) will highlight the earlier point regarding the "evergreen" aspect of multiples.

T A B L E   7-6

Television Broadcasting Industry Multiples

Years	Selling Multiple
1980s	10x–12x
Early 1990s	7x–8x
1995	10x–12x
1996	16x
1999*	18x

*The Viacom-CBS deal.

It should be noted that the EBITDA and FCF multiple methods correctly value a company as if it is completely unleveraged and it has no debt in the capital structure. The adding back of interest, taxes, and depreciation to the net earnings eliminates the relevance of whatever debt the company presently carries. This is the proper way to value a company, especially if you are a buyer, because the seller's chosen capital structure has nothing to do with the buyer and the capital structure she ultimately chooses. The company's present capital structure could be loaded with debt because the owner wants his balance sheet to look dreadful as he begins asset settlement negotiations as part of his upcoming divorce. Therefore, the company should be valued without regard to the company's existing debt. Once the buyer determines the value she wants to pay, she can agree to inherit the debt as part of her payment currency. For example, if the company's value is $5 million, the buyer agrees to pay it by assuming the $1 million of long-term debt that the seller owes and paying the $4 million balance in cash.

Multiple of Sales

This multiple is one of the more widely used valuation methods. Sales growth prospects and investor optimism play a major role in determining the level of the multiple to be used, and different industries use different multiples. In the food industry, businesses generally sell for one to two times revenue, but sales growth prospects can have an impact of raising or lowering the multiplier.

For example, Quaker Oats, a strategic buyer, paid $1.7 billion, or 3.5 times revenue, for Snapple in 1995 at a time when similar companies were being sold for a sales multiple of 2 or less. Quaker's rationale: It expected rapid growth of Snapple.

However, rapid growth did not happen. Two years later, Quaker sold Snapple to Triarc Cos. for $300 million, equivalent to a little more than 50 percent of its annual revenues of $550 million. Quaker's obvious overvaluation of Snapple was instrumental in the CEO's departure from the company. On the other hand, Triarc's owners were given the greatest compliment after buying Snapple when someone said, "They stole the company!"[18] In 2001, PepsiCo acquired Quaker for $13.4 billion.

Other industries commonly valued on a multiple of revenues include the funeral home industry, where companies sell for 1.5x to 2.2x revenues. Another industry is CPA firms. In 1996, American Express Co. began targeting small CPA firms for acquisition. The prices American Express paid ranged from 75 to 110 percent of the firm's revenues. But the most prominent industry that uses the multiple of sales model is technology, especially the Internet industry, which will be discussed in more detail later in this chapter.

The shortcoming of this method is that it ignores whether the company is making cash. The focus is entirely top line only. Therefore, this valuation method is best suited for those entrepreneurs who are focusing on growing market share by acquiring competitors. The idea is to buy new customers and rely on your own operational skills and experience to make each new customer a cashflow contributor. This method is best carried out by entrepreneurs who are well experienced in operating a profitable venture in the same industry as that in which the company is being acquired.

P/E Ratio Method

Another common valuation method that falls in the multiples category is the price-to-earnings ratio. The P/E ratio model is commonly used when valuing publicly owned companies. The P/E ratio is the multiplier used against the company's after-tax earnings to determine its value. It is calculated by dividing the company's stock price per share by the earnings per share (EPS) for the trailing 12 months. For example, a company with a stock price of $25 per share, 400,000 shares outstanding, and trailing 12 months of earnings of $1 million will have a P/E ratio of 10 calculated as shown in Exhibit 7-5. In the exhibit, the P/E of 10 means it costs $10 to buy $1 in profit, or conversely that an investor's return is 10 percent. This return compares very favorably with the 5.9 percent historical average returns of long-term bonds.[19]

E X H I B I T   7-5

Price-to-Earnings Calculation

Price per share/EPS
EPS = earnings/number of shares outstanding
$25/($1,000,000/400,000)
$25/2.5 = 10

The average historical P/E multiple for the Dow Jones Industrial Market and Standard & Poor's 500 is 14. In 1998, during the heart of the stock market rise, the S&P multiple was 28 and the Dow 22.[20] In late 2001, in the heart of the market crash, the S&P multiple was 23.5 and the Dow multiple was 57.3. If you exclude Honeywell (P/E of 731 due in large part to GE's attempted acquisition), the Dow multiple was 32.9. That multiple is higher than the historical averages for some good reasons. The Dow consists of larger blue-chip companies that tend to have less volatility, and during the economic downturn, investors were migrating to these safer companies. Consequently, the P/E multiples of these companies tended to be higher than normal. P/E multiples are published daily in the business sections of newspapers, showing the ratios for publicly traded companies in comparable businesses. Companies in the same industry may have different P/E multiples despite the fact that they have similar annual earnings and a similar number of outstanding shares. The difference may be due to the price of the stock. Investors may be willing to pay a higher stock price for one company due to its higher forecasted growth rate, the presence of more experienced management, the settlement of a recent lawsuit, or the approval of a new patent. In this example, the company with the higher stock price would have a higher P/E multiple and therefore a higher valuation. Thus, it can be concluded that when a company has P/E multiples that are higher than the industry average, it's primarily due to investors having a positive view of growth opportunities for the company and expecting relatively reliable earnings. Conversely, lower P/E multiples are associated with low growth, erratic earnings, and perceived future financial risk.

Be mindful of the fact that the use of P/E multiples is ideally for publicly owned companies. But P/E multiples are sometimes used to value private companies.

The ideal way to value a private company using a P/E multiple is to find a public company that is the best comparable. The most important criterion to look for is a company with exactly the same, or as close as possible, products or services. The objective is to select a company in the same business. The other important criteria are as follows:

- Revenue size
- Profitability
- Growth history and potential
- Company age

After determining the best comparable, the P/E multiple should be discounted. The reason? As stated earlier in this chapter, the value of a publicly owned company will always be higher than that of a private company with exactly the same revenues, profits, cashflow, growth potential, and age, due to liquidity and access to information. The result is that private companies are typically valued 15 to 25 percent lower than public companies. Therefore, the P/E multiple of a public company that is selected as the best comparable should be discounted accordingly by 15 to 25 percent.

MULTIPLE OF GROSS MARGIN

As a rule of thumb, the multiple against gross margins should be no higher than 2. Therefore, a company with revenues of $50 million and gross margins of 30 percent has a value of $30 million (e.g., $50 million × 0.30 = $15 million; $15 million × 2 = $30 million).

DIFFERENT INDUSTRIES USE DIFFERENT MULTIPLE BENCHMARKS

Before we close out the discussion of multiples, it is important to highlight the fact that different industries use not only different multiple numbers but also different benchmarks. They include the following:

- The hotel industry uses a multiple of rooms, where the multiple increases as the quality of the venture improves. For example, a Hilton International expert said, "A 4-star, 535 room hotel like the Drake should be viewed at $48.2 million, or $90,000 per room."[21]
- Distribution companies in the soft drink and alcoholic beverages industry are valued at a multiple of the number of cases sold.
- The pawnshop industry, which provides loans averaging $70 to $100 at annual interest rates ranging from 12 to 240 percent, typically uses one of two valuation methods: the multiple of earnings model and the multiple of loan balance model. There are over 15,000 pawnshops in the United States, and approximately 6 percent are publicly owned. These public pawnshops are valued at a multiple of 18.5 times earnings, which is significantly higher than the figures for private shops, which are valued at between 4 and 7 times earnings.

While this multiple of earnings valuation model is not unique to pawnshops, the model of a multiple of loan balance is. A pawnshop's loan balance provides evidence of the number of its customer relationships, which is its greatest asset. Thus, the multiple range commonly used to value a pawnshop is 2 to 4 of its outstanding loan balance. Rules of thumb are often used to make quick estimates of business values. The 2001 *Business Reference Guide*, published by the Business Brokerage Press, is a great resource for anyone involved in valuing, buying, or selling a privately held business. Table 7-7 is a sample of some businesses and the "rule-of-thumb" multiples outlined in the guide.

TABLE 7-7

Rule-of-Thumb Valuations

Type of Business	Rule-of-Thumb Valuation
Accounting firms	100–125% of annual revenues
Auto dealers	2–3 years net income + tangible assets
Bookstores	15% of annual sales + inventory
Coffee shops	40–45% of annual sales + inventory
Courier services	70% of annual sales
Day care centers	2–3 times annual cashflow
Dental practices	60–70% of annual revenues
Dry cleaners	70–100% of annual sales
Employment and personnel agencies	50–100% of annual revenues
Engineering practices	40% of annual revenues
Florists	34% of annual sales + inventory
Food and gourmet shops	20% of annual sales + inventory
Furniture and appliance stores	15–25% of annual sales + inventory
Gas stations	15–25% of annual sales
Gift and card shops	32–40% of annual sales + inventory
Grocery stores	11–18% of annual sales + inventory
Insurance agencies	100–125% of annual commissions
Janitorial and landscape contractors	40–50% of annual sales
Law practices	40–100% of annual fees
Liquor stores	25% of annual sales + inventory
Property management companies	50–100% of annual revenues
Restaurants (nonfranchised)	30–45% of annual sales
Sporting goods stores	30% of annual sales + inventory
Taverns	55% of annual sales
Travel agencies	40–60% of annual commissions
Veterinary practices	60–125% of annual revenues

Source: Business Brokerage Press via bizstats.com.

As one further point of reference, *The Newsletter of Corporate Renewal* suggests that the value of any company should be no more than 2x its gross margin dollars.[22] In conclusion, when valuing a company using any one of the aforementioned multiple models (i.e., revenues, cashflow, earnings, and gross margins), it should be noted that the multiples are not static. They are constantly changing or should be adjusted up or down, depending on several factors.

If an industry is experiencing a downturn, thereby making it a buyer's market, then the multiples will typically decline. The television industry is a perfect example. During the 1980s, television stations were selling for 10 to 12x EBITDA. By the turn of the decade, however, the multiples had gone down to 7 to 8. The reason? The country was in the early stages of a recession. Fewer advertising dollars were going to stations because of more competition from the new cable industry. Also the major networks decreased the amount of payments they were making to their affiliate stations. The combination of these factors created a buyer's market for network-affiliated television stations. By 1995, the multiples had changed again. The reason for the increase was aptly described in a *Chicago Tribune* article:

> Television stations normally sell for 8 to 10 times cashflow. But some of the recent sales sold at multiples of 15 to 20. A strong economy and an even more robust advertising market helped make TV stations virtual cash cows, producing profit margins ranging from 30 to 70 percent. The approach of a presidential election year in 1996 and the Olympic Games in Atlanta should provide further stimulus to the ad market."[23]

There are many factors that may justify the increase or decrease of a company's multiple relative to the industry's typical multiple. An example of multiples increasing occurred in the funeral home industry. Up to a decade ago, this industry was characterized by primarily small "mom and pop" businesses. These small businesses were selling for 2 to 3x EBITDA. But 10 years ago the value of companies in this fragmented industry of over 25,000 funeral homes began to change dramatically. Four companies, which are now publicly owned, began a fierce battle competing with one another to grow their companies rapidly by consolidating the industry. The four companies, Service Corp., Stewart Enterprises Inc., Loewen Group Inc., and Carriage Services, Inc., in many instances sought the same funeral homes, so that by the end of 1998 funeral homes were selling for 8 to 10x EBITDA.

In 1997, the industry saw the beginnings of the decline in these multiples because the growth began to slow. As one business analyst said, this industry is suffering from overvaluation of companies financed by too much debt that cannot be repaid due to an "outbreak of wellness"—fewer people are dying.[24] About 2.3 million people die each year in the United States, with a typical average annual increase of 1 percent. But for the first time in a decade, in 1997 that number decreased. There were 445 fewer deaths in 1997 compared with 1996. One interesting reason for this decline was the weather. Most people die in the harsh winter. The past few winters in the United States have been relatively mild. The industry's growth was also hurt by the increasing popularity of cremations, which cost half the price of traditional burials.[25]

The final example of an ever-changing multiple was that applied to high-growth Microsoft. From 1994 to 1996 Microsoft's multiple of revenues more than doubled from 6 to 14.[26]

ASSET VALUATION

In the past, the value of a company's assets had a great significance relative to the company's overall valuation. Today, most American companies do not have many tangible assets because each year fewer things are produced in the United States. Most are produced overseas in low-wage-paying countries.

The result is that over time the value of a company is dependent less on its assets than on its cashflow. Asset value tends to be the most meaningful in cases where financially troubled companies are being sold. In that case, the negotiation for the value of the company typically begins at the depreciated value of its assets.

CAPITALIZATION OF CASHFLOWS

Free Cashflow Method

The most complicated and involved valuation model is the free cashflow model, also known as the discounted cashflow or capitalization of cashflow model. It is a model that relies on projections filled with assumptions, due to so many unknown variables. Therefore, it is the model most commonly used to value high-risk start-ups.

Simply stated, free cashflow is a company's operating cashflow that is available for distribution to the providers of debt (i.e., interest and principal payments) and equity (i.e., dividend payments and repurchase of stock) capital. This is the cash that would be available after the operating taxes, working capital needs, and capital expenditures have been deducted.

Using this valuation method, one approach is to forecast the FCF like the Japanese do, for 25 years without regard to what happens later, because its discounted value will be insignificant. Another similar, more commonly used, approach is to separate the value of the business into two time periods—during and after an explicit forecasted period. The "during" period is referred to as the planning period. The "after" period is referred to as the residual.

The FCF valuation formula—Formula 7-4—is the sum of the present value (PV) of the free cashflow planning period and the present value of the residual value.

FORMULA 7-4

Free Cashflow Valuation

$$
\begin{array}{l}
\text{PV FCF planning period} \\
+ \ \text{PV residual value} \\
\hline
\textbf{FCF value}
\end{array}
$$

To calculate the PV FCF planning period, the following steps must be followed:

1. Determine the planning period. It is customarily 5 years.

2. Project, for 5 years, the company's earnings before interest and taxes (EBIT). The use of EBIT assumes that the company is completely unleveraged; it has no debt in its capital structure.

3. Determine the company's EBIT tax rate. This will be used to calculate the exact amount of adjusted taxes to be deducted. These are "adjusted" taxes because they ignore the tax benefits of debt financing, interest payments, since this model, as stated above, assumes a capital structure that does not include debt.

4. Determine the amount of depreciation expense for each of the 5 years. This expense can be calculated several ways:

a. Assume no depreciation expense because the capital expenditure for new assets and the corresponding depreciation will cancel each other out. If that assumption is made, then there should also be a zero for capital expenditures for new assets.

b. Using historical comparables, make the future depreciation expense a similar constant percentage of fixed assets, sales, or incremental sales.

c. Using the company's actual depreciation method, forecast the company's value of new assets from capital expenditures and compute the actual depreciation expense for each of the forecasted years.

5. Determine the needed increase in operating working capital for each year. The working capital required is the same as the net investment needed to grow the company at the desired rate. The working capital can be calculated as shown in Exhibit 7-6. The increase in working capital would simply be the change from year to year.

E X H I B I T   7-6

Working Capital Calculation

	Current operating assets excluding cash
minus	Current operating liabilities excluding debt
equals	**Working capital**

6. Determine the investment amounts for capital expenditures. Capital expenditures are made for two purposes. The first is for repairing the existing equipment in order to maintain the company's present growth. The other is for new equipment needed to improve the company's growth. As was stated in 4a above, the new asset cost can be zeroed out by the depreciation expense. Therefore, only the capital expenditure needed for maintenance would be highlighted. As stated earlier, that amount can be determined by using historical comparables.

7. Determine the company's expected growth rate (GR).

8. Determine the discount rate (DR). This rate should reflect the company's cost of capital from all capital providers. Each provider's cost of capital should be weighted by its prorated contribution to the company's total capital. This is called the weighted average cost of capital (WACC).

   For example, if a company is financed with $2 million of debt at 10 percent and $3 million of equity at 30 percent, its WACC or discount rate, can be determined as follows:

   a. Total financing—$5 million
   b. Percent of debt financing—40 percent ($2 million/$5 million)
   c. Percent of equity financing—60 percent ($3 million/$5 million)
   d. (Debt amount × debt cost) + (equity amount × equity cost)
   e. (0.40 × 0.10) + (0.60 x 0.30) + 0.22

   A final point: Please note that the tax shield benefit of the debt financing is incorporated in the WACC.

9. Input all the information in the FCF planning period formula, Formula 7-5.

FORMULA 7-5

Free Cashflow Planning Period

	EBIT
−	Tax rate
+	Depreciation
−	Increase in operating working capital
−	Capital expenditure
	FCF planning period

10. Once the FCF for each year is determined, a present value of the sum of the periods must be calculated. The

discount rate is required to complete the calculation
shown in Formula 7-6.

F O R M U L A   7-6

Present Value of Free Cashflow Planning Period

PV of FCF planning period:

$$\frac{\text{Year 1 FCF}}{(1 + \text{DR})} + \frac{\text{year 2 FCF}}{(1 + \text{DR})^2} + \frac{\text{year 3 FCF}}{(1 + \text{DR})^3} + \frac{\text{year 4 FCF}}{(1 + \text{DR})^4} + \ldots$$

Next, the present value of the residual must be determined. To do so, the first year's residual value must be
calculated by simply forecasting the FCF for year 6, the
first year after the planning period. Then all the information should be put into the PV residuals formula,
Formula 7-7.

F O R M U L A   7-7

Present Value Residuals

PV residuals:

$$\frac{\text{First year residual value/discount rate} - \text{growth rate}}{(1 + \text{discount rate}) \text{ \# number of years to discount back}}$$

The final number from this calculation should then be
added to the PV FCF number to determine the company's value.

Let's determine the value of Bruce.com using the FCF model.
The company is forecasting a conservative 10 percent growth rate.
Its WACC is 13 percent, and its tax rate is 52 percent. The forecasted
annual FCF is presented in Exhibit 7-7.

The PV of the FCF planning period is determined as shown in
Exhibit 7-8. With an estimated year 6 FCF valuation of $960,300, the
PV residual can be calculated using the equation in Exhibit 7-9.

Now we can determine the value of Bruce.com. As you can see in Exhibit 7-10, Bruce.com's value is $19,798,746.

E X H I B I T   7-7

Forecasted Annual Free Cashflow Calculation, in Thousands of Dollars

	2000	2001	2002	2003	2004
EBIT	$1398	$1604	$1789	$1993	$2217
− Tax (52%)	727	834	930	1036	1152
+ Depreciation	—	—	—	—	—
− Increase in working capital	56	144	158	175	191
− Capital expenditure	16	18	20	21	24
Forecasted annual FCF	**599**	**606**	**681**	**761**	**850**

E X H I B I T   7-8

Present Value of Free Cashflow Planning Period Calculation

PV of FCF planning period:

$$\frac{599}{(1 + 0.13)^1} + \frac{606}{(1 + 0.13)^2} + \frac{681}{(1 + 0.13)^3} + \frac{761}{(1 + 0.13)^4} + \frac{85}{(1 + 0.13)^5} =$$

$$\$530,088 + \$473,437 + \$469,655 + \$466,871 + \$461,956 = \$2,402,007$$

E X H I B I T   7-9

Present Value Residual Calculation

PV residual:

$$\frac{\$960,300/0.13 - 0.10}{(1 + 0.13)^5} = \frac{\$960,300/0.03}{1.84} = \$17,396,739$$

E X H I B I T   7-10

Valuation Calculation

$17,396,739	PV residual
+ 2,402,007	PV FCF
$19,798,746	Bruce.com valuation

It should be noted that 88 percent of the company's value comes from the residual value. Also, this FCF valuation formula is very sensitive to slight changes in the growth and discount rates. For example, if the discount rate were 0.17 instead of 0.13, an 18 percent difference, the value of Bruce.com would decrease by 57 percent to $8,430,776! The PV residual would be $6,264,187, and the PV FCF would be $2,166,589.

The criticisms of this model are that it is too theoretical and complex and is filled with uncertainties. The three major uncertainties are the FCF projections, discount rate, and growth rate. Nobody truly knows. It is all educated speculation. As Bill Sutter, (the venture capitalist at Mesirow Partners and a Stanford Business School graduate with a major in finance, who was mentioned earlier in this chapter) noted in a lecture to graduate business school students:

> Valuation is remarkably unscientific. You can take out your FCF models, Alcar models, talk about your capital asset pricing model and betas until you are blue in the face. I have not used any of those since I got out of business school. Frankly, that is not the way we operate. You can use it for your finance class but you are not going to use it out in the real world.

VALUING TECHNOLOGY AND INTERNET COMPANIES

In most instances, the valuation methods discussed throughout this chapter were not applicable when valuing start-up Internet and related technology companies. The P/E ratio method could not be used because the companies had no "E." Until 2000, Internet companies that had negligible or no present cashflow streams, and in most instances did not expect to get positive cashflow streams for years to come, had been valued at extremely high prices at the time they went public. Examples of this include Netscape, Yahoo!, and Amazon.com, to name just a few of the better-known brand names.

When Netscape, the Internet browser company, went public in 1996, over a 3-month period the value of its stock went from $28 to $171 per share despite the fact that the company had never made a profit. AOL eventually acquired Netscape.

In 1995, two Stanford Ph.D. students founded Yahoo!, the Internet search engine company. In 1996, with annual revenues of $1.4 million and profits of only $81,000, the company went public at a valuation of $850 million! In 1999, Yahoo's $19 billion market value was equivalent to that of CBS, which had 37 times the revenues of Yahoo! As discussed earlier, Yahoo! investors, rocked by the company's market capitalization collapse, have had little to yodel about recently.

Finally, the most famous e-commerce book company, Amazon.com, which went public in May 1997 at a value of $500 million, despite the absence of any historical, present, or near-term projected profits, once had a value greater than profitable Fortune 500 companies such as Sears, as noted earlier in this chapter. Another example: The Internet firm Epigraph had expected revenues of $250,000 in 1999 and $1.4 million in 2000. When asked when his company might become profitable, the founder responded, "Oh, come on. We're an Internet company!"[27]

In the late 1990s, the prices of Internet and technology companies soared enormously: Dell Computers rose 249 percent in 1998; Amazon.com went up 966 percent during the same year; and Yahoo! went up 584 percent, while eBay rose 1240 percent from its initial offering price. These valuations put in question whether or not conventional valuation methods were applicable in estimating the worth of Internet stocks. As one stockbroker noted, "I don't know how you value these things. It's a new set of rules. The Internet stocks are bizarre and outrageous."[28] And as we all discovered, many of those high-flying Internet stocks could be hazardous to one's health.

A prominent investor, Warren Buffett, the CEO of Berkshire Hathaway, who has forgone any significant investment in technology-related stocks, has also been baffled by their valuations. At a 1999 news conference he cheerfully closed a discussion of how he thought business schools should teach the principles of valuing companies by saying, "I would say for a final exam, here's the stock of any Internet company, what is it worth? And anybody who gave an answer, flunks."

Warren Buffett and others, who believed that Internet stocks were valued more on hope and on hype than on real numbers, were justifiably concerned that most Internet companies had high debt levels, few assets, and, most importantly, a limited, if any, history of profits. Despite this, investors were more than willing to pay premium prices for their stocks, with the expectation that these companies would eventually produce significant earnings. These high values were defended based on the assumption that the Internet had changed the way that business was to be conducted in the future.

Therefore, given all of this controversy, what was the best method(s) to use for valuing technology and Internet companies? Quite frankly, all of them had major drawbacks. The least practical method seemed to be a multiple of earnings or cashflow. As stated earlier, most of these companies had not only negative earnings but also negative cashflow. For example, in 1998 *Forbes* magazine identified what it called "the Internet landscape," which included 46 companies that covered the breadth of the Internet market, from semiconductor chips to sports commentary. Only 14 (or 35 percent) of the companies had at least a breakeven net income the previous 12 months. Despite this fact, $182 million was the value of the lowest company.[29]

Using the comparable valuation method also created problems. The process of borrowing a valuation from a similar company that had been priced by an acquisition or some other event did not work very convincingly either, says columnist Jim Jubak, especially given the fact that all Internet companies may be overpriced.[30] For example, two Internet services providers, Mindspring Enterprises Inc. and EarthLink Network Inc., were sold in 1998. Their selling prices translated into a value of $1500 per subscriber. In mid-1998, America Online (AOL), the largest and most prominent Internet service provider—now known as AOL Time Warner—had 14 million subscribers. If AOL were valued based on comparable subscriber rates, the company's value at the time would have been $21 billion, not the actual $14 billion. Thus, using the comparable method would have foolishly suggested that AOL was 33 percent undervalued!

Even the most popular and seemingly acceptable valuation method for the Internet industry, the multiple of revenues, had many justifiable critics. The rule of thumb was to use a multiple between 5 and 7 times a company's projected, not current, revenues to determine valuation. The multiple would go up or down depending on the company's revenue growth rates and gross margins.

Criticisms of this model included the fact that the 5 to 7 multiplier, for companies that had low or no profits, seemed grossly high when a company like Sears was valued at a revenue multiplier of 1 and a profitable media company such as Gannett was valued at a multiple of 5. The other problem was that the value was based on projected revenues, not present. If Amazon.com as of the third quarter, 1999 had been valued based on present revenues, the multiplier would have been an astonishing 20x. Even more astounding is that, because of the use of projected revenues, a company like Yahoo! had a $19 billion market value, similar to that of CBS television despite the fact CBS had revenues 37 times that of Yahoo!

Another example of the craziness of the revenue valuation model previously used to value Internet companies was a company called Rhythms NetConnections, a high-speed Internet access firm. Rhythms NetConnections, with revenues of $5.8 million, was valued at $3.1 billion, or 539 times revenue. In defense of this multiple, the founder said it was justified because Rhythms NetConnections was growing exponentially, doubling its size every quarter.[31] On August 1, 2001, Rhythms NetConnections and all of its wholly owned U.S. subsidiaries voluntarily filed for reorganization under Chapter 11.

To get a sense of perspective, let us look at the Standard & Poor's Industrial 400. If the companies on this list were valued based on multiple of revenues, their historical median from 1956 to 1997 is 0.9x. The highest it ever got during the 1990s was a frothy public market whopping 2.2 multiple of sales! The previous record multiple was 1.25x, in the mid-1960s.

The final criticism of the revenue method was based on the discovery that many Internet companies were reporting "virtual revenue." The revenue was not real. For example, the companies recognized as revenues the value of the ad space that they exchanged with each other for space on their sites. While the recognition of revenue in such a situation had to be offset by an expense on the income statement, the expense became irrelevant because valuation was based only on revenues. Since the expense was irrelevant, this practice encouraged companies to inflate the price of their bartered ad space. Another challenge to this practice was the fact that there was no guarantee that if the ad space was not bartered, it would have been sold. This bartering was very important to a company's reported revenue. Internet.com did not include bartered ads in its revenues. Its CEO, Alan Meckler, says that hurt the value of his company's stock, because competitors that included barter appeared to be doing better.[32] Exhibit 7-11 lists several public companies that according to their company reports, included bartered ads in their revenue in 1998.

E X H I B I T   7-11

Bartered Advertisements

Company	Percent of Revenue from Barter
CNet	6
Yahoo!	<10
EarthWeb	11
SportsLine USA	20

Not surprisingly, private companies planning to go public realized the value of recognizing barter. Deja.com, an online chat site that went public in 1999, reported 1998 revenues of $5 million. Over 25 percent of that reported revenue came from barter. After 6 years of no profits, Deja.com went out of business in 2001 and sold its assets to the search engine Google.

Given the fact that most Internet and e-commerce companies did not have earnings or positive cashflows, the commonly used and accepted valuation model was a multiple of revenues. Therefore, the companies were in constant aggressive pursuit of increased revenues to bolster their valuations. As stated earlier, this practice of rewarding revenues without regard to profit seemingly encouraged more companies to recognize "virtual revenue." The standard accounting rules, which have now been revised, vaguely stated that retailers that do not assume the risk of holding inventory are "business agents" and should book as revenue only the difference between what the retail customer pays and the wholesale price. Therefore, if a retailer charges a customer $200 for a bike that will be shipped to the customer directly from the manufacturer (i.e., drop-shipped) and the manufacturer charges the retailer $100, the amount of revenue recognized by the retailer should be the $100 difference, not $200.

The vagueness of the accounting rules resulted in Internet companies recognizing revenues differently. This inconsistency made some companies seem significantly larger than others. For example, Preview Travel's CFO, Bruce Carmedelle, said rival Priceline.com appeared to be 10 times larger though it "sells only a few more tickets than we do." At one time, Priceline.com counted as revenue what customers paid for airline tickets, while Preview counted only the commission it got from carriers.

This virtual revenue phenomena also occurred when a company generated sales by shipping inventory from its warehouse as well as by having the products shipped directly from its supplier's warehouse to the end customer. Ideally the revenue amounts should have been recognized differently. In the former case, the amount of revenue that should have been recognized was the total price the customer paid. In the latter case, where the product was being drop-shipped, the revenue recognized should only have been the difference between the retail and wholesale price. Xoom.com, now part of NBCi, was one of the companies that adhered to this practice. But many other companies such as Theglobe.com booked revenue the same in all cases, though some items came from company warehouses and others from suppliers.[33] Theglobe.com would soon see its world come crashing down. From its opening day high of $97 in 1998, the stock was delisted and trading for just 7 cents a share in late 2001. The technology industry, which came under justifiable criticism for overvaluation of companies without profits, began using the multiple of gross margins method. This method became more popular after it was realized that the multiple of revenues method encouraged these companies to generate revenue, without regard to gross, operating, or net profits. The result of the revenue method was the creation of companies such as Buy.com that sold products at prices below costs. This was sheer madness!

Table 7-8 lists the companies from *USA Today*'s Internet 100 with highest and lowest P/E multiples in 2000. Beginning in April 2000, the valuation of technology companies began declining rapidly, and as of this writing has not seemingly reached bottom. One of the results of this decline is that today there are significantly fewer millionaires in Silicon Valley than in the immediate past. In 1999, there was a record 159,000 millionaires. In 2001 there were approximately 136,000, a 15 percent drop![34]

T A B L E   7-8

USA Today Internet 100 Lowest and Highest P/E Multiple

Lowest	P/E	Highest	P/E
DLJ Direct	7.57	Infospace.com	599.3
Network Associates	6.98	Exodus Communications	634
Sterling Commerce	6.71	Vertical Net	854
Autoweb.com	6.62	Covad Communications	922
Autobytel.com	4.54	CMGI	1,228

Source: *USA Today*, February 14, 2000.

Another thing that positively affected the value of publicly traded Internet companies was the fact that they had "thin floats." This means that most of the company's stock was controlled by insiders such as the management team and other employees. Therefore, public investors held very little stock. The result was that it did not take a lot of buying by the public to increase the share price. Examples of companies with thin floats are listed in Exhibit 7-12. In contrast, companies with typical levels of stock held by the public include those listed in Exhibit 7-13.

E X H I B I T   7-12

Companies with Thin Floats, 1999

Company	Float
eHome	31%
Amazon.com	35%
Broadcast.com	35%
eBay	9%
Yahoo!	51%

E X H I B I T   7-13

Publicly Held Stock Levels

Company	Float
Microsoft	6%
AOL	8%
Adobe Systems	8%
Dell Computers	8%
Intuit	8%

Source: *Barron's*, December 21, 1998.

While we correctly criticized the looniness of valuations during the Internet craze, it is more important that the lesson learned be greater than a few jokes. The primary lesson learned is that whether one operates in a new economy, old economy, or future economy, financial fundamentals, relative to profitability and valuation, will always be important because they have passed the test of time.

NOTES

1. Schmidt, Julie, "Apple: To Be or Not to Be Operating System Is the Question," *USA Today*, September 24, 1996.
2. Stemberg, Thomas G., "Staples for Success," from *Business Plan to Billion-Dollar Business in Just a Decade Knowledge Exchange*, 1996.
3. Ibid.
4. Ibid.
5. Ibid.
6. Ibid.
7. Ibid.
8. Gupta, Udayan, "Companies Enjoy Privacy as Needed for Public Deals Ebbs," *Wall Street Journal*, December 17, 1995.
9. Tan, Kapin, "Multiples Jump, Yet Again, as LBO Firms Close Gap," *Buyout*, February 23, 1998, p. 1.
10. "Entrepreneurs Should Know," *Wall Street Journal*, May 21, 1998, p. R14.
11. National Venture Capital Association Home Page, August 6, 2001, http://www.nvca.org/.
12. *Buyouts*, February 22, 1999.
13. *The Private Equity Analyst*, April 2001, p. 54.
14. Gupta, Udayan, "Price Tag of Small Concerns Gets Bigger," *Wall Street Journal*, February 19, 1996.
15. *Forbes*, July 27, 1998, p. 112.
16. Gruner, Stephanie, "The Trouble with Angels," *Inc.*, p. 47.
17. Bill Sutter classroom presentation at Kellogg School of Management, March 10, 1999.
18. Dugan, Jeanne, "Will Triarc Make Snapple Crackle?" *BusinessWeek*, April 28, 1997.
19. *Wall Street Journal*, March 30, 1998.
20. *Forbes*, June 15, 1998.
21. *Crain's Chicago Business*, September 23, 1996.
22. *Newsletter of Corporate Renewal*, February 14, 2000.
23. Jones, Tim, "Rich Harvests in Television's Killing Fields," *Chicago Tribune*, October 22, 1995.
24. Edwards, Brian, and Mary Ann Sabo, "A Grim Tale," *Chicago Tribune*, October 29, 1999, Section 6N.
25. Ibid.

26. *Barron's*, September 15, 1997.

27. *Crain's Chicago Business*, September 27, 1999, p. 57.

28. *Forbes*, July 27, 1998, p. 112.

29. "Jubak's Journal: Putting a Price on the Future," *Forbes*.

30. Ibid.

31. McGough, Robert, "No Earnings? No Problem! Price-Sales Ratio Uses Rises," *Wall Street Journal*, November 26, 1999, pp. C1–2.

32. Krantz, Matt, "Web Site Revenue May Not Be Cash," *USA Today*, September 9, 1999, p. 1B.

33. Krantz, Matt, "Vague Rules Let Net Firms Inflate Revenue," *USA Today*, November 22, 1999, p. 1B.

34. *USA Today*, April 23, 2001, p. 18.

CHAPTER 8

Raising Capital

Money is always dull, except when you haven't got any, and then it's terrifying.

Sheila Bishop, The House with Two Faces (1960)

INTRODUCTION

As Gene Wang, a successful business owner, noted, for the entrepreneur in the capital-raising stage, there are four important things to do:

1. Never run out of money.
2. Really understand your business or product.
3. Have a good product.
4. Never run out of money.[1]

These are great words of advice; but for many entrepreneurs, accomplishing numbers 1 and 4 is easier said than done.

One of the most common complaints about entrepreneurship concerns money. Entrepreneurs repeatedly lament the fact that raising capital is their greatest challenge because there seemingly is never enough and the fund-raising process takes too long. These are not groundless complaints. Thomas Balderston, a venture capitalist, said, "Too few entrepreneurs recognize that raising capital is a continuing process."[2] Also, it is extremely tough, as it should be, to raise capital, be it debt or equity, for start-ups, expansions, or acquisitions. A Small Business Administration (SBA) study verifies this point. In 1995, there were over 300,000 small and medium-size companies seeking $30 billion in capital that went unfunded. Why is it so difficult to raise capital? The most logical reason is that capital providers are taking major risks in financing entrepreneurial ventures. Remember the statistic cited in Chapter 1? The success rate is only 20 percent! Given this fact, capital providers are justified in performing lengthy due diligence to determine the creditworthiness of entrepreneurs. It may seem sacrilegious for this author to say, but it must be said. Those who become entrepreneurs are not simply entitled to financing because they joined the club.

As stated in Chapter 1, one of my objectives for this book is to supply you with information, insights, and advice that will, I hope, increase your chances for procuring capital. Here are some words on the advice front: Since it is so tough to raise capital, the entrepreneur must be *steadfast and undeviating* in this pursuit. Recall from Chapter 2 that this is one of the traits of successful high-growth entrepreneurs. They are not quitters. They are thick-skinned enough such that hearing the word no does not completely deter or terminate their efforts. A great example of an entrepreneur with such perseverance is Howard Schultz, the CEO of Starbucks Coffee. When he was in search of financing for the acquisition of Starbucks, he approached 242 people and was rejected 217 times. He finally procured the financing, acquired the company, and today boasts a public company that has 3500 locations and more than 25,000 employees.

VALUE-ADDED INVESTORS

Howard Schultz and all other successful high-growth entrepreneurs know not only that it is important to raise the proper amount of capital at the best terms, but that it is even more important to raise it from the right investors. There is an old saying in entrepreneurial finance: Whom you raise money from is more important than the amount or cost. The ideal is to raise capital from "value-added" investors. These are people who provide you with value in addition to their financial investment. For example, value-added investors may give legitimacy and credibility to the company because of their upstanding reputation. Value-added investors also include those who help entrepreneurs acquire new customers, employees, or additional capital. A great example of an entrepreneur who understands the importance of value-added investors is the founder of eBay, who accepted capital from the famous venture capital firm Benchmark. Ironically, eBay really did not need the money. It has always been profitable. It took $5 million from Benchmark for two reasons. The first was that it felt Benchmark's great reputation would give eBay credibility. The second was that it wanted Benchmark, which had extensive experience in the public markets, to help eBay make an initial public offering (IPO).

Another great example of an entrepreneur who understood the importance of a value-added investor is Jeff Bezos of Amazon.com. When pursuing venture capital financing, Bezos rejected money from two funds that offered a lower valuation and better terms than KPCB, which he accepted. When asked why he took KPCB's lower bid, he responded, "If we'd thought all this was purely about money, we'd have gone with another firm. But KPCB is the gravitational center of a huge piece of the Internet world. Being with them is like being on prime real estate."[3]

In addition to investing $8 million, KPCB also helped persuade Scott Cook, the chairman of Intuit, to join Amazon.com's board. KPCB also immediately helped Bezos recruit two vice presidents and, in May 1997, helped him take Amazon.com public.

While the two aforementioned examples highlight only venture capitalists, it must be made perfectly clear that there are several other sources of value-added capital.

SOURCES OF CAPITAL

The source of capital that gets the most media attention is venture capital funds. But in reality, as Exhibit 8-1 shows, they are a small contributor to the total annual capital provided to entrepreneurs. Money from friends, family, and owners themselves is a bit more difficult to track. Table 8-1 examines the more formal sources of financing, and it shows that banks, with $179 billion in annual loans to small businesses, are the most active backers of entrepreneurs. The number 2 providers with $9.6 billion are nonbank financial institutions such as GE Capital and Prudential Insurance.

E X H I B I T   8-1

Sources of Small-Business Financing

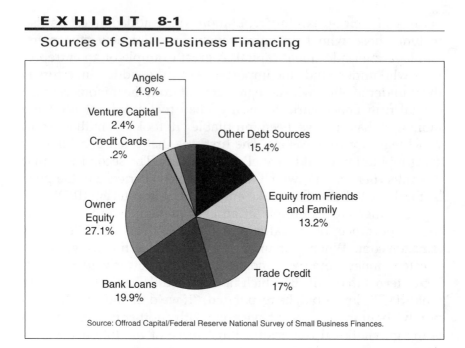

Source: Offroad Capital/Federal Reserve National Survey of Small Business Finances.

T A B L E   8-1

Capital to Entrepreneurs, 1996

$179 billion	Banks
96 billion	Nonbanks
30 billion	Angels
10 billion	Venture capitalists
20 billion	Other
$335 billion	Total capital

The fact that banks are more important to entrepreneurship than are venture capitalists can be further highlighted by the fact that even the most active venture capitalist will only finance 15 to 25 deals a year after receiving as many as 7000 business plans. The result is that in fiscal year 2000, after receiving approximately 8 million business plans, the entire venture capital industry invested in a record 5380 companies. This is akin to a pebble in the ocean when it is compared with banking. Arthur Andersen reported that each year approximately 37 percent of the 20 million-plus small-business owners apply for a commercial loan and bankers reject only 25 percent. Therefore, about 8 million people apply for commercial loans and 6 million, or 75 percent, are approved.

THE INVESTMENT IS IN THE ENTREPRENEUR

While there are many sources of capital, there are basically two ways to finance a business. The capital can be invested in the form of debt or equity. Be it debt or equity, the most important determinant of whether the capital will be provided is the entrepreneur and his or her management team. As venture capitalist Richard Kracum of Wind Point Partners said, "During the course of 70 investments we have made in many different kinds of situations over a 16 year period, we have observed that the quality of the CEO is the top factor in the success of the investment. We believe that the CEO represents approximately 80% of the variance of outcome of the transaction."[4]

The confirmation of the importance of the entrepreneur can be further supported by a statement from Leslie Davis, former vice president at South Shore Bank in Chicago, who said, "The most important thing we consider when reviewing a loan application is the entrepreneur. Can we trust him to do what he said he would do in his business plan?" Banks, just like venture capitalists, bet on the jockey. Now the horse (the business) can't be some run-down creature knocking on the door to the glue factory, but ultimately, financial backers have to trust the management team. What are investors primarily looking for in entrepreneurs? Ideally, investors prefer people who have entrepreneurial and specific industry experiences.

As Table 8-2 shows, investors rate entrepreneurs as "A," "B," or "C." They believe the best entrepreneur to invest in is the "A" entrepreneur, a person who has experience as an owner or even an employee in an entrepreneurial firm as well as experience in the industry that the company will compete within.

The second most desirable investment candidate is the "B" entrepreneur, who has experience in entrepreneurship or the industry, but not both.

The last category of people is the least attractive to investors. The person who falls into this category should try to eliminate at least one of the shortcomings prior to seeking capital. As one investor said, "There is nothing worse than a young person with no experiences. The combination is absolutely deadly." There is nothing a young person can do about age except wait for time to pass. But experience can be gained by working for an entrepreneur and/or in the desired industry.

T A B L E   8-2
Investor Ratings of Entrepreneurs

Rating	Experience
"A"	Entrepreneurship and industry
"B"	Entrepreneurship or industry
"C"	No entrepreneurship or industry

The financing spectrum in Exhibit 8-2 best depicts the financing sources typically used by start-up entrepreneurs. In Chapter 9, "Debt Financing," we will discuss each of these sources in greater detail. And at the end of Chapter 9, we will show how one entrepreneur became successful by using almost all of the sources. Using all of the sources is quite common for successful high-growth entrepreneurs.

E X H I B I T   8-2
Financing Spectrum

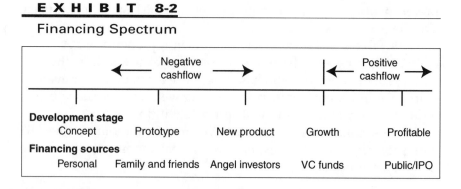

NOTES

1. *Chicago Sun-Times*, April 4, 1996, p. 44.
2. *Business Philadelphia Magazine*, November 1996.
3. *New Yorker*, August 11, 1997.
4. *Buyouts*, February 19, 2001, p. 56.

CHAPTER 9

Debt Financing

INTRODUCTION

Bill Gates has a rule that Microsoft, rather than incurring debt, must always have enough money in the bank to run for a year even with no revenues.[1] In 2001 Microsoft had $31.6 billion in cash on its balance sheet.[2] Unfortunately, 99.9 percent of entrepreneurs will never be able to emulate this financing plan. Therefore, they must be willing to pursue and accept debt financing.

Debt is money provided in exchange for the owner's word (sometimes backed up by tangible assets as collateral as well as personal guarantees of the owner) that the original investment plus a predetermined fixed or variable interest will be repaid in its entirety over a set period of time.

As we saw in Table 8-1, banks are by far the biggest source of capital for entrepreneurs on an annual basis. In June 2000, commercial banks had a total of $1.3 trillion in business loans outstanding (in other words, total loans and not just the notes written that year). Of that, 34 percent, or $437 billion, was in small-business loans (loans less than $1 million).[3]

In today's environment, lenders want to see a company's capital structure with debt equivalent to no more than four times EBITDA.[4]

TYPES OF DEBT

There are basically four types of debt. They are senior, subordi-nated (sometimes called sub debt), short term, and long term. The first two refer to the order of entitlement or preference that the lender has against the debt recipient. Senior debt holders have top priority over all other debt and equity providers. The senior hold-ers are the "secured creditors" who have an agreement that they are to be paid before any other creditors. If the company is dis-solved, the senior is entitled to be paid first and "made whole" as much as possible by selling the company assets. After the senior debt holder has been completely repaid, the remaining assets, if there are any, can go to the subordinated debt providers.

A lender does not automatically get the senior position simply because he or she made the first loan. The lender must request this position, and all other present and future lenders must approve it. This can sometimes be a problem because some lenders may refuse to subordinate their loan to any others. If the other lenders will not acquiesce, then the loan is generally not made.

Sub debt, also referred to as mezzanine debt, is subordinated to senior debt but ranks higher than equity financing. The term *mezza-nine* comes from the theater, where there are three levels, and the mid-dle level is always called the mezzanine. Both types of debt are used for financing working capital, capital expenditures, and acquisitions. Mezzanine financing usually occurs after senior lenders exhaust their lending capabilities. Finally, because it is in a subordinate position, mezzanine debt is typically more expensive than senior debt.

Mezzanine and senior debt, in addition to equity, constitute a company's capital structure, which describes how the company finances itself. Therefore, when a company's capital structure is highly leveraged, it means that it has a large amount of long-term debt.

Debt that is amortized longer than 12 months is considered long-term debt (LTD). It can be senior or mezzanine. It is high-lighted on the balance sheet under the long-term liabilities section. Loans for real estate and equipment are usually multiyear, long-term debt obligations.

In contrast, short-term debt (STD) is that which is due within the next 12 months. STD comes in two forms: a revolver debt, which is used for working capital, and current maturity of long-term debt. It is highlighted on the balance sheet under the current liabilities section. This debt typically has a higher cost than does long-term debt. Short-term debt is usually used to buy inventory and to fund day-to-day operating needs.

Let's look at the strengths and weaknesses of debt financing.

Pros:

- Entrepreneur retains complete ownership.
- Cost of capital is low.
- Loan payments are predictable.
- There is a 5- to 7-year payback period.
- Value-added lenders.

Cons:

- Personal guarantees required.
- Lender can force into bankruptcy.
- Amounts may be limited to value of assets.
- Payments due regardless of company's profits.

SOURCES OF DEBT FINANCING

The major sources of debt financing are personal savings, family and friends, angels, foundations, government, banks, factors, customer financing, supplier financing, purchase order financing, and credit cards. Let's review the sources in more detail.

Personal Savings

An entrepreneur's own money is often used to finance the company. This is especially true in the early stages of a start-up. One researcher found that "80% of the *Inc.* magazine founders he studied bootstrapped their ventures with modest funds derived from personal savings."[5] The primary reason behind this is that banks and other institutional debt providers do not supply start-up capital because it is too risky. Start-ups have no history of cashflow that can be used to repay the debt obligation.

Oftentimes the start-up investments are made in the form of equity instead of debt. But there are no rules that require such an equity investment. An entrepreneur's ownership stake does not have to come from his capital investment. In fact it should come from his hard work, called "sweat equity." My advice is that all investments made by the entrepreneur to his or her company should be in the form of debt at a reasonable interest rate. The repayment of this debt would allow the entrepreneur to receive capital from the company without the money being taxed because it was simply the return of the original investment. The interest payment would be deductible by the company, reducing its tax liability. The entrepreneur would be required to pay personal taxes on the interest earned.

All of this is more favorable to the entrepreneur than if the capital were invested as equity. In that case, if repaid by the company, it would be taxed at the investor's personal tax level, and any dividends would also be taxed. Unlike interest payments, dividends paid are not tax-deductible. Therefore, the company would receive no tax reduction benefits.

Family and Friends

As stated above, it is virtually impossible to procure debt financing for start-ups. Therefore, an obvious viable alternative is family and friends. The benefit of raising debt capital from this source is multifold. The money may be easier and faster to raise because the lenders are providing the capital for emotional rather than business reasons. They want to support the family member or friend. That was the case with Jeff Bezos's first outside lenders, who were his parents. Another benefit, especially with debt, is that if repayments cannot be made, these lenders may be more conciliatory than institutional lenders. Unlike the latter, they will not likely force the entrepreneur into bankruptcy if default on the loan occurs.

The negative aspects of procuring money from family and friends exceed the positives. First, these are typically not "value-added" investors. Second, they may not be "sophisticated investors," which we will discuss in more detail later in this chapter. They may not understand the risk of the investment nor the form. Regarding the first point, they may not really comprehend the fact that such an investment might be completely lost, yielding no capital return at all. They expect to be repaid no matter what happens. They may not realize that as a debt investor, they are not entitled to any ownership stake, only a predetermined interest payment and the return of their original investment. This usually becomes an issue when the entrepreneur is extremely successful in increasing the company's value. In such an instance many family members and friends may not be content with simply having their principal returned and earning interest on that money. They expect to share in the firm's value appreciation. In essence, they expect their debt to be treated as equity. If not, they feel cheated by their own child, grandchild, niece or nephew, or childhood friend.

This final point leads to the greatest problem with raising debt capital from family and friends. There is the threat of irreparably damaging or losing important personal relationships. As one professor said, "Remember these are people whom you eat Thanksgiving with, and it may not be safe to sit next to your uncle if you have lost all his money and he has sharp utensils in his hands."

In closing, my advice is to refrain from raising debt capital from family and friends. If this cannot be avoided, adhere to the following recommendations:

- Only raise money from those who can afford to lose the entire amount. Do not get money from a grandparent who has no savings and lives on a fixed government income. Make it clear to the family members that they may be putting their entire investment at risk; therefore, there is a chance it may not be repaid.
- Write a detailed loan agreement clearly highlighting the interest, payment amounts, and expected payment dates.
- The agreement should give the investor the right to convert any or all of the investment into company stock, thereby giving the investor an ownership stake if desirable.

  Or:

  The agreement should be that the investment is mezzanine financing, which is debt with equity. The investor receives all of the investment back, interest, *and* an equity stake in the company.

- Personally guarantee at least the amount of the investment and, at the most, the investment plus the amount of interest the investment could have gained had it been put in a safe certificate of deposit. Today that would yield approximately 4 percent.

Angel Investors

Angel investors are typically wealthy individuals who invest in companies. They are different from family and friends in that they do not usually know or have a relationship with the entrepreneur prior to the investment. Second, they are sophisticated investors, thoroughly understanding the risk of investment as well as comfortably being able to absorb a complete loss of investment.

Money from angels has been called the fastest-growing pool of risk capital in the country. In 1995 University of New Hampshire Professor William Wetzel estimated that there were 250,000 angel investors in the United States who annually provided $50,000 to $500,000 per deal in debt and equity to entrepreneurs. They funded 30,000 businesses at a cost of $20 billion. Two years later it was estimated that the amount of invested capital had increased 150 percent to $50 billion. While this increase in available capital obviously delighted entrepreneurs, it generated the opposite response from many in the institutional venture capital community. It created more competition for deals and increased valuations. Some venture capitalists called money from angels "dumb money," alleging that it was far less than value-added money. In my opinion, such insulting comments are simply sour grapes.

Why did so much capital come into the entrepreneurial marketplace? First, the decrease in the capital gains tax from 28 to 20 percent made more investment capital available. In fact, it was estimated that $10 billion of the $50 billion invested came from millionaires who gained their wealth from equity held in their own entrepreneurial venture. The tax decrease allowed them to keep more money that they then used for investments.

The other reason for the increase in angel capital was returns. Financing entrepreneurs were providing phenomenal returns to the venture capital community, and these investors also wanted to participate.

While most angels demanded equity for their investments, there were some who invested debt in companies that had "shaky credit" and that had been dumped by their banks. In those instances, the angels restructured the loans at significantly higher interest rates.

The positive aspect of getting debt financing from angels is that they can be more flexible on their terms than an institution like a bank. For example, the angel can make it a 10-year loan, whereas the typical maximum term of a bank's commercial loan is 5 to 7 years. Also, angel investors, unlike banks, make their own rules for lending. A bank may have a rule that a loan will not be provided to any applicant who has declared personal bankruptcy. The angel, on the other hand, uses his or her own discretion to determine if he or she wants to make a loan to such a person.

On the negative side, the cost of debt capital from angels is usually higher than institutional financing. It is not unusual for these investors to charge entrepreneurs 2 percent per month, which equals an astounding annual rate of 24 percent. Not only is such a rate higher than the 2 to 3 percent over prime that banks usually charge their best customers, but it is also greater than the 18 percent that some credit cards charge their customers. The other negative is that, unlike banks that cannot legally interfere with their customers' day-to-day business operations or strategy, the angel typically expects to be involved. For some entrepreneurs this may ultimately cause problems.

When most people think about formal organizations that provide debt capital, banks are the first ones that come to mind. But as stated earlier, there are other types of debt providers. Let's review and discuss a few of these nonbank sources of capital.

Foundations

Other interesting sources of capital for entrepreneurs are philanthropic organizations, including the Ford Foundation, the MacArthur Foundation, the Wieboldt Foundation, and the Retirement Research Foundation. Historically, these organizations have provided grants and loans only to not-for-profit entities. But since the beginning of the 1990s, they have broadened their loan activity to include for-profit companies that provide a social good.

Eligible companies would be those that explicitly state their intention to improve society by doing such things as employing former convicts, building homes in economically deprived areas, providing child-care services to single-income mothers, or offering computer training to low-income families. Specific examples include the MacArthur Foundation's loan to a Washington, D.C., publisher that tracks the economic policies of states. The loan was used by the company to purchase additional computers. Another example is the inventory loan that the Wieboldt Foundation made to a Chicago company called Commons Manufacturing, which makes window blinds that go into public housing.[6]

Foundations also provide grants to community development corporations (CDCs), which in turn use the money to provide business loans. The objectives of the CDCs are the same as foundations', which is to lend capital to businesses that provide a benefit to society. An example of such a CDC is Coastal Enterprises, an organization in Maine that provides capital to companies that employ low-income people in Maine.

These loans from foundations and CDCs are called program-related investments (PRIs). More than 550 organizations throughout the world provide PRIs, including those listed in Exhibit 9-1.

One of the attractive aspects of PRI loans to entrepreneurs is that interest rates can be as low as 1 percent with a 10-year amortization period. Another positive element is that the foundations can be considered to be value-added investors.

The Ford Foundation has the largest PRI program. The foundation's trustees allocated $160 million for PRIs. If more information about PRIs is desired, a great source is a book entitled *Program Related Investments: A Guide to Funders and Trends*.

E X H I B I T   9-1

Program-Related Investment Organizations

Bhartiya Samruddhi Investments and Consulting Services
Hyderabad, India

BRIDGE Housing Corporation
San Francisco, California

continued on next page

E X H I B I T   9-1

Program-Related Investment Organizations (continued)

Shorebank
Chicago, Illinois

Cooperative Housing Foundation
Silver Spring, Maryland

Corporation for Supportive Housing
New York, New York

Enterprise Corporation of the Delta
Jackson, Mississippi

MBA Properties
St. Louis, Missouri

MacArthur Foundation
Chicago, Illinois

Peer Partnerships
Cambridge, Massachusetts

Wieboldt Foundation
Chicago, Illinois

Government

Local, state, and federal government agencies have programs for providing loans to entrepreneurs. These programs typically are a part of a municipality's economic development or commerce department. Some government loans are attractive because they offer below-market rates. SBA and CAP (capital access program) loans are usually market-priced, which we will discuss later. They are provided to companies that are geographically located in the municipal area, that can prove the ability to repay, and, just as importantly, that will use the money to retain existing jobs or create new jobs. Regarding the retention of jobs, entrepreneurs in Chicago have accessed capital from the city for the acquisition of a company based on the fact that if they did not buy the company, someone else might do so and move it, along with the jobs, to another city. Other entrepreneurs have procured expansion debt capital with the agreement that for every $20,000 that the city provides, one new job will be created in 18 to 24 months. Practically every town, city, and state provides such job-related debt financing.

The negative aspect of these loans on the local and state levels is that they often take a long time to procure. A lot of paperwork has to be completed by the applicant, and the process can take as long as 12 months!

A great periodical for identifying economic programs is *The Small Business Financial Resource Guide*, which can be received free by writing to the U.S. Chamber of Commerce Small Business Center at 1615 H Street, NW, Washington, D.C. 10062. It can also be ordered online through MasterCard's web site at www.mastercard.com.[7]

Another drawback for some entrepreneurs is that the applicant must personally guarantee the loans. Personal guarantees will be discussed in more detail at the end of the discussion of debt.

Capital Access Program

One local government program that does not take so long is the capital access program (CAP). There are presently 20 states and 2 cities that participate. CAP is 15 years old and has provided 25,725 loans totaling nearly $1.5 billion. While it is a pittance compared with the annual $10 billion guaranteed by the SBA, CAP is rapidly becoming popular as it competes with SBA loans. The CAP loan product is a "credit enhancement," which induces banks to consider loan requests that might have otherwise been rejected due to deficiencies in collateral or cashflow.

Banks seemingly like this state government–sponsored loan program because the banks, not the government agency, set the terms, rates, fees, and collateral. They do not have to get approval from any other organization or agency.

Entrepreneurs like it for the same reason. The bank has the flexibility to approve a loan that may not qualify for SBA financing due to one reason or another. Another attraction is that entrepreneurs have stated that CAP financing is faster than SBA loans.

Small Business Administration Loan Program

Federal business loan programs fall under the authority of the U.S. Small Business Administration, which is the largest source of long-term small-business lending in the nation. Each year, the SBA guarantees loans totaling more than $10 billion. And since its inception in 1953, the agency has helped fund approximately 14 million businesses. The popularity of SBA loans comes from two primary reasons. First, the length of SBA loans can be longer than regular commercial loans. For example, an SBA guaranteed loan can be for as long as 10 years for a working capital loan versus 1 to 5 years normally. Second, the SBA guarantees loans to borrowers who cannot get financing elsewhere. It should be made perfectly clear that the SBA does not provide loans directly to entrepreneurs. It uses other financial institutions, banks and nonbanks, to do the actual lending. The SBA gives these approved institutions authority to represent it as a lender and will guarantee up to 80 percent of the loan. Therefore, for example, the lender, with the SBA's approval, provides a $100,000 loan to the entrepreneur. If the recipient defaults on the loan, the lender only has 20 percent at risk because the SBA guarantees the balance of the loan.

Most of the loans go to established businesses. Almost $3 billion is lent each year to new businesses. A few start-ups that received SBA loans are Ben and Jerry's, Nike, Federal Express, Apple Computer, and Intel.

Some people foolishly believe that they can default on the loan because there will be minimal consequences. Nothing could be further from the truth. Remember, all SBA loans are personally guaranteed. Second, the lender, despite the SBA guarantee, will doggedly pursue the payment of as much of the loan as possible before requesting SBA reimbursement. The lender's reputation is on the line, and if the lender's loan default rate becomes too high, the SBA will discontinue that bank's participation in the program.

SBA lenders fall under three categories: general, certified, and preferred lenders. The general lenders are those that have a small volume of deals or very little experience in providing SBA loans. Therefore, they must submit all of an applicant's loan information to the national SBA offices to obtain their approval before approving a loan. The process can take several weeks and even months. In contrast, the other types of SBA lenders can act faster.

The most active and expert lenders qualify for the SBA's streamlined lending programs. Under these programs, lenders are delegated partial or full authority to approve loans, which results in faster service from the SBA. Certified lenders are those that have been heavily involved in regular SBA loan-guarantee processing and have met certain other criteria. They receive a partial delegation of authority and are given a 3-day turnaround by the SBA on their applications (they may also use regular SBA loan processing). Certified lenders account for nearly one-third of all SBA business loan guarantees. Preferred lenders are chosen from among the SBA's best lenders and enjoy full delegation of lending authority in exchange for a lower rate of guarantee. This lending authority must be renewed at least every 2 years, and the SBA examines the lender's portfolio periodically. Preferred loans account for more than 10 percent of SBA loans.

To find a list of the SBA lenders in any state, contact the district or federal office at www.sbaonline.sba.gov or the SBA hotline at 800-827-5722. There is a publication for each state that is updated no more than every 2 years. It lists all the lenders and shows if they are general, preferred, or certified. The SBA also posts a state-by-state listing of SBA-preferred or -certified lenders online. It can be found at http://www.sba.gov/gopher/Local-Information/Certified-Preferred-Lenders/.

The SBA's most popular lending programs are the 7(a) Guaranteed, Fastrak, LowDoc, Microloan, and 504 Loan Programs. Before we look at each of these programs, let's discuss a few of the general highlights of SBA financing terms.

Depending on the program, loans can be amortized for as many as 25 years. Interest rates are no more than 2.75 percent over prime. The SBA charges the lender a fee between 3 and 3.5 percent of the loan, which is usually passed on to the loan recipient. And all investors with a stake of 20 percent or more of the company must personally guarantee the loan. Finally, if the loan is to be used to purchase another company, the seller must subordinate his or her financing of the company to the SBA. In fact, the SBA might require the seller to agree to "absolute subordination." In this case, no payments can be made to the seller as long as SBA money is outstanding.

There are eligibility requirements for all the loans. For example, because the SBA targets smaller companies, the applicant can't have a work force the size of GE. If the company is in manufacturing, it cannot employ more than 1500 people, and the maximum number of employees for a wholesale business is 100.

A few of the businesses that are ineligible for SBA financing include not-for-profit organizations and institutions, lending companies, investment firms, gambling companies, life insurance companies, religion-affiliated companies, and companies that are owned by non-U.S. citizens.

7(a) Guaranteed Loan Program   The majority of SBA loans are made under this program. In 2001, $9.8 billion was guaranteed, with an average loan of $230,000.[8] (Exhibit 9-2 shows the top five 7(a) loan markets by state.) Essentially, the 7(a) program is a conventional bank loan up to $2 million that receives an SBA guarantee. The SBA guarantees 80 percent of these loans up to $100,000, 75 percent between $100,000 and $1,333,333, and $1 million for loans between $1,333,333 and $2 million. The proceeds can be used to purchase commercial real estate, business equipment, and machinery. It can also be used to refinance existing debt, construction financing, and working capital.

There are personal net worth eligibility criteria for 7(a) loans. For example, for a $250,000 loan, the owner's net worth must be less than $100,000.

E X H I B I T   9-2

Top 5 SBA (7a) Loan Markets by State, 2001

Top States	Total Loans, in Millions
California	$1,994
Texas	$918
New Jersey	$851
Minnesota	$567
Virginia	$415
Source: SBA.	

Fastrak Loan Program   Fastrak loans are emergency loans up to $150,000. No paperwork is required by the SBA for these loans. The program allows companies to raise money within 48 hours. A company seeking this capital must have an impeccable credit rating because only 50 percent of the loan is guaranteed.

LowDoc Loan Program   This program was introduced in 1993 to simplify the application process. LowDoc stands for low documentation, and it is indeed that. A one-page application must be submitted for loans up to $150,000. An answer is given within 36 hours, and the loan application can be submitted electronically, via fax or online.

Microloan Program   Nonprofit groups such as community development corporations are the primary issuers of microloans. These are the smallest loans guaranteed by the SBA, at levels as small as $450. The maximum is $25,000, with the average loan being $10,000. Since 1992 the SBA has processed over 6500 of these loans, totaling $66 million.[9]

504 Loan Program   The 504 Loan Program is designed to provide financing for primarily long-term fixed assets, including commercial real estate and equipment and machinery. Unlike 7(a) loans, 504s cannot be used for working capital or inventory purchases. There are no eligibility restrictions on an owner's personal net worth.

Nonbank SBA Lenders

As stated earlier, the SBA guarantees loans made by banks as well as other financial institutions. These lenders compete by offering lower rates and faster loan approval. Exhibit 9-3 shows the nonbank lenders of SBA-backed loans in 2001. The SBA refers to these firms as SBLCs.

One such example of an SBLC is Allied Capital. This firm, which is publicly traded, has provided over 800 loans in the amount of $600 million. The following are examples of its lending criteria:

- $1.40 earnings for every $1 in fixed costs.
- Long-term debt of no more than four times the company's shareholders' equity.
- Great management.

EXHIBIT 9-3

Nonbank (SBLC) Loan Volume, Fiscal Year 2001

	# Loans Approved	Gross $ Approved	SBA $ Approved	Average Loan Approval Amount
CIT Small Business Lending Company*	1,217	$578,023,800	$418,510,246	$474,958
Business Loan Center, Inc.	564	$371,664,500	$272,573,567	$658,980
The Money Store Investment Corp.	462	$292,357,800	$209,836,774	$632,809
GE Capital Small Business Finance Corp.	527	$224,561,256	$165,352,521	$426,112
Amresco Independence Funding, Inc.	196	$174,345,500	$120,390,462	$889,518
Small Business Loan Source, Inc.	93	$66,971,000	$49,908,120	$720,118
Heller First Capital Corporation†	95	$65,203,900	$44,243,002	$686,357
Commercial Capital Corporation	77	$40,324,900	$30,144,878	$523,700
Allied Capital SBLC Corporation	58	$36,077,800	$26,440,670	$622,031
CitiCapital Small Business Finance, Inc.	135	$33,032,200	$24,781,358	$244,683
First Western SBLC, Inc.	25	$10,639,813	$7,986,760	$425,593
Grow America Fund, Inc.	26	$7,552,215	$5,760,430	$290,470
Transamerica Small Business Capital, Inc.	14	$7,447,000	$5,398,865	$531,929
Loan Source, Inc.	4	$550,000	$442,500	$137,500
Total SBLC loan approvals in FY 2001	3,493	$1,908,751,684		$546,451

* CIT has since been purchased by Tyco.

† GE Capital purchased Heller Financial for $5.3 billion in August 2000. (*BusinessWeek Enterprise*, March 2, 2001, p. 6).

Regarding the final point, William Walton, the company's chairman, said, "You have to start with management. Over the years we've discovered that a good entrepreneur can often achieve more than what the numbers suggest."[10]

Unfortunately, as of this writing, the number of nonbank lenders is decreasing. Banks have lowered their rates to a point at which the nonbanks can no longer compete. One reason that banks have been able to do this is because their cost of capital is lower than that of nonbanks. Banks use the deposits they have, whereas nonbanks must get their money from the public capital markets. Another reason is that banks are using their commercial loans as "loss leaders." They will sacrifice returns on the business loans to increase the number of customers who use many of their other services, such as online banking, personal savings, loan accounts, and cash management programs. Nonbanks that have departed from or significantly decreased their loan business include Heller Financial and The Money Store.[11]

Banks with SBA Loan Programs

Approximately 50 percent of the 9000 banks (down from 14,000 in 1997) in the country use the SBA's guaranteed loan program. The certified lender status is held by 600 banks and the preferred lender status by 161 banks. The Small Business Administration produces an annual report on the small-business lending activities of the nation's leading commercial banks. The SBA analyzes lending patterns and ranks "small-business-friendly" banks in every state. The SBA says its goal is to give small businesses an easy-to-use tool for locating likely loan sources in their communities. It's also to nudge banks to compete more aggressively for small-firm customers. The report is a great resource for entrepreneurs trying to determine which banks will be more likely to lend a sympathetic ear and, more importantly, some cash for your business! The searchable database is available online at http://www.sbaonline.sba.gov/advo/stats/lending/2000/. At the same site, you can also find a state-by-state searchable database for "microbusiness-friendly" banks—banks with significant lending activity in loans under $100,000.

Advice for Getting an SBA Loan

It has been estimated that the SBA will approve less than 50 percent of requested loans. Some advice for improving your chance of obtaining an SBA-guaranteed loan is provided below.

- *Clean up personal financial problems.* Most of the loans are rejected due to applicants' poor personal credit history. Before applying, the entrepreneur should reduce credit card debt as well as the number of credit cards. Financiers are aware of these numbers and view holding too many negatively. Finally, before applying the entrepreneur should check with major credit bureaus and make sure there are no errors on his or her credit reports. The bureaus are EquiFax (800-685-1111), Trans Union (610-690-4909), and TRW (800-422-4879). A copy of a report may cost up to $25, but it is well worth it.

- *Realistically define goals.* Apply for a specific dollar amount, and identify in detail how the funds will be used. Develop realistic, logical financial pro formas that show under the worst-case scenario that the debt can be repaid. At a minimum, most lenders want to see that a company's annual cashflow is 1.25 times its total annual loan (principal and interest) obligations. Do not plug in numbers! Do not ask for money that cannot be forecasted to be paid back.

- *Begin early.* Apply for financing at least 6 months before the money is needed.

- *Work with experienced lenders.* Apply to institutions that have certified or preferred lender status.

- *Submit an excellent business plan.* Follow the guidelines and advice presented in Chapter 3 regarding the development of a business plan. Make sure the entire plan, especially the executive summary, is well written, clear, and thorough. Just as important, check and recheck all numbers, making sure they are correct and the math is perfect. All numbers must add up.

- *Collect preapplication information.* Loans for existing and start-up businesses require much of the same information, including:

- The personal tax returns for the past 3 years of all investors with at least 20 percent ownership
- The personal financial statements for all investors with at least 20 percent ownership
- The ownership documents, including franchise agreements and incorporation papers

A few pieces of information are needed for an existing business that are not needed for a start-up and vice versa:

For an existing company:
- Past 3 years of tax returns
- Interim financial statements
- Business debt schedule

For a start-up company:
- Business plan
- Potential sources of capital
- Available collateral

- *Do not lie.* Never lie. An entrepreneur's greatest asset is his or her reputation.

Banks without SBA Loan Programs

Historically, banks without SBA programs (those that use personal guarantees as their primary collateral), which include community development banks, have not been viewed as great friends to entrepreneurs. The reason is because most were asset-backed lenders that determined the loan amount by a strict formula such as 80 percent of the value of accounts receivable plus 20 percent of inventory and 50 percent of fixed assets. Given this formula, start-ups could never get loans, and companies with tangible assets were limited to the amount mandated by the formula regardless of the true amount needed.

Fortunately, with the "entrepreneur generation" of the mid-1990s came the advent of an increasing number of banks that were cashflow lenders like the SBA. This happened for two main reasons. One reason was that bankers realized that, unlike in the past, businesses that were being created had no large tangible assets. In particular, these were technology companies that carried little inventory and, in many cases, had virtually no equipment and machinery. Their greatest valued asset was their intangible "intellectual property." Therefore with fewer assets to use as a collateral, banks changed with the times and began focusing on cashflow and management. This point was supported by a comment from John Timmer of the former First National Bank of Chicago (now Bank One), who said, "We quit studying things like inventory aging and receivables and have begun to focus on things like the credit history of the entrepreneur who runs the business."[12]

The other reason why cashflow loans to entrepreneurs became inviting to banks was because banks had to find a new customer base to replace the big corporations, which were using bank financing less. *Inc.* magazine described this phenomenon beautifully in an article that said:

> For once, small businesses will be the apple of lenders' eyes. For all of their robust balance sheets, banks have increasingly fewer customers to lend to as big corporations have been forging their own global financing channels and downsizing companies have less need to borrow. The banking system is not that relevant anymore to middle market and large corporations. Well ain't that a shame? Like many large commercial lenders, Bank of Boston disdained small businesses until recently. Not only are we willing, ready and able to lend to small businesses, but we are anxious to do so also."[13]

Another prominent bank that befriended entrepreneurs was Bank of America. In 1999 it began offering "fledgling firms a Visa card with a $50,000 line of credit and said it would lend nearly $200 billion to small companies in the coming decade."[14]

One of the leading banks lending to entrepreneurs was, and is, Wells Fargo; in fact, it's among the top five small-business lenders in the country. Why does it do it? It does it for all the right reasons. First and foremost, it's profitable to do it. In 1997, Wells Fargo's earnings from small business lending more than doubled since 1995.[15] In 1995, it earned $108 million on its small-business lending portfolio, up 61 percent from the previous year and generating a stellar 32 percent return on equity on this portfolio.[16]

Community Banks

Many of the most small-business-friendly regional banks have been purchased by huge domestic banks or by foreign banks attempting to establish a presence in the United States. Bank consolidations continue to impact loans to small businesses. An FDIC working paper suggested that bank consolidation has been linked to lower loan growth in rural areas, and that markets experiencing merger activity by larger banks had lower loan growth than markets experiencing no consolidation.[17] Unlike the large banks, community banks have always been a friend to entrepreneurs. These are typically small independent banks that specialize in certain targeted lending. There are over 5000 such banks in the country. To find out who and where they are, contact the Independent Banking Association of America at 800-422-8439 or info@ibaa.org. A sampling of community banks is presented in Exhibit 9-4.

EXHIBIT 9-4

Various Community Banks

Community Bank	Investment Focus
Enterprise Federal Savings Bank	African-American churches
Prince Georges County, Maryland	
Net Bank	Internet users
Alpharetta, Georgia	
Michigan Heritage Bank	Equipment leasing
Novi, Michigan	
Pacifica Bank	Asian small-business community
Bellevue, Washington	
First Truck Bank	Small and women-owned businesses
Charlotte, North Carolina	

Personal Guarantees

One of the greatest drawbacks to debt financing from banks for many entrepreneurs is the personal guarantee, which is collateralized by all assets including one's home. While such a guarantee is not required of loans from all capital sources, it is for any SBA financing. Leslie Davis, a former commercial lender, said that it is not unusual for entrepreneurs to say, "I cannot agree to personally guarantee the loan because my spouse will not let me." In those cases she immediately rejects the loan, because, as she explains, "If the spouse does not completely believe in the entrepreneur, why should we?" One of the greatest fears that entrepreneurs have is losing their homes. Bankers estimate that at least 90 percent of first-time business owners use their homes as collateral. These are the entrepreneurs *and* spouses who are completely committed. Should they worry? Yes and no. If the borrower defaults and a personal guarantee is backed partially or completely by the home, the lender has the legal right to sell the home in order to recoup its investment. But private banks and the SBA typically attempt to work with the entrepreneur to develop a long-term repayment plan that does not include selling the house. This point was supported by an SBA director who said, "Our position as far as personal residences is to try to work with the individual borrower as much as possible. We look at the home as collateral of the last resort. We certainly don't want to retain assets, especially not residential real estate."[18] Therefore it is good advice to communicate regularly with the lender after providing a personal guarantee, so if the loan becomes a problem, it can be restructured prior to default. Loan officers have been trained to receive bad news. They do not necessarily like it, but they like surprises even less. Keep the loan officer informed. The loan officer wants you to repay the loan and succeed, and will help if you pursue the problem early. Even when default is inevitable or occurs, the loan officer will still help you as long as you communicate, are open with information, are willing to negotiate, and agree to a payment plan that could take 10 to 15 years. Most importantly, demonstrate a "good-faith effort" to work things out.

The worst thing you can do when facing default is to become difficult, noncommunicative, or threatening. Do not attempt to negotiate by threatening that you will declare bankruptcy if the lender does not give you what you want. Such threats usually upset the lender, and if you carry the threat out, it will be more harmful to your future than to the lender's. In such combative cases, the lender will not only pursue the home that was collateralized, but also seek to garnish any future earnings that the entrepreneur may have to fulfill the entire debt obligation.

Try to work things out. As stated in Chapter 1, most successful high-growth entrepreneurs fail at least two times. Give yourself another chance by making the bad experience a win-win situation for you and the financier. The financier wins by receiving payment, and you win by keeping a strong reputation and putting yourself in the position to receive financing from the same lender for future deals. As one bank executive explained, "If you've had some financial trouble in the past, it doesn't mean that I'll turn you down. I'll be curious about how you responded to the trouble."[19]

Nonbank Financial Institutions without SBA Loan Programs

Many nonbank financial institutions without SBA programs also provide long-term debt financing to entrepreneurs. Included in this group are national insurance companies such as Northwestern Mutual and Prudential. Their loans can be used for working capital, business acquisitions, and equipment and machinery. These institutions tend to have higher minimum loan levels than banks that service entrepreneurs. For example, Prudential's loan level ranges between $10 and $15 million. Another difference from traditional bank lending is that if they were a subordinated lender, the loan would only be for 1 to 1.5 times EBITDA. As the senior lender, nonbank financial institutions will be similar to banks lending as much as three times EBITDA. Another attraction is that these institutions are not asset lenders; they are cashflow lenders. As one supplier said, "We don't look at collateral upfront. We look at management's work history, and then the cash flow of the business. Banks don't usually do that."[20] The final significant difference is one of their main attractions; be it senior or subordinated debt, they can amortize the loan over 15 years! This compares very favorably with the maximum 7 years that banks traditionally offer.

CREATIVE WAYS TO STRUCTURE LONG-TERM DEBT

Debt is usually structured such that it is amortized over 5 to 7 years, with interest and principal payments due each month. For the first-time or inexperienced entrepreneur, it is recommended that you ask for terms that are more lenient. The purpose is to give you a little breathing room immediately after procuring the loan, so that your entire focus can be on operating the company and not becoming a slave to servicing debt. The options for repaying the debt could include:

- Making payments quarterly or semiannually.
- Making interest payments only each quarter, with a principal balloon payment at the end of year 5 or year 7.
- Making no payments at all until 3 to 6 months following the loan closing; then paying interest only for the balance of the fiscal year, followed by quarterly payments of interest and principal for 5 to 6 years.
- With SBA loans you can structure fixed principal and interest monthly payments even with a variable rate. If interest rates go down, you pay down the principal faster. If interest rates rise, you'll have a balloon payment at maturity.

These are only a few suggestions that every entrepreneur should consider pursuing. As is obvious, it frees up a lot of cash in the early stages—cash that the entrepreneur can use to solidify the financial foundation of the company. These options, or any variation of them, are not typically automatically offered by the lender. The entrepreneur must ask for them during negotiations.

LONG-TERM DEBT RULES TO LIVE BY

In summary here are a few final pieces of advice relative to debt financing:

- Always take the maximum number of years allowable for repayments. Try to include a no-prepayment penalty clause in the agreement.
- Get a fixed versus a floating rate of interest. Know what your future payments will always be.
- Expect loan application rejection. Do not be "thin-skinned."
- After getting the loan, keep your investors informed. Send them monthly or quarterly financial statements, and if possible, send out a quarterly status report. Invite lenders to visit your business at least once a year. A few of these

suggestions may actually be required as stipulated in your loan documents.

- When things go wrong—renegotiate.
- Keep excellent and timely financial statements. Historical statements should be readily available at any time. They should be neatly stored in an organized filing system.
- Once the loan application has been submitted, expect to hear via telephone from a loan officer before or after normal working hours. This is one of the ways to evaluate the working habits of the entrepreneur. Does he or she come in early and stay late? Is he or she an 8:00 a.m. to 5:00 p.m. person? (To prove you are not the latter, call the loan officer at 6:00 a.m. or 9:00 p.m. and leave a message on his voice mail that you are in your office and working and thought he might be doing the same, because you had a question for him.)

DEBT FINANCING FOR WORKING CAPITAL

Up to this point the sources of capital discussed could have been used for business acquisitions, start-ups, or working capital. As stated before, most entrepreneurs find access to working capital their greatest problem. Therefore, in addition to the aforementioned sources, here are other sources of debt financing specifically for working capital.

Factors

Factoring firms, or factors, are asset-based lenders. The asset that they use for collateral is a company's accounts receivable (AR). By way of example, a company sells its AR, at a discount, to a factor. This allows the company to get immediate cash for the products shipped or services rendered. The usual agreement is that when the product is shipped, a copy of the shipping document, called the bill of lading, along with the invoice is faxed to the factor. Typically, within 48 hours, 60 to 80 percent of the invoice amount is deposited by the factor into the client's account. When the customer pays the bill, which is usually remitted to the factor per instructions on the invoice, the factor takes the 60 to 80 percent that it had advanced to the client plus 2 to 6 percent for the use of its capital. The balance is sent to the client.

There are two types of factors in this $90 billion annual industry—recourse and nonrecourse. The former buys accounts receivable with the agreement that it will be reimbursed by the client for receivable that cannot be collected. The latter type takes all of the risk of collecting the receivables. If it is not paid, the client has no obligations to the factor. Obviously the fees charged by nonrecourse factors are greater than those for recourse factors.

Regardless of the type, before an agreement can be reached with a client, the factor investigates the creditworthiness of the client's customers. In most instances the factor will "cherry-pick," or select, certain customers, rejecting the accounts of others. The rejected customers are those that have a history of slow payment.

There are a few factoring firms like Quantum in New York, whose president said, "We don't require the client to use us any more than he needs us. He can use us for one invoice and never again."[21] For most firms, though, factoring is not a one-shot deal. These firms negotiate 6 to 12 month agreements with their clients.

Let's look at a few of the pros and cons of this working capital financing.

Pros:

- Access to immediate cash.
- Do not give up equity.
- Approximately 1-week quick application and approval process.

Cons:

- Expensive. 2 percent per month equals 24 percent annually.
- Length of relationship.
- A company's existing debt covenants may forbid the company from using this capital, because it is the selling of assets.
- Some customers may perceive your firm is in financial trouble if they are asked to remit payment to a factoring firm.

How can an entrepreneur find a factor? Usually the factor will find you. Once you go into business, factors will begin sending you unsolicited requests via mail to use their services. The postcard or letter will not call it factoring, but working capital or inventory financing.

There are more than 200 factoring firms in the country. The Edwards Directory of American Factors lists them all. This directory can be found in the library, or it can be ordered at a cost of $250 by calling 800-963-1993. Also, Alana Davidson, the principal of IBC Funding, a factoring broker, has written a paper entitled "Ten Frequently Asked Questions about Factoring." It can be obtained free of charge by writing to IBC Funding, 3705 Ingomar Street, NW, Washington, D.C. 20015.[22]

Advice for Using Factors

- Factors are ideal for businesses in industries with inherent long cash gaps such as the health care industry, where insurance companies are notoriously slow in paying claims, or the apparel industry, where producers must buy fabrics 6 to 9 months before they use it.
- Factors are also ideal for companies experiencing or forecasting rapid growth.
- And they are ideal for companies that cannot get capital from anywhere else.
- But factors should only be used by companies that have included the cost of factoring in their price. Otherwise, the cost of factoring could eliminate all of the company's profits. In fact, one factor suggested that the only firms that should use this financing are those with at least 20 percent gross margins.[23]
- Ultimately, cheaper forms of capital should replace factor financing. It is too expensive to use on a long-term basis.

Customer Financing

The idea that a customer could be a provider of debt may seem odd, but it is indeed possible and has happened many times. Customers are willing to provide capital to suppliers who provide them with a high-quality or unique product they may not be able to buy somewhere else. This financing can be a direct loan or a down payment on a future order. That is the financing that Robert Stockard, the owner of Sales Consultants of Boston (SCB), an executive recruiting firm, received from his largest customer, MCI. When the telecommunications giant needed a temporary sales force of 1200 people to nationally launch its new calling plan, Friends and Family, it hired SCB. Rather than approach a bank for additional working capital to finance this larger than usual job, Stockard persuaded MCI to make a 10 percent down payment on the $2.5 million contract.[24]

Entrepreneurs like Stockard, who successfully procure working capital from customers, show that anything is possible if you simply ask. An investor who is also a customer is a value-added investor.

But raising capital from a customer has a few drawbacks that should be considered first. One is that you may chance losing customers who are competitors with your investor. Another is that, as an investor, your customer could get access to key information about your company and use it to become your competitor.

Still another negative is that once a customer is an investor, the customer knows more about the true state of operations. This exposure to the company's internal operations may cause the customer to seek another supplier if the customer thinks the company is poorly managed.

Finally, the additional insight that a customer has may make it tough for a supplier to increase prices since the customer now knows the cost of the product. Therefore be careful when accepting capital from customers.

Supplier Financing

Suppliers are automatically financiers if they give credit to their customers. The simplest way that entrepreneurs improve their supplier financing is by delaying the payment of their bills. This is called "involuntary extended supplier financing." But sometimes a supplier will graciously agree to extend its invoice terms to help a customer finance a large order that, in turn, helps the supplier sell more goods.

And there are other instances where a supplier will give a direct loan to its customer. That was the case when Rich Food Holdings, a grocery wholesaler in Richmond, Virginia, loaned $3 million to Johnny Johnson, a grocery chain owner, "to buy my buildings, equipment and groceries. In exchange, I agreed to purchase 60% of my inventory from them."[25]

Like customer financing, supplier financing has a few negative aspects. The first is that the supplier may require you to purchase most or all of your products from it. This causes a problem when it has poor delivery, poor quality, and higher prices.

Another problem may be that because your supplier is an investor, other suppliers that are the supplier's competitors may refuse to continue to do business with you.

Purchase Order Financing

Although they may seem alike, factoring and purchase order financing are two different things. The first provides financing after the order has been made and shipped. The latter provides capital at a much earlier stage—when the order has been received. There are many businesses that have orders they cannot fill because they cannot buy inventory. This working capital is used to pay for the inventory needed to fill an order. It is a great resource for companies that are growing fast but that do not have the capital to buy additional inventory to maintain growth. That was the case with Jeffrey Martinez, the president of Ocean World Fisheries USA in Florida. His company is an importer of shrimp and crab from Latin America. His customers were giving him purchase orders at a rapid pace. He, in turn, was generating orders to his supplier faster than collecting receivables, which created a cash shortage and diminished the speed at which he could buy more inventory. In addition, his suppliers expected to be paid immediately upon delivery. He had to pay for inventory before he got paid. Martinez explained his working capital problem this way: "We're able to sell all the shrimp and crab we could import and more. But when suppliers put the product in a container, they expect to be paid immediately."[26] His solution? He procured inventory using purchase order financing from Gerber Trade Finance in New York, which allowed him to pay for his inventory at delivery.

This type of financing is designed for companies that cannot get a traditional loan from a bank or finance company because they may carry too much long-term debt. It is ideal short-term financing for companies that do not hold inventory for long, such as importers, wholesalers, and distributors.

Like factoring, purchase order financing is not cheap. The lender charges fees that range from 5 to 10 percent of the purchase order's value, and payment is due in 30 to 90 days.[27]

Purchase order financing is riskier than factoring because the collateral is inventory, which may get damaged, be poorly produced, or get spoiled. Therefore, banks and other traditional financiers have not wholeheartedly embraced this type of debt financing.

Besides Gerber, two additional purchase order financiers are Bankers Capital and Transcap Trade Finance. Both are located in Northbrook, Illinois.

Credit Cards

The final source of debt working capital is from credit cards. But before proceeding, let me offer a stern warning about using credit cards. *Be careful!* The abuse of credit cards can be one of the entrepreneur's easiest and quickest ways to go out of business.

In 1999, Americans charged over $1.1 trillion on their credit cards. The top four cards are Visa, Mastercard, American Express, and Discover. It is estimated that 78 million U.S. households have at least one credit card. In 1997 alone, 450 million cards were issued. There are only 270 million men, women, and children in the entire country. The industry loses billions of dollars each year to bills that will never be paid. In fact, about $5 out of every $100 charged will be written off by card issuers as bad debt. Despite this fact, in 1999 the industry mailed 2.9 billion card solicitations. This was equivalent to 14 solicitations for every adult in the country!

One group that has been increasingly receptive to these solicitations is entrepreneurs. A 1999 Arthur Andersen survey of small and midsize businesses showed that in 1998 almost half, 47 percent, of the owners used credit cards to finance their companies. In 1997, the rate was 34 percent, and it was 17 percent in 1993. During the same time, commercial bank loans were obtained by 45 percent of the owners in 1998 and 38 percent in 1997. In fact, 1998 was the first year that more entrepreneurs used credit cards for financing than bank loans.[28]

Entrepreneurs have embraced credit card use for several reasons. First and foremost, credit cards are very easy to get, as proved by the statistics just cited. Second, the card allows easy access to as much as $100,000 in cash advances without having to explain how the money will be spent. The final reason is that if used methodically and strategically, credit cards can provide inexpensive capital.

Regarding this final point, there are two ways that the capital can be cheap. The first is by using cards that offer introductory rates as low as 3.9 percent. The second is a situation where the capital could be provided as an interest-free short-term loan. That occurs when the bill is paid off each month during the grace period.

According to an Arthur Andersen survey, this interest-free lending was being taken advantage of by almost 60 percent of credit card–using entrepreneurs in 1997 that regularly paid their bills each month. A year later the number had dropped dramatically to 38 percent.

This change highlights one of several negative aspects of using credit cards for working capital. One large bill comes due every month compared with several small bills from many suppliers when paying by check. It is easier to juggle the payments of several small bills when cash is short than it is one large bill.

This problem leads to the next issue, and that is the assessment of expensive late-payment penalties. In 1997 the government lifted restrictions on maximum penalty charges, resulting in credit card issuers charging whatever late fee they wanted, even if the bill was paid one day after the grace period. The Consumer Action Organization's research found that banks made 74 percent more on late fees in 1998 than in 1995. This increase came from several changes. Banks that charged $7 in 1995 increased that amount to $29 in 1998. Late fees were also imposed earlier. Many banks allowed a 5- to 15-day leniency period after the due date. In 1998 that policy was discontinued. The last change was the reduction of the usual 25 days a cardholder had between receiving a bill and the due date, called the grace period.[29]

One thing that has not changed is the high interest rates. While many used low introductory rates to lure new customers, once these rates expired in 3 to 6 months, the traditionally high credit card rates of 12 to 20 percent took effect. This is very expensive money because of the high rates and the fact that the interest charges are compounded. Getting behind on credit card payments can put an entrepreneur in a deep financial hole. The worst is when the debt is so past due that the interest costs are being compounded and late penalties added such that payments never decrease the principal. A situation like this can harm the entrepreneur's personal credit because he or she is liable, not the business.

Another challenge in using credit cards other than for cash advances is finding suppliers that will accept them. Suppliers that might have credit card payment capabilities have an aversion to accepting credit cards because the suppliers have to pay the issuing institution 2 to 4 percent. This in effect reduces the price they charge you.

The final negative is that the use of personal credit cards for business purposes is a violation of the customer-cardholder agreement you sign.

If you are not dissuaded from using a credit card, here are a few suggestions:

- Pay the entire bill before the end of the grace period to eliminate interest charges or late fees. Payment means the money must actually be received and not simply "in the mail."
- All cards do not have grace periods. Only use those that do.
- Know how long your grace period is. That is the amount of time a lender allows before charging interest on the balance due. Some grace periods are as few as 20 days. If the bill is paid in full before the end of the grace period, no interest is charged. You should know that federal law says that credit card bills must be received no later than 14 days before the grace period ends.
- Refrain from getting cash advances if interest is charged immediately after the money is given regardless of whether the account is paid in full during the grace period. In addition to interest charges, most credit card companies charge a 2 to 5 percent fee of the total cash

advance. Only use cards that treat cash advances like other charges that you make.

- Find out your credit card statement closing date. It is the date in every month where billing for that month ends. Therefore, if your statement closing date is the 10th of every month and you have a 20-day grace period, complete payment must be received and paid by the 30th of the month in order to avoid interest payments.

- When using the card to pay suppliers, get an agreement with them that no matter when you make the actual purchase, they will bill the credit card on the day following your statement closing date. Using the example in the item above, that date would be the 11th of the month. Therefore, that charge will not show up until you receive the bill that closed on the 10th of the next month. With a 20-day grace period added to that, you could get a 50-day interest-free loan.

Let's use a more detailed example to illustrate this point. The Perkins Company purchases 60 widgets from the Steinharter Company for $1000 on October 14. The Perkins Company's closing statement date is the 29th of each month. Therefore, the Perkins Company charges the payment on October 30. On November 29, the charge is sent to the Perkins Company by the issuer. The 20-day grace period ends December 18. The Perkins Company pays the entire bill at the bank on December 17. The result is that the Perkins Company received an interest-free $1000 loan for 62 days, from October 14 to December 17.

In closing—*be careful!* Credit card companies are constantly changing things. One such change could be your closing statement date or the number of days in your grace period. Unnoticed changes in either could result in your owing a complete month's worth of interest because your payment was 1 day late. Finally, just as with any other contract, make sure to read the fine print and know what obligations you and your business must fulfill.

NOTES

1. *Time*, January 13, 1997, p. 49.
2. *Red Herring*, September 15, 2001, p. 92.
3. SBA Office of Advocacy. "Small Business Lending in the United States," June 2000.
4. *The Private Equity Analyst*, April 2001.
5. *Five Myths about Entrepreneurs*, p. 19.
6. *Crain's Chicago Business*, November 6, 1996.
7. *Inc.*, February 1998, p. 80.
8. *Small Business Administration*, October 2001.
9. *Chicago Sun-Times*, June 30, 1998, p. 42.
10. *BusinessWeek*, March 2, 1998.
11. *Crain's Chicago Business*, August 13, 2001.
12. *Crain's Chicago Business*, December 1996, p. 22.
13. *Inc.*, January 1998.
14. *USA Today*, July 30, 1999, p. 2B.
15. *USA Today*, April 14, 1998, p. 14a.
16. *BusinessWeek*, April 15, 1998, p. 98.
17. SBA Office of Advocacy, "Small Business Lending in the United States," June 2000.
18. *Nation's Business*, July 1996, p. 45R.
19. *Inc.*, June 1987, p. 150.
20. *Crain's Chicago Business*, December 1996, p. 22.
21. *Black Enterprise*, July 1999, p. 40.
22. *Nation's Business*, September 1996, p. 21.
23. *Black Enterprise*, July 1999, p. 40.
24. *Forbes*, December 28, 1998, p. 91.
25. *Black Enterprise*, March 1998, p. 84.
26. *Chicago Sun-Times*, July 17, 2001, p. 47.
27. *Crain's Chicago Business*, March 13, 2000.
28. *USA Today*, November 19, 1998.
29. *Parade Magazine*, January 3, 1999, p. 13.

CHAPTER 10

Equity Financing

INTRODUCTION

Equity capital is money provided in exchange for ownership in the company. The equity investor receives a percentage of ownership that ideally appreciates as the company grows. The investor may also receive a portion of the company's annual profits, called dividends, based on his or her ownership percentage. For example, a 10 percent dividend yield or payout of a company's stock worth $200 per share pays an annual dividend of $20.

Before deciding to pursue equity financing, the entrepreneur must know the positive and negative aspects of this capital. They are:

Pros:

- No personal guarantees required.
- No collateral required.
- No regular cash payments required.
- Value-added investors.
- Equity investor cannot force business into bankruptcy.
- On average, companies with equity financing grow faster.

Cons:

- Dividends not deductible.
- New partners.

- Typically very expensive.
- Entrepreneur can be replaced.

SOURCES OF EQUITY CAPITAL

Many of the sources of debt capital can also provide equity capital. Therefore, for those common sources, what was stated earlier in the book about them also applies here. When appropriate, a few additional issues might be added in this equity discussion. Otherwise please refer to Chapter 9.

PERSONAL SAVINGS

When an entrepreneur personally invests money into the company, it should be in the form of debt, not equity. This will allow the entrepreneur to recover his or her investment with only the interest received being taxed. The principal will not be taxed, as it is viewed by the IRS as a return of the original investment. This is in contrast to the tax treatment of capital invested as equity. Like interest, the dividend received would be taxed, as well as the entire amount of the original investment, even if no capital gain is realized.

Finally, the entrepreneur's equity stake should come from the person's hard work in starting and growing the company, not the person's monetary contribution. This is called sweat equity.

FRIENDS AND FAMILY

Equity investments are not usually accompanied by personal guarantees from the entrepreneur. Such assurances may be required by the entrepreneur when receiving capital from friends and family in order to maintain the relationship if the business fails.

But this may be a small price to pay in order to realize an entrepreneurial dream. Start-up capital is virtually impossible to obtain except through friends and family. Dan Lauer experienced this firsthand when he was starting his company, Haystack Toys, in 1988. He raised $250,000 from family and friends after quitting his job as a banker. He went to family and friends after 700 submission letters to investors went unanswered.[1]

ANGEL INVESTORS

Wealthy individuals usually like to invest in the form of equity because they want to share in the potential growth of the company's valuation. There is presently and has always been a dearth of capital for the earliest stages of entrepreneurship—the seed or start-up stage. Angel investors have done an excellent job of providing capital for this stage. Their investments are typically between $25,000 and $150,000. In return, they expect high returns (minimum 38 percent IRR), similar to what venture capitalists get. Since they are investing in the earliest stage, they usually also get a large ownership in the company because the valuation is so low.

As was stated in Chapter 9, many angel investors are former successful entrepreneurs. One of the prominent former entrepreneurs who has gone on to become an angel investor is Mitch Kapor, who in 1982 founded Lotus Development, the producer of Lotus 1-2-3 software, which is now a division of IBM. Since he became an angel in 1994, one of his most successful investments was in UUNet, the first Internet access provider.

But angel investing has never been limited to just former entrepreneurs. In fact, Apple Computer got its first outside financing from an angel, who had never owned a company. He was A. C. "Mike" Markkula, who gained his initial wealth from being a shareholder and corporate executive at Intel. In 1977 he invested $91,000 into Apple Computer and personally guaranteed another $250,000 in credit lines. When Apple went public in 1980, his stock in the company was worth more than $150 million.[2]

This is one of several reasons why the number of angel investors increased so dramatically over the past decade—*returns!* The publicity surrounding successful entrepreneurial ventures oftentimes included stories about the returns investors received. These stories, coupled with research led many wealthy individuals to the private equity industry. And while the anecdotal stories themselves are quite impressive, the more seductive story is empirical research that compares returns for private equity firms with returns for several other investment options. As Table 10-1 shows, a 1998 study by Morgan Stanley Research determined that from 1945 to 1997 the average annual returns for private equity firms were greater than for all other investment options.

T A B L E   10-1

Average Annual Returns, 1945–1997

Sector	Returns, %
Private equity	16.7
Emerging market stocks	15.6
Small stocks	14.9
S&P 500	12.9
International stocks	11.4
Real estate	8.0
Commodities	7.8
Corporate bonds	5.8
Long-term bonds (Treasury)	5.5
Silver	5.0

The second reason behind the increase in angel capital was an increase in the number of wealthy people in the country who had money to invest. For example, from 1995 to 2000 the number of millionaires in America increased from 5 million to 7 million people. Many of these gained their wealth through successful technology entrepreneurial ventures.

The final reason for the explosion in angel capital was the change in federal personal tax laws. In 1990 the capital gains tax was decreased from a maximum of 28 percent to 20 percent. Thus people were able to keep more of their wealth, and they used it to invest in entrepreneurs.

Interestingly it was rumored that one of the groups that strongly lobbied against this change was institutional investors. These are private equity firms, not individual investors. They challenged the change because they correctly predicted it would hurt their business. They believed that as more money became available to entrepreneurs, a company's valuation would inevitably increase and there would be more competition. Rich Karlgaard, the publisher of *Forbes* magazine, made this same point:

> In my cherubic youth I used to wonder why so many venture capitalists opposed a reduced capital gains tax. Then I woke up to the facts. Crazy as it sounds, even though venture capitalists stand to benefit individually by reduced capital gains taxes, the reduced

rates would also lower entry barriers for new competition in the form of corporations and angels. That might lead to—too much venture capital.[3]

Despite private equity firms' complaints, clearly for the entrepreneur, the increase in available capital was a huge positive. A few other positive aspects of angel equity capital for entrepreneurs are as follows:

- Seed capital is being provided. Most institutional investors do not finance this early stage of entrepreneurship.
- Many of the angels have great business experiences and therefore are value-added investors.
- Angel investors can be more patient than institutional investors who have to answer to their limited partner investors.

But there are also a few negative aspects to raising money from angels:

- Potential interference. Most angels want not only a seat on the board of directors, but also a very active advisory role that can be troublesome to the entrepreneur.
- Limited capital. The investor may only be able to invest in the initial round of financing due to limited capital resources.
- The capital can be expensive. Angels typically expect annual returns in excess of 25 percent.

Regarding this final point, here is what an angel investor said about his expectations:

> I expect to make a good deal of money—more than I would make by putting my capital into a bank, bonds, or publicly traded stocks. My goal, after getting my principal back, is to earn 33% of my initial investment every year for as long as the business is in operation.
>
> My usual understanding is that for my investment I own 51% of the stock until I am paid back, whereupon my stake drops to 25%. After that we split every dollar that comes out of the business until I earn my 33% return for the year.[4]

Despite the drawbacks, most entrepreneurs who successfully raise angel capital do not regret it. As one entrepreneur said,

"Without angel money, I wouldn't have been able to accomplish what I have. Giving up stock was the right thing to do."[5]

As investors have seen the potential for huge returns, the number of angel investors has increased dramatically, and they have become easier to contact. There are forums in almost every region of the country similar to the Midwest Entrepreneurs Forum in Chicago. At this event, held the second Monday of each month, entrepreneurs make presentations to angel investors. There are also at least a half-dozen angel-related Web sites, including The Angels Forum (www.angelsforum.com) in Silicon Valley and SourceCapitalnet.com (www.sourcecapitalnet.com) in New York. The SBA started ACE-NET (www.ace-net.org) in 1998. Its official name is the Access to Capital Electronic Network, created to help bring entrepreneurs and angels together online.

PRIVATE PLACEMENTS

When entrepreneurs seek financing, be it debt or equity, from any of the sources mentioned up until now, that financing is called a private placement offering. That is, capital is not being raised on the open market via an initial public offering, which will be discussed later in this chapter. The capital is being raised from select individuals or organizations that meet all of the standards set by Regulation D, which was an amendment to the U.S. Securities Act of 1933. The rule says "neither the issuer nor any person acting on its behalf shall offer or sell the securities by any form of general solicitation or general advertising. This includes advertisements, articles or notices in any form of media. Also, the relationship between the party offering the security and the potential investor will have been established prior to the launch of the offering."[6] All of this simply means that an entrepreneur cannot solicit capital by standing on the corner trying to sell stock in his company to any passersby. He also cannot put an ad in a newspaper or magazine recruiting investors. He must know his investors, directly or indirectly. Potential investors in the latter category are known through the entrepreneur's associates, such as his attorney, accountant, or investment banker.

The final part of the regulation says that the fund-raising efforts must be restricted to "accredited investors only." These investors are also known as sophisticated investors. Such an investor has to meet one of the three following criteria:

- An individual net worth (or joint net worth with spouse) that is greater than $1 million
- An individual income (without any income of a spouse) in excess of $200,000 in each of the two most recent years and reasonably expect an income in excess of $200,000 in the current year
- Joint income with spouse in excess of $300,000 in each of the two most recent years and reasonably expect to have joint income in excess of $300,000 in the current year

Prior to accepting investments, the entrepreneur must get confirmation of this "sophisticated investor" status by requiring all the investors to complete a form called the Investor Questionnaire. This form must be accompanied by a letter from the entrepreneur's attorney or accountant stating the fact that the investors meet all of the accreditation requirements.

Violation of any part of Regulation D could result in a 6-month suspension of fund raising or something as severe as the company being required to immediately return all of the money to the investors. Therefore, the entrepreneur should hire an attorney experienced with private placements before raising capital. Table 10-2 summarizes the Regulation D rules restrictions.

As stated earlier, sources of capital for a private placement are angel investors, insurance companies, banks, family, and friends, as well as pension funds and private investment pools. There are no hard-and-fast rules regarding the structure or terms of a private placement. Therefore, private placements are ideal for high-risk and small companies. The offering can be for all equity, all debt, or debt and equity. The entrepreneur can issue the offering or use an investment banker.

The largest and most prominent national investment bankers that handle private placements are Merrill Lynch, J.P. Morgan, and CS First Boston. These three bankers raise a total of over $30 billion annually for entrepreneurs. Regional investment bankers are better suited for raising small amounts of capital.

T A B L E   10-2

Regulation D Rules Restrictions

Amount of Offering	$1 million	$1 million– $5 million	Unlimited (Emphasis on Nonpublic Nature, Not Small Issue!)
Number of Investors	Unlimited	35 plus unlimited accredited investors	35 plus those purchasing $150,000
Investor Qualification	None required (no sophistication requirement)	• Accredited— presumed qualified • 35 nonaccredited— no sophistication requirement	Nonaccredited purchasers must be sophisticated—must understand risks and merits of investment; accredited presumed to be qualified
Manner of Offering	General solicitation permitted	No general solicitation	No general solicitation
Limitations on Resale	No restrictions	Restricted	Restricted
Issuer Qualifications	No reporting companies; no investment companies; no "blank-check" companies; no "unworthy issuers"	No investment companies; no issuers disqualified under Reg. A; no "unworthy issuers" (Rule 507)	None (except for Rule 507 "unworthy issuer")
Information Requirements	No information specified	If purchased solely by accredited, no information specified; for nonaccredited—info required: (a) Nonreporting companies must furnish similar info as in a registered offering or Reg. A offering, but modified financial statement requirements (b) Reporting companies must furnish specified SEC documents, plus limited additional info about the offering	
SEC Rules	Rule 504	Rule 505	Rule 506

When hiring an investment banker, the entrepreneur should expect to pay a fixed fee or a percentage of the money raised (which can be up to 10 percent) and/or give the fund-raiser a percentage of the company's stock (up to 5 percent). One important piece of advice is that the entrepreneur should be extremely cautious about using the same investment banker to determine the amount of capital needed and to raise the capital. There is a conflict of interest when the investment banker does both for a variable fee. Whenever only one investment banker is used for both assignments, the fee should be fixed. Otherwise use different companies for each assignment.

SHOPPING A PRIVATE PLACEMENT

After the private placement document has been completed, it must be "shopped" to potential investors. The following describes the process of shopping a private placement.

1. Make an ideal investor profile list (have net asset requirement).
2. Identify whom to put on actual list.
   - Former coworkers with money.
   - Industry executives and salespeople who know your work history.
   - Past customers.
3. Call candidates and inform them of the minimum investment amount.
4. Send a private placement memorandum outlining the investment process only to those not intimidated by the minimum investment expressed during the call.
5. Contact other companies where your investor has invested.

CORPORATE VENTURE CAPITAL

In the 1990s large corporations embraced entrepreneurship with the same interests as individuals. This was surprising because it was assumed that corporations with their reputations for stodgy bureaucracy and conservatism were "anti-entrepreneurship." Their primary relationship with the entrepreneurship world came as investors. Since 1997, as Exhibit 10-1 shows, the number of corporate venture funds and the dollars available for investing exploded.[7] As mentioned earlier in the chapter, private equity firms were seeing remarkable returns, and corporations wanted a piece of that action.

E X H I B I T   10-1

Corporations with Venture Programs

Year	Number of Corporations	Total Capital, $ billions
1997	70	1.3
1998	108	1.7
1999	203	6.3

Another equally important reason for the explosion in corporate venture funds was that corporations were investing in companies with products or services related to their industry. Such strategic investments were a part of corporations' research and development programs. They were seeking access to new products, services, and markets. For example, cable television operator Comcast Corp. established a $125 million fund to invest in companies that would "help it understand how to capitalize on the Internet." Comcast wanted to bring its cable TV customers online and also saw potential to put its QVC shopping channel on the Internet.[8]

The final reason that such prominent corporations as Intel, Cisco, Time Warner, and Reader's Digest (see Exhibit 10-2 for a more detailed list) created their funds was to find new customers. As one person described it, "Corporations are using their venture-backed companies to foster demand for their own products and technologies."[9] Two companies implementing that strategy were Andersen Consulting and Electronic Data Systems. Both companies invested in customers that used their systems integration consulting services.

Traditional venture capitalists love for their portfolio companies to receive financing from corporate venture capitalists. The primary reason is because the latter are value-added investors. In fact, three of the most successful venture capital firms—Accel Partners; Kleiner, Perkins, Canfield and Byers (KPCB); and Battery

Ventures—have wholeheartedly endorsed the use of corporate funds. This point was made by Ted Schlein, a partner with KPCB, who said, "Having a corporation as a partner early on can give you some competitive advantages. The portfolio companies are after sales and marketing channels."[10]

E X H I B I T   10-2

Various Corporations with Venture Programs

- Andersen Consulting
- AOL Time Warner
- Chevron Corporation
- Coca-Cola Corporation
- Comcast Corporation
- Electronic Data Systems Corporation
- Fujisawa Pharmaceutical Corporation
- Intel Corporation
- Lucent Technologies
- MCI World Com
- Microsoft
- Oracle Corporation
- Reader's Digest Association
- Sun Microsystems
- Texas Instruments
- Toys R Us

PRIVATE EQUITY FIRMS

Many of the sources of equity financing that have been discussed up to this point are from individuals. But there is an entire industry filled with "institutional" investors. These are firms that are in the business of providing equity capital to entrepreneurs, with the expectation of high returns.

This industry is commonly known as the venture capital industry. But venture capital is merely one aspect of private equity. The phrase *private equity* comes from the fact that money is being exchanged for equity in the company and it is a private deal between the two parties—investor and entrepreneur. For the most part, all of the terms of the deal are dependent on what the two parties agree to. This is in contrast to public equity financing which occurs when the company raises money from an initial public offering. In that case, all of the aspects of the deal must be in accordance with the Securities and Exchange Commission (SEC) rules. One rule is that financial statements of a public company must be published and provided to the investors quarterly. Such a rule does not exist in private equity deals. The two parties could make any agreement they want, i.e., financial statements sent to investors every month, quarterly, twice a year, or even once a year.

PRIVATE EQUITY: THE BASICS

It is important to note that owners of private equity firms are also entrepreneurs. These firms are typically small companies that happen to be in the business of providing capital. Like all other entrepreneurs, they put capital at risk in pursuit of exploiting an opportunity and can go out of business.

LEGAL STRUCTURE

Most private equity firms are organized as limited partnerships or limited liability companies. These structures offer advantages over general partnerships by indemnifying the external investors and the principals. The structures also have advantages over a C corporation because they limit the life of the firm to a specific amount of time (usually 10 years), which is attractive to investors. Furthermore, the structures eliminate the "double taxation" on distributed profits.

The professional investors who manage the firm are the general partners (GPs). The GPs invest only 1 to 5 percent of their personal capital into the fund and make all of the decisions. External investors in a typical private equity partnership are called limited partners (LPs). During the fund-raising process, LPs pledge or commit a specified amount of capital for the new venture fund. For most funds formed today, the minimum capital commitment from any single LP is $1 million; however the actual minimum contribution is completely at the discretion of the firm. The commitment of capital is formalized through the signing of the partnership agreement between the LP and the venture firm. The partnership agreement details the terms of the fund and legally binds the LPs to provide the capital that they have pledged.

Getting Their Attention

GPs rely on their proprietary network of entrepreneurs, friendly attorneys, limited partners, and industry contacts to introduce them to new companies. GPs are much more likely to spend time looking at a new opportunity that was referred to them by a source they find trustworthy than by other sources. A business plan that is referred through their network is also less likely to be "shopped around" to all the other venture capitalists focused on a particular industry segment. GPs want to avoid getting involved in an auction for the good deals because bidding drives up the valuation. In the course of a year, a typical private equity firm receives thousands of business plans. Less than 10 percent of these deals move to the due diligence phase of the investment.

BUSINESS PLAN REVIEW

Most firms use a screening process to prioritize the deals they are considering. Generally, associates within a firm are given the responsibility of screening new business plans based on a set of investment criteria, developed over time by the firm. These criteria are grounded in the characteristics of completed deals that have been successful for the firm in the past. Several of the parameters used to screen business plans are:

- Industry
- Growth expectations
- Phase in life cycle
- Differentiating factors
- Management
- Terms of the deal

An entrepreneur can expedite the process by creating a concise, accurate, and compelling document that addresses the key concerns of an investor. The ability of the entrepreneur to effectively communicate his or her ideas through a written business plan is critical to receiving funding for the project.

Once a deal passes the first screen by meeting a majority of the initial criteria, a private equity firm begins an exhaustive investigation of the industry, the managers, and the financial projections of the potential investment. Due diligence may include hiring consultants to investigate the feasibility of a new product, doing extensive reference checking on management including background checks, and undertaking detailed financial modeling to check the legitimacy of projections. The entire due diligence process taxes from 30 to 90 days in a deal that receives funding.

MANAGEMENT

Most GPs list management as their most important criteria for the success of an investment. The management team is evaluated based on attributes that define its leadership ability, experience, and reputation, including:

- Recognized achievement
- Teamwork
- Work ethic
- Operating experience
- Commitment
- Integrity
- Reputation
- Entrepreneurial experience

GPs use a variety of methods to confirm the information provided by an entrepreneur, including extensive interviews, private detectives, background checks, and reference checks. During the interview process, the entrepreneur must provide compelling evidence of the merits of the plan and of the management team's capability in executing it. Therefore, the management team must clearly and concisely articulate the product or service concept and be prepared to answer an in-depth series of questions. Additionally, the interview process provides an indication to both sides of the fit between the venture capitalist and the entrepreneur. A good fit is critical to the potential success of the investment because of the difficult decisions that inevitably need to be made during the life of the relationship.

Some firms believe in the strength of management so much that they invest in a management team or a manager before a company exists. Often, these entrepreneurs have successfully brought a company to a lucrative exit and are looking for the next opportunity. Some venture firms give these seasoned veterans the title "entrepreneur in residence," and fund the search for their next opportunity.

Ideal Candidate

Again, private equity from institutional investors is ideal for entrepreneurial firms with excellent management teams. Their companies should be predicted to experience or are experiencing rapid annual growth of at least 20 percent. The industry should be large enough to sustain two large successful competitors. And the product should have:

- Limited technical and operational risks
- Proprietary and differentiating features
- Above-average gross margins
- Short sales cycles
- Repeat sales opportunities

Finally, the company must have the potential to increase in value in 5 to 7 years such that the investor can realize his/her minimum targeted return. Coupled with this growth potential must be at least two explicit discernible exit opportunities (sell the company or take it public) for the investor. The entrepreneur and investor must agree upon the timing of this potential exit and the strategy in advance. For example, an ideal entrepreneurial financing candidate is one who knows that he wants to raise $10 million in equity capital for 10 percent of his company and expects to sell the company to a *Fortune* 500 corporation in 5 years for 7 times the company's present value. This tells the investor that she can exit the deal in year 5 and receive $70 million for her investment.

When an entrepreneur goes after private equity funding, he or she should know what kind of returns are expected. The institutional private equity industry and the targeted minimum internal rates of return are noted in Exhibit 10-3.

E X H I B I T   10-3

Targeted IRR for Private Equity Investors

Private Equity Investor Type	Targeted IRR
Corporate finance	20–40%
Mezzanine funds	15–25%
Venture capital funds	38–50%

Again, private equity investors make their "real" money when a portfolio company has a liquidation event: The company goes public, merges, recapitalizes, or gets acquired. Depending on the equity firm and its investment life cycle, the fund's investors typically plan to exit anywhere between 3 and 10 years after the initial investment. Among other things, investors consider the time value of money—the concept that a million dollars today is worth more than a million dollars 5 years from now—when determining what kind of returns or IRR they expect over time. Exhibit 10-4 provides an approximate cheat sheet for the entrepreneur. As the exhibit shows, an investor who walks away with 5 times his or her initial investment in 5 years has earned a 38 percent IRR.

E X H I B I T   10-4

Time Value of Money IRR on a Multiple of Original Investment over a Period of Time

	2×	3×	4×	5×	6×	7×	8×	9×	10×
2 years	41	73	100	124	145	165	183	200	216
3 years	26	44	59	71	82	91	100	108	115
4 years	19	32	41	50	57	63	68	73	78
5 years	15	25	32	38	43	48	52	55	58
6 years	12	20	26	31	35	38	41	44	47
7 years	10	17	22	26	29	32	35	37	39

During the 1990s, there was an explosion in the number of private equity firms formed. According to *Stanley Pratt's Guide to Venture Capital*, the number of firms in the United States nearly doubled from 698 in 1990 to 1353 in 2000. Why? You know the answer! Returns! In 1999, a record setting year for IPOs, returns on venture capital averaged 165 percent. As we saw in Table 10-1, private equity returns have historically outpaced all other investments. Exhibit 10-5 offers a closer look.

E X H I B I T   10-5

Private Equity Returns Compared with the S&P 500*

	3 Months	1 Year	3 Years	5 Years	10 Years	20 Years
Venture capital funds (net return after fees)	−6.3%	37.6%	64.8%	48.0%	29.9%	19.9%
All buyout funds (net return after fees)	−2.5%	9.7%	14.3%	17.4%	16.6%	19.2%
Mezzanine funds (net return after fees)	−0.2%	14.9%	10.8%	11.1%	12.4%	11.7%
All private equity	−4.0%	20%	30.3%	28.3%	22.1%	19.3%
S&P 500† (dividends reinvested)	−27.8%	−8.7%	12.3%	18.3%	17.5%	15.7%

* "U.S. Venture Quarterly Returns Dip into the Red for the First Time Since 1998 but Still Show Healthy Return for the Year," *Venture Economics News*, April 9, 2001.

† S&P 500 returns from http://www.economagic.com.

INTERNATIONAL PRIVATE EQUITY

Over the last decade private equity firms have been established throughout the world. Both the number of funds and the amount of capital that has been raised in Europe, Latin America, and Asia have dramatically increased each year. Most of the money, estimated to be 60 to 70 percent, has come from investors in the United States, including pension funds, insurance companies, endowments, and wealthy individuals. Several of the international funds are highlighted in Exhibit 10-6. Capital raised in 1998 was $24 billion in Europe, $5 billion in Asia, and $3.6 billion in Latin America.

E X H I B I T   10-6

Various International Private Equity Firms

Latin America	Europe	Asia
Exxel Capital Partners	Merlin Ventures	SOFTBANK Capital
GP Capital Partners	Early Bird Ventures	Attractor Investors
CVC/Opportunity Equity Partners	3i	Vertex Management

ADVICE FOR RAISING PRIVATE EQUITY

Derrick Collins, a general partner at Polestar Capital, gives the following advice to entrepreneurs interested in obtaining equity capital:

- Do your homework. Seek investors with a proclivity to your deal. Only approach those who are buying what you are selling. Pursue capital from firms that explicitly state in their description an interest in your industry, the size of the investment you want, and the entrepreneurial stage of your company.
- Get an introduction to the investors prior to submitting the business plan. Find someone who knows one of the general partners, limited partners, or associates of the firm. Ask person to call on your behalf to give you an introduction and endorsement. This action will maximize the attention given to your plan and shorten the response time.

If the suggested steps above result in a meeting with a private equity investor, John Doerr, a general partner at KPCB, suggests the following:

> After the first meeting with the venture capitalist, you might say "I'd like a yes or no right now, but I understand you will need more than one meeting. So what's your level of interest, and what's the next step?" Frankly, you'd prefer a swift no to a long drawn-out maybe. Those are death.[11]

INCREASING SPECIALIZATION OF PRIVATE EQUITY FIRMS

There has been an increasing trend toward private equity firms specializing in a particular industry or stage of development. Firms can be categorized as either generalists or specialists. Generalists are more opportunistic and look at a variety of opportunities from high-tech to high-growth retail. Specialized firms tend to focus on an industry segment or two, for instance software and communications. Notice that these are still very broad industries. Specialization has increased for several reasons. First, in an increasingly competitive industry, venture capitalists are competing for deal flow. If a firm is the recognized expert in a certain industry area, then it is more likely that the firm is exposed to the deal. Additionally, the firm is better able to assess and value the deal because of its expertise in the industry. Finally, some specialized firms are able to negotiate lower valuations and better terms because the entrepreneur values the industry knowledge and contacts that a specialized firm can provide. Entrepreneurs should keep this in mind when raising funds. As important as it is for entrepreneurs to target the correct investment stage of a prospective venture capital firm, it is equally important that they consider the industry specialization of the firm.

IDENTIFYING PRIVATE EQUITY FIRMS

As noted earlier in this chapter, one of the best resources for finding the appropriate private equity firm is *Stanley Pratt's Guide to Venture Capital*, which lists companies by state, preferred size of investment, and industry interests. Two additional resources are available online:

1. The National Venture Capital Association at www.nvca.org or 703-351-5269
2. VentureOne at ventureone.com

Another online source is the W. Maurice Young Entrepreneurship and Venture Capital Research Centre. It produces the Venture Capital Web Links site. Over 150 web sites, including 71 sites filled with lists of investors, are highlighted.

The final suggestion is to pursue the opportunity to make a presentation at a venture capital forum such as the Springboard Conference for female entrepreneurs and the Mid-Atlantic Venture Fair, which is open to entrepreneurs in all industries and all stages of the business cycle. These are usually a 2-day event where entrepreneurs get a chance to present to and meet local and national private equity providers. Typically the entrepreneur must submit an application with a fee of approximately $200. If selected to make a 10 to 15 minute presentation, an additional fee of $500 or so may be required. The National Venture Capital Association should be contacted to find out about forums and their locations, times, and dates.

SMALL-BUSINESS INVESTMENT COMPANIES

The federal government, through the SBA, also provides equity capital to entrepreneurs. Small-business investment companies (SBICs) are privately owned, for-profit equity firms that are licensed and regulated by the SBA. SBICs invest in businesses employing fewer than 500 people and showing a net worth not greater than $18 million and after-tax income not exceeding $6 million over the two most recent years. There are approximately 410 SBICs in the country, and in 2000, they invested $5.5 billion in 3050 small businesses nationwide. The deals averaged $1.2 million, but the median investment was less than $250,000.[12]

SBICs were created in 1957 for the purpose of expanding the availability of risk capital to entrepreneurs. Many of the first private equity firms were SBICs. And many of the country's successful companies received financing from an SBIC. They include Intel, Compaq Computer, and Outback Steakhouse. They also include some notable debacles like the venture begun by Susan MacDougal, who used her $300,000 to invest in a little real estate project called the Whitewater Development Corporation. In most ways, SBICs are similar to traditional private equity firms. The primary difference between the two is their origination and financing. Anyone can start a traditional private equity firm as long as he or she can raise the capital. But someone interested in starting an SBIC firm must first get a license from the SBA. Interest in creating an SBIC comes from the attractive financing arrangement. For every dollar raised by the general partners for the fund, the SBA will invest $2. Therefore, if the general partners obtain $25 million in commitments from private sources, the SBA will invest $50 million, making it a $75 million fund.

SBICs invest $200,000 to $4 million in each deal. They tend to focus on growth-stage companies versus pure start-ups.

Included under the SBIC program are specialized small-business investment companies (SSBICs). They are similar to SBICs in every way except they tend to make smaller investments, and most importantly, they are created specifically to provide investments in companies owned by socially and economically disadvantaged entrepreneurs.

The newest SBIC-related entity is the new markets venture capital (NMVC) program. It was created to provide equity capital to entrepreneurs with companies in rural, urban, and specially designated low- and moderate-income (LMI) areas. As many as 20 NMVCs are expected to get licensing approval in the next 2 years.

Clearly, the comprehensive SBIC program has been a strong contributor to the emergence and success of entrepreneurship in America. It has increased the pool of equity capital for entrepreneurs, as well as made equity capital available to underserved entrepreneurs. The general private equity industry has a reputation for only being interested in investments in technology entrepreneurs. In contrast, SBICs have a reputation for doing "low-tech" and "no-tech" deals. Both reputations are unfounded. Traditional private firms such as Thoma Cressey Equity Partners invest in later-stage, "no-tech" companies, and SBICs such as Chicago Venture Partners invest in technology companies.

A free directory of operating SBICs can be obtained by calling the SBA Office of Investments at 202-205-6510 or going online at http://www.sba.gov/INV/opersbic.html. There is also a national SBIC trade association. Its directory costs $35 and can be obtained by calling 202-628-5055 or contacting the association online at www.nasbic.org.

INITIAL PUBLIC OFFERINGS

Every year hundreds of entrepreneurs raise equity capital by selling their company's stock to the public market. This process of selling a typical minimum of $5 million of stock to institutions and individuals is called an initial public offering (IPO) and is strictly regulated by the SEC. The result is a company that is "publicly owned." For many entrepreneurs, taking a company public is the ultimate statement of entrepreneurial success. They believe that entrepreneurs get recognized for one of two reasons: having a company that went bankrupt or having one that had an IPO. Timing is everything with an IPO issue. The late 1990s were record-breaking days of glory, the later half of 2000 was the beginning of a slowdown, and 2001 was deadly.

When a company "goes public" in the United States, it must meet a new standard of financial reporting as regulated by the Securities and Exchange Commission. All the financial information of such a company must be published quarterly and distributed to the company's shareholders. Therefore, due to the SEC's public disclosure rules, everything about a publicly owned company is open to potential and present shareholders. Information such as the president's salary and bonus, the company's number of employees, and profits are open to the public, including competitors.

This source of capital was extraordinarily popular during the 1990s. From 1970 to 1997, entrepreneurs raised $297 billion through IPOs. More than 58 percent of this capital was raised from 1993 to 1997.[13] In 1999 and 2000, entrepreneurs were the highly sought-after guests of honor at a record private equity feast. The money flowed, and entrepreneurs could, in essence, auction off their business plans to the highest bidders. Average valuations of high-tech start-ups rose from about $11 million in 1996 to almost $30 million in 2000.[14] But by the summer of 2000, as the NASDAQ began to crash, venture capital investments began to slow dramatically. As Table 10-3 shows, the boom began its slide in 2000 when the public markets became less interested in hyped technology companies that had no foreseeable chances of making profits. According to research by PricewaterhouseCoopers, in the first 3 months of 2001, venture capitalists reduced their investments in high-tech start-ups by $6.7 billion—a 40 percent drop from the previous quarter. In the first quarter of 2001, 21 companies went public compared with 123 in the same quarter a year earlier. And by late 2001, the IPO market was down dramatically.

T A B L E   10-3

Number of Initial Public Offerings

	Annual U.S. IPO Volume	
	Amount Raised, $ Millions	No. of IPOs
1990	5,294	154
1991	16,950	331
1992	26,752	524
1993	46,186	703
1994	27,998	585
1995	36,921	571
1996	51,427	823
1997	44,259	590
1998	40,391	368
1999	70,816	512
2000	71,175	396
2001*	27,502	61
Total	465,670	5,618

*As of 10/01.

Source: Dealogic, the global banking research firm.

For firms that are still committed to going public with an IPO issue during sluggish times, patience better be a core competency. Venture Economics, a research firm that follows the venture capital industry, studied the time it takes a company to go from its first round of financing to its initial public offering. In 1999, a company took an average of 140 days; 2 years later that average has surged to 487 days—a jump of 247 percent.

1990s IPO Boom

The stock market boom of the 1990s was historic. In 1995 Netscape went public despite the fact it had never made a profit. This was the beginning of the craze of companies going public even though they had no profits. In the history of the United States there has never been another decade that had as many IPOs or raised as much capital. *Barron's* called it one of the greatest gold rushes of American capitalism.[15] Another writer called it "one of the greatest speculative manias in history."[16]

The frothy IPO market was not limited to technology companies. On October 19, 1999, Martha Stewart took her company public and the stock price doubled before the end of the day. Vince McMahan, the owner of the World Wrestling Federation, took his public the same day. Disappointingly, the results were not as good as Martha's. The stock only increased a puny 48.5 percent by the day's end! In 2000, when many Internet companies were canceling their initial public offerings, Krispy Kreme donuts was the second best-performing IPO of the year.[17]

Because the public markets were responding so positively to IPOs in the 1990s, companies began racing to go public. Before 1995, it was customary for a company to have been in business for at least 3 years and have shown 4 consecutive quarters of increasing profits before it could do an IPO. The perfect example was Microsoft. Bill Gates took it public in 1986, over a decade after he founded it. By the time Microsoft went public, it had recorded several consecutive years of profitability.

But as stated earlier, the IPO of Netscape in August 1995 changed things for the next 5 years. In addition to having no profit, Netscape was very young, having been in business for only 16 months. By the end of 1999, the Netscape story was very common. "The average time from initial financing to an IPO was 18 months."[18] The absurdity was best described by a Wall Street analyst, who said, "Major Wall Street firms used to require four quarters of profits before an IPO. Then it went to four quarters of revenue, and now it's four quarters of breathing."[19]

This IPO euphoria created unparalleled wealth for entrepreneurs, especially those in Silicon Valley's technology industry. At the height of the boom in 1999, it was reported that Silicon Valley executives held $112 billion in stock and options. This was slightly more than Portugal's entire gross domestic product of $109 million.[20]

As all of the aforementioned information shows, entrepreneurs were using IPOs to raise capital for the company's operations as well as to gain personal wealth.

PUBLIC EQUITY MARKETS

After a company goes public, it is listed and traded on one of several markets in the United States. Over 13,000 companies are listed on these markets. The three major and most popular markets are the New York Stock Exchange (NYSE), the American Stock Exchange (AMEX), and the National Association of Securities Dealers Automated Quotations (NASDAQ). Let's look at each in greater detail.

NYSE

With its start in 1792, the New York Stock Exchange is the oldest trading market in the world. It also has the largest valuation. These two facts are the reason the NYSE is called the "Cadillac of securities" markets. Companies listed on this market are considered the strongest financially of companies on the three markets. In order to be listed on the NYSE, the value of the company's outstanding shares must be at least $18 million. And its annual earnings before taxes (EBT) must be at least $2.5 million. Companies listed on this market are the older, more venerable companies such as General Electric, Sears, and McDonald's. In 2000 Microsoft moved to the NYSE from the NASDAQ.

AMEX

The American Stock Exchange is the world's largest market of foreign stocks and the second largest trading market. The market value of a listed company must be at least $3 million, with an annual EBT of $750,000. In this market, traders buy and sell stocks, options, and derivatives in person at auctions. In 1998 the AMEX and NASDAQ markets merged and took the name NASDAQ-AMEX Market Group. At the time, the total market value of all companies listed on both markets was $2.2. trillion, compared with $11.6 trillion for the NYSE.[21]

NASDAQ

The NASDAQ market opened in 1971 and was the first electronic stock market. More shares are traded at an average of 1.8 billion per day over this market than any other in the world.[22]

The minimum market value for companies listed on this market is $1 million. There is no minimum EBT requirement. That is why this market with over 5000 listings is the fastest-growing market in the world. The NASDAQ is heavily filled with tech, biotech, and small-company stocks. Trading on this market occurs via telephone and computer. All the technology companies that went public since 1995 did so on the NASDAQ market.

Reasons for Going Public

Entrepreneurs take their companies public for several reasons. The first is to raise capital for the operations of the company. Because the money is to be used to rapidly grow the company, the equity capital provided from an IPO may be preferred over debt. In the instances of the tech companies in the 1990s that had negative cashflow, they could not raise debt capital. Only equity financing was available to them.

Even if a company can afford the debt capital, some entrepreneurs prefer capital from an IPO because it can be relatively cheap. In fact, the cost of the capital can be lower than that of debt. The explanation is very simple math.

Over the history of the Dow Jones, the average P/E ratio is 14. This means investors are willing to pay $14 for every $1 of earnings. Therefore, the cost of this capital is only 7 percent ($1/$14—about 2 percentage points less than the cost of debt today, which at prime plus 2, is approximately 9 percent.

Another reason for going public is because it might be easier to recruit and retain excellent employees by combining publicly owned stock with their salaries. This allows employees to personally benefit when the value of the company increases from their hard work.

Still another good reason is that an IPO provides the entrepreneur with another form of currency that can be used to grow the company. In the 1990s the stock of a company was being wisely used as currency. Instead of buying other companies with cash, many buyers paid the sellers with their stock. The seller would then hold the stock and benefit from any future increases in value. In fact, many deals did not close or were delayed in closing because the seller wanted the buyer's stock instead of cash. This was the case when Disney purchased the ABC network. Disney wanted to pay cash, but the ABC team held out until they received Disney stock. Their reasoning was that $1 worth of Disney's stock was more valuable than $1 cash. They were willing to take the risk that, unlike cash, which depreciates due to inflation, the stock would appreciate.

The final reason for going public is to provide a liquidity exit for the stockholders, including employees, management, and investors.

Reasons for Not Going Public

Taking a company public is extremely difficult. In fact, less than 20 percent of the entrepreneurs who attempt to take a company public are successful.[23] And the process can take a long time—as long as 2 years.

Also, the cost of completing an IPO is very expensive. The typical cost is approximately $500,000. Then there are additional annual costs that must be incurred to meet SEC regulations regarding public disclosure, including the publication of the quarterly financial statements.

By the time most companies go public, they have received financing from family and friends, angels, and at least two rounds from institutional investors. As a result, most founders will be lucky if they retain 10 percent ownership. The exception to this rule is Bill Gates, who owns approximately 20 percent of Microsoft.[24] Another is Jeff Bezos, who owns 41 percent of Amazon.com. In late 2001, with his company's stock tanking, that stake was worth just under $1 billion.

One of the greatest criticisms of going public is that most of the stock is owned by large institutional investors, which have a short-term focus. They exert continual pressure on the CEO to deliver increasing earnings every quarter.

The final reason for not going public is that while stock sold by the company can be immediately used for operations, stock owned by the key management team cannot be sold immediately. SEC Rule 144 says that all key members of the company cannot sell any of their stock. These key members are officers, directors, and inside shareholders, including venture capitalists, who own "restricted stock." These are stocks that were not registered with the SEC. This is in contrast to the shares of stock issued to the public at the IPO. These stocks are unrestricted.

The holding period for restricted stock is 2 years from the date of purchase. At that time the restricted stockholders may sell their stock in any 3-month period as long as they do not sell more than 1 percent of the total number of shares outstanding.[25] For example, if the entrepreneur owns 1 million shares of the 90 million shares of outstanding common stock, he or she may not sell, in a 3-month period, any more than 900,000 shares of the stock.

Control

One negative myth about going pubic is that if the entrepreneur owns less than 51 percent of the company, he or she loses control. This is not true. Founders including Bill Gates, Jeff Bezos, and Michael Dell own less than 51 percent of their companies, but they still have control. The same is true of the Ford family, which only owns 6.5 percent of Ford Motor Company. The key to control is to have influence on the majority of voting stock. Some stock may be nonvoting stock, a.k.a. capital stock. The entrepreneur with his or her family and board members may own virtually none of the nonvoting stock but a majority of the voting stock. This fact, along with the entrepreneur being in a management position and being the one who determines who sits on the board of directors, keeps him or her in control.

The IPO Process

As has been stated earlier, taking a company public can be expensive and time-consuming for the entrepreneur. But when done right and for the correct reasons, it can be very rewarding.

While it can take up to 24 months to complete an IPO, investment banking firm William Blair and Company said that 52 to 59 weeks is the norm.

Bessemer Venture Partners, a leading venture capital firm, accurately described a simplified step-by-step IPO process:

1. Entrepreneur decides to take the company public to raise money for future acquisitions.
2. Interviews and selects investment banks (IBs).
3. Meets with the IBs that will underwrite the offering.
4. Files the IPO registration with the SEC.
5. SEC reviews and approves the registration.

6. IBs and entrepreneur go on "road show."

7. IBs take tentative commitments.

8. IPO.

Let's discuss these steps in more detail.

IPO Decision

The entrepreneur's decision to do an IPO can be made almost the day the person decides to go into business. Some entrepreneurs articulate their plans for going public in their original business plan. In starting the business, one of their future objectives is to own a public company.

Others may decide to go public when they get institutional financing. The venture capitalist may only provide them financing if they agree to go public in 3 to 5 years. In such a case, the entrepreneur and the investor may make the decision.

Another way that entrepreneurs decide to go public is when they review their 3- to 5-year business plan and realize that their ability to grow as fast as they would like will be determined by the availability of outside equity capital—greater than what they can get from institutional investors.

Interviews and Selection of Investment Banks

Once the decision has been made to go public, the entrepreneur must hire one or more investment banks to underwrite the offering. This process of selecting an IB is called the "bake-off." Ideally several IBs that are contacted by the entrepreneur will quickly study the company's business and afterwards solicit, via presentations and meetings, the entrepreneur's selection of their firms. The IB's compensation is typically no more than 7 percent of the capital raised.

Underwriter(s) Meetings

After the IBs are selected, the entrepreneur will meet with the underwriters to plan the IPO. This process includes determining the company's value, the number of shares that will be issued, the selling price of the shares, and the timing of the "road show" and the IPO.

In typical public offerings the underwriters buy all of the company's shares at the initial offer price and then sell them at the IPO. When underwriters make this agreement with the entrepreneurs, this is called a firm commitment.

There are also underwriters that make "best-efforts" agreements. In this case they will not purchase the stock but will make every effort to sell it to a third party.

IPO Registration

The entrepreneur's attorney must file the registration statement with the SEC. This is a two-part document. The first part is called a prospectus and discloses all the information about the company, including the planned use of the money, the valuation, a description of management, and financial statements. The prospectus is the document given to potential investors.

The first printing of this prospectus is called a *red herring* because it contains warnings to the reader that certain things in the document might change. These warnings are printed in red ink.

The second part of the document is the actual registration statement. The four items disclosed are:

- Expenses of distribution
- Indemnification of directors and officers
- Recent sales of unregistered securities
- Exhibits and financial statement schedules[26]

SEC Approval

The SEC reviews the registration statement in detail to determine that all disclosures have been made and that they are correct and easy to comprehend. The reviewer can approve the statement, allowing the next step in the IPO process to commence; delay the review until changes are made to the statement that satisfies the reviewer; or put a "stop order," which terminates the statement registration process with a disapproval decision.

The Road Show

Once approval has been obtained for the registration statement, the entrepreneur and IB are free to begin the marketing process to potential investors. This is called the road show, where the entrepreneur makes presentations about the company to the potential investors that the IB has identified.

Investment Commitments

During the road show, the entrepreneur makes a "pitch" for why the investors should buy the company's stock. After each presentation the IBs will meet with the potential investors to determine their interest. The investors' tentative commitments for an actual number of shares are recorded in "the book" that the IB takes to each road show presentation.

The IB wants to accumulate a minimum number of tentative commitments before proceeding to the IPO. IBs like to have three tentative commitments for every share of stock that will be offered.[27]

The IPO

On the day that the IPO will occur, the investment bank and the entrepreneur will determine the official stock selling price and number of shares to be sold. The price may change from the time they began the road show to the day of the IPO, due to interest in the stock. If the tentative commitments were greater than a 3-to-1 ratio, then the offering price may be increased. It may be lowered if the opposite occurred. That is exactly what happened to the stock of Wired Ventures, which went public in 1996. Originally the company wanted to sell 4.75 million shares at $14 each. By the date of the IPO, it made the decision with its IB, Goldman Sachs, to reduce the offering to 3 million shares at a price of $10 per share. One of the reasons for this change was due to the fact that hours before the stock had to be officially priced for sale, the offer was still undersubscribed by 50 percent. Even at this lower price, though, the IPO never took place. Wired Ventures was not able to raise the $60 million it sought, and it incurred expenses of approximately $1.3 million in its attempt to go public.

Choosing the Right Investment Banker

As the preceding information shows, the ability to have a successful IPO is significantly dependent on the IB. The most critical importance of an IB is its ability to value the company properly, assist the attorney and entrepreneur in developing the registration statement, help the entrepreneur develop an excellent presentation for the road show, access its database to reach and invite the proper potential investors to the presentation, and sell the stock. Therefore, the entrepreneur must do as much as possible to select the best IB for his or her IPO. A few suggestions are as follows:

- Identify the firms that have successfully taken companies public that are similar to yours in size, industry, and amount to be raised. A great resource to find these companies is published by Securities Data Publishing (212-765-5311), entitled *Going Public: The IPO Reporter*.

- Select experienced firms. At a minimum the ideal firm has underwritten two deals annually for the past 3 years. The firms that are underwriting eight deals per year, or two each quarter, may be too busy to give proper attention to your deal. Also eliminate those that have deals that consistently took over 90 days to get registration approval.

- Select underwriters that price the deal close to at least its first day closing. If they price the stock too low such that by the end of the first day the stock increased dramatically in price, then the entrepreneur sold more equity than needed. For example, if the initial offering was 1 million shares at $5 per share and closed the first day at $10 per share, then the stock was underpriced. Instead of raising $5 million dollars for 1 million shares, the entrepreneur could have raised the same amount for 500,000 shares had the underwriter priced the stock better.

- Select underwriters that file planned selling prices close to the actual price at the initial offering. Some underwriters file at a price and then try to force the entrepreneur to open at a lower price so that they can sell the stock and their investors can reap the benefits of the increase. This practice, when it is done, usually occurs a day or so prior to the IPO, where the underwriter threatens to terminate the offering if the price is not reduced. To minimize the chances of this happening, the entrepreneur should only select underwriters that have a consistent pattern of filing and bringing the stock to the market at similar prices.

- Select underwriters that have virtually no experiences with failing to complete the offering. Companies that file for an IPO, but do not make it, are considered "damaged goods" by investors.

- Get an introduction to the investment banker. Never cold-call the banker. The company's attorney or accountant should make the introduction.[28]

THE FINANCING SPECTRUM

There's an old dog food commercial that features a frolicking puppy changing before our eyes into a mature dog. The commercial reminds pet owners that as their dogs grow, the food that fuels them needs to change too. Businesses are the same way with equity financing. As a business evolves from an idea into a mature company, the type of financing it requires changes. At the beginning of Chapter 8, the steps in which many successful high-growth entrepreneurs raised their equity capital were highlighted in the financing spectrum.

An actual entrepreneur who raised money from almost all of the sources of capital on that spectrum was Jeff Bezos. Exhibit 10-7 shows when Bezos raised capital and from whom.

E X H I B I T   10-7

Jeff Bezos Financing Spectrum

07-94	10-94 and 02-95	12-95	1996	05-97
Amazon.com concept	Amazon.com incorporation and launch	Amazon.com operating	Amazon.com growing	Amazon.com exponential growth
↓	↓	↓	↓	↓
■ Capital from personal savings	■ Capital from mother and father	■ Capital from angels	■ Capital from venture capitalist	■ Capital from IPO
– $15,000 interest-free loan	– 582,528 shares common stock sold to father for $100,000	– Raised $981,000 at $5 million premoney valuation	– $8 million from KPCB at $52 million premoney valuation	– Raised $54 million
– $10,000 equity investment for 10 million shares of common stock	– 847,716 shares common stock sold to mother for $144,000			

DIRECT PUBLIC OFFERINGS

In 1989 the SEC made it possible for companies seeking less than $5 million to raise it directly from the public without going through the expensive and time-consuming IPO process described earlier. Aptly named, this direct process is called a direct public offering, or DPO. In a DPO, shares are usually sold for $1 to $10 each without an underwriter, and the investors do not face the sophisticated investor requirements. Forty-five states allow DPOs, and the usual legal, accounting, and marketing fees are less than $50,000.

There are three DPO programs that have been used by thousands of entrepreneurs. The programs are:

1. Rule 504, a.k.a. Regulation D, which is also called the Small Corporate Offering Registration, a.k.a. SCOR
2. Regulation A
3. Intrastate

The SEC can be contacted at 202-942-4046 to procure a free pamphlet entitled "Q & A: Small Business and the SEC—Help Your Company Go Public." Let's discuss each in more detail.

- *Small Corporate Offering Registration.* In the Small Corporate Offering Registration or SCOR program, the entrepreneur has 12 months to raise a maximum of $1 million. Shares can be sold to an unlimited number of investors throughout the country via general solicitation and even advertising. One entrepreneur who accessed capital via a DPO was Rick Moon, the founder of Thanksgiving Coffee Co. Rick raised $1.25 million in 1996 for 20 percent of his coffee and tea wholesaling company that had annual revenues of $4.6 million. He aggressively advertised the offering to his suppliers and customers on his web site, in his catalog, on his coffee-bean bags, and on the bean dispensers in stores.[29]
- *Regulation A Offering.* Under the Regulation A program an entrepreneur can raise a maximum of $5 million in 12 months. Unlike SCOR where no SEC filings are required, this offering must be filed with the SEC. Otherwise all the attributes assigned to SCOR are applicable to Regulation A. Dorothy Pittman Hughes, the founder of Harlem Copy

Center with $300,000 in annual revenues in 1998, began raising $2 million under this program by offering stock for $1 per share. The minimum number of shares adults could buy was 50; for children the minimum was 25.[30]

- *Intrastate Program*. The intrastate program requires companies to limit the sale of their stock to investors in one state. This program has other significant differences from SCOR and Regulation A. First there are no federal laws limiting the maximum that can be raised or the time allowed. These two items vary by state. The other difference is that the stock cannot be resold outside the state for 9 months.

The DPO is best suited for historically profitable companies with audited financial statements and a well-written business plan. Shareholders are typically "affinity" groups that are somehow tied to the company, including customers, employees, suppliers, distributors, and friends. After completing a DPO, the company can still do a traditional IPO at a later date. Real Goods Trading Company did just that. In 1991, it raised $1 million under SCOR. Two years later it raised an additional $3.6 million under Regulation A. Today its stock is traded over the NASDAQ market.

DPOs have a few negative aspects. First, it is estimated that over 70 percent of those who register for a DPO fail, for various reasons. But the greatest drawback is the fact that there is no public market exchange like the NYSE for DPO stock. This type of exchange brings sellers and buyers together, and that does not exist for DPOs. Therefore, the ability to raise capital is negatively affected by legitimate concerns on the potential investors' part that their investment cannot be made liquid easily. Another problem is that the absence of a market leaves the market appreciation of the stock in question. One critic of DPOs said, "There is no liquidity in these offerings. Investors are stepping into a leg-hold trap."[31] As a result, DPO investors tend to be long-term-focused. Trading of the stock is usually arranged by the company or made through an order-matching service that the company manages. The shareholders can also get liquid if the company is sold, the owners buy the stock back, or the company does a traditional IPO.

Because this is a book about finance, and not one about law, we have intentionally avoided a long discussion of the legal aspects of entrepreneurship. That doesn't mean that you should ignore the legal ins and outs of running a business or getting one started. One great resource that comes highly recommended from my students is the book *The Entrepreneur's Guide to Business Law* by Constance Bagley and Craig Dauchy.

NOTES

1. *BusinessWeek*, January 8, 2001, p. 55.
2. *Forbes ASAP*, June 1, 1998, p. 24.
3. *Forbes*, January 10, 2000, p. F.
4. *Inc.*, July 1997, p. 48.
5. *Crain's Chicago Business*, March 9, 1999, p. SB4.
6. *BUYOUTS*, February 8, 1999, p. 23.
7. *The Corporate Venturing Report*, Premiere Issue, 2000, p. 24.
8. *The Private Equity Analyst*, August 1999, p. 36.
9. Ibid., p. 34.
10. Ibid.
11. *Fast Company*, February 1998, p. 86.
12. *Los Angeles Times*, May 7, 2001.
13. *Directorship Inc.*, Fall 1998, p. 1.
14. *The Economist*, May 3, 2001.
15. *Fast Company*, January 2000, p. 50.
16. Chancellor, Edward, *Devil Take the Hindmost: A History of Financial Speculation*, May 1999.
17. *Boston Globe*, February 21, 2001.
18. *USA Today*, June 22, 2000.
19. Ibid., December 23, 1999.
20. *Time*, September 27, 1999.
21. *Chicago Sun-Times*, November 3, 1998, p. 45.
22. Ibid., September 3, 2000, p. 47A.
23. *The Wall Street Journal*, April 6, 2001, p. C1.
24. *USA Today*, January 21, 1999.
25. *The Entrepreneur's Guide to Going Public*, p. 297.

26. Ibid., p. 202.
27. *Inc.*, February 1998, p. 57.
28. *Success*, January 1999, p. 20.
29. *Inc.*, December 1996, p. 70.
30. *Essence*, May 1998, p. 64.
31. *USA Today*, April 29, 1997, p. 4B.

CHAPTER 11

Financing for Minorities and Women

INTRODUCTION

As noted in the beginning of the book, minority- and women-owned firms are fast becoming powerful economic forces in the small-business world. Minority-owned businesses grew more than four times as fast as U.S firms overall between 1992 and 1997, increasing from 2.1 million to 2.8 million firms.[1] The following statistics come from a report by the U.S Commerce Department's Census Bureau in 2001 and are worth considering:

- Minority-owned firms generated $255.9 billion in annual revenue.
- While Hispanics controlled the largest share of firms owned by minorities, Asian and Pacific Islander–owned firms had the largest share of minority-owned business revenues—52 percent.
- Men were owners of approximately 55 percent of the firms owned by each of the four minority groups (African Americans, Asian and Pacific Islanders, Hispanics, and Native Americans). African Americans had the largest percentage of firms owned by women—38 percent.

- Of all minority-owned firms, 59 percent were in the services and retail trade industries, accounting for 43 percent of all receipts.

As I also mentioned in the beginning of the book, my mother, Ollie Mae Rogers, was the first entrepreneur that I ever met, and accordingly I have a tremendous amount of respect for women entrepreneurs. As noted earlier, women-owned businesses conservatively total more than 5.4 million companies, employ 7.1 million people, and generate more than $800 billion in revenues every year.

Needless to say, minority and women entrepreneurs have played the game of catch-up brilliantly, and they have forced the traditional small-business infrastructure to change. Thank God we are past the era when women could not get a loan without the signature of their husbands and it was legal to reject a loan application from a person simply because of his ethnicity or race! The laws that made such gender and racial discrimination legal have had a profound effect on minority and women entrepreneurship. The inability to access capital from other than personal savings, family, friends, and angels retarded the growth of most entrepreneurs from these two sectors. Given the absence of growth capital from financial institutions, these entrepreneurs, in essence, were involuntarily relegated to a life as mom and pop, or lifestyle, entrepreneurs. The legacy is that we have virtually no major corporations that were founded by minorities or women.

And while there are federal laws that prohibit gender and racial discrimination in debt and equity financing, it is sad to report even today that minority and women entrepreneurs are receiving a pittance of all the capital provided to entrepreneurs.

Still there are an increasing number of investment firms that are focusing in on all kinds of niches, and these firms are an important resource. For example, there are specialized firms that target entrepreneurs who are female, are minorities, or are in industries such as consumer goods, food products, banking, and sports. There are even firms that will only invest in companies in certain geographical regions such as the New England region or rural areas. A few of these specialized firms are listed in Exhibit 11-1.

Niche Equity Investment Firms

Name	Targeted Investments
Belvedere Capital Partners	Community banks in California
IMG/Chase Sports Capital	Sports related companies
Village Ventures	Underserved areas, nonmajor cities
Bastion Capital	Hispanic entrepreneurs
Capital Across America (CXA)	Women-owned businesses

MINORITIES—DEBT FINANCING

The history regarding the success rate of minority entrepreneurs raising institutional equity and debt capital is worse than that of women. Research by Professor David Blanchflower of Dartmouth College showed that the loan rejection rate was significantly higher for minority entrepreneurs than for whites, as is shown in Exhibit 11-2.

E X H I B I T   11-2
Denial Rates for Business Lending

All categories	28.8%
White	26.9%
Hispanic	35.9%
Black	65.9%

The result of this high rejection rate is that minority-owned companies use personal financing more. SBA data suggest that 37 percent of all businesses use bank credit, but only 27 percent of minority business owners do so.[2] Of those businesses, 15 percent of black owners and 33 percent of Hispanic owners use commercial bank credit. The Federal Reserve Bank of Chicago found that 12 percent of the minority entrepreneurs it surveyed had received debt financing from banks. The other 88 percent used their own capital or money from family and friends.[3]

ADVICE

Minority entrepreneurs seeking debt capital should approach the institutions that are friends to minorities. Those firms include community development banks and large banks such as Wells Fargo. In 1995 Wells Fargo committed to invest over $2 billion in minority entrepreneurs.

Another excellent source is SBA lenders. The Milken Institute reported that "the total number of SBA loans made to Hispanic and black-owned businesses has tripled since 1992 and quadrupled for Asian businesses. The SBA's total share of loans going to minority entrepreneurs has increased from 15 percent in 1992 to 24 percent in 1998."[4]

MINORITIES—EQUITY FINANCING

Less than 1 percent of all equity capital provided by institutional investors has gone to minority entrepreneurs. Virtually all of that capital has come from firms that are associated with the National Association of Investment Companies (NAIC). These NAIC-related firms explicitly target investments in minority-owned companies. Some also invest proactively in women entrepreneurs. More than 75 NAIC firms in the United States have invested since 1986 over $3 billion in approximately 18,000 companies. About a decade ago most of these were government-backed SBICs. Today most are private funds.

Almost every high-growth, successful, minority-owned company has received financing from an NAIC-affiliated firm. A few of the equity capital recipients are listed in Exhibit 11-3.

Equity capital has also been made available to minority entrepreneurs by angel investors. One such group is called the Access to Capital Group. It is a Dallas-based group of minority investors that can be contacted at 877-408-1ACG.

ADVICE

Minority entrepreneurs seeking equity capital should contact the NAIC at www.naichq.org to get a complete listing of the member funds. A few are presented in Exhibit 11-4.

E X H I B I T   11-3

Various Equity Investments from NAIC Member Firms

Company	Minority	Description	NAIC Member
Radio One	Black	Public company (NASDAQ: ROIA). Largest minority-owned broadcasting company	TSG Capital
Black Entertainment Television	Black	Former public company (NYSE: BTV) Acquired by Viacom	Syncom
Z-Spanish Media	Hispanic	Largest Spanish-language media network	TSG Capital
Watson Pharmaceuticals	Asian	Public company (NYSE: WPI)	Polestar Capital
BioGenex Laboratories	Indian		Pacesetter

E X H I B I T   11-4

Various NAIC Members

NAIC Member	Location	Phone
Black Enterprise/Greenwich Street Equity Fund	New York, NY	212-816-1189
Opportunity Capital Partners	Fremont, CA	510-795-7000
TSG Capital	Stamford, CT	203-352-1860

WOMEN—DEBT FINANCING

Throughout history, women have always had a tough time getting debt capital from institutions such as banks. As we stated in Chapter 1, women own approximately 26 percent of all non-farm U.S. businesses, but the Milken Institute reports that, as of October 2000, women received only 12 percent of all credit provided to small businesses.[5] A symptom of this problem may be the fact that, according to research by the National Foundation for Women Business Owners (NFWBO), fast-growth firms owned by women, compared with those owned by men, are less likely to have commercial bank loans. The research showed that 52 percent of male-owned companies had loans versus only 39 percent for females.

One of the ways women combat this problem is by using personal credit cards for their business's debt-financing needs. NFWBO's information showed that 32 percent of women-owned companies compared with 21 percent of those owned by males used their credit cards.[6]

ADVICE

Women seeking debt financing should approach institutions that want to do business with women. Those firms include SBA lenders and banks such as Wells Fargo, which in 1994 committed to loan $1 billion to women entrepreneurs. A year later, Wells Fargo became so convinced that financing women entrepreneurs was a great strategy that it increased its commitment to $10 billion to be invested over a 10-year period. This additional commitment came after the NFWBO published research showing that investing in women entrepreneurs was sound business because they had a better chance of repaying business loans. This fact was proved from information showing that on average, women-owned companies stay in business longer. Specifically, nearly 75 percent of women-owned firms founded in 1991 were still in business 3 years later compared with 66 percent for all U.S. firms.[7]

In addition, the SBA has increasingly supported women's businesses. Over the past 7 years, SBA-guaranteed loans to women have tripled to 48,000 loans annually, worth a total of $9 billion. While this increase in activity is to be applauded, it should be noted that there is still room for improvement on SBA loans. From October 1999 to June 2000, the SBA guaranteed $9.83 billion in loans. Only $1.57 billion, or less than 16 percent, went to women.[8] A few other institutional debt sources of capital for women entrepreneurs are listed in Exhibit 11-5.

WOMEN—EQUITY FINANCING

Until last year (2000), women entrepreneurs had never received more than 2 percent of all institutional equity capital. In 2000, they received 4.4 percent.[9] According to a study commissioned by the Center for Women's Business Research (formerly National Foundation for Women Business Owners), women entrepreneurs

E X H I B I T   11-5

Various Women-Focused Institutional Debt Sources

Source	Description/Contact
Capital Across America	Mezzanine-stage financing
Count-Me-In for Women's Economic Independence	An online lending program
FleetBoston Financial's Women Entrepreneurs' Connection	Small-business-banking program
SBA, Office of Women's Business Ownership	800-8-ASK-SBA
Wells Fargo Bank	800-359-3557, ext. 120
Women, Inc.	$150 million loan fund, 800-930-3993

who seek or have obtained equity capital find the sources of funding three ways: word of mouth (60 percent of recipients, 49 percent of seekers), their own networks of business consultants (50 percent of recipients, 42 percent of seekers), and investors who have sought them out (38 percent of recipients, 39 percent of seekers).[10]

ADVICE

My advice would be the same as with the debt capital sources. Go to sources interested in doing business with women. Exhibit 11-6 lists equity funds that target women entrepreneurs.

E X H I B I T   11-6

Women-Focused Private Equity Firms

Source	Description/Contact
Women's Growth Capital Fund	
Three Guineas Fund	San Francisco
Telecommunications Women's Growth Capital	Washington, DC
Viridian Capital Partners	San Francisco–based SBIC
Juno Partners	New York–based buyout firm

In addition to the funds cited in the exhibit, there are venture fairs for women seeking equity capital. The most prominent is the

Springboard Conference where entrepreneurs make presentations to investors. The first was held in January 2000. Since then, others have been held in Boston and Chicago. At the inaugural conference, 27 female entrepreneurs made presentations to 300 investors. By the end of March, 26 of 27 entrepreneurs, who were individually seeking $1 million to $30 million, procured capital. The total raised by these entrepreneurs was $266 million.[11]

Another great source of equity capital is angel investors. Exhibit 11-7 lists those investors interested in financing women entrepreneurs.

E X H I B I T   11-7

Various Women-Focused Angel Investors

Source	Description/Contact
Women's Collateral Worldwide, Inc.	215-564-2800
Seraph Capital Forum	125 Seattle-based women
WomenAngels.net	National Network

While things are improving for both women and minorities, it is not fast enough. Poor access to capital for these two groups is hurting America. Former SBA chief Aida Alvarez stated it beautifully when she said: "Businesses owned by women and minorities are multiplying at a faster rate than all other U.S. businesses. If we don't start investing now in the potential of the businesses, we will not have a successful economy in the new millennium."[12]

CONCLUSION

My alma mater, the Harvard Business School, recently asked me to sit on a panel to discuss entrepreneurship. All the other panelists were current entrepreneurs, and the questions eventually focused on the future of entrepreneurship: Given the tough economic times, was this really the right time to consider starting a business? Everyone else on the panel shook his or her head no. By now, I think you can guess my answer: Of course this is the right time to start a business! In every recession, depression, and downturn that this country has ever seen, entrepreneurship has been the engine of growth. After the terrorist attack on September 11, 2001, the airline industry alone laid off more than 100,000 workers. Which *Fortune* 500 company do you think will hire all those pink slip recipients? If anyone is waiting for the big companies with thousands of employees to fill a cloudy day with sun, and turn around these tough times, he or she is in for a long and disappointing wait. Entrepreneurs hold the keys to the next generation of *Fortune* 500 companies. Of course the capital is constrained, and investors are more skeptical than they have been. In many ways, that's good news. It means that only the best companies—those with the best ideas and the best managers—will get financial backing. I'm a firm believer that good managers make better decisions when times are tough. And tough times make better managers. Expenditures are scrutinized more carefully, cashflow gets a closer look, innovative partnerships are born, and managers learn once again that execution is everything.

Is this the right time for you? Only you can answer that question. Volkswagen has a catchy marketing campaign that tells consumers, "On the road of life, there are drivers and passengers. Drivers wanted." For future entrepreneurs, the worst thing that you could do to yourself is to spend your life kicking the tires and wondering whether or not you should have taken a risk, cut the safety net, and taken the plunge. Entrepreneurship is about passion, vision, focus, and sweat, and no swing of the stock market will ever change that. Around every corner is the next idea, the next dream, and the next business opportunity. I wish you well on your adventure.

NOTES

1. U.S. Department of Commerce news release, July 12, 2001.
2. Small Business Administration, "Minorities in Business," 1999, p. 4.
3. *Crain's Chicago Business*, February 15, 1999, p. 17.
4. *The Minority Business Challenge*, Milken Institute, September 25, 2000, p. 34.
5. "Economic Prosperity, Women and Access to Credit," Milken Institute p. 3.

6. "Entrepreneurial Vision in Action: Exploring Growth among Women- and Men-Owned Firms," the National Foundation for Women Business Owners, February 2001, p. 20.
7. National Foundation for Women Business Owners, October 17, 1996.
8. Ibid.
9. *USA Today.com*, August 14, 2001, http://www.usatoday.com.
10. *Women Entrepreneurs in the Equity Capital Markets: The New Frontier*, National Foundation for Women Business Owners, 2001.
11. The Kauffman Center Report on Women Entrepreneurs.
12. *Chicago Sun-Times*, March 24, 1999, p. 69.

GLOSSARY

A Entrepreneur: An investor rating for an entrepreneur. The A entrepreneur has both experience in entrepreneurship, as an owner or an employee in an entrepreneurial firm, as well as experience in the company's industry.

Accounts Payable: Money that is owed to suppliers.

Accounts Receivable: Money that is owed by customers.

Accounts Receivable Collection System: A system that allows the entrepreneur to do business with customers who may not have a credit history or even those who have a bad credit history.

Accrual Accounting Method: An accounting method that measures the performance and position of a company by recognizing economic events regardless of when cash transactions happen.

Acquisition: A company that is inherited or bought.

Amortization: The deduction of expenses over a specific period of time.

Angel Investors: High-net-worth individuals or wealthy families who invest capital in debt and/or equity entrepreneurial firms.

B Entrepreneur: An investor rating for an entrepreneur. The B entrepreneur has either experience in entrepreneurship as an owner or an employee in an entrepreneurial firm, or experience in the company's industry.

Bake-Off: The process of selecting an investment bank.

Balance Sheet: A company's financial statement that reports its assets, liabilities, and net worth at a specific time.

Blue Sky Projection: Financial projections that are simply pulled "out of the air."

C Entrepreneur: An investor rating for an entrepreneur. The entrepreneur has neither experience in entrepreneurship as an owner or an employee in an entrepreneurial firm nor experience in the company's industry.

Capital Call: A formal notification from the private equity firm to its limited partners indicating that a specific amount of capital is to be transferred to the firm within a specified time period (typically 30 days).

Cash Accounting Method: An accounting method where revenues are recognized only when the cash is received, and expenses are recognized only when the cash is disbursed, thereby reducing the company's profit before taxes and consequently the taxes paid.

Cashflow: The amount of cash a company generates and uses during a period.

Cashflow Cycle: Measures the number of days it takes to convert inventory and receivables into cash.

Cashflow-to-Debt Coverage Ratio: Measures if a company's cash can meet its debt service. A 1.25:1 ratio minimum should be targeted.

Cashflow Ledger: Provides a summary of the increases (inflow) and decreases (outflow) in actual cash over a period of time.

Cash Gap: The number of days between the supplier's payment of cash for goods and services used to generate revenues and the receipt of payments from customers for those goods and services.

Collection Ratio: Measures the quality of the accounts receivable. It shows the average number of days it takes to collect receivables. The ideal is to get paid as quickly as possible. Also known as days receivable.

Commitment Letter: Summarizes the agreement between the venture capitalist and the entrepreneur regarding the key business points and deal parameters.

Comparables: Public and private companies with valuation characteristics (e.g., amount of revenues, growth rate, etc.) similar to those of the company that is being valued.

Comparables Analysis: The process of identifying companies with similar valuation characteristics and using this information to approximate the valuation of a potential investment.

Compounded Annual Growth Rate (CAGR): Used to discuss the rate of growth of money over a certain period of time—the interest rate. Compounding means you earn interest on the initial investment in addition to the interest earned each year, or the actual dollars of growth.

Contribution Margin: Revenues minus variable costs.

Corporation: The most common form of business organization, in which the total worth of the organization is divided into shares of stock, each share representing a unit of ownership.

Cost of Goods Sold (COGS): Cost of the raw material and direct labor required to produce the product that generates a company's revenue.

Cost of Services Rendered: Cost of the direct labor required to produce the service that generates a company's revenue.

Current Assets: Represents cash, accounts receivable, inventory, marketable securities, prepaid expenses, and other assets that can be converted to cash within 1 year. Appears on a company's balance sheet.

Current Liabilities: The amount owed for interest, accounts payable, short-term loans, expenses incurred but unpaid, and other debts due within 1 year. Appears on a company's balance sheet.

Days Inventory Carried: Measures the average amount of daily inventory being carried.

Days Payable: Measures the speed at which a company is paying its bills.

Days Receivable: *See* Collection Ratio.

Deal Flow: The companies or concepts that are potential venture capital investments.

Debt Financing: Capital that is loaned to a company and is returned to the investor over a period of time through principal and interest payments.

Debt Obligation: An amount of money owed from one person or firm to another.

Debt/Equity Ratio: Measures the degree to which the company has leveraged itself relative to its value.

Depreciation: An expense recorded to reduce the value of a long-term tangible asset.

Direct Public Offering (DPO): A capital-raising process for companies seeking less than $5 million. The companies raise the capital directly from the public without having to go through the expensive and time-consuming IPO process.

Discount Rate: The capital gain required to make an investment in a given stock worth the associated risk.

Discounted Cashflow: Future cashflows multiplied by a discount rate to obtain present values.

Due Diligence Process: An investigation or audit of a potential investment.

Earnings: The net income for a company during a specific period.

Earnings before Interest and Taxes (EBIT): The cash available to service debt (principal and interest), pay taxes, buy capital equipment, and/or return to shareholders after paying all of a company's operating expenses.

Earnings before Interest, Taxes, Depreciation, and Amortization (EBITDA): The cash generated by the company after paying all of the expenses directly related to its operations, and therefore, the cash available to pay for nonoperational expenses such as taxes, principal, and interest payments on debt. To determine EBITDA, one must utilize the income statement.

Employee Stock Ownership Plan (ESOP): An organized plan for employees of a company that allows them to buy shares of its stock.

Entrepreneur: One who organizes, manages, and assumes the risks of a business or enterprise.

Entrepreneurial Spectrum: Describes different types of entrepreneurs (e.g., start-up entrepreneur, acquirer, etc.).

Equity: The value of the funds contributed by the owners (the stockholders) plus the retained earnings (or losses).

Equity Capital: Capital that is invested or available for investment in the ownership of a company. Also known as risk capital or venture capital.

Evergreen Multiple: A valuation multiplier that is constantly changing or should be adjusted up or down, depending on several factors.

Executive Summary: A summary of the main information in the detailed business plan. It should be concise (i.e., no longer than two pages), be clear and simple to understand, and present a good summation of the most relevant information needed by potential investors.

Exit Strategy: The process by which an owner or investor liquidates his or her ownership in a business (e.g., merger, acquisition, public offering, etc.).

Factor: A lender that uses a company's accounts receivable for collateral.

Factoring Firm: *See* Factor.

Financial Projections: Projections of future revenues, expenses, profits, assets, and liabilities.

Financing Expenses: The interest payments paid on loans to the business.

Financing Spectrum: The steps in which entrepreneurs raise capital.

Franchise: A right or license granted to an individual, group, or business to market a company's goods or services in a particular territory.

Free Cashflow (FCF): The operating cashflow of a company available for distribution to the providers of debt (interest and principal payments) and equity (dividend payments and repurchase of stock) capital. Also known as the discounted cashflow or capitalization of cashflow method model.

Gross Margin: Measures the gross profit margin the company is achieving on sales.

High-Growth Entrepreneur: An entrepreneur who is proactively looking to grow annual revenues and profits exponentially.

Income Statement: It records the flow of resources over time by stating the financial condition of a business at the end of a period, usually a month, quarter, or year. Also known as the profit and loss, or P&L, statement.

Initial Public Offering (IPO): The first time a company sells shares of its stock to the public. Also known as going public.

Institutional Investors: Accredited companies, organizations, and investment firms that invest capital in entrepreneurial companies.

Intangible Asset: An asset that is not physical in nature, including a company's customer list, patents, and name.

Interest: The charge for the privilege of borrowing money, typically expressed as an annual percentage rate. Also refers to the amount of ownership a stockholder has in a company, usually expressed as a percentage.

Interest Rate: The monthly effective rate paid (or received if you are a creditor) on borrowed money. Expressed as a percentage of the sum borrowed.

Internal Rate of Return (IRR): The return on an investment with consideration to the length of the period of the investment.

Inventory: An asset on a company's balance sheet. Can be raw materials, finished items already available for sale, or those in the process of being manufactured.

Inventory Turns: Measures the number of times inventory is sold and replenished during a time period. It measures the speed at which inventory is turned into sales.

Investment: The outlay of money, usually for income or profit.

Investment Agreement: Has four principal business objectives. First, it establishes the detailed terms of the investment and the specific provisions of the financing (warrants, preferred stock, etc.). Second, it creates and regulates the operation of the enterprise through required covenants such as the submission of periodic financial statements or the maintenance of key financial ratios. Third, it provides fundamental disclosures during the investment process through representations and warranties. Finally, it establishes the conditions that must exist prior to the investment being made by the venture capital firm. Also known as the term sheet.

Leveraged Buyout (LBO): The acquisition of a company primarily financed through debt.

Liquidity Ratio: Measures a company's ability to meet its short-term payments.

Lock-Up Period: The period after an initial public offering when company insiders are prohibited from selling their shares. Lock-up periods typically last 180 days.

Long-Term Assets: The value of a company's property, equipment, and other capital assets, less depreciation.

Long-Term Debt: Debt that is repaid over a period that is more than 1 year.

Long-Term Liabilities: A company's liabilities for leases, bond repayments, and other items due in more than 1 year.

Management Buyout (MBO): A leveraged buyout where the acquiring group is led by the firm's management.

Mezzanine Capital: Subordinated debt with equity warrants.

Multiple of Cashflow: A number that is multiplied by the company's cashflow to determine the company's value.

Multiple of Free Cashflow: A number that is multiplied by the company's FCF to determine the company's value.

Multiple of Gross Margin: A number that is multiplied by the company's gross margin to determine its value.

Multiple of Revenue: A number that is multiplied by the company's revenue to determine its value.

Net Income: A company's total earnings, reflecting revenues adjusted for costs of doing business, depreciation, interest, taxes, and other expenses.

Net Operating Income: Measures income generated from operations without regard to the company's financing and taxes.

Net Profit Margin: Measures the net profit margin that the company is achieving on sales.

Net Working Capital: A measure of the company's ability to pay its bills or the company's short-term financial strength.

Net Worth: The difference between a company's total assets and total liabilities. Also known as stockholders' equity.

Nonrecourse Factor: A factor that buys accounts receivable with the agreement that it will assume all of the risk of collecting the receivables.

Operating Expenses: The tangible and intangible (depreciation and amortization) expenses required to operate the day-to-day activities of a company. Also known as sales, general, and administrative expenses.

Operating Plan: Information provided in the business plan that explains the day-to-day operations of the company.

Postmoney Valuation: A company's value, using whatever method the entrepreneur chooses, before the investment. It means the premoney valuation plus the amount of the equity investment.

Premoney Valuation: A company's value, using whatever method the entrepreneur chooses, before the investment.

Price-to-Earnings (P/E) Ratio: Measures the price investors are willing to pay for a company's stock for each dollar of the company's earnings.

Private Placement: The sale of a bond or other security directly to a limited number of investors, which avoids the need for SEC registration if the securities are purchased for investment as opposed to resale.

Private Placement Memorandum: A capital-raising document that is used for a private placement.

Pro Formas: Financial statements with at least 3 years—one current and two future—of financial projections and three scenarios—a best, worst, and most likely case.

Proactive Analysis: An analysis of financial statements that is used by entrepreneurs to better manage their company, influence the business decisions of a company's managers, and attract capital from investors and creditors.

Profit and Loss (P&L) Statement: *See* Income Statement.

Public Equity Market: A marketplace in which shares, options, and futures on stocks, bonds, commodities, and indexes are traded (e.g., NYSE, NASDAQ, etc.).

Purchase Order Financing: Capital that is provided to a company using existing sales orders as collateral.

Quick Ratio or Acid Ratio: Measures liquidity and assesses whether current bills can be paid without selling inventory or other illiquid current assets.

Recourse Factor: A factor that buys accounts receivable with the agreement that it will be reimbursed by the client for receivables that cannot be collected.

Regulation A: A Federal Reserve Board regulation that exempts small public offerings, valued at less than $1.5 million, from most registration requirements with the SEC.

Retained Earnings: The percentage of net earnings not paid out in dividends but retained by the company to be reinvested in its core business or to pay debt.

Return on Equity: Measures return on invested capital.

Return on Investment (ROI): The amount earned on a company's total capital, expressed as a percentage.

Revenues Analysis: The analysis of a company's historical annual revenue.

Risk Capital: *See* Equity Capital.

Road Show: A promotional presentation by an issuer of securities to potential buyers about the desirable qualities of the investments.

Securities and Exchange Commission (SEC): A federal agency that regulates the U.S. financial markets. The SEC also oversees the securities industry and promotes full disclosure in order to protect the investing public against malpractice in the securities markets.

Senior Debt: Debt whose terms in the event of bankruptcy require it to be repaid before subordinated debt holders receive any payment.

Series A Investment: The first round of investments.

Series B Investment: The second round of investments.

Short-Term Debt: Debt that is repaid over a period that is less than 1 year.

Simple Interest: The rate of growth relative to only the initial investment or original principal of a loan.

Small-Business Investment Company (SBIC): A privately owned equity investment firm that is licensed and regulated by the SBA.

Small Corporate Offering Registration (SCOR): A direct public offering where the entrepreneur has 12 months to raise a maximum of $1 million.

Sole Proprietorship: A business organization that is unincorporated and has only one owner.

Specialized Small-Business Investment Company (SSBIC): Privately owned equity investment firm that is licensed and regulated by the SBA. Underserved markets, including minority and women entrepreneurs, are targeted.

Start-Up: A company that is created on the basis of an idea, product, or service.

Statement of Cashflow: Explains changes in cashflows resulting from operations, investing, and financing activities.

Strategic Buyers: Corporate buyers that purchase companies for strategic synergistic reasons and typically are willing to pay more than other investors in all sectors.

Subordinate Debt: Debt over which senior debt takes priority. In the event of bankruptcy, subordinated debt holders receive payment only after senior debt claims are paid in full. Also known as sub debt.

Tangible Assets: An asset that has physical form.

Taxes: A levy on corporations or individuals enforced by a level of government to finance government activities.

Term Sheet: *See* Investment Agreement.

Thin Float: A public equity offering where most of the company's stock is controlled by insiders such as the management team and other employees.

Valuation: Estimate of the worth or price of a company.

Value-Added Investor: An equity or debt investor that provides supporting services (e.g., professional services, staff recruitment, referrals, advice, etc.) in addition to providing capital.

Venture Banks: Banking institutions that provide equity capital.

Venture Capital: *See* Equity Capital.

Venture Capital Method: A process in which a potential investment is valued by first forecasting the future value of an investment at exit and then discounting that value to the present using a large discount rate.

Working Capital: Current assets minus current liabilities.

APPENDIX A

The following table looks at the national averages for corporate gross profit, net income, and return on equity. The data were compiled by BizStats.com using 4.7 million U.S. corporate income tax returns.

TABLE A-1

Industry Profitability—Corporations

Construction	Total Active Corporations	Cost of Goods Sold, %	Gross Profit, %	Net Income as % of Sales	Net Income as % of Book Equity
General building contractors	180,935	85.3%	14.7%	1.9%	22.1%
Operative builders	1,843	69.2%	30.8%	4.0%	14.7%
Heavy construction contractors	23,071	77.8%	22.2%	3.2%	11.1%
Plumbing, heating, and A/C	50,435	71.3%	28.7%	2.6%	24.3%
Electrical contractors	35,076	71.1%	28.9%	3.6%	29.0%
Other special trade contractors	196,423	66.3%	33.7%	3.3%	28.6%

continued on next page

T A B L E   A-1

Industry Profitability—Corporations (continued)

Retail trade	Total Active Corporations	Cost of Goods Sold, %	Gross Profit, %	Net Income as % of Sales	Net Income as % of Book Equity
Building material dealers	20,171	73.4%	26.6%	3.4%	15.6%
Hardware stores	10,677	67.4%	32.6%	0.6%	4.1%
Garden supplies	12,502	72.2%	27.8%	2.1%	14.9%
General merchandise stores	9,835	70.3%	29.7%	2.8%	13.1%
Grocery stores	45,534	75.6%	24.4%	1.4%	18.4%
Other food stores	27,374	61.8%	38.2%	2.1%	20.9%
Motor vehicle dealers	42,289	88.3%	11.7%	0.8%	17.5%
Gasoline service stations	31,376	84.5%	15.5%	0.7%	11.7%
Other automotive dealers	33,953	72.2%	27.8%	2.0%	15.8%
Apparel and accessory stores	39,420	58.7%	41.3%	3.5%	15.3%
Furniture and home furnishings stores	48,678	64.7%	35.3%	1.6%	9.5%
Eating and drinking places	215,393	43.3%	56.7%	2.5%	15.0%
Drugstores and proprietary stores	17,619	74.7%	25.3%	2.3%	8.9%
Liquor stores	14,407	80.0%	20.0%	1.0%	11.5%
Other retail stores	204,705	64.9%	35.1%	2.1%	12.2%

Wholesale trade	Total Active Corporations	Cost of Goods Sold, %	Gross Profit, %	Net Income as % of Sales	Net Income as % of Book Equity
Groceries and related products	29,201	86.2%	13.8%	1.0%	15.5%
Machinery, equipment, and supplies	55,650	75.3%	24.7%	3.4%	20.5%
Motor vehicles and automotive equipment	27,667	77.8%	22.2%	1.3%	9.5%
Furniture and home furnishings	9,978	70.4%	29.6%	3.3%	28.6%
Lumber and construction materials	16,413	82.0%	18.0%	1.8%	17.0%
Toys, sporting, and photographic goods	12,537	72.0%	28.0%	2.6%	26.8%
Metals and minerals	6,377	89.5%	10.5%	1.6%	9.0%
Electrical goods	30,004	81.1%	18.9%	1.0%	8.2%
Hardware, plumbing, and heating equipment	14,301	75.8%	24.2%	2.7%	15.6%

continued on next page

T A B L E   A-1

Industry Profitability—Corporations (continued)

Wholesale trade	Total Active Corporations	Cost of Goods Sold, %	Gross Profit, %	Net Income as % of Sales	Net Income as % of Book Equity
Other durable goods	53,381	79.4%	20.6%	1.7%	13.6%
Paper and paper products	11,362	76.0%	24.0%	1.4%	5.5%
Drugs and drugstore sundries	5,997	87.5%	12.5%	0.8%	5.4%
Apparel, piece goods, and notions	18,656	75.3%	24.7%	3.2%	21.2%
Farm-product raw materials	7,723	92.7%	7.3%	0.6%	4.5%
Chemicals and allied products	9,079	77.7%	22.3%	1.9%	11.9%
Petroleum and petroleum products	13,828	88.9%	11.1%	1.1%	7.8%
Alcoholic beverages	4,615	74.7%	25.3%	3.1%	22.3%
Other nondurable goods	43,985	79.0%	21.0%	2.1%	17.5%

Services	Total Active Corporations	Cost of Goods Sold, %	Gross Profit, %	Net Income as % of Sales	Net Income as % of Book Equity
Hotels and other lodging places	30,636	41.3%	58.7%	4.4%	9.8%
Personal services	95,807	30.8%	69.2%	5.4%	17.9%
Advertising	35,693	43.9%	56.1%	2.7%	14.8%
Miscellaneous business services	407,400	35.7%	64.3%	4.8%	16.8%
Auto repair and services	98,333	44.3%	55.7%	1.3%	9.4%
Miscellaneous repair services	51,292	56.4%	43.6%	3.3%	21.2%
Motion picture production and distribution	20,925	46.5%	53.5%	2.7%	2.6%
Motion picture theaters	1,711	28.8%	71.2%	2.5%	5.7%
Other amusement and recreation services	102,948	32.2%	67.8%	4.7%	9.4%
Offices of physicians	127,872	4.5%	95.5%	1.2%	38.7%
Offices of dentists	47,344	3.6%	96.4%	3.6%	77.1%
Offices of other health practitioners	39,721	12.6%	87.4%	5.2%	61.2%
Nursing and personal care facilities	15,303	12.0%	88.0%	1.1%	5.1%
Hospitals	1,493	9.9%	90.1%	1.5%	1.4%
Medical laboratories	6,567	19.8%	80.2%	-5.6%	-12.9%
Other medical services	45,299	35.9%	64.1%	0.5%	2.3%
Legal services	72,848	1.6%	98.4%	4.8%	101.5%

continued on next page

TABLE A-1

Industry Profitability—Corporations (continued)

Services	Total Active Corporations	Cost of Goods Sold, %	Gross Profit, %	Net Income as % of Sales	Net Income as % of Book Equity
Educational services	23,810	22.7%	77.3%	1.7%	11.6%
Social services	21,400	16.7%	83.3%	1.9%	13.0%
Membership organizations	14,971	43.2%	56.8%	3.1%	6.7%
Accounting and auditing services	42,037	9.8%	90.2%	5.4%	66.5%
Miscellaneous services	218,629	34.1%	65.9%	2.1%	10.5%

Manufacturing	Total Active Corporations	Cost of Goods Sold, %	Gross Profit, %	Net Income as % of Sales	Net Income as % of Book Equity
Meat products	3,843	85.4%	14.6%	1.7%	11.0%
Dairy products	1,180	75.6%	24.4%	2.3%	14.3%
Preserved fruits and vegetables	730	65.0%	35.0%	5.9%	13.0%
Grain mill products	1,352	62.8%	37.2%	6.1%	17.5%
Bakery products	5,354	56.0%	44.0%	3.8%	19.4%
Sugar and confectionery products	884	64.8%	35.2%	6.3%	12.6%
Malt liquors and malt	35	42.2%	57.8%	10.1%	19.5%
Alcoholic beverages, except malt liquors	1,407	58.2%	41.8%	14.6%	4.3%
Bottled soft drinks and flavorings	653	52.5%	47.5%	9.8%	21.2%
Other food and kindred products	4,218	74.2%	25.8%	3.2%	10.1%
Tobacco manufacturers	45	39.5%	60.5%	0.0%	0.0%
Weaving mills and textile finishings	1,477	75.4%	24.6%	2.8%	9.4%
Knitting mills	552	74.3%	25.7%	3.0%	11.0%
Other textile mill products	3,048	75.4%	24.6%	3.6%	13.7%
Men's and boys' clothing	1,391	69.7%	30.3%	7.0%	22.5%
Women's and children's clothing	4,468	72.0%	28.0%	2.6%	16.8%
Other apparel and accessories	5,852	68.3%	31.7%	1.3%	9.7%
Miscellaneous fabricated textile products	5,154	72.8%	27.2%	2.3%	11.0%
Logging, sawmills, and planing mills	11,694	77.4%	22.6%	1.1%	2.9%
Millwork, plywood, and related products	4,318	76.7%	23.3%	2.2%	5.4%

continued on next page

T A B L E   A-1

Industry Profitability—Corporations (continued)

Manufacturing	Total Active Corporations	Cost of Goods Sold, %	Gross Profit, %	Net Income as % of Sales	Net Income as % of Book Equity
Other wood products	6,394	74.4%	25.6%	5.1%	25.3%
Furniture and fixtures	11,372	66.4%	33.6%	0.0%	0.0%
Pulp, paper, and board mills	293	71.6%	28.4%	1.9%	3.2%
Other paper products	3,749	69.2%	30.8%	5.9%	17.2%
Newspapers	5,936	31.7%	68.3%	14.9%	25.2%
Periodicals	4,825	42.3%	57.7%	1.9%	4.5%
Books, greeting cards, and other publishing	11,890	35.1%	64.9%	5.9%	5.2%
Commercial and other printing services	29,942	61.5%	38.5%	3.9%	18.0%
Industrial chemicals, plastics and synthetics	4,219	67.8%	32.2%	7.4%	12.5%
Drugs	2,536	43.2%	56.8%	15.4%	22.8%
Soaps, cleaners, and toilet goods	3,056	61.9%	38.1%	11.5%	33.7%
Paints and allied products	533	56.5%	43.5%	7.0%	19.0%
Agriculture and other chemical products	3,159	68.8%	31.2%	5.0%	11.3%
Petroleum refining	224	78.8%	21.2%	6.6%	10.7%
Petroleum and coal products	1,151	71.7%	28.3%	-1.8%	-9.4%
Rubber products, hose, and belting	1,933	67.7%	32.3%	5.7%	22.8%
Miscellaneous plastics products	10,363	69.4%	30.6%	4.8%	19.1%
Footwear, except rubber	191	64.0%	36.0%	4.0%	14.2%
Leather and leather products	1,203	70.7%	29.3%	1.6%	6.8%
Glass products	1,199	60.3%	39.7%	5.8%	14.6%
Cement, hydraulic	226	60.7%	39.3%	14.3%	23.9%
Concrete, gypsum, and plaster products	4,730	65.8%	34.2%	8.2%	28.4%
Other nonmetallic mineral products	3,571	65.5%	34.5%	4.0%	11.9%
Ferrous and primary metal products	2,189	75.6%	24.4%	2.5%	8.2%
Nonferrous metal industries	2,050	81.1%	18.9%	4.4%	11.2%
Metal cans and shipping containers	209	78.8%	21.2%	1.8%	4.2%
Cutlery, hand tools, and hardware	3,059	59.2%	40.8%	13.4%	24.0%
Plumbing and heating, except electric	995	65.1%	34.9%	7.5%	15.4%
Fabricated structural metal products	9,448	73.3%	26.7%	5.8%	21.2%

continued on next page

T A B L E   A-1

Industry Profitability—Corporations (continued)

Manufacturing	Total Active Corporations	Cost of Goods Sold, %	Gross Profit, %	Net Income as % of Sales	Net Income as % of Book Equity
Metal forgings and stampings	4,916	74.3%	25.7%	5.1%	22.7%
Coating, engraving, and allied services	3,468	62.7%	37.3%	6.4%	25.3%
Ordnance and accessories	970	70.3%	29.7%	6.4%	33.2%
Miscellaneous fabricated metal products	23,529	68.0%	32.0%	6.4%	25.5%
Farm machinery	1,984	62.9%	37.1%	8.8%	27.7%
Construction and related machinery	2,457	72.4%	27.6%	7.9%	24.4%
Metalworking machinery	9,635	65.2%	34.8%	6.1%	19.8%
Special industry machinery	3,481	66.3%	33.7%	4.5%	12.8%
General industrial machinery	4,385	64.5%	35.5%	8.1%	19.6%
Computers and office machines	3,782	62.2%	37.8%	8.2%	26.4%
Other machinery, except electrical	7,157	70.6%	29.4%	4.7%	16.6%
Household appliances	718	73.7%	26.3%	3.2%	15.1%
Radio, TV, and communication equipment	3,182	63.3%	36.7%	4.6%	14.9%
Electronic components and accessories	12,407	66.4%	33.6%	8.1%	17.9%
Other electrical equipment	7,816	58.4%	41.6%	8.2%	13.2%
Motor vehicles and equipment	2,789	77.2%	22.8%	3.6%	11.1%
Aircraft, guided missiles, and parts	870	76.5%	23.5%	5.2%	21.1%
Ship and boat building and repairing	2,066	74.0%	26.0%	3.8%	10.5%
Other transportation equipment	1,438	74.7%	25.3%	5.5%	17.2%
Scientific instruments, watches, and clocks	3,169	67.3%	32.7%	6.7%	17.3%
Optical, medical, and ophthalmic goods	5,028	51.0%	49.0%	6.3%	10.7%
Photographic equipment and supplies	186	51.6%	48.4%	9.2%	21.8%
Miscellaneous manufacturing	31,315	61.6%	38.4%	4.8%	15.4%

continued on next page

T A B L E   A-1

Industry Profitability—Corporations (continued)

Transportation and public utilities	Total Active Corporations	Cost of Goods Sold, %	Gross Profit, %	Net Income as % of Sales	Net Income as % of Book Equity
Railroad transportation	780	28.1%	71.9%	3.1%	2.1%
Local and interurban passenger transit	18,155	19.6%	80.4%	2.0%	10.8%
Trucking and warehousing	82,313	29.4%	70.6%	2.6%	14.4%
Water transportation	8,911	52.6%	47.4%	4.5%	10.7%
Air transportation	8,680	22.3%	77.7%	5.4%	22.4%
Pipelines, except natural gas	280	40.8%	59.2%	32.8%	116.1%
Other transportation services	48,373	63.5%	36.5%	1.6%	12.2%
Telephone and other communication services	17,302	26.5%	73.5%	7.3%	9.2%
Radio and television broadcasting	8,787	19.9%	80.1%	2.6%	3.1%
Electric services	963	46.1%	53.9%	11.7%	10.9%
Gas production and distribution	1,081	79.7%	20.3%	0.3%	0.7%
Combination utility services	126	44.6%	55.4%	10.5%	13.2%
Water supply and other sanitary services	13,661	27.8%	72.2%	5.6%	9.9%

Finance, insurance, and real estate	Total Active Corporations	Cost of Goods Sold, %	Gross Profit, %	Net Income as % of Sales	Net Income as % of Book Equity
Mutual savings banks	206	20.6%	79.4%	222.7%	17.5%
Bank holding companies	5,225	0.8%	99.2%	78.4%	8.8%
Banks	3,820	0.4%	99.6%	21.9%	11.2%
Savings and loan associations	1,803	5.4%	94.6%	59.3%	17.1%
Personal credit institutions	3,804	20.4%	79.6%	13.7%	6.6%
Business credit institutions	2,387	1.5%	98.5%	18.3%	9.3%
Other credit agencies	25,845	12.6%	87.4%	26.2%	12.3%
Security brokers and services	10,468	2.2%	97.8%	21.8%	17.8%
Commodity brokers and dealers	14,944	8.1%	91.9%	12.4%	17.7%
Life insurance companies	1,685	74.1%	25.9%	7.0%	8.5%
Mutual property and casualty insurance companies	1,723	67.0%	33.0%	7.6%	8.1%

continued on next page

TABLE A-1

Industry Profitability—Corporations (continued)

Finance, insurance, and real estate	Total Active Corporations	Cost of Goods Sold, %	Gross Profit, %	Net Income as % of Sales	Net Income as % of Book Equity
Stock property and casualty insurance companies	3,648	68.4%	31.6%	6.2%	5.3%
Insurance agents, brokers, and services	78,717	15.4%	84.6%	8.6%	18.3%
Real estate operators and building lessors	219,034	12.5%	87.5%	10.4%	5.6%
Lessors of mining, oil, and similar property	1,636	0.0%	100.0%	121.9%	20.2%
Lessors of railroad and other real property	3,594	0.0%	100.0%	34.1%	9.2%
Condominium management and housing associations	47,259	7.8%	92.2%	-3.2%	-2.2%
Subdividers and developers	64,645	75.4%	24.6%	3.1%	4.5%
Other real estate services	181,963	21.4%	78.6%	4.4%	8.2%
Small-business investment companies	8,284	0.0%	100.0%	7.6%	2.0%
Other holding and investment companies	54,088	36.8%	63.2%	68.7%	6.7%

Agriculture, forestry, and fishing	Total Active Corporations	Cost of Goods Sold, %	Gross Profit, %	Net Income as % of Sales	Net Income as % of Book Equity
Agricultural production	91,164	52.8%	47.2%	2.5%	6.5%
Agricultural services, forestry, and fishing	71,950	61.2%	38.8%	2.4%	14.7%

Mining	Total Active Corporations	Cost of Goods Sold, %	Gross Profit, %	Net Income as % of Sales	Net Income as % of Book Equity
Copper/lead/gold/silver ores	1,159	55.7%	44.3%	-0.6%	-0.3%
Other metal mining	527	73.9%	26.1%	5.1%	6.3%
Coal mining	1,521	68.9%	31.1%	3.9%	3.8%

continued on next page

T A B L E   A-1

Industry Profitability—Corporations (continued)

Mining	Total Active Corporations	Cost of Goods Sold, %	Gross Profit, %	Net Income as % of Sales	Net Income as % of Book Equity
Crude petroleum and natural gas	13,772	58.3%	41.7%	6.3%	4.1%
Oil and gas field services	12,208	48.2%	51.8%	13.5%	16.3%
Crushed stone, sand, and gravel	3,414	62.6%	37.4%	7.0%	6.1%
Other nonmetallic minerals	396	71.1%	28.9%	2.6%	4.0%

Source: BizStat.com.

APPENDIX B

The following table notes a number of U.S. funds that target minority markets.

TABLE B-1

U.S. Funds Focused on Minority Markets

Firm Name	Location	Industry or Other Specialty	Stage	Geographic Focus	Contact Information
21st Century Group	Dallas, TX	Diversified	Diversified	National	Kelvin Walker (kwalker@hmtf.co)
Ascend Venture Group	New York, NY	Businesses leveraging emerging technologies	Early, expansion, later	Northeast, West Coast	Felicia Allen (fallen@ascendventures.com)
Atlantic Coastal Ventures, LP	Washington, DC	Converging technologies	Early, expansion, later	Northeast, Southeast	Walter Threadgill (wthreadgill@atlanticcv.com)
Black Enterprise/ Greenwich Street	New York, NY	Telecom, consumer goods, media financial services	Expansion, acquisition buyouts and successions	National	Ed Williams (ed.a.williams@citi.com)
Blue Capital Management, LLC	New York, NY/ Los Angeles, CA	Healthcare, business services, manufacturing, distribution	Expansion, later, acquisition	National	Robert Taylor (roberttaylor@bluecapital.com)
Broadcast Capital, Inc.	Washington, DC	Communications	Expansion, later, acquisition	National	John Oxendine (broadcap@aol.com)
Dearborn Capital Corporation	Dearborn, MI	Automotive suppliers, service, manufacturing, processing	Expansion, later, acquisition	Midwest	William Lang (wlang2@ford.com)
East Coast Venture Capital	New York, NY	Transportation	Expansion	National	Zindel Zelmanovitch (fstart@aol.com)
Fairview Capital Partners	Farmington, CT	Private equity fund of funds, diversified	Diversified	National	Edwin S. Shirley (eshirley@fairviewcapital.com)
Fleet Development Ventures	Boston, MA	Diversified	Diversified	National	Daniel Coleman (daniel_e_coleman@fleet.com)
Fulcrum Venture Capital Corporation	Culver City, CA	Diversified	Expansion, later, acquisition	National (West Coast emphasis)	Brian Argrett (brian@fulcrumventures.com)
Ibero American Investors Corporation	Rochester, NY	Diversified	Expansion, later, acquisition	National	Domingo Garcia (domingo@iberoinvestors.com)

continued on next page

TABLE B-1

U.S. Funds Focused on Minority Markets (continued)

Firm Name	Location	Industry or Other Specialty	Stage	Geographic Focus	Contact Information
ICV Capital Partners	New York, NY	Food processing, consumer products & services, industrial manufacturing, healthcare	Expansion, later, acquisition	National (emphasis on urban areas)	Grace Bianchi (gbianchi@icvcapital.com)
LaSalle Bank	Chicago, IL	Diversified	Diversified	National	Torrence Moore (torrence.moore@abnamro.com)
Medallion Capital, Inc.	Minneapolis, MN	Diversified	Expansion, acquisition	National	Dean Pickerell (dpickerell@medallioncapital.com)
Miami Ventures Asset Management, LLC	Miami, FL	Diversified	Diversified	National	John Hall (Jhall@mvfunds.com)
Milestone Growth Fund	Minneapolis, MN	Diversified	Expansion, later, acquisition	National (primarily Minnesota)	Judy Romlin (jromlin@milestonegrowth.com)
MMG Ventures	Baltimore, MD	Health care, information technology, telecommunications	Expansion, later, acquisition	Mid-Atlantic	Stanley Tucker (stanley.tucker@mmggroup.com)
Momentum Ventures	Washington, DC	Franchise development and expansion, education e-commerce applications	Diversified	Mid-Atlantic	Lloyd Arrington (nedcoedfc@aol.com)
New Vista Capital	Palo Alto, CA	Technology	Early, expansion	National	Frank Greene (fgreene@nvcap.com)
Nogales Investors, LLC	Los Angeles, CA	Diversified (with the exception of tech and real estate)	Expansion, later	National (West Coast emphasis)	Luis Nogales (lnogales@noglesinvestors.com)
Opportunity Capital Partners	Fremont, CA	Health care, information technology, telecommunications	Early, later, acquisition	National (West Coast emphasis)	Peter Thompson (jpt@ocpcapital.com)
Pacesetter Capital Group	Dallas, TX	Diversified	Early, later, acquisition	National (Southwest emphasis)	Donald Lawhorne (drl@pacesettercapital.com)
Pharos Capital Group, LLC	Dallas, TX	Healthcare, technology, business services	Expansion, later	National	Kneeland Youngblood (kyoungblood@pharosfunds.com)
Polestar Capital Partners	Chicago, IL	Applied technology, manufacturing	Early, expansion	National (Midwest emphasis)	John Doerer (jd@polestarvc.com)
Progress Investment Management	San Francisco, CA	Private equity fund of funds, diversified	Diversified	National	Thurman White (thurman@progressinvestment.com)

continued on next page

333

T A B L E B-1

U.S. Funds Focused on Minority Markets (continued)

Firm Name	Location	Industry or Other Specialty	Stage	Geographic Focus	Contact Information
Provender Capital Group	New York, NY/ Los Angeles, CA	Specialty dinance, multi-unit operations, specialty retail, consumer goods	Expansion, later, acquisition	National	Frederick Terrell (fterrell@provender-capital.com)
Quetzal/JP Morgan Partners	New York, NY	Communications, media	Expansion, later	National	Lauren Tyler (Lauren.Tyler@JPMorganPartners.com)
Reliant Equity Partners	Chicago, IL	Automotive, manufacturing, consumer & industrial products, health care, telecommunications	Buyout & recap, growth equity, buy & build	National	Carr Preston (cpreston@reliantequity.com)
SB/Shorbank Capital Corporation	Chicago, IL	Diversified	Expansion, later	National	David Shryock (dave@sbpartners.com)
Smith Whiley & Company	Hartford, CT/ Chicago, IL	Diversified products & services, communications & technology	Special situations (equity & mezzanine debt)	National	Gwendolyn Iloani (iloanig@smithwhiley.com)
Southern Africa Enterprise Dev. Fund	Johannesburg, RSA	Diversified	Diversified	Southern Africa	Steven Weddell (rkelley@saedf.org.za)
Syncom Management Company, Inc.	Silver Spring, MD	Communications (broadcast, pcs, broadband, Internet)	Early	National	Herbert Wilkins, Sr. (hwilkinssr@syncomfunds.com)
Telecommunications Development Fund	Washington, D.C.	Communications	Seed & early	National	Ginger Lew (ginger.lew@tdfund.com)
Triad Capital Corporation	New York, NY	Diversified	Expansion, acquisition	National (including Puerto Rico)	Marcial Robiou (mrobiou@bcf-triad.org)
TSG Capital Group	Stamford, CT	Communications, manufacturing, specialty retail	Buyout	National	Cleveland Christophe (cleve@tsgcapital.com)
Bank of America*	Chicago, IL	Diversified	Diversified	National	Ed Powers (edward.powers@bankofamerica.com)
Edwards & Angell, LLP*	West Palm Beach, FL	Legal Services	N/A	National	Pamela Robertson (probertson@ealaw.com)
Goldman Sachs Urban Investment Group*	New York, NY	Diversified	Diversified	National	Richard Roberts (richard.roberts@gs.com)
Leventhal, Senter & Lerman, PLLC*	Washington, D.C.	Legal Services	N/A	National	S. Jenell Trigg, Esq. (strigg@lsl-law.com)

INDEX

the world
book of
CHILDREN'S
GAMES

the world book of

written and designed by

CHILDREN'S
GAMES

ARNOLD ARNOLD

WORLD PUBLISHING
TIMES MIRROR
NEW YORK

Published by The World Publishing Company
Published simultaneously in Canada
by Nelson, Foster & Scott Ltd.
First printing—1972

Library of Congress catalog card number: 77-142134
ISBN 0-529-00778-9
Printed in the United States of America

WORLD PUBLISHING
TIMES MIRROR

Contents

To Gail, Francis, Marguerite
and Geoffrey;
to Buster, to the chipmunks,
to the ducks and to the turtles;
to the trees, to the grass,
to the wind on the water;
to the sun, to mud puddles and
to the lines on concrete pavements;
and to all the people and things
that awaken me to playfulness.

Introduction

This book addresses itself to parents, to teachers, to recreational, park, playground, and street supervisors of children's play, and to children. It includes selected indoor and outdoor games, other than formal sports, for children from preschool through elementary school ages. Older children and teen-agers can similarly enjoy some of these. I have made the selection and adapted the rules with special consideration of today's child life at home, in the school, and in the community.

There is a special need for this book at this time. Family life and childhood traditions are now threatened with destruction in an environment that is essentially hostile to child development. Crowded cities, suburbs, and schools; the lack of safe play spaces and fresh air; and TV addiction conspire to destroy the spirit of spontaneous play and the culture of childhood.

In her introduction to Alice Gomme's *The Traditional Games of England, Scotland and Ireland,* the folklorist Dorothy Howard expresses the hope that with republication of this classic, "children's folk lore is climbing the ladder of academic and scholarly respectability on this side of the ocean." But at the same time she deplores "appropriating old games and revamping them to fit supervised play programs . . . to transmit by book the old games and play ways which children have transmitted to children on playgrounds for hundreds of years."[21]

It is obviously preferable when children can perpetuate this culture from generation to generation by word of mouth. But Miss Howard, like so many others, seems strangely unsympathetic to the restrictions placed on today's children by a hazardous society that inhibits their humanizing development and the spontaneous perpetuation of play culture. And so I have attempted to rescue a portion of this lore that is applicable by today's child from being abandoned entirely to the folk-lorist, to the cultural anthropologist, and to "academic respectability." It must remain the property of children, even when it needs to be kept alive for them by adults.

A definition of game-playing is difficult because it overlaps in some areas with play with toys. Much of children's play with toys is exploratory; some involves *role-playing*. But all game-playing involves acting out. A game can therefore be roughly classified as an activity in which the child assumes a particular role, as aggressor or defender, and characteristics of models outside himself. The common ground in play as in games is, in the words of the historian Johan Huizinga, "doing a thing for the sake of the thing itself."[23]

I have left out a number of game categories quite deliberately. Some seemed inappropriate to wide application by today's children. Others are so specialized that they should be, as some are, the subject of books of their own. Games with tops, games involving songs and stories, and string and finger games like Cat's Cradle are excluded, although I refer to them in the text and in the bibliography.[19, 22]

Each game in this book is prefaced with information that suggests the lowest age group to which it might be introduced. I am generally opposed to any age-grouping of activities, books, records, or toys, since each child differs from the next in development and in experience. But these games are predominantly group games, and so some average age-grouping seemed advisable. Games should be introduced to younger age groups on a trial basis. They must be halted or modified when children demonstrate their lack of enjoyment or their immaturity by being unable to cooperate, or when losing still overwhelms them.

Most of today's adults no longer know the large repertoire of childhood games with which previous generations were familiar. Spontaneous play opportunities were already restricted in their childhood. Our young parents and teachers are the first generation to have spent a large part of their growing years before TV sets. They therefore have little play and game information that they can transmit to their children. Teenagers, even when younger children have contact with them, suffer an even greater lack of informal game experience.

Until the beginning of this century the more mature children in the family predominantly cared for the younger ones. Preschoolers could observe their older brothers and sisters at play in fields, in gardens, in playgrounds, and in relatively safe residential streets. Two hundred years ago, the games of children past infancy were identical to those played by adults on village greens in the summer and before the hearth in winter. Children needed only to imitate what they saw their elders do all around them.

The industrial revolution first interrupted this general playfulness. The eighteenth-century German educator Friedrich Froebel recognized that such a lack of models might inhibit children's learning and maturation. He

suggested a system of education involving games—
"mother play"—that he hoped might serve as a substitute for spontaneous childhood culture. But it was soon
turned into a regimen of formal learning by the school-
masters and parents of that day.

Lately, play has been rediscovered as a learning in-
strument. But now it threatens to turn into yet another
form of child manipulation, of teaching the child "cog-
nitive" information, while neglecting the socializing
and experiential aspects of play.

Before a child can benefit from formal education, he
needs development of self-expression, inner controls,
coordination, and the faculties of whimsy, humor, curi-
osity, and foresight.[2] He must experience leadership
and learn to appreciate the need for submitting to rules.
He must be allowed to succeed and to learn how to
accept failure gracefully. He needs the enjoyment of
active participation in rewarding activities and of total

absorption. Games can help a child acquire some of these qualities and skills. Informal games allow every child, regardless of his talents or weaknesses, to participate as an equal with other children and to enjoy experiences that are essential to his future learning.

Many of today's school sports are organized so as to exclude all but the most able performers. The rest of the student body watches from the sidelines, a habit that is reinforced at home before the TV set. As a result, many are denied physical exercise and a foundation for social and academic learning. At the same time our children are severely regimented at home and in school, despite the lip service given to their emancipation. Adults vacillate from permissiveness to authoritarianism. Neither treatment allows children the exercise of making choices or of formulating rules for themselves in trial situations. Only a child who has these experiences early and often in play can learn to make distinctions between what is playful and what is merely ludicrous, or between aggressive pursuit of goals and antagonism.

As repeatedly stressed in the following chapters, children should be encouraged to make up and to agree to rules of their own invention, rather than to merely follow those that are given. Only then can they learn the fundamental rule that no game, nor any aspect of life, can be enjoyed without rules.

The "no-rule" idea that is central to many of today's youth attitudes is the product of their relative inexperience in social play. Today's child never has sufficient experience in play to realize that "no rules allowed" is in itself a rule. In order to play "the no-rule game" a whole raft of new rules naturally follow, whether or not anarchic players admit to them.[4]

I have included historic sidelights concerning the origins of some of the games I have adapted. Telling children about their history can help them establish a bond with the past. It will give them incentives for carrying this heritage forward into the future.

The following notes and comments are especially addressed to those who organize or supervise children's games at home or in school.

The Role of the Play Supervisor

An experienced teacher usually knows how much direction and supervision is required to organize groups of children. But despite this knowledge and the best of intentions, many manage to turn game-playing in class or in the playground into a form of discipline or even punishment. The role of the game supervisor should be restricted to suggesting and initiating play, helping children acquire the required skills, furnishing materials, and acting as arbiter when they are unable to manage on their own.

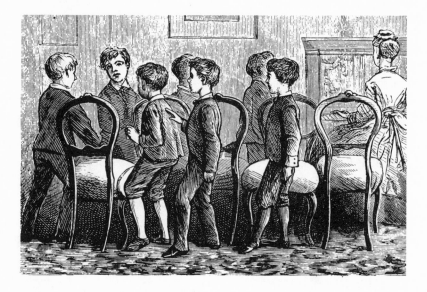

Preschool children need a great deal of help when they first play group games. They cannot be *made* to play. Regimentation will certainly kill their enthusiasm and their ability to learn how to handle the materials of play, how to follow rules, and how to take their turn. Older children should be encouraged to adapt given rules and to make up others, to improvise, and to regulate themselves and each other. They must be given opportunities to operate within their group as leaders and as followers. The presence of a respected and unobtrusive adult or teen-ager can serve as a regulating influence on school-age children's play.

The Rules of Games

Except in formal sports, like baseball, basketball, or football, that are governed by standard regulations, and especially when children are not especially sports-minded, it is best to encourage them to formulate rule variations by agreement among themselves. Stimulate group discussions beforehand on how the game is to be played. But insist on elimination of any rule that discriminates against unpopular, smaller, or weaker players, or that might lead to inflicting pain or causing damage.

Some play supervisors feel that a major lesson of game-playing for children is their submission to ordained rules. But in many instances, this merely leads to resistance or to passivity. Children can only recognize the value of rules and respect those that apply to games and to life in general if they are given opportunities for inventing rules and for trying them out.

Winning and Losing

It is important to realize that children below the age of 5 or 6 find it extremely difficult to accept the idea of losing. Organize game variations that involve neither winning nor losing. In game-playing by children of any age greatest emphasis should be placed on exuberance and on the fun of playing. Children, especially today, are sufficiently competitive without being driven to succeed even in their informal games. The very nature of games is competitive. Nothing is wrong with providing outlets for beneficial aggressive behavior.

But considerable damage can result from making winning seem the sole value, ahead of any others that are implicit in game-playing. So in most instances, do not reward the child or team who wins and do not condone forfeits or punishment of losers. Victory in a game won through skill and competence should be a sufficient reward. Losing should not lead to a sense of defeat. Instead, it can stimulate greater effort, or better co-ordination, or more concentration, or finer cooperation on the next occasion.

The play supervisor should suggest group games for young children in which each can experience accomplishment. And at a party, such as a birthday party, the adult in charge should arrange things so that each child wins something, if prizes are to be given. The idea is to make all the children happy, rather than to pit one against the next.

For these reasons among others, a number of variations are suggested for many of the games listed. Some require a losing member of a team to be "out" of the game when he fails or is tagged. Alternate rules allow such an "out" player to join the opposing side, the last remaining player of his original team being the winner. Other possibilities are to keep each team's turn "at bat" to a short period of time. Then the "out" players re-enter the game without a long wait. Still another option is the starting of a smaller side game for those who are eliminated from the larger one for the time being. Allowing a number of players to stand around aimlessly while the rest are at play can lead to unhappiness.

The informed play supervisor should address himself to issues such as these instead of becoming deeply involved in the game itself. If the game palls and interest lags, the supervisor should suggest another activity. This book contains dozens of possible games for every age group, and in using them the children may invent variations of their own. The leader should never insist on completing a given number of rounds of the same game before allowing a change of activity. This is how children lose interest in games and why they feel regimented by adults.

Counting Out, Choosing Team Captains and Sides

The tendency among many who organize and supervise games is to choose team captains or to allow each team to elect its own. In the first instance children sus-

pect favoritism, whether or not they are justified. In the second, teams may choose a leader merely because he is the most powerful member of that group. He may intimidate or bully the rest.

More important than fostering leadership in favored or in seemingly dominant children is to give every child a chance to experience authority and responsibility. Assign an order of play in which every player is a leader in turn. This is preferable to leaving the choice to children, to chance, or to counting out in which adroit youngsters can always manipulate the odds.

The following are some of the favored methods of selecting a player to be "it," choosing leaders, or deciding the order of play that children usually use when they play without supervision.

1. *Tossing a Coin.* Players are required to guess "heads" or "tails" of a coin flipped by one player. The first player to guess correctly is "it" or the first to play, and so on. Team selections can be made by all children flip-

ping coins, the "heads" joining one team and the "tails" the other. If the game requires equal-sized teams, coin-tossing continues among the larger team, until both are evened out.

2. *Drawing Straws.* The game organizer, or one of the players, holds a number of straws (or blades of grass, ribbons, or strings) in his hand. All but one are the same length. He holds them so that the rest of the players cannot tell which is the odd-sized one. Each player chooses one straw. That player who picks the odd-sized one is "it," goes first, or becomes leader of one of the teams. To choose teams, the game organizer selects an equal number of short and long straws and holds them out as before. Players are divided according to which size straw they pick.

3. *Odds or Evens.* The game organizer, or one of the players or team captains, holds out a number of fingers on both hands, behind his back, out of sight of the rest of the players. Each of the other players in turn then guesses whether the number of stretched-out fingers is odd or even, to decide teams, order of play, and so on. The game organizer can let each player see the number of his outstretched fingers after he has made his guess, and may then change the number for the next player.

4. *Racket Toss-up.* In games requiring a racket, the choice of first turn, team membership, or leadership of teams can be decided by flipping the racket and letting one side or the other determine the results, according to the side facing up at each toss.

5. *Hand-over-Hand.* In games requiring a bat (like Rounders), captains and order of play may be decided by one player tossing the bat to the next, who must catch it. The first player then grasps the bat directly above the hand of the second, who in turn grasps the next higher position with his other hand, and so on. The player whose hand comes closest to the top of the bat, still grasping it, but not placing any part of his hand beyond it, wins that decision, or joins a particular team.

6. *Playing-Card Choice.* If available, a deck of regular playing cards, one dealt to each player, may decide team captain, sides, or order of play. After one card has been dealt to each player, the player holding the highest card goes first, or becomes team captain, and so on. Sides can be chosen by putting those holding red cards on one team and those holding black cards on the other.

7. *Counting Rhymes.* Nursery and other special rhymes have been used from time immemorial to count out sides, to determine playing order, and to choose team leaders. One player recites the verse while the rest stand around in a circle. The reciting player points his finger at any player, chosen supposedly at random, and moves that finger from player to player on each succeeding word—(or it might be done on syllables or letters). The player to whom his finger is pointing at the last word of the counting rhyme is "it," the team leader, or the member of one team. For choosing sides, the counting out continues until the first team, equal in number to the remainder, is chosen. Any experienced child can cheat easily in counting out. He can choose on

Introduction

whom the last syllable falls, knowing with which player to start, or, as often happens, by skipping a child as he recites and points.[20] Following are a few old and common counting rhymes:

Eena, mena, mina, mo,
Catch an outlaw by the toe;
If he hollers, let him go,
Eena, mena, mina, mo !

Intery, mintery, cutery, corn,
Apple-seed and briar-thorn,
Wire, briar, limber lock,
Three geese in a flock;
One flew east, one flew west,
One flew over the cuckoo's nest
O-U-T, out !

Apples and oranges, two for a penny,
Takes a good scholar to count as many;
O-U-T, out goes she [or he].

Monkey, monkey, bottle of beer,
How many monkeys are there here?
1, 2, 3,
You are he [or she].

As I went up the apple-tree,
All the apples fell on me;
Bake a pudding, bake a pie,
Did you ever tell a lie?
Yes you did; you know you did,
You broke your mother's teapot lid.
L-I-D, that spells, lid.

Cheating

Cheating in games is more often a time-honored custom than a frowned-on practice in many adult societies. The unpardonable crime, in most cultures that accept cheating, is being caught in the act. But it is considered the height of cleverness to get away with it unnoticed. We also accept this practice in real life, though we insist on entirely different standards of behavior from our children, who naturally resent it.

It is far better to dramatize the socially disruptive effect of cheating than to moralize about it to children. Games are an ideal vehicle to teach this lesson. This concept is implied in the ritual and customs of those societies that realistically accept cheating as allowable behavior in real life as in games, subject to given rules. The shaming of those who are caught in the act serves better to inhibit cheating than a blanket prohibition.

For these reasons I suggest that you invite players, old enough to appreciate this idea, to cheat at games with the understanding that they may suffer banishment from the game if they are caught. Occasionally encourage a game in which all are invited to cheat without penalty. The game is bound to be sufficiently chaotic and unpleasant so that the players themselves will request an end to this rule.

Organizing the Game

Whether parent, street worker, professional teacher, or teen-ager, the game supervisor has a number of clearly defined responsibilities:

1. Become familiar with the requirements and rules for each game to be played. Furnish all the necessary equipment and materials before the game begins.

2. Have an understanding of children, their talents, abilities and disabilities.

3. Suggest only games that are within the competence of the age groups involved, and that are appropriate to their size, strength, and experience. Steer children away from games that are too complicated or too difficult at their stage of development.

4. Avoid overenthusiasm. Children rapidly spot and distrust fake enthusiasm and artificial cheer.

5. Be prepared to participate as a regular player, subject to all rules, including those that may seem to detract from adult dignity, if you are needed to even up teams. Otherwise watch from the side lines.

6. Help children who may not be as competent and well-coordinated as their age mates by assigning them jobs or positions that allow them the exercise of whatever skills they possess. A handicapped child may enjoy being timekeeper, scorekeeper, or referee in a game in which he himself cannot participate. Overlook mistakes of individual children, or quietly correct them without interrupting the game. Don't embarrass children or scold them in front of the others for an inadvertent infraction of rules, or error in play.

7. Explain one game at a time, and have the children play one or more trial games that don't "count" before the actual game begins. Have a number of alternate games and the required equipment available in advance, in case the children do not like the first game you suggested.

8. Let the children rest between games, as their ages and energy dictate.

9. Select games in a chronology of difficulty, starting with the simplest, and working up to more challenging ones as the children's skills improve through practice.

Special Suggestions for Preschool Children's Games

Preschool children cannot follow complicated rules. Choose games for young age groups that develop individual skills, like ball-throwing or hitting a target with a beanbag, rather than competitive team games. Gather preschool children around you as you explain what is expected and give demonstrations of what is to be done. Pick out one or two able children and allow them to demonstrate what you showed them. Then gradually involve more and more of the rest, until all or most of them are in the game. Have alternate activities ready for those who choose not to participate. Keep alert for the time when the interest of the playing children seems to wane. Then suggest that they vary game-playing with another activity, unless the children themselves insist on playing longer.

Preschool and early-grades children find it difficult to await taking turns. Some feel discriminated against when they are "it," though they may have enjoyed playing while others were "it." It is best to keep such children out of team games, until they can observe game-playing long and often enough to submit willingly to the discipline required to play them. Never force a child to participate.

Plan the time-span of such games to be short, and keep groups or teams small, so that all have a turn before the majority tire of the game. It is better to play several short rounds than to insist on a single long one.

Age Grouping

The games listed in this book state approximate age groups. But your knowledge and observation of the children in your charge are the best indicators of which games they are ready to play. Simplify the rules or change the game if it proves too difficult.

Regulation Games

This book includes only games that can be played informally at home, in classrooms, in schoolyards or backyards, on playgrounds, in parks, on play-streets and fields, or on beaches. Ample rule manuals for formal sports and regulation games exist for those who wish to learn to play them. The informal games listed in this book are a useful preparation for those that involve throwing, kicking, or other coordination. They have special appeal not only to young children, but also to older ones who are not especially athletic.

How to Use the Age, Place, and Materials Index of Games

In each chapter throughout this book, games are grouped in an ascending order of complexity. To facilitate location of games that are appropriate for particular age groups, all but the Strategic Games are listed

in the index at the end of this book, showing category, number of given variations, age group, the minimum number of required players, needed equipment, and the place where they can be played—indoors, at home, in the classroom, or in the gym; outdoors, on the beach, in the grass, in a car, on paved street or playground— and page number.

The age grouping of these games furnishes rough guidelines only, as experience and such developmental differences as size, strength, coordination, and intelligence vary from child to child and from group to group.

The Strategic Games are listed only by name, by the number of required players, and by page number, in an order of family relationships. They can be played wherever a game diagram can be scratched into the ground, drawn on a sidewalk or on a piece of paper.

These games are generally unsuitable for children below school age. Even older children need to play the more elementary games many times before they can develop the insight, planning ability, and logic required for the more difficult ones.

I

Ball, Bowling, Beanbag, and Balloon Games

The playing ball is probably the simplest and most readily available toy that lends itself to the greatest variety of games for a child alone or for children in groups. Any two or more children who meet for the first time, whether or not they speak the same language, will find an ordinary playing ball an immediate bridge to understanding.

The origins of ball games and sports go back many centuries. Most have evolved slowly through the ages. For example basketball, "invented" in 1892 in Springfield, Massachusetts, by Dr. James Naismith, was really adapted from a Floridian Indian game. The ball, the solid sphere and the inflated skin, predates historical times.

The first ball was probably a stone or a pebble, thrown as much as a weapon as for tests of skill. Its use in play was most likely a preparation for hunting, defense, or attack. A smooth, rounded stone obviously felt better in the hand and could be thrown farther than a jagged one. When it landed it rolled, so it lent itself better to games of skill in which control, rather than sheer strength, determined success. Many thousands of years must have gone by before man discovered that he himself could shape and polish stones, and so turn them into perfect spheres. A ball of this type which is more than 5,000 years old is exhibited in London's British Museum.

Only one or two isolated tribes exist anywhere in the world to whom the ball as a toy or as a weapon is unknown. Most civilizations have, at one time or another, attributed magical qualities to this shape and to games in which balls were used. One African society in the former French Cameroons still believes that during times of drought, girls can invoke rainfall through ritual ball-game playing.[6] In medieval times, choir boys played similar religious games.

A mural in an ancient Egyptian tomb at Beni Hasan shows two girls tossing a ball back and forth. In his epic *Odyssey*, the Greek poet Homer tells of ball games at the time of the siege of Troy. During the period in which Alexander the Great ruled, Athenians erected a statue to that ruler's favorite ball-player. Julius Caesar and Emperor Augustus were eager ball-players, as was Harun al-Rashid of *A Thousand and One Nights* fame. The Celts of pre-Christian Ireland played ball as a part of their religious rites. Neighboring villages contested for the possession of the sun, as represented by a ball made of an inflated goat-bladder. And the game of Handball is still a national sport in Ireland.

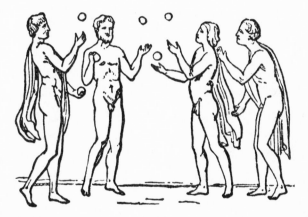

The citizens of European towns in the Middle Ages were so fond of ball games that they built special high-ceilinged arenas called "ball houses." Here they could play regardless of weather or season. The same halls were also used for singing and dancing contests. From this practice came the designations *ballad*, *ballet*, and *ball*—songs and dances that took their names from the places in which they were performed.

Today's spectators at ball parks and in front of TV sets may become noisily agitated or jubilant when their favorite teams lose or score. But their excitement is nothing compared to the enthusiasm or degree of spectator participation common at ball games in France in the seventeenth century. The game then popular was similar to Football. It led to serious injuries, fractures, and sometimes worse fates to both players and fans. Whole towns and villages would battle each other and at times feud for years over the outcome of games. Thus, in 1639, the French King Charles V banned all public games by royal decree. But they were so popular that even this prohibition had little effect.

Hurling, originally played by the Romans, and taken up by the British in the fifteenth century, gave birth to many of the rules of today's sports, such as Handball, Football, and Rugger. In the English version, houses that were miles apart were designated as goals. Players ranged over the countryside, converging on the ball-carrier "so as you shall sometimes see twenty or thirty lie tugging together in the water [of shallow streams and ditches] scrambling and scratching for the ball."[32]

Camp was the name of a football game known in England as early as the fourteenth century and not very different from the Greek and Norse Common Ball, or Ball Battle, and other games in which players were often severely wounded and sometimes killed. The name of this game probably came from the medieval German word *Kemp*, which meant warrior or champion. There the game of *Kemping*, played until late in the nineteenth century, consisted of one team of men hurling wooden balls, loaded with lead, against another team. The interrelationship of these various games is illustrated by the fact that nineteenth-century schoolboys in Massachusetts spoke of "camping" a ball, meaning to kick it.

The extremes of violence to which the games of five and six hundred years ago led in England caused them to be outlawed there as they were in France. King Edward III attempted to do so in 1349, giving as the excuse that ball-playing interfered with the practice of Archery among the population. King James I tried again to forbid such games in the seventeenth century, declaring that "From this court I debarre all rough and violent exercises, as the foot-ball, meeter for lameing than making able the users thereof."[32]

Balls have in various times and places been made of papyrus, plaited rushes, stone, marble, wood, pottery, terra cotta, and animal hides or cloth filled with hay, kapok, shavings, sawdust, and seeds. American Indians in pre-Columbian times played with balls made of sewn deer hides. And Japanese children, on special holidays, are still given balls made of tightly wadded tissue paper wound round with colored string. While the sap of the rubber tree was long used in South America and Africa for a variety of purposes, the invention of the solid bouncing ball had to await the discovery, early in the nineteenth century, of the process of vulcanizing rubber. Though many of today's sports balls are still made of rubber or have a rubber core or bladder, plastics are replacing this material in the manufacture of most balls for children.

Histories of some ball games, played by individuals or in groups, in which the ball is thrown, kicked, headed, rolled, or struck with a stick, mallet, bat, or racket, are treated briefly in the rules to certain games included in this selection. But no matter how a ball is used in play, it is a most satisfactory toy. It is not surprising that we enjoy it so much. It is symbolic of the globe on which we live.

PITCH BALL

Ages: **4 and older.**

Number of players: **2 or more.**

Equipment: **3 beanbags (or soft rubber balls, table tennis balls, or golf balls); chalk; wastebasket.**

Place: **Indoors (classroom or any other room or gym) or outdoors.**

A starting line is marked with chalk, a stick, or a tape, six feet or more from the wastebasket. Players line up behind the chalk line, each one stepping up to it in turn. The first player receives three balls (or whatever other equipment is used) at each turn, and tries to pitch them into the wastebasket, one at a time. He scores according to the number he manages to toss inside. The next player, and each in turn, is given the three balls and plays as did the first. That player wins who gets the highest score. This game can be played for one or for several rounds.

Variation: Many different targets can be used, including several pots and pans, lined up side by side, each of which is assigned a different score value. A target can be made out of a corrugated box into the top of which several holes have been cut, each hole large enough for the pitched ball to pass through. Each hole can be given a different score value. Or, if beanbags are used, a three-concentric-ring target can be drawn on the floor, the center ring marked 100, the second ring 50, and the outer ring 20. Players score either when their bag is tossed so that it is inside one of the target areas, without touching any of the drawn circles, or, when played by younger children, if the bag lands on one of the lines.

BELL BALL

Ages: **5 and older.**

Number of players: **1 or more.**

Equipment: **Medium-sized inflated ball (or hollow rubber ball, beanbag, or inflated toy balloon); a bell on a string, ribbon, or stick.**

Place: **Outdoors—the bell is hung on a limb or on the branch of a tree, or from any other projection, 6 feet above the ground. Indoors—only a beanbag or balloon should be used.**

A line is marked off at a distance from the bell, from which each player throws, that will both challenge him and at the same time allow him a fair chance of hitting the bell with the ball, beanbag, or balloon. Each player may have a number of turns, agreed to before the start of the game. Each time a player hits the bell, he scores one point. The highest-scoring player wins.

PATSY BALL

Ages: **6 and older.**

Number of players: **1 or more.**

Equipment: **Small, bouncing rubber ball.**

Place: **Outdoors on hard ground or pavement.**

Each player in turn pats the ball between bouncing it on the ground. He scores according to the number of times he pats the ball without allowing it to bounce more than once between pats. Whenever a player misses, the ball is passed to the next player, if any, and so on. That player wins who can keep the ball bouncing and pat it alternately the greatest number of times.

Variation: The player is allowed to pat the ball only with his left (or right) hand. Another method is for the player to pat the ball alternately with his left and right hands between bounces.

SEVENS

Ages: **6 and up.**

Number of players: **1 or more.**

Equipment: **Small, bouncing rubber ball.**

Place: **Outdoors or gym.**

The object of this game is for each player to catch and throw the ball in 7 (or more or less) set ways without fumbling or dropping it. At any point at which the player fails to follow the agreed upon sequence, or drops the ball, he stops and surrenders the ball to the next player. He scores himself according to the number of catches and throws he completes successfully before dropping the ball or mixing up the sequence.

The name of this game and the reason for restricting the number of throws to seven are probably connected with the magic assigned to particular numbers in primitive religions. The number 7, in ancient myth, has been assumed to have magical qualities. This, like many other myths, has survived in children's play. So there is no reason why the number of sequences for each turn cannot be altered to more or less, according to the attention span and skill of players at different ages and stages of development.

Following are some sequences commonly used:

1. Throw the ball up against a wall and catch it 3 times.
2. Throw the ball up into the air 3 times, clapping your hands after each throw and before you catch it.
3. The same as (2) above, but clap your hands behind your back before you catch the ball.
4. The same as (2) above, but clap your hands, and then touch each shoulder with your opposite hand before you catch the ball.
5. Throw the ball up in the air 3 times with your left hand, catching it in your right hand each time it returns.
6. The same as (5) above, but reverse hands: throw with your right; catch with your left.
7. Throw the ball 3 times with one hand from behind your back, up over your head, and catch it with the other hand in front. Then repeat, using opposite hands for catching and throwing.
8. Bounce the ball on the ground 3 times, turn completely around, and catch it each time before it bounces again.
9. Bounce the ball on the ground with your right

hand, and lift your left leg over it before you catch
it on the rebound. Do this 3 times with one hand
and leg. Then do it 3 times using your other hand
and leg.
10. Throw the ball into the air 3 times, reciting:
"Peter Piper picked a peck of pickled peppers"
before catching it each time.
11. Throw the ball into the air. Let it bounce off your
head before catching it.
12. Beat the ball down onto the ground 3 times in
succession and then catch it.
. . . and so on.

PASS THE BALL

Ages: **6 and older.**

Number of players: **6 or more.**

Equipment: **Medium-sized inflated ball.**

Place: **Outdoors with ball. Indoors with toy balloon.**

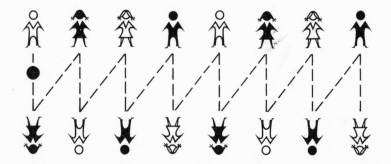

Players line up in two equal rows, facing one another,
as far apart as they can throw and catch the ball. The
first player, at the head of either line, throws the ball

to that player directly opposite him, who returns it
to the player in the opposite row, second in line from
the first. Play continues until the last player has caught
the ball. He then returns it, and play continues in the
opposite direction, and so on, for a number of rounds
determined before the start of the game.

Any player who drops the ball at his turn steps back
one step (or shoe's length for very young or inexperienced players). After three such fumbles and backward steps, that player is out of the game.

When a player has stepped back, but manages to catch
and return the ball without dropping it in the following
two consecutive turns, he may step into line again, or
one step forward, whichever is the lesser distance. That
side wins which has the largest number of players remaining in line at the end of the game.

Variation 1: Players are divided into two equal teams,
each of which forms a circle, each player standing 5
feet or more from the next. The players then throw the
ball from one to the next around the circle. Each team
plays with its own ball. All other rules of the original
game remain as before.

Variation 2: Players are divided into two equal teams.
Each team divides in half. Half the players on one team
form a single line, standing alternately next to half the
players on the opposing team. The remaining players
form a similar line, each player facing a member of
the opposing team in the first line (see diagram). The

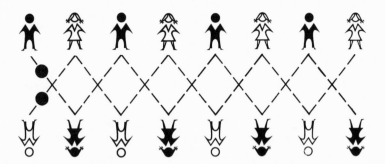

opposing team members at one end of the two lines are given a ball each. Each throws the ball to his own next team member diagonally opposite him. When each ball reaches the last team member in line, play continues in the opposite direction. Play continues for as many rounds, from one end of each line to the other, as agreed upon before the beginning of the game. That team wins whose first player has the ball in hand at the end of the agreed-upon number of rounds.

CALL BALL

Ages: **6 and older.**

Number of players: **5 or more.**

Equipment: **Small, soft, bouncing rubber ball.**

Place: **Outdoors or gym.**

Each player is given a special name—in the case of 7 players, each becomes a "day of the week." One of the secondary benefits of a game like this one is that it can be used by a parent or teacher to reinforce memory. Children are much more likely to remember the days of the week or the months of the year used in play than by sitting in a classroom or at home, trying to memorize them by rote.

The first player "up" bounces the ball off the ground or floor as hard as he can, calling out the name of any other player as he does so. All other players are loosely grouped around him. As soon as the ball leaves the first player's hand, all other players scatter. That player whose name is called must try to catch the ball before it bounces a second time. If he succeeds, he is next "up," and bounces the ball, as did the first player "up." If the player whose name was called fails to catch the ball in time, he loses one point and calls "STOP." All other players must stand wherever they are. The named player then aims the ball at any other player, except at that player who called his name. If another player is struck or tagged with the ball, he loses one point and is "up" at that turn. If no player is tagged, then the player whose name was called by the first player loses another point, and the first player is "up" once more. Any player who loses three points is out of the game. The last remaining player or players win the game.

Variation 1: If a windowless wall is available, the first "up" player may bounce the ball at the wall, calling out any other player's name. That player must try to catch the ball after the first and before the second bounce on the ground. The rest of the rules stand.

Variation 2: A square, large enough to hold all players including the first "up" player, is drawn on the ground or floor. All except the "up" player may run out of the square as soon as the ball is thrown. They return for each "up" turn. The rest of the rules remain the same.

TAG BALL

Ages: **6 and older.**

Number of players: **3 or more.**

Equipment: **Handball (or volleyball, basketball, or large inflated ball).**

Place: **Outdoors or gym.**

One player is "it," and is given the ball, while the rest scatter. "It" tries to tag any other player by throwing the ball. The tagged player then changes places with "it" and continues in turn. A player may only be considered tagged if the ball hits him before it bounces. Players may return the ball to "it" to speed up the game. All players may run, including "it."

Variation 1: A player may be considered "tagged" if the ball touches him even after it has bounced one or more times.

Variation 2: In a game of 12 or more players, several players may be designated "it" at the same time, playing with a single ball that they may pass to each other; or each being given one ball, they may throw it to one another to facilitate tagging. Only that player who throws the ball that tags an opposing player may change places with him.

DODGE BALL

Ages: **6 and up.**

Number of players: **Two teams of 6 or more players each.**

Equipment: **Handball (or basketball or medium-sized inflated ball).**

Place: **Outdoors or gym.**

Players are divided into two equal teams. One team forms a circle large enough to allow the members of the second team to move and run freely inside it. One member of the outside circle team is given the ball. A time limit is set during which each team serves as the circle team. For a game involving 6 to 10 members on each team, 3 to 5 minutes per inning is sufficient. The object of the game is for members of the outside circle team to "tag" inside team members with the ball. Circle team members may pass the ball to each other before aiming for inside team members. Any tagged inside team member leaves the game.

Inside team members may move about and try to dodge the ball. Circle team members may run into the circle only to recover the ball, but may not try to tag an inside team member with it until they have returned to their places on the outside circle. At the end of each inning, the tagged players who are out of the game are counted. That team wins which has tagged the largest number of opposing players at the end of the number of innings agreed upon.

Variation: Tagged players, instead of being out of the game, join the outside circle players for the rest of that inning. The last remaining inside player is the winner for his team.

SCHOOL BALL

Ages: **6 and older.**

Number of players: **12 or more.**

Equipment: **One hollow rubber ball (or beanbag or toy balloon).**

Place: **Indoors (classroom or any other room, using beanbag or balloon only). Outdoors or gym (using any kind of medium-sized ball).**

Players sit in rows on chairs or at their school desks or tables, or stand in line, one behind the other, or in a circle. The ball, beanbag, or balloon is never thrown, but passed by hand from one player to the next as rapidly as possible. Any player who fumbles and drops it is out of the game. (When played standing in a circle or in line, any player who is "out" may be required to sit down in his place.) Each player must accept the ball and pass it on as rapidly as he can.

Played in a room or when all players are seated, the players close ranks or move up to adjacent seats as others drop out of the game. The last remaining player wins.

Variations (a large number of variations are possible in playing this game):

Number of players: **10 or more per team.**

Place: **Outdoors or gym.**

1. Each team of players lines up in a single row, parallel to the next team. Or each team may form a circle. The first player in each row or circle holds one ball, bean bag, or balloon. At the word "Go" from the supervisor or from one player designated as the "starter," he passes (or throws) the ball to the next player, and so on down the line or around the circle. The last player in line (or the player who is the last next to the first player in a circle) runs to the head of the line (or runs once around the circle) and passes the ball to the next, in the same manner as did the first player. That team wins whose first player first returns with the ball to his original position.

2. Each team of players lines up in its own row, one behind the next, each straddling his legs as wide as possible. The first player passes the ball between his legs to the next, and so on down the line to the last player. The rest of the rules in (1) above remain the same.

3. Each team of players lines up in a row or in a circle. The players pass the ball backward overhead from one to another. All other rules remain the same as in (1) above.

4. Two teams line up, each in a row, each 20 feet or more from a basketball hoop (or a wastebasket, when the game is played by young children). The game is played as before, except that the last player in each row at each turn, must run to a marked line ahead of the basket, as soon as he receives the ball. He must then throw it and get it into the basket successfully. If he

fails, he must keep trying until he has succeeded, and only then may he return with the ball to his place as the first in line, passing the ball back to the next player behind him, who passes it on until it is in the hands of the last player in line, who plays as did the first. The rest of the rules remain the same as in (1) above.

5. Two or more teams line up, each in a row, as before. The first member of each team stands at a marked place, 20 or more feet ahead of his line, facing the second player. He throws the ball to that player of his own team and then runs to the back of his line. The second player, on catching the ball, runs to the marked place, faces his team, and throws the ball to the player facing him, and so on. That team wins the game whose first player to throw the ball stands once more at the marked place, after all other team members have had their turns. If either thrower or catcher drops the ball, that play must be repeated.

6. Play begins as in (2) above. When the ball is passed back to the last player in a row, all players about-face at his command. They then pass the ball back to the first player, as before. That team wins whose first player first receives the ball on completion of its passage in both directions.

7. Any of these games may be played with several balls, bean bags, or balloons, used by each team at the same time. The last player at his turn must wait until he has received as many balls as are in play. All other rules remain the same as in (1) above.

CATCH THE BALL

Ages: **7 and older.**

Number of players: **12 or more.**

Equipment: **Basketball (or football, large inflated ball, beanbag, or inflated toy balloon).**

Place: **Outdoors or gym.**

All players but one form a circle. The remaining player stays inside the circle. The players forming the circle pass the ball to one another at random, being allowed to throw it from one side of the ring to the other. The inside player tries to intercept the ball or to knock it out of the hands of any other player. If he succeeds, he then changes places with the last player to touch or hold the ball. If any player who is part of the circle drops the ball in the process of throwing or catching it, whether or not this is due to interference from the inside player, he also changes places with the inside player.

Variation: The same rules apply, except that all players must kick the ball to each other and may not touch it with their hands. A further variation that allows the inside player to intercept the ball by both foot and hand is not recommended. It could lead to injury.

ODD BALL

Ages: **7 and older.**

Number of players: **12 or more.**

Equipment: **Handball (or basketball, football, or large inflated ball).**

Place: **Outdoors or gym.**

All players but one form a circle, each with his feet spread apart as far as is comfortable. Each player's right foot touches the next player's left, all around the circle. The extra player is given the ball and goes into the center of the circle. It is his object to throw (or kick) the ball out of the circle between players' legs. He may not throw (or kick) over the players' heads. The circle players may try to stop the ball with their hands, without moving the position of their feet. Any player among those forming the circle who loses his balance changes places with the center player. If the center player manages to throw (or kick) his ball outside the circle, he changes places with that player between whose legs the ball passed, or with the player to the right of the gap between the legs of 2 adjacent players, when the ball escapes the circle in this manner.

Variation: Instead of being placed in the center, the extra player stays outside the circle and tries to throw (or kick) the ball into the circle, as before. All other rules remain the same.

THROW AND GO

Ages: **7 and older.**

Number of players: **5 or more.**

Equipment: **Small or medium-sized rubber ball (or tennis ball); sticks (or tent pegs)—numbering one less than the number of players.**

Place: **Outdoors on soft ground.**

Field: Lay out a circle at least 10 feet in diameter. Mark the center of
       the circle. Make a number of holes, one less than the number of
       players, more or less evenly spaced around the circumference of the
       circle. Holes should be at least 5 feet apart, 3 inches deep, and
       about 4 inches in diameter.

The first player "up" stands in the center of the circle
and holds the ball. Each of the rest of the players, with
stick in hand, chooses one hole. Every player stands
behind his hole, just outside the circle. At the word
"Go" from the "up" player in the middle, the rest race
once around the circle until each returns to his original
hole and places his stick into it.

As soon as he says "Go," the "up" player may throw
or roll the ball, aiming for one of the holes. If the ball
lands in an empty hole, the "up" player changes places
with the one whose hole it is. If the "up" player misses,
or if all players have their sticks in their holes on
completion of their runs, or if the ball rolls into a hole
in which a returned player has already placed his
stick, the "up" player must continue to resume play as
before, to call "Go" and to throw his ball, until he succeeds in landing his ball in an empty hole.

Variation: Stool Ball
Place: Indoors.

All the rules of Throw and Go apply, except that players
sit in a circle on stools or chairs. Instead of throwing
his ball into a hole, the "up" player tries to strike an
unoccupied chair while its occupant races around the
circle. This version of the game is very old, and proba-

bly originated in England. William Bradford, the five-time governor of Plymouth Colony, discovered children playing Stool Ball one Christmas day, took away their ball, and henceforth prohibited all game-playing in the colony on this or any other holiday.

CHASE BALL

Ages: **8 and older.**

Number of players: **Any number, divided into two more or less equal teams.**

Equipment: **Handball (or basketball, volleyball, or large, inflated rubber ball).**

Place: **Outdoors or gym.**

This is an informal playground game in which players on the same team pass the ball back and forth to each other, while the opposing players try to intercept the ball and, if able to do so, pass it to members of their own team. This game is most frequently an informal school-recess game in which no scores are kept.

CENTER BALL

Ages: **8 and older.**

Number of players: **10 or more.**

Equipment: **Volleyball (or handball, basketball, or large inflated ball).**

Place: **Outdoors or gym.**

All players but one stretch out both arms to form a circle, in which each player stands at double arms' length from the next. After the circle is formed, players lower their arms to normal position. The odd player stands in the middle of the circle, holding the ball. He throws it at any player, and then runs outside the circle. The receiving player must catch it and run with it to the center of the circle, where he puts it down. If he fails to catch the ball, he becomes the odd player, and the former odd player takes his place in the circle. If the receiving player catches the ball and places it in the center, he must try to tag the odd player by hand before the latter can return to the middle of the circle and touch the ball. If the receiving player succeeds in tagging the odd player, the odd player must throw and run once more. If the odd player touches the ball in the center before he is tagged, the receiving player then becomes the odd player. The game continues as before.

PIGGYBACK BALL

Ages: **10 and older.**

Number of players: **12 or more.**

Equipment: **Large handball (or volleyball, basketball, inflated rubber ball, beanbag, or inflated toy balloon).**

Place: **Outdoors on soft ground only.**

The players are divided into two equal teams. One becomes the "horse" team, the other the "rider" team for the first inning. The horses carry the riders piggyback. One mounted rider is given the ball and must throw it to any other mounted rider, and so on. When any rider fumbles and drops the ball, all riders dismount at once and scatter. The nearest horse may then pick up the ball and throw it to any other horse or at any rider in order to tag him with it. The horses may attempt to tag a rider with only a single throw at their turn. If the horses fail to hit a rider, all riders remount, and the game continues as before. If a rider is tagged by a horse, then riders and horses change places and the horses mount the riders for the next inning, and so on.

AMERICAN INDIAN BALL GAMES

Lacrosse is the most famous American Indian ball game still played today. But the Indians of Florida once played a game that was a forerunner of today's Basketball. A wicker basket was fixed to the top of a pole so that, when the ball was thrown into it properly, it turned around and around the pole. That player won who managed to turn the basket around the pole the largest number of times at a single throw.

The following are the rules for an ancient Indian game that can lead to rough scrimmages. Firm rules about allowable and disallowed body contact should be clearly spelled out, understood, and agreed to by all players before the start of the game.

HIGHBALL

Ages: **12 and older.**

Number of players: **12 or more.**

Equipment: **Handball (or volleyball, basketball, or large inflated ball); tape or chalk.**

Place: **Outdoors.**

A field, 60 feet by 20 feet or larger, is marked off and divided by a center line at the halfway point of the 60-foot lines (see diagram).

All players are grouped about the center of the field. One player, chosen by lot, is given the ball. He throws it high into the air and tries to catch it as it returns. Any other player may catch the ball if he can. A player who catches the ball runs with it to score one point if he crosses the line at either end of the field while carrying the ball.

Any player may tackle the ball-carrier, according to the rules, and if he captures the ball, may try to score. A ball-carrying player may, if he feels himself threatened, pass the ball to any other player, whom he then pursues with the rest. Whenever a point is scored, the game resumes as it started, the scoring player being given the throw into the air. That player wins who scores the largest number of points within a time period agreed to before the start of the game.

BOWLING

The modern game of Bowling probably originated in Europe in the Middle Ages. The earliest known games

were similar to the present-day Italian game of Bocce, in which one player throws out a small wood or metal ball. He, and then each additional player in turn, tries to bowl three larger balls as close to the first as possible. Only that player scores whose balls come closest to the first. And only those balls belonging to the winning player count that are closer to the first ball than those of any other player. The medieval woodcut below shows that at that time the pins consisted of cones toward which players tossed or rolled their balls.

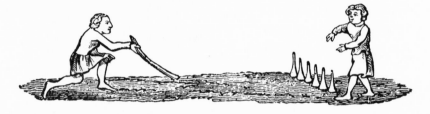

More "pins" were added to these games until, in time, a variety of such games were standardized, among them our regulation Bowling and Curling-on-the-Ice.

One example of how some of the seemingly meaning-less names of games originated is Kayle-pins, an early

form of Nine-pins. It was later known as Kettle, or
Kittle-pins, which eventually turned into the game of
Skittles.

Bowling-on-the-Green, an English invention, was a
game enthusiastically played by King Henry VIII.
This version of the game led to the construction of
indoor bowling alleys that soon became hangouts for
criminals and dens of all sorts of skulduggery. Therefore, in the sixteenth century, King Henry's son, Edward VI, closed down all bowling alleys in England.

Among the games popular at the time was one called
Half-Bowl. This game was played with one-half of a
solid wooden bowling ball. It was delivered down a
short, smooth alley toward a circle of 15 pins. The half-
ball had to be spun so that it skittered around the circle
of pins, entering the circle from the side away from
the player, to knock down as many pins as possible.

About 1780, the magistrates of London once more banned Bowling, citing the most popular games by name. This led to the revival of an older game, Nine Holes, one that the magistrates had neglected to specify in their edict. Players called it Bubble-the-Justice, in the mistaken hope that they had outfoxed the law.

STAKE BALL

Ages: **7 and older.**

Number of players: **6 or more.**

Equipment: **Handball (or volleyball, basketball, or large inflated ball); a set of bowling pins (or Indian clubs, large soda bottles, sticks, or tent pegs) one less than the number of players; chalk or marking stick.**

Place: **Indoors or outdoors.**

Bowling pins (use sticks or tent pegs on soft ground) are set up 10 to 15 feet apart. A circle, 4 feet in diameter, is drawn or scratched around each bowling pin.

One player enters each circle containing a bowling pin. The remaining player, chosen by lot, becomes "it," and may stand anywhere, but must be at least 6 feet from the nearest player at the start of the game. He is given the ball. His object is to kick the ball so that it knocks down a bowling pin (or hits a stick stuck into the ground). The players inside their circles try to protect their own bowling pins as well as they can, keeping at least one foot inside their own circles at all times. When "it" knocks down a bowling pin, he changes places with the player in whose circle it stood. A player who leaves his circle, if spotted by "it," is challenged and becomes "it," changing places with his challenger.

Variation: This variation is played without bowling pins or stakes. The object of "it" is to tag a player who is outside his circle by throwing the ball at him. Players who beckon to each other may run and exchange circles. Each player who succeeds in doing so without being "tagged" scores one point. A tagged player changes places with "it" and becomes "it," until he has tagged another player outside his circle. That player wins who reaches a given score, or who has the highest score at the end of a time period agreed to before the start of the game.

BALL BOWLING

Ages: **7 and older.**

Number of players: **1 or more.**

Equipment: **Handball (or volleyball, basketball, or large inflated ball); 2 bowling pins (or Indian clubs or empty soda bottles); chalk or tape.**

Place: **Indoors or outdoors.**

The bowling pins are set up 15 feet or more from a starting line marked by tape or chalk. Bowling pins should be set up sufficiently far apart to allow the ball to pass between them (see diagram). The object is for each player, at his turn, to aim and roll the ball from the starting line so that it passes between the two pins without knocking down either of them. Knocking down one pin and still rolling the ball between them costs a player 1 point. Rolling the ball between them and knocking down both pins costs him 2 points.

Knocking down one pin, but failing to roll the ball between the two pins, costs a player 3 points. Failure to roll the ball between both pins and failure to knock down at least one pin costs him 4 points. That player wins who has the lowest score at the end of the number of innings agreed to before the beginning of the game.

BATTLE BALL

Ages: **8 and older.**

Number of players: **Two teams of 5 or more players each.**

Equipment: **Handball** (or volleyball, football, basketball, or large inflated ball); as many **Indian clubs** (or bowling pins, empty tin cans, or empty soda bottles) as the number of players; **tape** or **chalk**.

Place: **Outdoors** or **gym.**

A field, 40 feet by 15 feet, is staked out. It is divided by a center line halfway between the 40-foot lines, and two lines parallel to the center line, 4 feet from each end of the field (see diagram). Half the Indian clubs (or whatever equipment is used) are placed, evenly spaced, at least 2 feet apart, in each end zone between the lines. In a game of more than 8 players per team, the clubs should be lined up in two evenly spaced rows in each end zone.

Each team occupies and remains in one-half of the field. Players may not stand in the end zones or cross into them at any time during the game. If team captains are chosen, each may place his players in positions he deems most advantageous. Each team in turn, in alternate innings, is given the ball for the first throw. The object of the game is for each team to knock down as many of the Indian clubs as possible in the end zone of the opposing team by aiming the ball over the heads of or past the opponents. The ball may be passed among team members and intercepted by the opposing team. Each Indian club knocked down counts one point. An inning may end either when all Indian clubs of one side are knocked down, or at the end of a time period agreed to before the start of the game. That team wins which scores the largest number of points at the end of an even number of innings.

Variation: 2 or 4 balls may be used, equally divided between the teams at the beginning of the game.

RICOCHET

Ages: **8 and older.**

Number of players: **1 or more.**

Equipment: **Handball (or volleyball, basketball, or large inflated ball); 10 bowling pins (or Indian clubs or large empty soda bottles); chalk or tape.**

Place: **Indoors or outdoors.**

All 10 bowling pins are set up in a circle, 5 to 6 feet from a wall, with room for the ball to pass between them. A starting line, about 20 feet from the wall and facing the circle of bowling pins, is marked with tape or chalk (see diagram).

Each player, at his turn, rolls or throws the ball against the wall so that it bounces or rolls back into the circle of bowling pins, knocking over as many as possible. Each pin downed at one turn scores one point for that player. Pins downed *before* the ball has hit the wall score against that player, each downed pin counting as minus one point. Pins are set up again between each player's turn. That player wins who scores highest in the number of innings agreed to before the start of the game.

BALL GAMES WITH STICKS, BATS, MALLETS, OR RACKETS

The earliest version of Golf, played with a small, hard ball made of leather stuffed with feathers, was known in the days of ancient Rome. It was driven by players armed with a club that was curved at one end. The medieval game of Goff gave the modern one its name. Rules similar to those for Goff applied to a game called Bandy Ball in the fourteenth century, and to Stow Ball, popular in Europe in the sixteenth and seventeenth centuries.

Polo, played by teams of horsemen who try to score goals by driving a puck with mallets, originated centuries ago in Persia, where such a game was played with rackets and a hard leather ball. This game, like the jousting tournament of armored knights, though a mock battle, was taken most seriously by its players. And a similar game is still played by today's Afghan tribesmen. They compete for possession of the body of a beheaded calf, with which they score by carrying it on horseback across a goal line.

The ancestors of modern croquet were the seventeenth-century game of Pall-Mall, and an earlier one called Ring Ball, both of which originated in England.

Club Ball, first recorded in 1344, was the forerunner of Rounders, once a formal game in England, which led to the rules and methods of play for Baseball. The British game of Cricket shares the same beginnings.

The game that gave birth to Tennis, Badminton, and Squash was probably first played in France without a racket. The ball was struck with the open palm—sometimes heavily gloved, at other times bare. In 1424, a French woman named Margot was a champion of this game. Played with rackets, Tennis became a favorite among the nobility of Europe. The ledgers of England's King Henry VII testify that players, then as now, lost balls that they drove outside the courts: "Item for the king's loss at tennis, twelvepence; for the loss of balls, threepence."

TRAP BALL

Ages: **9 and older.**

Number of players: **2 or more.**

Equipment: **Soft, small rubber ball (or soft baseball or tennis ball); baseball bat (or stick); 1 trap (see illustration).**

Place: **Outdoors.**

A circle, 20 feet or more in diameter, is marked around the trap in the center. The first player, chosen by lot, steps up to the trap with a bat in hand. He strikes

the trap with his bat, releasing the ball. He must hit the
ball with his bat while it is in the air. The rest of the
players stay outside this circle. If the player up at bat
fails 3 times in a row to strike the ball outside the
circle, or if he strikes the ball outside the circle, but it
is caught by one of the other players before it falls
to the ground, he loses his turn either to the next
batter chosen by lot, or to the player who caught the
ball.

If the batter hits the ball outside the circle and no one
catches it before it strikes the ground, he scores 1 point
and continues at bat until he either misses 3 turns at
bat in succession, or is caught out. The highest-scoring
player wins after all players have had their turns at
bat.

Variation 1: The batter drops his bat on the ground as
soon as he has hit the ball beyond the circle. If the ball

is not caught, the player who picks it off the ground may throw it at the bat inside the circle, from the spot at which he picked up the ball. If he hits the bat, or if it is agreed that he need only come within 2 feet of the bat, the batter is "out," and that player becomes the next batter "up."

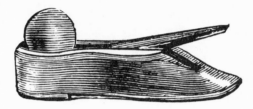

Variation 2: The ball may be thrown by a player, chosen by lot, if no trap is available. Only the pitcher may catch the ball, *inside the circle*, and, if he is able to do so before the struck ball hits the ground, may take his turn at bat. The other players must stay outside the circle, but may catch the batter out, as in the original game.

HAND TENNIS

Ages: **12 and older.**

Number of players: **2, or two teams of 2 players each.**

Equipment: **Fives ball (or golf ball), and 1 padded glove for each player (or a small, soft hollow rubber ball or tennis ball that can be struck with the ungloved hand).**

Place: **Handball court or an area enclosed by a two- or three-sided windowless wall, at least 15 feet high, marked by a line at the players' chest height.**

This game, now played in England as the game of
Fives, when played against a single wall, is much like
Handball. The first player, chosen by lot, throws the
ball up into the air and bats it with his hand against
the wall (in a single-wall game); or into a corner above
the marked line, so that it first strikes both walls before bouncing onto the ground (in a court with more
than one wall). The second player, or one member of
the second team, must similarly bat the ball with his
hand before it bounces, or before it bounces more than
once on the ground, letting it strike one or more walls
above the line before it falls to the ground. The game
continues until one player misses returning the ball
before it strikes the ground twice. Each such "miss"
scores 1 point for the opponent or for the opposing
team. That player or team wins which first scores 21
points.

BALL GAMES THAT REQUIRE MARKED
COURTS OR PLAYING FIELDS

Prehistoric men undoubtedly found that throwing or
practicing other skills required for their own or for
tribal defense or support could be practiced in play.
But I doubt that they could play formal games until
they were able to understand "that their struggles with
nature, with predators and with other men were not
haphazard encounters. They [first] had to discover that
there was a possibility of design and of planning for
the exigencies of daily life. Once man realized that he
was not just a plaything of chance, he could begin to
plan his moves, foresee probable results, and take luck
into account as one of the components.

"Man probably did not take long to discover how to scratch his plan into the soft earth, using sticks or pebbles to show the position of hunters and prey, attackers and defenders." Early man may also have deduced the need for rules from a recognition of this possibility of planning. "And so the first game [using a playing field] may have been invented."[2] Eventually, tribal chiefs may have thought of the idea of using live men in planning these strategies. It is a small step from this kind of planning to have the men act out their roles in mock combat or hunt. Within historical times, the princes and maharajas of India played Chess and Pachisi in this manner, laying out life-sized game boards in the courtyards of their palaces. Many of these games became a part of religious ritual, in which the stakes sometimes were a matter of life and death for the participants.

The following ball games, descendants of these early games, require playing fields that can be improvised indoors and out, using tape or ribbons, chalk lines, or sticks and stones to mark boundaries and goals.

BALLOON BALL

Ages: **6 and older.**

Number of players: **Two teams of 6 or more players each.**

Equipment: **Inflated toy balloon; tape (or string or twine).**

Place: **Indoors in classroom or any other room.**

Two lengths of string, tape, ribbon, or twine are strung 6 feet from the floor, from wall to wall, one at each end

of the room, 2 or more feet from end walls, with sufficient room left for both teams to stand or sit, evenly
distributed, facing each other, in the center of the
room (see diagram).

The balloon is tossed into the center of the room. The
object of the game is for teams to score by slapping the
balloon across the opponents' goal (as represented by
the ribbon *behind* each team). Each time the balloon
drifts between the ribbon and the wall, it scores 1 goal
for the opposing team. That team wins which scores the
greatest number of goals in a given time period, or that
first reaches a number of goals agreed to before the
start of the game. At the scoring of a goal, the game
resumes as at first.

Variation 1: The ribbons may be strung across the four corners of the room, two belonging to each team (see diagram). All other rules remain as before.

Variation 2:

Ages: **7 and older.**

Number of players: **Two teams of 8 or more players each.**

Place: **Outdoors** or **gym.**

A field, 20 by 30 feet (or larger, depending on the ages and number of players), is marked out and divided by a center line halfway at the 30-foot lines (see diagram).

Each team lines up facing the other, about 1 foot from the center line (see diagram). The balloon is tossed into the center, between both teams, who then try, by striking it, to drive it across the line marking the end zone of the opposing team. Team members may cross into each other's territory, once the balloon is released among them. It may never be carried in the hand or held, but must at all times be struck or pushed. Each time the balloon crosses the end zone on one side or the other, the opposing team scores, and play resumes as at first, both teams lining up at the center line, the team that scored the last point being given the balloon. That team wins which scores the largest number of points in a time period, or achieves a point score agreed to before the start of the game.

ROLL BALL

Ages: **7 and older.**

Number of players: **6 or more.**

Equipment: **Softball (or small, bouncing rubber ball); 5 pebbles (or bottle caps) for each player; metal spoons for digging.**

Place: **Outdoors on soft ground.**

Players line up as closely as possible, in a single line. Each digs a hole at his feet, about half again as large and half as deep as the circumference of the ball to be used. A line is marked, 10 feet (or more for older players) away from, but centered on, the line of holes (see diagram).

One player, chosen by lot, leaves his hole and stands at the mark. The rest of the players stay behind their respective holes. The first "up" player tries to roll the ball into any of the holes. The player into whose hole the ball rolled (even if it is the ball-roller's own) must pick it up. The rest of the players scatter. The player who picked up the ball now tries to "tag" any other player by throwing the ball at him. A tagged player must place one of his pebbles into his own hole, and then take his turn at the mark as the next ball-roller.

If the player into whose hole the ball rolls fails to tag another player, he places one of his pebbles in his own hole and takes his turn at the mark. As soon as any player has placed the fifth pebble in his own hole, he is out of the game. That player wins who stays in the game longest.

HOLE BALL

Ages: **7 and older.**

Number of players: **1 or more.**

Equipment: **Baseball (or small, rubber ball); small digging tool (or metal spoon).**

Place: **Outdoors on soft ground.**

Using your own shoe length as a 1-foot measure, pace out a straight line about 42 feet long. Mark a starting point at one end of the line. Then dig a hole, 3 or 4 inches deep and half again as wide, 10 feet from the starting point. Another hole is dug, 4 feet from the first, then three others, each spaced out 8 feet from one another, all along the line (see diagram).

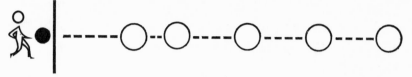

The first player bowls the ball from the starting point to the first hole. If he manages to sink the ball into the first hole, he may continue by lifting the ball out of the hole and bowling from that hole to the next, and so on. He loses his turn at any hole in which he fails to sink the ball on the first try (or more, if agreed to before the start of the game). Each player scores according to the number of holes he successfully fills with his ball at successive innings. That player wins who has the highest score at the end of the number of innings agreed to before the start of the game.

RELAY BALL

Ages: **8 and older.**

Number of players: **12 or more for each of two even-numbered teams.**

Equipment: **2 handballs (or volleyballs, basketballs, footballs, or large inflated balls); tape or chalk.**

Place: **Outdoors or gym.**

A field is staked out as shown (see diagram). Each team is divided into two equal groups and lined up as shown (see diagram). The first player in one of each team's lines is given a ball. At the signal to start, the two first-in-line players of each team race toward the other end of the field, tossing the ball from one to the other. On reaching (touching with one foot or crossing) the end line, both players of each team return, continuing to pass the ball between them as before. The ball must be passed at least 4 times on each lap.

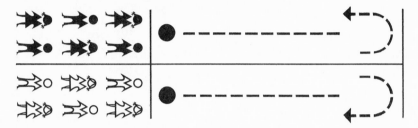

On their return to the starting line, whichever player has the ball at that time passes it to one of the next two team members, who continue the game as before, and each then stands last in his respective line. That team wins whose first two players first stand at the head of their respective lines again, after all other players have run the course.

Variation: This game can be played so that the ball is kicked between players, but never touched by hand.

CORNER GOAL BALL

Ages: **9 and older.**

Number of players: **6 or more for each of two teams.**

Equipment: **Handball (or volleyball, basketball, or large inflated ball).**

Place: **Outdoors or gym.**

A field, 25 feet by 40 feet, is staked out and divided by a center line into halves, each 25 feet by 20 feet. Four-foot squares, one at each corner of the field, serve as goals (see diagram).

All but 2 players of each team line up 4 feet from, and on opposite sides of, the center line. The 2 remaining players on each team stand, one each, in the corner goals in the half of the playing field occupied by the opposing team (see diagram). The ball is given to one member of whichever team is chosen by lot to begin the game. The object is to throw the ball over the heads of the opposing team to one of the two goalkeepers who are members of the throwing team. The opposing team tries to intercept the ball and scores in the same manner.

Goalkeepers may step beyond their 4-foot-square goals, provided they keep one hand (or foot) inside the goal. Each time a goalkeeper captures the ball, he scores 1 point for his team. He then tries to throw the ball back to his own team. Team members may pass the ball to each other, and may intercept the throw from the goalkeeper to his own team, provided they do not reach or step inside the goal lines or into the opposing team's half of the playing field. The winning team is the one with the highest score at the end of a given time period.

The game can also be played so that the team wins which first scores 20 (or more, or less) points.

Variation: Agreement is made before the game about whether players may or may not wrest the ball from a goalkeeper who has captured it, before he touches the ground inside his goal with the ball in order to score.

ROUNDERS

Ages: **9 and older.**

Number of players. **Two teams of 9 players each for the conventional game; more players can be added to each team, up to a total of 12 or 14 players per team.**

Equipment: **Softball; baseball bat (or stick); tape or chalk.**

Place: **Outdoors.**

A five-sided field is marked off, 25 feet per side, with bases at four of the corners. Home base is marked at the fifth corner; a pitcher's line is drawn 12 feet from home base (see diagram).

The players are divided into two teams, a member of each tossing for first side at bat. The fielding team selects a pitcher for the first inning, and the batting side tosses to determine batting order.

The fielders stand at various locations, outside the field of play. No fielder may stand between the pitcher and the man at bat. The batter stands next to home base. The pitcher throws the ball underhand. The player at bat may refuse any ball; but if he tries to hit a pitched ball, it counts as one of the three tries to which he is entitled. If he fails to hit the ball after three tries, he is "out." If he hits a ball, he must drop his bat and run to his right to the first corner base, or beyond if he thinks that he can successfully reach second, third, fourth, or home base, and if these are unoccupied.

Only one batter at a time may occupy any single base. When a batter has hit the ball, the man on second base must run toward third, and so on. Those players who occupy bases must try to reach at least the next base whenever a hit is made. Only by returning to home base, after having safely reached all other bases, does a batter score a run for his side.

If any member of the fielding team, including the pitcher, catches the ball before it strikes the ground, the batter, and all players who are "off" base, are out of the game for that inning. Any player who has started to run from one base to the next may attempt to return to his last base before such a ball is caught. Any fielder may throw the ball and try to hit a runner with it. If the ball hits the batter, or any other runner who is between bases, before he reaches a base or has one foot on it, that batter or runner is also out of the game. Fielders may throw the ball to each other and to the pitcher to try to tag any batter running between bases. They may also chase a runner and tag him by touching him with the ball. However, no fielder may catch and hold a runner so that another fielder may tag him.

When all members of the team first at bat have completed their turns, whether or not they occupy bases, that inning ends and the teams switch sides. The game continues as before. That team wins which has scored the largest number of runs during its inning, or after the number of innings agreed to before the start of the game.

Variation: Players should decide before the game whether base-stealing is allowed, when the next base is unoccupied.

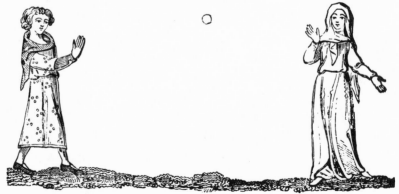

II

Marble Games

The children of ancient Rome used nuts for playing games similar to some of the marble games described here. Originally, these were children's versions of bowling games they saw their elders play. As these games became popular, special marbles were made for young players, first of stone and clay, later of marble, agate, and glass. Devotees have invented a long list of names for the various kinds, ranging from "bosses," "bonzes," "aggies," "glassies," "alleys," "baries," "poppos," and "stonies," to "taws." Marble game crazes have waxed and waned periodically. During one of the peak periods in England, around 1860, an anonymous Victorian described marbles rapturously as "glass spheres holding a twisted spiral of filament, thin music translated into colored glass, crimson with pale blue, fire with Canary, emerald with rose. The similar sphere of the eye, however juxtaposed to the harder crystal, peers in vain through the twisted colors to see a heart."

Shooting marbles requires a certain amount of skill and concentration, the symptoms of which one can see in the little boy scrunched close to the ground, marble in hand, poised to shoot, eyes fixed on the target, neck stretched, chin out and teeth clenched over the lower lip. I recall the passion with which these games were played in my childhood. A gaming fever possessed us, born of greed or despair as one's hoard swelled or shrank inside the little marble bag each of us clutched to himself with miserly mania.

In the first half of this century, marble playing was taken sufficiently seriously that an Official Set of State and Interstate Rules was drawn up by a Conference of Recreation Executives from 60 New Jersey and Pennsylvania cities. I can imagine these paunchy, middle-aged men, thrashing out, compromising and settling, in smoke-filled caucus, the 31 rules for the official game of marbles, in addition to a set of definitions of terms that include: " 'Hysting,'—the act of raising the hand from the ground in shooting (Forbidden)." So, no hysting, please.

The following marble games and their rules have been distilled and adapted from those most popular in the past. Any of these games can be played, won, or lost according to one of two ways. The first depends on a winning score based on the number of points scored or games won, in which captured marbles are returned to every player at the end of each game. The second, in which some players may "lose all their marbles," is a game of "winner take all," or at least as many as he can capture. The first kind of game is for fun, the second "for keeps," or "in earnest." I recommend the former for children below school age and for any who cannot stand losing their treasured marbles. And of course, children should be encouraged to adapt the given rules in any way on which they can agree.

In many marble games, players shoot from a mark, called the "taw," some distance from their targets. A 4- to 6-foot distance is ample for preschool children. But the distances can be increased for games played by older and more skilled players. The established manner of shooting marbles consists of holding the marble in the hollow made by pressing the thumb against the forefinger, an inch or two off the ground, and flicking the thumb to propel the little ball forward. This is called "knuckling down" (see illustration below). A less favored method is to rest the marble on the floor or the ground and to flick it with the forefinger toward its target.

Some of the games depend for their outcome on how close a player can bring his marble to a target or to an opponent's marble. Such games are difficult for smaller children or when played on rough ground. The rules may be adapted so that the winning player is the one

whose marble comes within a "span" of his target, or
closer—a span being that player's hand's breadth, with
fingers stretched out, from the tip of the thumb to the
end of the little finger.

The order in which players shoot their marbles is most
often decided by each player's throwing or shooting
one marble toward a marked line or circle, the nearest
to the line or the closest to the center of the circle being
first, the next closest second, and so on.

BOUNCE EYE

Ages: **5 and older.**

Number of players: **2 or more.**

Equipment: **An equal number of marbles for each player; chalk or stick for marking lines.**

Place: **Indoors** or **outdoors.**

A circle about 1 foot in diameter is drawn on the ground or the floor. Each player places 2 or more marbles in a heap in the center of the circle. Each player in turn stands close to the circle and drops one of his other marbles straight down, from eye-level height. His object is to aim this marble so that it strikes the largest number of marbles and knocks them out of the circle. After the drop, the player captures any marbles which he has knocked outside the circle, and recovers his shooter. If he fails to knock any marbles out, his shooter is added to those remaining in the circle. The game ends when no marbles remain in the circle.

MARBLE SHOOT

Ages: **6 and older.**

Number of players: **Any number.**

Equipment: **An equal number of marbles, all of the same size, for each player; chalk or stick for marking line.**

Place: **Indoors** or **outdoors.**

A starting line is marked on the floor or the ground with chalk or a stick. The first shooter, chosen by lot, shoots out his marble from behind the starting line. The second player shoots his marble in the same manner, attempting to hit the first player's marble. If he succeeds, he pockets both the opponent's marble and his own. If he fails, the third player (or the first, in a game of only 2 players) aims for either marble, and, if he strikes one, may continue until he misses or until he has captured all marbles on the field. If no marble remains on the ground, the next player shoots out a marble and the game continues as at first. That player wins who captures the largest number of his opponents' marbles.

Variation 1: On agreement before the game, the second player captures the first player's marble if his shot comes within a "span" of it.

Variation 2: The target consists of 4 marbles arranged as shown (see diagram below), 3 marbles touching, set out in a triangle, forming the base for a fourth, placed on top. This is the "castle." Each player in turn builds a castle with his own marbles for the next player. If the shooter hits the target from a given distance and dislodges the top marble, he captures all 4. If he fails to do so, he loses his shooter to the player who built the castle.

Variation 3: The "castle" can also be constructed by placing a regular playing die on top of the foundation. If a player fails to dislodge the die, he forfeits his shooter to the player who built the castle. If he hits the castle, the player who built the castle pays him as many marbles as the number shown uppermost on the die after it has rolled off.

Variation 4: A large "castle" can be made by placing 9 marbles at the base, then 6, then 4, and then 1 (or a die) on top.

Variation 5: The "keeper" method used in Marble Bridge (see p. 89) can be employed in these "castle" games. The castle-keeper is selected and "pays" according to the number of marbles scattered beyond a small circle. The "keeper" wins the shooter of any player who fails to score.

TARGET

Ages: **6 and older.**

Number of players: **Any number.**

Equipment: **An equal number of marbles, all of the same size, for each
player; chalk or stick for marking line.**

Place: **Indoors or outdoors.**

A shooting line is marked on the floor or the ground
with chalk or a stick. Each player contributes a given
number (3 to 6) of his own marbles, which he sets up,
along with an equal number from each other player,
in a circle or row, at a distance from the shooting line.
Each player in turn shoots one marble into this target.
A player takes as many marbles as he hits at his turn,
and recovers his own shooter. If he fails to hit any, he
leaves his shooter where it falls. That player wins who
captures the largest number of marbles in the number
of turns agreed to before the start of the game.

RING GAME

Ages: **6 and older.**

Number of players: **Any number.**

Equipment: **An equal number of marbles, all of the same size, for each
player; chalk or stick for marking line.**

Place: **Indoors or outdoors.**

A shooting line is marked on the ground or the floor
with chalk or stick. Each player contributes an equal
number of marbles to make up a circle of 16 or more

marbles, set up with plenty of space between them. A larger marble or target is set in the center. The first player, chosen by lot, shoots from the shooting line, marked some distance from the circle, and tries to hit the center target. If he fails to do so, his shooter remains where it lies. If he succeeds in hitting the target, he may then try to hit any of the marbles set up in the circumference of the circle, by shooting his marble from where it lies. He collects any marble he hits, other than the center marble, and removes it from the game.

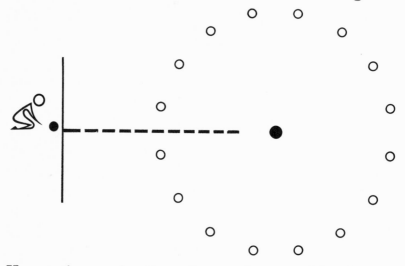

He continues shooting, from wherever his shooter lands, for as long as he hits and pockets another marble. His turn ends when he fails to hit another marble. Each player takes his turn in the same manner. Any player may also aim for any shooter marbles left in the ring by previous players. Or he may win shooters outside the ring by hitting them. When all marbles, except the target, have been won, each player again contributes an equal number for the next game. A new first player is selected, and the game resumes as before.

SHOOT OUT

Ages: **7 and older.**

Number of players: **Any number.**

Equipment: **An equal number of marbles, all of the same size, for each
player; chalk or stick for marking line.**

Place: **Indoors or outdoors.**

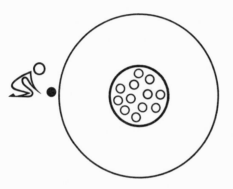

A large circle, 3 feet or more in diameter, is drawn on
the floor or the ground. A smaller circle, 4 to 5 inches in
diameter, is drawn in the center of the large one. Each
player places an equal number of marbles inside the
small circle. Players shoot from the edge of the large
circle, and may not extend their hands inside it to play.
Each player (using his remaining marbles) tries to
shoot as many of the marbles as possible out of the
large circle. Each player shoots in turn, continuing to
shoot from where his shooter lands, for as long as he
fires at least one marble outside the large circle. When
a player fails to shoot any other marble out of the large
circle at his turn, even if his shooter has gone outside
the large circle, play passes to the next player, and so
on. Any player's shooter marble left in the large circle
at the end of his turn may be shot out by following

players or by himself, at his next turn. A player captures all marbles which he shoots outside the large circle. Play continues until all marbles have been captured.

MARBLE BOCCE

Ages: **7 and older.**

Number of players: **2 or more.**

Equipment: **Each player should have 6 marbles of the same color, and each player's color should be different; 1 large target marble; chalk or stick for marking line.**

Place: **Indoors or outdoors.**

The first player shoots out the large target marble from a marked starting line. He then shoots one of his marbles, trying to come as close to the target marble as possible. Each player shoots one marble in turn, until all have played their 6 marbles. A player may dislodge the target marble or any other player's marbles, or even his own that he previously shot. The player's object is to try to get as many as possible of his marbles closer to the target than those of any other player. After every player has shot all 6 marbles, the player whose marble lies closest to the target is the only one who scores. He receives 1 point for that marble, and 1 point for every other marble that lies closer to the target than any opponent's marble does. The player who first scores 21 or more points in succeeding games is the winner.

Variation 1: The target marble is placed 6 inches from a wall. All rules remain the same, except that each player's marble must be shot against the wall and bounce off it, before coming to a halt as close to the target as possible. A shooter marble that comes to rest before it hits the wall is removed from the game at once. That player loses his turn and may not shoot that marble during that inning.

Variation 2: Instead of setting out a target marble, players draw a line some distance from a shooting line from which all players shoot. That player who comes closest to the line in successive turns wins all the marbles.

Variation 3: Lean a flat board against a wall. Each player in turn rolls his marble down the board toward the target marble. All other rules remain the same.

NINE HOLES

Ages: **7 and older.**

Number of players: **2 or more.**

Equipment: **An equal number of marbles for each player; equipment for digging holes in ground; stick for marking line.**

Place: **Outdoors on soft ground.**

Three rows of 3 small holes each are dug in the ground, forming a square. Each hole should be an equal distance (6 to 9 inches) from each adjacent hole (see diagram). Each hole should be large enough to hold 6 to 8 marbles.

Each player contributes an equal number of marbles, so that the center hole contains the most marbles, and twice as many marbles are in each of the 4 corner holes as are in any of the remaining 4. For example, if there are 3 players, each may contribute 10 marbles. Four marbles are placed in each corner hole, 2 in each of the other 4 outside holes, and 6 in the middle.

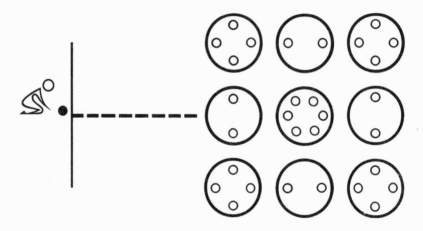

Players shoot from a line marked a given distance from the holes. Each player in turn aims 1 marble per turn toward the holes. If his marble falls into a hole, he captures all marbles in it. If he misses landing his shooter in a hole, it is added to the store in the nearest hole. If a marble lands exactly between holes, or if the nearest hole is too full, then it is placed into any empty hole, or into that hole containing the least number of marbles. If, after the beginning of the game, a player's shooter lands in an empty hole, he must add as many marbles from his own stock as that hole contained at the beginning of the game. The game ends when all holes are empty. The player who captures the largest number of marbles is the winner.

MARBLE BRIDGE

Ages: **7 and older.**

Number of players: **2 or more.**

Equipment: **3 marbles for each player; an arched bridge, cut out from shirt boards, containing 9 or more holes (see illustration). Arches should be cut large enough for marbles to go through. Each arch is numbered at random. Chalk or stick for marking line.**

Place: **Indoors or outdoors.**

Players shoot from a marked line, a given distance from the bridge. Each player shoots all three of his marbles at each turn. A marble scores only if it passes all the way through an arch. The sum of the numbers of the arches through which he is able to shoot his marbles is the player's score at that turn. The winner is the player who has the highest score at the end of a number of turns agreed to before the start of the game.

Variation: Each player starts with an equal number of marbles. One player is chosen "bridge-keeper" by lot. Each player in turn shoots one marble at the bridge. If he scores by shooting his marble through one of the arches, the bridge-keeper must "pay" him the number written over that arch. If he misses, he surrenders his shooter to the bridge-keeper. After each player has shot his marble, he who shot first becomes bridge-keeper, and so on until all players have had their turns.

PICKING THE PLUMS

Ages: **7 and older.**

Number of players: **2, or two teams of up to 4 players each.**

Equipment: **An equal number of "target" marbles for each player or team, plus 3 "shooter" marbles per player or team; chalk or stick for marking lines.**

Place: **Indoors or outdoors.**

Three parallel lines, 4 feet long and 8 inches apart, are drawn on the floor (or scratched lightly into the ground); the shooting lines for each player or team are determined by one player's starting from the center line and pacing off an equal number of steps (12 or more) in each direction. Each side sets up its target marbles between the center line and the outside line closest to the opponent.

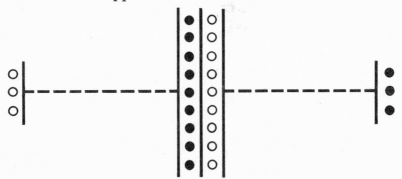

Each player (or each team's players in turn) fires 3 marbles at the target marbles of the opponent. The opposing players or teams take turns shooting. The object is for each player to shoot the opponent's target marbles across the center line. A player or team captures any opponent's target marble which is moved across the center line. Each player or team recovers its own 3 shooter marbles between turns. The game ends when one player or team has captured all of the opponent's target marbles.

Variation: Only two parallel lines are drawn. Each player contributes an equal number of marbles to be set up in a straight row between the lines. Players shoot from opposite sides, capturing marbles they shoot beyond the opponent's line.

III

Button Games

Many of the marble games listed in the previous section can also be adapted to be played with buttons that are tossed, rolled on their edges, or snapped, one against another, as in the game of Tiddlywinks (see illustration) (see Marble Games: Marble Shoot; Target; Nine Holes, etc.). The following button games are especially useful at parties or on occasions when no other materials for play are at hand. Flat stones or coins can be substituted for buttons in many of these games.

Buttons also lend themselves to making an instant toy that was popular over one hundred years ago, but is unknown to many contemporary children. Required materials are a button that has at least two holes in it, and a thread or thin string, 24 to 30 inches long. Thread the button through one hole in one direction and through the second in the other (see illustration) and tie the ends of the thread together. If the child puts the forefinger of each hand through the loops, one finger on each side of the button, and twists the string a few times, he can make the button spin rapidly back and forth, by alternately pulling and relaxing his hold on the string. If the button is large enough, it will make a humming sound. The same toy can be made by cutting a cardboard disk and punching two holes in it, $\frac{1}{8}$ inch apart, on both sides of the center.

BUTTON-STRINGING CONTEST

Ages: **4 and older.**

Number of players: **2 or more.**

Equipment: **An equal number of large buttons with large holes for each player; 1 length of light string or thread on which buttons can be strung without difficulty; 1 button is tied to the end of each string or thread.**

Place: **Indoors.**

Each player tries to string his buttons as quickly as possible. This game can be played for a given period of time, allowing each player to string, unstring, and restring all of his buttons several times in succession. The winner is the player who is able to do this the greatest number of times in the set time period.

KNOCK 'EM DOWN

Ages: **6 and older.**

Number of players: **1 or more.**

Equipment: **1 medium-sized button (or a coin or flat stone); 1 wooden stake or stick, sufficiently flat at one end so that the button can be balanced on it; an equal number of pebbles for each player (or sticks, each 6 inches long).**

Place: **Outdoors on soft ground.**

A circle, 2 to 3 feet in diameter, is marked on the ground; the stake is set in the center, with the button balanced on top of it; a line is marked 6 feet from the stake (or farther for older players).

Standing at the mark, each player in turn throws his pebbles or the short stick at the button, and tries to knock it off the top of the stake so that it falls outside the circle. The winner is the player who succeeds the most times in a given number of turns. The objective, of course, is to aim at the top of the stake.

SNIP-SNAP or TIDDLYWINKS

Ages: **6 and older.**

Number of players: **2 or more.**

Equipment: **3 medium-sized buttons (preferably all of the same size, but a different color for each player); 1 large button; chalk or stick for marking lines.**

Place: **Indoors or outdoors.**

A starting line and a finish line are marked, 8 to 10 feet apart.

Each player lines up his buttons at the starting line, next to those of the other player or players. Then each player in turn, using the large button, snaps his own buttons toward the finish line. If one player manages to snap his button so that it falls on and partially covers an opponent's button in front of the finish line, he captures that button. That player wins who first reaches the finish line with the largest number of his buttons.

Variation: This same game can be played using a hole, rather than a finish line, as the target.

SNAP PEBBLE

Ages: **6 or older.**

Number of players: **2 or more.**

Equipment: **10 or more small, flat buttons or stones; chalk or small stick.**

Place: **Indoors** or **outdoors.**

One player scatters the buttons or pebbles on the ground. The first player, chosen by lot, draws a line (with chalk or stick) between any 2 buttons. He then flicks 1 of these 2 buttons with his index finger across the line, trying to hit the other. If he succeeds he takes the struck button out of the game, draws another line, anywhere between any 2 remaining buttons, and continues as before. He loses his turn only when he fails to hit another button for which he aims. The second player then takes his place and the game continues in turn. That player wins who has collected the largest number of buttons when only a single button is left on the ground.

LONDON

Ages: **7 and older.**

Number of players: **2 or more.**

Equipment: **Large sheet of brown wrapping paper, 30″x40″ or larger; chalk, crayon or stick; 2 large buttons, or one marble, Ping-Pong ball or small ball made of wadded tissue paper.**

Place: **Indoors or outdoors.**

If played indoors, tape the wrapping paper onto the floor. On it, draw the diagram shown below, using either crayon or chalk. Out of doors, scratch the same diagram into soft ground or draw it, using chalk, on pavement.

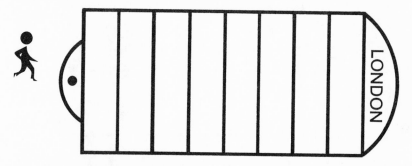

The first player kneels before the base line of the diagram and propels his playing piece in the following manner. If buttons are used, snap one against the other; if a marble is used, flick it with an index finger; if a Ping-Pong ball or a tissue ball is used, blow on it, or flick it like the marble.

A player loses his turn when his playing piece lands on a line or outside the game diagram. If it lands on a space between the lines, he draws a small circle in that

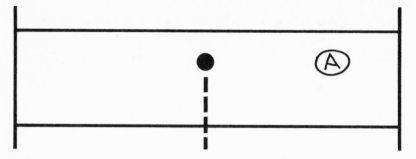

space, marks it with his initial, and resumes play as before until he loses his turn. If the playing piece lands in a space that is occupied by a circle with his initial in it, at any turn, he draws a small oval under the circle (see diagram), next one leg, and thereafter another, each time his counter lands in that same space. The first player to complete three such armless figures in any space, draws in the arms at that turn and "owns" it (see diagram) no matter how many incomplete figures, drawn by other players, occupy it. Any other player who, in his turn, lands in such an "owned" space, loses his turn.

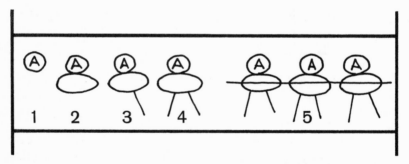

Players may only add to or complete their own figures on landing on any space in their respective turns. Whenever a player lands on "London" he may, at that turn, add one feature to any one of his own figures that occupies any space on the diagram, including drawing the arms of a completed set of three or starting a new one in any space that is not yet "owned." That player wins who "owns" the greatest number of spaces when all are "owned."

TOSS-UP

Ages: **8 and older.**

Number of players: **2 or more.**

Equipment: **An equal number of buttons for each player (each player should have a different color, if possible); 1 large button or pebble, used as a target; stick for marking line.**

Place: **Outdoors, against a windowless wall.**

A mark is made 6 to 10 feet from the wall.

The first player, chosen by lot, stands at the mark and tosses the target button or pebble so that it bounces off the wall and lands a distance away from it. He then begins the first round, in which each player in turn stands at the mark and bounces one of his own buttons off the wall. The object is to make the button land within a "span" (see Marble Games, introduction) of the target. The player who comes closest wins all the other buttons thrown in that round. If no player comes within a "span" of the target, players continue for another round, leaving the target and all previously thrown buttons in place. Otherwise a new round is started like the first, the target button being rethrown for each round, the second player in the first round becoming the first in the second, and so on.

If any player's button does not strike the wall before
it lands, that player is disqualified from winning the
round, even if his button comes closest to the target.
His button is captured, along with the rest, by the
winner of that round.

IV

Hop, Skip, and Jump

In an era when most children spend a great deal of time sitting—on school buses, in school, at home in front of their TV sets, radios and record players, in movies and, at later ages, in cars, it seems a good idea to keep their circulation going from earliest ages on, by encouraging vigorous exercise in play. The following games have been selected because of their relative informality and the few, if any, materials that are needed to play them. Further, these are games that do not require given or large teams. Two or more children can play wherever they happen to find themselves.

Most of these games are ancient. It should be kept in mind that before the end of the last century, most people in Europe, as in the Americas, lived on farms and away from urban centers. Especially in the United States, rural children were largely isolated from contact with others of their own ages. The farms were far apart from one another. Thus, the games that these children played among themselves were adaptable to wide age groups and were not dependent on given-sized teams or rigid rules. These same games are also ideal for present-day play streets in crowded cities, or for informal play when children casually meet in playgrounds and parks, and whenever they gather outdoors.

HOPSCOTCH

Ages: **5 and older.**

Number of players: **1 or more.**

Equipment: **A stick to scratch the diagram into soft ground, or chalk for pavement; a pebble, a small piece of wood, or a shell as the counter that, in most English-speaking countries, is called the "potsie."**

Place: **Outdoors.**

Countless versions of this game exist and are played around the world. Patricia Evans discovered at least 19 different ones played by children in San Francisco in 1955.[15] An ancient Hopscotch diagram has survived the centuries, inscribed in the pavement of the Forum in Rome. The game is known as *Marelles* in France, as *Tempelhüpfen* in Germany, and by the name of *Ekaria Dukaria* in India. Russian, Scandinavian, and Chinese children enjoy the same game played with minor variations.

The game of Home (see diagram) is played by throwing the "potsie" into space number 1, jumping with the right foot into 8, hopping with the left foot into 2, with the right into 7, never keeping both feet on the ground, until the first player has arrived at "Home." Here he can put both feet down. He returns, left foot into 5, right foot into 4, in turn, until he arrives at 1. Here he retrieves his "potsie" while standing on one foot and then jumps out.

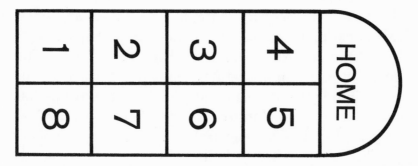

If the "potsie" lands on a line, or when a player steps on a line, he is out and must start at his next turn as at first. But when a player completes the full round, he continues by throwing his "potsie" into space number 2, completes a full round of hopping as before, jumps out, and then continues until he has thrown his "potsie" into every space from 1 through 8, except "Home," hopping the full circuit each time. If he completes all rounds without fault, he closes his eyes and throws the "potsie" aiming for "Home." If it lands inside without touching a line, he goes through the diagram once more, eyes closed, first stepping into 1 and 8 with both feet at the same time, next into 2 and 7, all the way to "Home" and back again. If he completes this round without stepping on any lines, picking up his "potsie" on "Home" and finally jumping out, he has won that game and a new round begins.

Variation 1 (see diagram): The first player throws his "potsie" into 1, hops with both feet into 1 and 2, respectively, then hops with one foot into 3, and continues, hopping alternately with two feet and with one until he reaches 12 and then returns, hopping in the same manner in the opposite direction. If he completes this round successfully without stepping on any lines, this same player aims his "potsie" at 2, hops all the way through the diagram once more as before, picking up his "potsie" on his return trip, when he reaches the space into which it was thrown and so on, until he has thrown the "potsie" into all the numbered spaces. That player wins who completes the whole round of throws and hops successfully. He loses his turn whenever his "potsie" or a foot lands on a line.

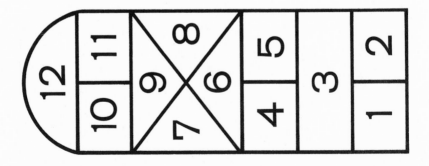

Variation 2: The following diagrams show different Hopscotch diagrams used by children of the past and present, with and without numbers, played by hopping on a single foot, on both, or alternately on one and then on both. The rules are more or less similar to those described above.

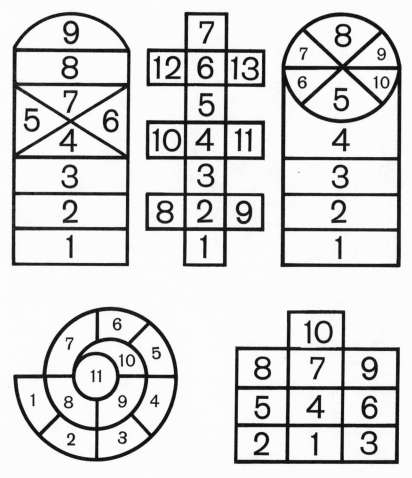

Variation 3: An old English version of this game requires each player to kick the "potsie" from square to square as he hops into it, starting at 1, hopping up to 12 on one foot and back again to 1 and then out. On completing this round he goes through the next as before, carrying the "potsie" on the back of his hand, next on his forehead, next bent over on the small of his back, then on the right shoulder, and finally on his left shoulder. If, on the first or on any succeeding round, he kicks the "potsie" onto a line, or when, on succeeding rounds, he drops it or if he steps on a line, he is out and must await his next turn.

ROPE-SKIPPING

Ages: **6 and older.**

Number of players: **1 or more.**

Materials: **Skip-rope.**

Place: **Outdoors.**

Rope-skipping by individual children and groups is sometimes accompanied by the singing of game rhymes,

of which the following is typical. The rope is swung
and the player skips, keeping the rhyme's beat:

> Mother, Mother, I am sick,
> Call for the doctor, quick, quick, quick.
> In came the doctor, in came the nurse,
> In came the lady with the alligator purse.
> Out went the doctor, out went the nurse,
> Out went the lady with the alligator purse.

Joseph Strutt, the early-nineteenth-century author of
the book *Sports and Pastimes of the People of England*,
describes rope-skipping as follows:

> This amusement is probably very ancient. It is performed by a
> rope held at both ends, that is, one end in each hand, and
> thrown forwards or backwards over the head and under the
> feet alternately. Boys often contend for superiority of skill in
> this game, and he who passes the rope about most times
> without interruption is the conqueror. In the hop season, a
> hop-stem stripped of its leaves is used instead of a rope, and
> in my opinion is preferable.[32]

Variation 1: Two players turn the rope slowly at first,
then faster, while a third skips until he (or she) trips
or misses a skip. Then one of the others takes his place.
Players keep score of the number of times each manages to skip successfully before tripping.

Variation 2: The two players who hold the rope ends
swing it from side to side, instead of turning it in a
complete circle as before. The third player skips—
either with both feet together, or first with one foot
and then with the other.

Variation 3: CHASE THE FOX: A game for 5 or more players. Two turn the rope. One of the other players is chosen the leader. The rest must follow and do exactly what the leader does in their turn. The following sequence is typical:

a) The leader "runs," but does not skip, through the rope while it is up high. The rest follow in turn.

b) The leader jumps into the turning rope, skips once, and then jumps out again. The rest follow.

c) The leader jumps into the turning rope, skips twice . . . and so on.

The first player to trip on the rope takes the place of one of the rope-turners.

Variation 4: One player turns the rope and skips. A second player runs through the rope while it is up high and, facing the rope-turning player, skips with him once and runs out. Each of the other players follows in turn.

Variation 5: Two players turn the rope. A third runs in, carrying a stone or pebble. He places the stone on the ground and picks it up again at each alternate skip.

Variation 6: Two players turn two ropes at the same time in either the same or opposite directions. The other players, in turn, are required to skip both ropes.

Variation 7: One player turns and skips the rope himself (or two rope-turners swing it for a third). But the rope must pass twice beneath the skipper's feet at each leap.

COCK-FIGHTING

Ages: **6 and older.**

Number of players: **2 or more.**

Place: **Outdoors.**

Each player stands on one foot and grasps his other by the ankle in one hand. Both players hop around and bump into each other, attempting to knock the opponent off balance. That player wins who forces his opponent off balance, to let go of his foot, or to place both feet on the ground.

This and the following games can be played by any number of participants, the winner of each round opposing the next player, or the winner of rounds opposing each other, or as a free-for-all.

Variation 1: Players hop on one foot, with arms folded across their chests.

Variation 2: Each of 2 opposing players squats on his haunches, putting his arms around his knees and clasping his hands firmly. Players hop as before, trying to unbalance one another.

Variation 3: Players squat as above. But they are required to face each other with toes touching, throughout the contest.

Variation 4: Draw a circle around each 2 opposing players. Without using the free hand (placing it behind their backs) in the first game cited above, or playing according to any of the other versions, that player wins who forces his opponent to touch or to cross the circle.

LEAPFROG

Ages: **6 and older.**

Number of players: **2 or more.**

Place: **Gym** or **outdoors.**

Caution players not to make fists while leaping over another's back, to make "firm" backs, and to stand rigid and still while others leap over them.

One player makes a "back" by bending forward and down, and by placing his hands on his knees to make a "high back," or elbows on knees to make a "small back," as demanded by each leaping player. The second player then leaps over the first and makes a "back" in turn at about 5- or 6-foot distance from the first. The first player then leaps over him, and so on. In a game of more than 2 players, the first and second players remain in place until the third has jumped; all 3 then remain in place until the fourth has jumped, and so on, until all players are making "backs" at the same time. The last player in line, who leaped first, then straightens up, leaps over all others and makes a "back" again at the head of the line. The game continues for as long as players agree.

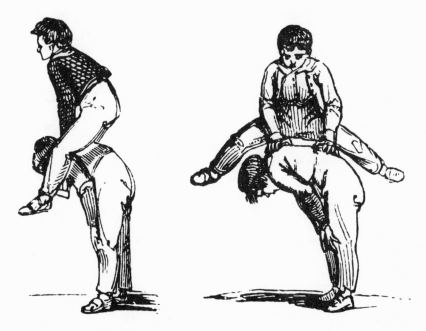

Variation: Leapfrog can also be played as a race game. Players divide into two or more equal teams and commence, as before, on the word "Start" from the referee.

Players only leap over those of their own team. That team wins whose last player first completes jumping over all of his teammates and stands first in line ahead of his team.

HOPPING BASES

Ages: **6 and older.**

Number of players: **12 or more (must be an even number), divided into two equal teams, plus one "it" player.**

Place: **Outdoors.**

A playing field is marked, 60 feet (or more) long and 15 feet (or more) wide. A 3-foot circle is marked in the center for "it" (see diagram).

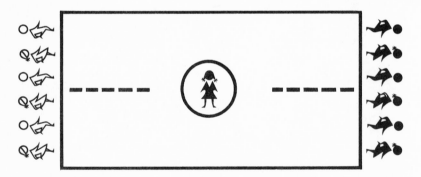

"It" is chosen by lot. The members of each team line up on opposing base lines of the field. "It" stands in a circle in the center. At the command from "it," the members of both teams start hopping on one leg, from one end of the field to the other. "It" may stand on both legs as long as he stays in his "castle." But in order to tag the hopping players, he must leave his castle and hop like the rest. All tagged players, and any player who puts his other foot down, are "out," with the exception of "it." If he puts his other foot down, he must return and step inside his castle before venturing forth once more to tag players. Any player who reaches the opposing base is "safe." The game ends when all players have reached opposite base lines or have been captured by "it." Then a new "it" is chosen for the next game.

Variation 1: The same playing field is used, but without castle or "it" player. Two equal teams line up on the base lines on opposing sides of the field and, on the word "Go," hop on one foot toward the opposite side of the field. Opposing team members try to unbalance each other. Any player who loses his balance or puts his other foot down is considered captured by the opposing team and must go to the base line toward which that team hops. Any team member who has crossed the opposite base line is safe. But any captured player may be rescued by any member of his own team who hops up to him and touches him. The team wins which crosses the opposing base line with the greatest number of its members.

Any player may hop back to his starting boundary line to take a rest. Once he crosses the opposing line, he may not re-enter the game.

Variation 2: In another version of the latter game described above, players of each team merely sally forth to capture opponents, returning them to their original starting base. That team wins which captures the largest number of opponents.

Variation 3: All players line up at one end of the field and hop on either right or left foot (determined before the start of the game) toward the opposite finish line. The player who crosses the opposing end-zone line first is the winner. Any player who puts his other foot down during the race is out of the game.

Variation 4: One player is chosen to be "it." All players, including "it," grasp their own right feet with their right hands and hop. "It" tries to tag another player in this manner. None of the players, including "it," may put both feet on the ground except when standing still. If "it" has both feet on the ground while tagging a player, it doesn't count. If he puts his foot down or lets go of it while chasing a player, he is required to tag two players before he is released. Only the second tagged player changes places with him. "It" may be required to tag more than two, depending on the number of times he is seen putting his other foot down, or releasing his hold on it, while chasing another player. Any other player is required to change places with "it," if "it" sees him putting his other foot on the ground or releasing his hand hold on it while hopping.

OBSTACLE HOP

Ages: **7 and older.**

Number of players: **2 or more.**

Materials: **Stones (or pegs).**

Place: **Outdoors on soft ground.**

The stones or pegs are placed to mark an obstacle course. Players must hop, on one leg, in and out of the stones or pegs in a given manner (see diagram) from start to finish. One player hops at a time. Each player is timed. The player who completes the course in the shortest time period is the winner. Any player who loses his balance while on the course, or whose other leg touches the ground, is out of the game.

Originally, blindfolded players were required to dance on one foot around a number of eggs laid out over a piece of ground, a dance floor, or a stage. Anyone who stepped on an egg was the loser. Such egg-hopping dances were common in the days of the English poet Chaucer (d. 1400), and were still in vogue during the reign of Queen Elizabeth I.

JUMP UP

Ages: **7 and older.**

Number of players: **2 or more.**

Materials: **8-foot string (or light rope), with a paper bag attached that contains a quantity of sand sufficient to allow the bag to be swung in a circle steadily (see illustration).**

Place: **Outdoors.**

One player, chosen by lot, stands in the middle, holding the end of the rope. The other players stand in a circle around him, close enough so that, when the center player swings the rope with the bag attached, they must hop to avoid it. Any player who fails to jump in time, and whose legs become caught in the rope, is out of the game. The last player to remain in the game changes places with the player in the middle for the next round.

V

Race, Tag, and Catch Games

The Olympic Games, held for more than 1,000 years, from 776 B.C. to A.D. 394, in the valley of Olympia in Greece, originally featured just a single event—the 200-yard dash. The Roman emperor Theodosius banned these quatri-annual games because of bitter quarrels between his regime and that of the Greeks. The Olympics were not revived until 1896, and with the exception of the World War I and II years, have been held every four years since.

Men have run races from and with predators and each other, and for sport, since time immemorial. Children have raced on their way to and from school, and in fields and parks, on the beach and in gardens and play-grounds. They have also invented variations on this simple activity that, in most instances, requires nothing but rules and a pair of legs.

FOOT RACES

Ages: **4 and older.**

Number of players: **2 or more.**

Equipment: **See individual variations.**

Place: **Outdoors** or **indoors.**

The simplest form of foot-racing merely requires that a start and a finish line be marked at a distance, in a straight line or on a circular track. Players line up at the start and race at a given signal. The winner is the player who first crosses the finish line at the end of the course, or after covering several laps.

Variation 1: EGG RACE

Equipment: **1 large spoon** and **1 egg for each player.**

Players race as above, except that each is required to hold an egg in a spoon in one hand, and carry it from start to finish. That player wins who first crosses the finish line with his egg intact on the spoon. No player may use his other hand to hold or steady the egg. Any player is out of the game if he drops his egg or uses his other hand to steady either spoon or egg. This game may also be played as a relay game (see Relay Races,

p. 141), or with table tennis balls or other small balls carried on spoons as substitutes for eggs.

Variation 2: SACK RACE

Equipment: **1 potato sack for each player; twine, sufficient to tie the sack at the waist of each player.**

Each player steps into a sack, tying it around his waist. Players hop from start to finish line. Any player who falls may get up and continue to hop. The player who crosses the finish line first is the winner.

STOOP TAG

Ages: **4 and older.**

Number of players: **8 or more (up to about 12).**

Place: **Indoors or outdoors.**

All players but one form a circle. The extra player stands in the center. The players in the circle skip round and round, singing any song they know or reciting any common nursery rhyme. As soon as they have finished, all must stoop (or sit) down. The player in the center tries to tag any player before he stoops (or sits) down after each rhyme or song has ended. The tagged player must then stand in the center. The first center player joins the circle, and the game continues.

MUSICAL CHAIRS

Ages: **4 and older.**

Number of players: **8 or more.**

Equipment: **Chairs—1 less than the number of players; piano (or radio or record player).**

Place: **Indoors.**

Chairs are set up back-to-back in two more or less equal rows. The players line up, forming a circle around the chairs. One other person is required to play or to start and to stop the music. At the start of the music, all players start walking or running around the island of chairs. Whenever the music stops, each player must try to sit in an empty chair. No two players may occupy the same chair. The player who is left standing is out of the game. Another chair is removed before the music begins again. At the resumption of the music, players get up and walk or run as before—and so on. The player who manages to sit in the last remaining chair wins the game.

FOLLOW THE LEADER

Ages: **5 and older.**

Number of players: **6 or more.**

Place: **Indoors or outdoors.**

Players line up, one behind the other, without touching or holding one another. The first in line is chosen by lot. All others are required to follow him wherever he goes, doing exactly what he does and imitating his every gesture. If he hops, they hop, etc. Any player who fails to "follow the leader" is out of the game. It is best to play each "turn" of this game for a predetermined time period, at the end of which a new leader is chosen. Those players win who remain in line at the end of each round.

Variation: Players line up side by side, holding hands. The leader starts out as before. Whenever any player fails to "follow the leader," he changes places with the player next to him who is closer to the end of the line. If two players release hands, both players change places with the next two who are closer to the end of the line. Any player who reaches the end of the line is out of the game. The rest of the rules remain the same.

HOOP GAMES

Ages: **5 and older.**

Number of players: **1 or more.**

Equipment: **Hoop and stick.**

Place: **Outdoors.**

The earliest hoop game was probably invented by children playing outside a cooper's shop in the Middle Ages, or perhaps even earlier. There they may have picked up one of the iron hoops with which coopers bound wooden slats to form barrels. Finding that the hoops could be controlled by wooden sticks, the children made up all sorts of racing games, one of which is described below. Children have played with hoops ever since, except for an interval between the early part of this century and the appearance of the Hoola Hoop in the nineteen-fifties. Typical of many children's pastimes, this simple toy—no different from its predecessors, except that it was made of plastic tubing—was suddenly rediscovered and became a temporary fad.

Players line up in a row and race toward a given, pre-determined finish line (and back, if the ground is restricted in length). Each drives and guides his hoop with his stick. Any player whose hoop falls to the ground is out of the game. The first player to cross the finish line wins.

Variation 1: Hoop games can also be played as relay games (see Relay Races, p. 141).

Variation 2: A course is set up, marked by a number of gates consisting of 2 stones placed close together, but far enough apart that a hoop can be driven between them. A finish line is marked. Each player in turn must drive his hoop from one end of the course to the other, steering it through each gate. Any player who fails to clear a gate or who upsets his hoop before reaching the finish line is out of the game.

TAG

Ages: **5 and older.**

Number of players: **3 or more.**

Place: **Outdoors** or **gym.**

One player is chosen "it," and tries to chase and tag any of the others. As soon as he tags another player, the tagged player becomes "it," and so on.

Variation 1: Same rules as above, except that when a player runs between "it" and the player being chased, "it" *must* chase the intercepting player.

Variation 2: Known as Touch Tag. In this game, players agree beforehand on a common material— wood, metal, or any other. Whenever a chased player touches the specified material, he is safe for the time being, until "it" chases another player.

Variation 3: Carry Tag requires an object that is passed from player to player. "It" may only chase and tag a player who holds the object. The object must always be in sight when carried by one of the players.

Variation 4: The first "it" tags another player, who becomes "it," as usual. When the new "it" tags another player, he must at the same time hold his hand over the place on his body where the first "it" tagged him. The newly tagged player must do the same, and so on.

Variation 5: Each group of 3 players forms a line, each player grasping the waist of the player in front of him. It is the object of "it" to attach himself to the last player of any group of 3 players. If he succeeds in so

doing, the first in line of that group becomes "it." Any player in a group of 3 who lets go of the person in front of him becomes "it," whether or not his group has been tagged.

Variation 6: One player is chosen to be "it," and another as the "runner." The remaining players form a circle, each holding the hands of his neighbor. "It" stands inside the circle and the "runner" outside at the start of the game. On the word "go" from the "runner," he himself runs round the circle, dodging in and out between players, while the "it" player tries to tag him. The players in the circle must raise their arms or make room for either to pass. But "it" must follow the "runner" precisely through the same openings in the circle and he must imitate exactly what the "runner" does, jumping, rolling on the floor or ground, hopping on one leg, or whatever he chooses to do. When "it" manages to tag the "runner," the latter joins the circle; the player who was "it" in the former round becomes the "runner" for the next, choosing any player in the circle to be "it" for the next round.

Variation 7: Shadow Tag is an outdoor, sunny-day version, in which one player is selected to be "it." The rest scatter, but they must remain in sunny or well-lit places. "It" tags any other player when, having chased him, he manages to step on his shadow. A tagged player becomes "it" in turn.

FOX AND RABBIT

Ages: **5 and older.**

Number of players: **10 or more.**

Place: **Indoors** or **outdoors.**

Players divide into groups of four. One of the remaining players is chosen as "it," and the other as the "spare rabbit." Three of each group of four form a circle (the rabbit warren) by placing their hands on each other's shoulders. The fourth member of each group becomes a "rabbit" and squats in the center of the circle. "It" is the "fox" and he attempts to tag the "spare rabbit," who may run into any warren for safety. The fox may not follow him or reach inside. But that rabbit who is already inside the warren into which the "spare rabbit" ran for safety must then leave it at once, to be chased by the fox. At no time may more than one rabbit remain in any warren. The players forming any circle must allow the "spare rabbit" to enter whenever he chooses to do so. The rabbit who must then run away becomes the "spare rabbit" and, though he may choose any other warren for safety in the same manner as the first, he may not return to his original warren at that turn. Any tagged rabbit changes places with the fox.

POTATO RACE

Ages: **5 and older.**

Number of players: **2 or more.**

Equipment: **Use 6 or more potatoes—the same number—for each player's line. Other objects, like pebbles or Ping-Pong balls, can be used in their stead; chalk or stick for marking lines; empty carton or wastebasket for each player or team.**

Place: **Indoors or outdoors.**

Mark a start line and place one row of potatoes for each player at right angles to the start line, each potato 4 or 5 feet from the next. Place the carton or wastebasket at the end of each line. All players line up at the start line, one behind each row of potatoes. On the word "go" from the referee, each runs forward, picks up the first potato only, runs to the basket, drops or throws it in, and then returns for the next potato, and so on. The player wins that round who first drops the last of his potatoes in the basket.

Variation: This game may also be played as a relay game. Divide the players into equal teams, each of which lines up behind its own line of potatoes. Every line must contain as many potatoes as the number of players on each team. The first player, having dropped his potato into the basket, returns and tags the next player in line, who runs forward to do the same, and so on. The team wins whose last player first drops the last potato into his own team's basket and who returns, tagging the first player of his team.

PAIR RACE

Ages: **5 and older.**

Number of players: **13 or more—it must be an odd number.**

Place: **Indoors or outdoors.**

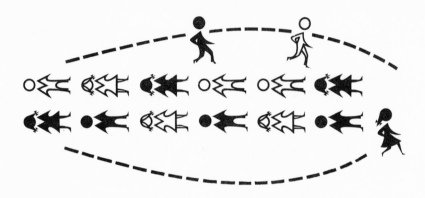

Players pair up, holding hands, and stand in line. The odd player, chosen by lot to be "it," stands aside. At his command, "Last pair go," the last pair in the row of players split up and run toward the head of the column on opposite sides, trying to avoid being tagged by "it."

If either member of the pair is tagged, "it" and the tagged player make a pair at the head of the column. The other partner of the first pair then becomes "it," and the game continues as before. If "it" fails to tag either member of a pair before they hold hands again at the head of the column, he must continue to be "it" for the next turn, and so on.

CAT AND MOUSE

Ages: **5 and older.**

Number of players: **12 or more.**

Place: **Outdoors** or **gym.**

All but 2 players form a circle. They may not hold hands. Of the remaining players, one is chosen "cat," and the other "mouse." The cat stands inside the circle, and the mouse remains outside. The object of the cat is to try to get outside the circle to "tag" the mouse. It is the object of the players in the circle to try to prevent the cat's escape. The mouse may not ever enter the circle. The game ends when the mouse has been tagged, or if the cat is unable to escape the circle after a pre-determined time period.

BUTTERFLY HUNT

Ages: **6 and older.**

Number of players: **Two teams of 12 or more each.**

Place: **Outdoors** or **gym.**

One team is designated as butterflies, the other as hunters. The hunters try to capture the butterflies by encircling them and joining hands to close the net. Captured butterflies are out of the game for that turn. Hunters may repeatedly net as many butterflies as they can at one inning. At the end of the time period allowed for one inning, captured butterflies score for the capturing team. Teams change places alternately for succeeding innings. The winning team is the one which has scored the largest catch at the end of a given number of innings.

LION AND GAZELLES

Ages: **6 and older.**

Number of players: **8 or more.**

Place: **Outdoors** or **gym.**

One player is chosen as the lion, and a place is marked for his den. The rest of the players are gazelles, who have a marked safety zone, some distance from the lion's den, within which they cannot be captured. All the gazelles start walking toward the lion, approaching closer and closer. The lion may dash out of his den at any time to chase one of the gazelles, who then tries to run back to his safety zone. If a gazelle is tagged before he reaches safety, he is captured by the lion and remains in his den. If he reaches his safety zone before being tagged, the lion loses 1 point. The game is played for a given time period, or until all the gazelles are captured. The last gazelle to be captured then becomes the lion.

BLIND MAN'S BUFF

Ages: **6 and older.**

Number of players: **8 or more.**

Place: **Indoors** or **outdoors.**

All players but one form a circle, facing inward. The extra player is blindfolded and placed in the center. The rest of the players hold hands and skip in a circle. The "blind man" may call "stop" at any time, on which signal the players in the circle must stand in place. The blind man then points in any direction. The player closest to the blind man's pointed finger must step into the circle and try to keep away from the blind man. If the blind man tags him, he must stand still while the blind man touches his face and tries to guess his name. (Alternate rule: The blind man may ask the tagged player any one question other than his name.) If the blind man is able to guess the player's name, he is released, and the tagged player takes his place. If the blind man fails to guess the player's name, the game continues as before, the tagged player returning to his place in the circle.

RACE FOR THE EMPTY SPACE

Ages: **6 and older.**

Number of players: **12 or more.**

Place: **Outdoors** or **gym.**

All players but one stand in a circle facing inward. The remaining "it" player runs outside the circle and tags any player. The tagged player and "it" must then run around the circle in opposite directions until they meet. On meeting, they grasp hands and swing each other once around in a circle, and then continue to run as before. The first player to reach the space vacated by the tagged player is safe. Whichever player remains becomes "it," and play continues as at first.

HAND-HOLD TAG

Ages: **6 and older.**

Number of players: **6 or more.**

Place: **Outdoors or gym.**

One player is selected as "it." The rest of the players scatter. "It" tries to tag one of the others. Whenever he succeeds, he and the tagged player join hands, and they seek to tag any of the others. Each tagged player joins the "it" line. The last remaining untagged player is the winner.

HANDKERCHIEF TAG

Ages: **6 and older.**

Number of players: **10 or more.**

Place: **Outdoors or gym.**

All players but one form a circle, facing inward. "It," chosen by lot, runs around the outside of the circle, carrying the handkerchief. He drops the handkerchief behind any player in the circle. That player must pick up the handkerchief and chase "it," trying to tag him before he can safely run to the vacant place in the circle. "It" must run once around the circle before he may occupy the vacant place. If "it" is tagged, the second player returns to his place in the circle and gives the handkerchief back to "it." "It" must then drop the handkerchief behind another player, who chases him as before.

If "it" runs to the vacant place without being tagged, the chasing player becomes "it," and so on. The game continues for a given time period.

COUNTING OUT CATCH

Ages: **6 and older.**

Number of players: **10 or more.**

Place: **Outdoors** or **gym.**

Players agree to a number, considerably greater than the number of players. They line up in a circle and start counting off, starting with any player chosen by lot. Counting off continues until the determined number is reached. The player who counts off that number is "it." All other players scatter. "It" must catch or tag any other player before he is released from being "it." The players agree to a new number, count off, and continue to play as before.

Variation: This same game can also be played using the alphabet, one letter being chosen for each turn. Or the States of the Union can be used, one state being agreed upon as determining "it." In this event, each player must name a different state in turn. He has 10 seconds to think of a state that hasn't been named before, or he must name the chosen one. The rest of the rules remain as before.

MAN IN THE MIDDLE

Ages: **6 and older.**

Number of players: **10 or more.**

Equipment: **Two sets of markers or tape to indicate end zones and mid-point.**

Place: **Outdoors or gym.**

One player is chosen by lot to be the "Man in the Middle." The rest are divided into two more or less equal teams. End zones are marked 40 yards or so apart (less for younger players), and another marker is placed halfway between them. Markers or tape should also indicate side boundaries. The Man in the Middle stands at the midpoint, and the teams line up one each at the end zones.

At the word "go" from the Man in the Middle, each team starts running toward the opposite end zone, keeping within boundaries. The Man in the Middle may also leave his place, and he tries to tag as many of both teams as he can before they cross their respective end zones. Each tagged player must go directly to the mid-point and await the end of that turn. When all players who were not tagged have returned to their end zones, the Man in the Middle returns to his starting point, and the game begins anew on his shout of "go," except that all tagged players now aid him in tagging team members as they cross from one end zone to the other. The last player to be tagged is the winner.

Variation 1: This game may be played in a play-street, the edges of the sidewalk being the end-zone boundaries. Or all players may line up on one side of the street (or field) and try to run to the opposite side at the command of the Man in the Middle.

Variation 2: Players are divided into three equal teams. Two teams line up on one side of the street or playground respectively. The third team lines up in the center. The members of the third team must hold hands. All other players may run individually. On the word "go," the two teams on opposite sides of the street or playground try to cross over and change places. The team in the middle tries to tag as many players as possible while the others are crossing. Any tagged player is out of the game. The game ends after a given time period, or when all members of the two crossing teams are captured. Teams then change places, and one of the other two teams becomes the "Team in the Middle." The game should continue for at least three rounds, giving each team one turn in the middle. The team that captures the largest number of opponents wins.

This is a variation of a game called Barley Break, played for centuries by the children of England and Scotland.

THREE'S A CROWD

Ages: **6 and older.**

Number of players: **24 or more.**

Place: **Outdoors** or **gym.**

All but two players stand in pairs, one player behind another, to form a double circle, facing inward. The remaining two players, chosen by lot, are "it," who does the chasing, and the "catch-me" player, who runs from him. Both players start from opposite sides of the circle and may run on either or both the inside or the outside of the circle in either direction, or may dodge between the players forming the double circle.

Whenever the "catch-me" player feels himself threatened, he may stand directly behind any one of the couples that form the circle. When he does so, the front player of that couple becomes the "catch-me" player and must run from "it." If "it" tags the "catch-me" player before he stands safe, they change places. The game continues for a predetermined time period.

Variation 1: All but two players, chosen by lot, are divided into couples, each player facing and holding both hands with his partner. "It" then chases the other extra player and tries to tag him. If the chased player ducks under the arms of any couple, he is safe in the "cage" so formed. But the person whom the chased player faces must then release his hold and run from "it" until he is either safe in a "cage" or tagged. Any tagged player must chase "it" in turn. Any "caged" player takes the place of the person whom he faces. (See also Fox and Rabbit.)

Variation 2: Two players—one to be "it" and the other to be the "runner"—are chosen by lot. The remaining players pair off and each pair links arms. On the word "Start" from the "runner," "it" chases and tries to catch him. The runner may seek safety by linking arms with any couple, at which moment the member of that couple with whom he does not link arms must release his partner to become the "runner" in turn. Any tagged player changes places with "it," who then becomes the "runner."

NUMBER

Ages: **6 and older.**

Number of players: **11 or more.**

Equipment: **Cards or sheets of paper, at least 6" x 9", marked with one number each, from 1 to a number one less than the number of players.**

Place: **Indoors.**

One player is chosen to be "it." The rest sit in a circle, each holding one card, number side facing the center of the circle. "It" then calls out any two numbers shown on the cards. The 2 players holding these numbers must get up and try to change places without being tagged by "it." A player whose number has been called may not return to his original place, but must run or dodge, inside or outside the circle of players, until he gains the place of the other player or until he is tagged. "It" changes places with a tagged player.

Variation: This game can be played without numbers, using the names of players, with letters of the alphabet marked on cards, or with numbers as above, for which "it," instead of calling out two marked numbers, must name them, each multiplied by two (or three or more, as agreed to before the start of the game). In other words, when "it" calls 4 and 6, 2 and 3 must try to change places. (See also Number Games.)

COUNT TO TEN

Ages: **6 or older.**

Number of players: **4 or more.**

Place: **Indoors** or **outdoors; mark off two parallel lines, 20 to 75 feet apart.**

One player, chosen to be "it" by lot, stands on one line with his back to all others who are lined up toeing the other line. "It" counts to ten as rapidly as possible. While he counts, the other players may advance as many paces as possible toward the line on which "it" stands, by putting one foot directly in front of the other for each step. At the count of ten "it" may turn around. The other players must then stand stock-still. If "it" can catch any player moving or taking a step when he turns around, that player must then return to the starting line and the game resumes as before. The first player to cross the line on which "it" stands changes places with him. Then "it" joins the rest of the players and the game starts again as at first.

I SPY

Ages: **7 and older.**

Number of players: **6 or more.**

Place: **Outdoors.**

One player is chosen as "it." He must remain near a tree or other goal, facing it with his eyes closed while he counts out loud to 100 (or any other number agreed upon). The other players hide. When "it" reaches his last number, he opens his eyes, leaves the goal, and tries to find the other players. As soon as he spots another player, he must call out his name. Both then run toward the goal. If "it" reaches the goal first, the second player becomes the "spy." If the second player reaches the goal first, he is safe, and "it" must continue to find and race other hidden players.

Variation: Other simple hide-and-seek games for younger children can include indoor and outdoor hiding games without the "race" feature of the above version.

HAND IT OVER

Ages: **7 and older.**

Number of players: **Two teams of 12 or more each.**

Place: **Outdoors or gym.**

Players are divided into two teams—cops and robbers. The robber team selects an object that can be carried in a pocket of one of the players without being visible to the opponents. The robber team lines up on one side of the playground or street and, on command, crosses over to the other side, running, walking, and dodging the opposing "cop" team that is in the middle of the field. It is the object of the "cops" to tag as many robbers as possible before they reach the other side of the playground. The cops must demand, and a captured player who has it in his possession must give up, the hidden object. If one of the captured players has the hidden object, the cops win, teams change places, and the game resumes as before. If none of the captured robbers has the hidden object, the remaining robbers cross over once more as before. Captured players are out of the game for that turn.

Each crossing from one side to the other scores for the robber team. That team wins which has captured the robber holding the hidden object in the least number of cross-over runs, in the number of turns agreed on before the start of the game.

RELAY RACES

Ages: **7 and older.**

Number of players: **Two or more teams of 6 or more players each.**

Equipment: **Stick (or cloth, ball, or Indian club) for each team; markers for starting and goal lines.**

Place: **Outdoors or gym.**

Each team lines up behind its own starting line. The first player is given the ball (or other object). On a given signal, each team's first player races toward the goal line, touches or crosses it, and returns to the front of his team's line. He passes the ball to the next player of his team, then goes to the end of the line. The second player runs to the goal line and back, and passes the ball to the third player, and so on. That team wins whose last player is first to return to his team's starting line with the ball. *Note:* The distance between starting and goal lines should be determined according to the ages and stamina of the players.

Variation 1: Instead of carrying an object, each player may merely slap the hand of the next player on his return to the starting line.

Variation 2: The goal line consists of a circle of Indian clubs that the first player must knock down. The second runner must set them up again before he returns to his team; the third player knocks them down again, and so on.

Variation 3: Hurdle Relay: The first two players of each team hold a rope or stick between them, low enough so that any other player can jump over it. The rest of the players of each team line up 6 or 7 feet from the hurdle. Each player must jump the hurdle and then return to the end of the line. When all team members have jumped, the player first in line takes the place of one hurdle holder, who goes to the end of the line. The players in line then run and jump as before. After all team members have jumped once more, the new player first in line takes the place of the hurdle holder who has not yet jumped, and the game continues as before. The winner is the team whose last player is first to return to the end of the line, after all team members have both jumped the hurdle and taken a turn at holding it.

Variation 4: In any of the above relay games, players may be required to hop on one or two legs, instead of running. Or the relays may be run piggyback, the first player carrying the second, who, on returning to the starting line, carries the third, and so on.

Variation 5: Instead of carrying a ball, each team's first player is given a word, a sentence, a number, or a sequence of numbers to memorize. On returning to his team after running the course, he passes this message on to the next player, and so on. That team wins whose last runner is first to return to his team and who recites the correct message, as given to the first player.

Variation 6: Other stunts each relay racer may be required to perform can include: balancing a pencil in his palm while he runs or walks; taking off his shirt and putting it on again at the goal line before he returns to his team; taking off and putting on his shoes, and so on. Or each team member may be required to perform some physical stunt at the goal line before returning to his team—such as climbing a rope, turning a somersault, skipping a rope 6 times, etc.

Variation 7: The last player in each team's line calls out an object at each turn that the front member of the opposite team must run to and touch before returning and tagging the next team member in line. The last player in line must call out the next objective for his opposing team's next runner before the first runner returns to his starting line.

Variation 8: Players divide into two equal teams. Each team's members sit in a row or circle of their own. On the word "Start" from the referee, the first player of each team, chosen by lot, races all around his own team's row or circle of players and returns to his seat. As soon as he is seated, the next player gets up and completes the course, and so on, until all players of one team have run and are seated once more. That team wins whose last player to run returns to his seat.

GREEN AND BLUE

Ages: **7 and older.**

Number of players: **Two teams of 6 or more each; 1 referee.**

Place: **Outdoors** or **gym.**

The referee is chosen by lot. The two teams, one called Green, the other Blue, line up 8 to 10 paces apart, with their backs to each other. A finish line is marked 30 or more paces ahead of each line of players. The referee stands between teams.

The object of whichever team is called by name (Blue or Green) by the referee, is to race to the finish line facing the opposing team—i.e., to the line behind the called team's backs. The other team tries to tag as many runners as possible before they reach the finish line.

If the number of runners reaching the finish line is greater than the number tagged, the running team wins. If the tagged number is greater, the pursuing team wins. Succeeding turns continue as at the start of the game.

SLAP TAG

Ages: **7 and older.**

Number of players: **Two teams of 6 or more players each.**

Place: **Outdoors** or **gym.**

Each team lines up, with arms outstretched, behind a line 20 or more yards from the opposite team. One member of either team is selected to start running toward the opposing team. When he reaches the opposite side of the field, he slaps the hand of any player, and tries to run back and cross his own starting line. The slapped player chases him and tries to tag him.

If the first player is tagged before he crosses his own starting line, he is captured and is out of the game. Whether or not the second player tags the first, he in turn slaps the hand of an opposing player, who chases him back to his own finish line. The game continues until all the members of one team are captured, or for a predetermined time period, at which time the team with the largest remaining number of players is the winner.

SEND-OFF

Ages: **7 and older.**

Number of players: **Two teams of 6 or more players each.**

Place: **Outdoors or gym.**

The two teams, one designated Green, the other Blue, line up separately in parallel lines. The first player of the Blue team stands 50 or so paces ahead, facing both lines. It is the object of the first player of the Green team to intercept and tag the first Blue team player before the latter can return and touch the last player in line on his own team. If the player is tagged, he changes teams and stands at the end of the Green team's line, playing in turn like the rest. If the first Green player fails to tag the first Blue player, he then changes teams and stands at the end of the Blue team's line.

On the following turn, a Green team player stands 50 or so paces ahead of both teams. Then it is the turn of the Blue team player next in line to try to tag him. The game continues either for a predetermined time period, or until one side has tagged and captured all players.

PRISONERS' BASE

Ages: **7 and older.**

Number of players: **10 or more players divided into even-numbered teams.**

Place: **Outdoors** or **gym.**

Each team gathers in opposing fields. On the word "Start" from the referee, members of each team try to cross into the opponents' field and to reach the "prison" on that side. When any player enters or manages to touch or to put one foot into an opponent's prison, if he is not tagged before he does so, *and only if that prison is empty*, the inning ends with a score of 1 point for that player's side. The game then resumes as at first.

A player may be tagged and imprisoned by the tagging side while he is inside the opponents' field. All prisoners can be freed when a player of the same side as the prisoners' manages to reach that prison without being tagged and touches any one prisoner inside the prison. Prisoners may lean out of each prison to be touched by a member of their own side, provided they keep at least one hand or foot inside the prison.

Released prisoners and the player who released them must return to their own side of the playing field, while all other players stand in place. All then continue to play as before. But at the end of each inning all players, except prisoners who are not released, must return to their respective sides.

The game continues for a given number of innings or for an agreed-upon time period. That team wins which scores the largest number of innings at the end of a game or has imprisoned all members of an opposing team.

Variation: Small sticks or pebbles are placed inside each team's prison. Whenever a player reaches the opposing team's prison, and if no prisoners are inside it, he may take one stick and try to return it to his own side without being tagged, placing it inside his own team's prison. If he is tagged before crossing into his team's territory, he loses the stick and he and it are returned to the prison of the team from which he took it. All other rules remain as before. That team wins which either succeeds in liberating all sticks from an opponents' prison or imprisons all opponents.

POISON

Ages: **7 and older.**

Number of players: **12 or more.**

Equipment: **Chalk or stick to mark a circle.**

Place: **Outdoors or gym.**

All players form a circle. A smaller circle is drawn or marked inside this circle, leaving about 4 feet between it and the circle of players. All players link arms and then try to force one another to step onto or into the inner circle. The first player to do so becomes "it," while the others shout "poison" and run away. "It" must tag any of the others to end that round, and the game resumes as before. All players agree on a "safe" material before the start of the game—stone or wood—that, when any player stands on or touches it, provides a safe haven against being tagged by "it." No player may carry this material with him while he is running.

Variation 1: This game may also be played by placing Indian clubs to form the inner circle. The object is then to force any other player to knock down the first one to become "it." The game proceeds as before.

Variation 2: Either game can be played without the "tag" ending. On stepping on or across the inner circle or on upsetting an Indian club, that player is "out" for that round. The circle of players then re-forms and the game proceeds as before. When the number of players is reduced so that no circle can be formed, those remaining hold hands and run round the inner circle as before. That player wins who succeeds in forcing his last remaining opponent to step onto or into the circle, or to upset an Indian club.

ABOUT FACE

Ages: **7 and older.**

Number of players: **11, 18, 27, or 38.**

Place: **Indoors** or **outdoors.**

In a game of 11 players, all but 2 form a square forma-tion in ranks of three (see diagram). In a game of 18, all but 2 form a square in ranks of four, as before, and so on. The 2 remaining players toss up to decide who will be "it" and who will be the "runner." The rest of the players hold hands, forming parallel lines in a single direction (see diagram). "It" and the "runner" start in different ranks. On the word "Go" from the "runner," "it" chases him up and down and around the ranks trying to tag him. But the "runner" may, at any time before he is tagged, call "About face,"

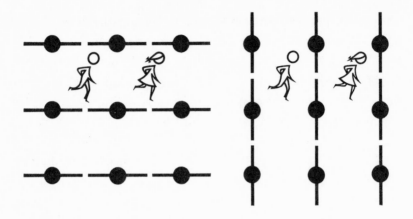

at which time all players in the ranks are required to turn ninety degrees in either direction to hold hands with their new partners to the right and left (see diagram). This regrouping of ranks can prevent the "runner" from being tagged. When the "runner" is tagged, he and "it" choose 2 others from the ranks to take their places and they in turn join the rest. The game continues until all players have taken turns at being either "it" or "runner."

Variation: The "runner" may be required to call either "Right turn" or "Left turn," so that all players in the ranks face in the same direction at all times.

INDOOR TAG

Ages: **7 and older.**

Number of players: **8 or more.**

Equipment: **Chairs or pillows for all but 2 players.**

Place: **Indoors.**

Clear all furniture from the room, except chairs (or pillows), sufficient for all but 2 players. Line up chairs or pillows in two or more equal rows, leaving ample space between the rows and between rows and walls. One player is chosen by lot to be "it" and another to be the "runner." The rest sit down on the chairs or pillows, all facing in one direction, being sure to keep their feet out of the rows to their left and right, keeping parallel aisles in one direction unobstructed. "It" stands in the center in front of the seated players. The "runner" stands in the center behind them. On the word "Go" from the runner, "it" chases and tries to tag him. Both may only run up and down the open aisles and around the front and back of the seated players, but never across the rows. When tagged, the "runner" changes places with "it."

The "runner" may seek safety by standing behind any of the rows of seated players, shouting "Safe." "It" must then stand still until the foremost player in that row has gotten up from his seat and all players in that row have moved up one seat, giving the former "runner" the opportunity to sit in the last and vacated chair in the row. The game then continues as before, "it" being able to chase the new "runner," as soon as all players are seated again. The game is played for a time period agreed to before the start.

HUNT THE FOX

Ages: **7 and older.**

Number of players: **10 or any larger number of even-numbered players.**

Equipment: **Chalk.**

Place: **Outdoors** or **gym.**

Mark a double circle divided by as many diameters as half the number of players minus 2 (see diagram). One player, chosen by lot to be the hunter, stands in the center. The rest are foxes who, all but one, stand, each to one den, where the diameters meet the outer circle. The remaining fox, chosen by lot, has no den and stands anywhere on the outer circle.

On the word "Start" from the referee, each fox must leave his own den and run to any other along any of the marked lines. He may not run to either den directly to the left or to the right of his first one. The odd fox may run along any line to any den. At the same time the hunter leaves the center and attempts to tag any fox who has not yet found a den. The hunter may only run along the paths. Once a fox or the hunter has started along a path, neither may turn back. But either can change direction whenever he comes to an intersection of paths. The first tagged fox changes places with the hunter and the game resumes as at first. When the hunter is unable to tag any fox before all but one have found a den, the referee declares a new "start" and all foxes must exchange dens once more.

CIRCLE-GO-ROUND

Ages: **7 and older.**

Number of players: **12 or more.**

Equipment: **Chalk or stick.**

Place: **Outdoors or gym.**

Draw or mark a large circle, 20 or more feet in diameter. Players form around the circle, each facing the back of the one in front of him. On "Start" from the referee, all run round the circle. Each player tries to overtake the one in front of him, passing him on the outside and tagging him while he passes. Any tagged player is out of the race. That player wins who overtakes and tags the last but one player.

Variation: The referee may say: "Turn about" at any point of the game, requiring all runners to run in the opposite direction. He may do so as often as he chooses during the game.

WHEELBARROW RACE

Ages: **7 and older.**

Number of players: **4 or more.**

Place: **Indoors on a rug or outdoors on soft ground.**

Mark a start and finish line 15 or more feet apart. Players pair off and line up behind "start." Each pair decides who shall play the part of the wheelbarrow first. The wheelbarrow player gets down on his hands and knees. The second player of each team picks up his partner's feet and, on the word "Start" from the referee, guides his wheelbarrow toward the finish line. The "wheelbarrow" must walk all the way on his hands only. On arriving at the finish line, the players of each team change places, he who first wheeled the wheelbarrow becoming the wheelbarrow in turn. Each pair then returns to start as before, as quickly as possible. That pair wins the game which first crosses the "start" line.

HARE AND HOUNDS

Ages: **9 and older.**

Number of players: **6 or more.**

Equipment: **A bag of scraps of colored paper (or a piece of chalk).**

Place: **Outdoors—must be in a park or other large area.**

One player is chosen as Hare and is given the scraps of
paper or the chalk. He is given a start of 5 minutes,
after which the other players may follow. The Hare
must mark his course after every 100 steps, by making
an agreed-upon mark with the chalk or by dropping
a piece of colored paper where it can be seen. He may
double back or otherwise try to deceive his pursuers.
The Hound who manages to track down the Hare and
tag him is the winner.

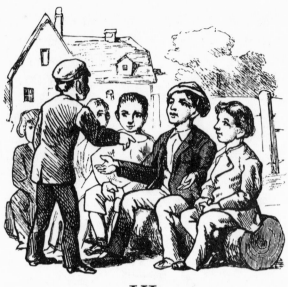

VI

Word Games for Home, Outing, or School

Many children have a difficult time learning to read because no one ever taught them to play with words. Certainly such play makes the use of words more appealing at early ages. Besides being fun, it helps children enlarge their vocabularies. At the very least, it stimulates them and gives parents and teachers one additional means of encouraging learning.

Word games, used at home and in school, can relieve the monotony of repetition and be substitutes for rote learning. They can dramatize a lesson or punctuate it so that children feel that learning is not exclusively serious; it can also be amusing.

Some of these games need nothing other than a lively imagination. They can be played in a car, on the beach, at the dinner table, or any place away from home where no materials are available. Others require paper and pencils, and can be fun for children of different ages at a party or in school. They can be converted into blackboard games in a classroom, for which the teacher is both the stimulator and the referee.

Consider, for the moment, that babies learn to speak by literally playing with sounds. By imitating them, by playing repetitive games like Patty Cake or "This little pig went to market," by crooning, talking, and singing to them, a parent encourages early speech. And, when properly stimulated, children learn at an amazing rate. This simple method of learning through play is often forgotten once a child reaches the ages at which formal education begins—today, as early as nursery school or kindergarten. And while a certain amount of drill is essential to some aspects of learning, it is more important that the child is able to apply whatever he learns. Word games dramatize the benefits of a large and varied vocabulary. Those games that allow teaching of fact or principle can be arranged so that the child is not numbed by repetition.

Finally, word games can show children that play does not require "things" or toys. For the most part, play depends on the child's own ingenuity and his knowledge of game and play lore. Man's fascination with words, with riddles and conundrums antedates the Oracle at Delphi. And play with words and ideas is an exclusively human preoccupation. So if you want your child to express himself and to play with words and ideas, he'll need to be shown some of the simple and traditional ways in which children and adults have used language in games.

Many of these word games can help children to learn to observe, classify, and order their experiences. Others can teach them to follow directions or how to give them. At the very least, these games can awaken a consciousness that orderly and systematic methods of thought and action can lead to gratifying success by the shortest route.

These games and their rules, like all others, require adaptation to the abilities, development, and experience of individual children or groups. They can unlock and unfold a child's ability to express himself imaginatively. Such games can enable him to convert into active play what he sees and hears around him, what was read to him and what he has been shown, in real life, at home, in school, on outings, and on TV.

Obviously, game-learning should not be the exclusive method employed, nor does all learning lend itself to translation into games. But certainly some aspects of learning can be eased and made more attractive, and can be combined with the teaching of social skills and self-expression.

WHO AM I?

Ages: **4 and older.**

Number of players: **6 or more.**

Place: **Indoors or outdoors.**

One player is chosen by lot to be "it." He is blindfolded, or turned away from the rest against a wall or a tree. The referee points to any one other player who must then say at once: "Peter Piper picked a peck of pickled peppers" (or some other agreed-to phrase or nursery rhyme). "It" must then try to identify that player by name, without seeing him. If he succeeds, he changes places with that player. If he fails, the game continues as at first, with the referee choosing another player to be identified, until "it" guesses a player's identity.

Variation: The blindfolded player stands in the center of a circle made by the other players, who dance or run around him. They must stop and stand still when the blindfolded player commands them to do so. The blind-folded player then points in any direction with his finger. That player at whom he points must then leave the circle to stand about 1 foot in front of the blind-folded player, who asks him to make a noise like a given animal—to bark like a dog, to moo like a cow, or to meow like a cat. The blindfolded player must then guess that player's identity. If he succeeds, he changes places with that player. If he fails, the player returns to the circle and the game resumes as at first.

COOPERATIVE TALE

Ages: **4 and older.**

Number of players: **2 or more.**

Place: **Indoors** or **outdoors.**

One player—or an adult—starts a story by telling a few sentences, e.g., "Once upon a time I went to the Zoo...." Each following player, in turn, adds whatever he wishes to the last player's sentence, e.g., "The keeper had left a cage door open...." "And so, just as I got there, a bear walked out..." and so on.

NURSERY RHYME BEE

Ages: **5 and older.**

Number of players: **2 or more.**

Place: **Indoors** or **outdoors.**

The first player recites the first line of any nursery rhyme. Each following player, in turn, recites the next line, or portion of a line, until the whole nursery rhyme is completed. The following player starts with the first line of any other such poem, and so on. It is best not to keep scores or to pit preschool children against one another competitively in this kind of game.

BIRD, INSECT, OR FISH

Ages: **5 and older.**

Number of players: **2 or more.**

Place: **Indoors** or **outdoors.**

Each player chooses one category—bird, insect, or fish —at every turn. The next player is required to name one member of that species. For example, if the first player says, "Fish," the second might reply, "Catfish." If the second player gives a correct answer, he then demands that the third player name any member of a species that he chooses, and so on. Any player who fails to name a member of a requested species or who gives an incorrect answer, may not, at that turn, ask the next player to name an animal. Or play may continue without penalty, after discussion of any wrong choice.

If children are too inexperienced to play this version, simpler classifications can be chosen, like "four-legged animals, two-legged animals, and animals that swim" or "things with wheels and things that walk." The object of the game is less to inform than to encourage children to classify what they know.

Variation 1: Each player is assigned an animal sound that he can identify and imitate, or a single child can represent a number of animals. Then tell a story, weaving in all the animals the child or the children have been taught to imitate, mentioning each as often as possible. Whenever such an animal is mentioned, the child is required to make the appropriate noises.

Variation 2: Players form a circle or decide on a given order of play. The first player makes an animal noise. The next player must guess it. If he guesses incorrectly, he loses his turn. If he guesses correctly, he in turn makes an animal noise that the next player must identify, and so on. Any player who wishes may make a nonsense noise or other noise that is not made by an animal. If the next player says, "Nonsense," he continues in turn. But he loses his turn if he either fails to guess it, or identifies this noise incorrectly as one made by an actual animal.

Variation 3: The same game may also be played using transportation noises, sounds of the city, or sounds of the country. All rules of *Game Variation* 2, above, remain as before.

BECAUSE

Ages: **5 and older.**

Number of players: **2 or more.**

Place: **Indoors** or **outdoors.**

The first player describes any event in the simplest way, e.g., "The toast burned." The second player is required to give a reason, e.g., "Because the toaster was turned up too high." The third player (or the first, in a game of 2) must then state a probable effect—"And everyone had charcoal for breakfast." The next player starts with a new statement, and so on.

Players should be encouraged to state cause or effect as rapidly as possible. Any answer can be challenged by other players and must be defensible.

THE ABC GAME

Ages: **5 and older.**

Number of players: **2 or more.**

Place: **Indoors** or **outdoors.**

The first player is chosen by lot. He names any letter of the alphabet. Each of the other players in turn must name, within 15 seconds (or any other agreed-to time period), a word that begins with that letter. Any player who fails to do so is out of the game. Once each child has taken his turn, the next player (chosen by lot or by agreement among players) names any other letter of the alphabet, and so on. No player may use a previously mentioned word. The last remaining player is the winner.

Variation 1: This game can be limited to cities, countries, nouns, verbs, flowers, animals, or any subject with which the children are familiar.

Variation 2: "It," chosen by lot, thinks of any object that is in sight and names its color only. Each player in turn then tries to guess what it is. That player who first names the correct object becomes "it," chooses another object, names its color, and asks the rest to guess what it is, and so on.

Variation 3: This game can be played by requiring "it" to name the first letter of the name of any object that is in sight. The game is played as above.

Variation 4: These are simple games that can be adapted to use on trips in cars and by older players, by using objects that the car passes while the game is played.

SIMON SAYS

Ages: **5 and older.**

Number of players: **3 or more.**

Place: **Indoors** or **outdoors.**

One player is chosen "it" and becomes "Simon." The rest of the players either line up opposite him or form a circle around him. "Simon" then performs gestures and describes them. *Example:* He touches his left ear with his right hand. He then says: "Simon says: 'Touch your left ear with your right hand.'" The other players must do exactly what he says and does. But, interspersed with describing what he does, "Simon" may also say one thing and do another. When this happens, the players are always required to do what he says, but not what he does. For example, if he says: "Simon says: 'Touch your left ear with your right hand,'" but he touches his toes instead, the other players must touch their left ears with their right hands. Any player who touches his toes instead is out of the game. When all players but one are out of the game, the remaining player changes places with "Simon," and the rest of the players re-enter the game and the game resumes as as first.

Variation: Players sit in a circle. The first is given a pencil or a spoon. He holds or taps it in any way he chooses, saying: "Anyone can do that." He then passes the spoon to the next player. That player must copy what the first player did, and then do something else with the spoon, saying to the next player: "Anyone can do that," and so on. Any player who fails to do exactly what the player before him did, is out of the game for that round.

ALL BIRDS FLY

Ages: **6 and older.**

Number of players: **6 or more.**

Place: **Indoors** or **outdoors.**

Each player, starting with one chosen by lot to be "it" first, is given 10 turns to say: "All birds fly." He then names either a bird or any other animal or object and, flapping his arms while he speaks, says, for example: "Eagles fly," or "Tables fly," and so on.

Whenever he names an actual bird, all other players must flap their arms. But the object is to catch others unaware, so that they flap their arms even when the first player says: "Elephants fly." The naming player should vary actual birds with other animals or objects in a random order.

Any player who flaps his wings when anything other than a bird is named is out of the game for the remainder of that "it" player's 10 turns. He re-enters the game when it is the next player's turn to be "it." That player wins who is able to make the largest number of players drop out during his 10 turns as "it." Airplanes, and people, objects, or animals that can be transported by plane, do not count as "birds."

Variation: The identical game can be played, with each player saying: "All fish swim," and then naming either a fish or a swimming mammal, saying, "Whales swim," or mentioning some other object or animal that cannot swim, while he flaps his arms. The rest of the rules remain the same. Ships, and people, objects, or animals that can be transported by ship, do not count as "fish."

HOW MANY WORDS?

Ages: **6 and older.**

Number of players: **6 or more.**

Place: **Indoors or outdoors.**

One player is selected to be "it," and another as timekeeper. "It" leaves the room, while all other players, including the timekeeper, decide on any letter of the alphabet. "It" is then invited back into the room and is told which letter was selected. While the timekeeper counts to 30, or to any other number agreed to before the start of the game, "it" must recite as many words as he can think of that begin with the given letter. He must stop when the timekeeper stops counting. The number of words he was able to recite that begin with the given letter are his score for that turn.

Another is chosen to be "it," and the game continues as before, until all players have been "it" in turn. That player wins who has the highest score at the end of the game.

THE EATING AND DRINKING GAME

Ages: **6 and older.**

Number of players: **2 or more.**

Place: **Indoors** or **outdoors.**

Players sit in a circle or decide on a given order of play. The first player, chosen by lot, tells the next what he wants to eat or drink. *Example:* "I want to eat an egg." The next player must state where the food or drink originated: "A hen [or a chicken] laid it." He then goes on to tell the next player what he would like to eat, and so on.

Any player who cannot name the origin of the food or drink, loses that turn, may not tell the next player what he wants to eat or drink, and scores 1 point. That player wins who, at the end of a given number of turns, or at the end of a predetermined time period, has the fewest points.

Variation 1: This game can be played by allowing each player to state that he wants a given object. The following player is required, as before, to name that object's origin.

Variation 2: The object of each player is to ask a question that requires a Yes or No answer from the next. If the next player cannot answer or fails to answer correctly, he loses a turn and 1 point. The rest of the rules remain the same. It is the object of each player to ask his question in such a way that the next has difficulty answering him, or to ask a nonsense question that sounds as if it made sense.

Variation 3: Every player in turn may ask each of the other players one or more different questions at his turn. Anyone who uses the words Yes or No in his answer loses 1 point. That player wins who, after all have had their turn at asking questions, has the least number of points.

WHAT IS MY JOB?

Ages: **6 and older.**

Number of players: **2 or more.**

Place: **Indoors** or **outdoors.**

The first player describes a job, naming only tools and an end-product, without defining the occupation itself, e.g., "I use a hammer and a saw and I make tables. What is my job?" The second player must then define that occupation by title, e.g., "A carpenter." If he answers correctly, he asks the next player (in a game of more than 2 players) or the first (in a game of 2) to name an occupation that he describes in the same manner as the first player did. The game continues in turn. Any player who fails to give a proper difinition, or one who asks the question in an unanswerable fashion, loses his turn.

Variation: Players may be asked, at their turn, to act out an occupation in pantomime. All other rules remain as in the game described above.

TAKE A TRIP

Ages: **7 and older.**

Number of players: **2 or more.**

Equipment: **Blackboard and chalk; paper and pencil for each player.**

Place: **Indoors.**

The teacher, or a player chosen by lot, writes a story on the blackboard, leaving out all nouns, leaving empty spaces in their place, and marking each space with a number.

Example:

1 went to 2 in order to find a 3 ! When he came to 4 , he went into the 5 and spoke to a 6 ! . . . and so on.

Each child either draws a picture or writes down a noun. He numbers it according to the space into which it is supposed to fit. At the end of an agreed-to time period, each player reads the whole story or sentence, including the nouns he has drawn or written, each placed into its proper space.

ALPHABET QUESTIONS

Ages: **7 and older.**

Number of players: **2 or more.**

Place: **Indoors** or **outdoors.**

Players sit in a circle or decide on a given order of play. The first player, chosen by lot, asks the next in line a question about any object, animal, plant, person, or place, the name of which begins with the letter "A." *Example*: "If I lived in *A*merica, what would I want to be?" The next player in turn must answer him with a sentence that makes sense and has an answering word (noun or adjective) beginning with the same letter. *Sample Answer*: "I'd want to be an *A*stronaut."

If the second player answers correctly, he may then ask the next player any other question, the noun of which begins with the letter "B." *Example*: "If I were a *B*at, what would I be?" The next player must answer as before, except that this time, the noun or adjective must begin with the letter "B." *Sample Answer*: "I'd be *B*lind in daylight." Play continues thus in turn until the whole alphabet has been completed.

Any player who fails to answer a question as required within a given time period, or who answers incorrectly, loses his turn to ask the next question and scores 1 point. That player wins who at the end of the game has the least number of points.

QUESTION AND ANSWER

Ages: **7 and older.**

Number of players: **2 or more.**

Place: **Indoors or outdoors.**

The first "it" is chosen by lot. He chooses any animal, occupation, object, or place (e.g., horse, carpenter, house, or farm) and asks each of the other players in turn one question in connection with his chosen subject. All of his questions must be asked so that they can be answered with *Yes* or *No* or *Sometimes*. If a player answers *"No,"* he must be prepared to give the right explanation. *Example*: If "it" has chosen horses, he may ask the next player: "Do horses live is the country?" *Answer*: "Sometimes." "It" then asks the third player: "Do horses eat meat?" *Answer*: "No, they eat grass, hay, oats, etc." It is, of course, the object of "it" to try to trip up his opponents.

Any player who gives the wrong answer is out of the game for that inning. Questions continue until only one of the other players is left. He then becomes "it" in turn, and the other players re-enter the game.

OBSERVATION

Ages: **7 and older.**

Number of players: **2 or more.**

Equipment: **Paper and pencil for each player; a number of small, common objects.**

Place: **Indoors.**

All players remain outside the classroom or living room. Meanwhile, one player chosen by lot, or the teacher, places a number of objects on a table inside the room. The number and variety of the objects to be arranged depend on the ages and experience of the players.

Each player then returns to the room alone, and stays in it for an agreed length of time, looking at the heaped objects on the table. He then leaves the room, and once outside, writes down all the objects that he saw and can remember. The player or players win who can accurately remember, name, and describe one or more qualities of each object that was heaped on the table. For very young players, it is sufficient that each remember the objects only. Older players may be required to try to remember each object's color, etc.

Variation: Instead of requiring players to leave the room, the designated first player or teacher may place the objects in a large paper bag. This bag is passed around the room or class. Each player is then required to reach into the bag, but may not look into it. He may feel the objects in the bag for 20 seconds, and then must pass it on to the next player. When all players have had their turns, each then either recites or writes down the objects that he can identify and remember.

To avoid disputes among players, they may agree to be blindfolded in turn for playing the "paper bag" variation of this game. When the game is used as a classroom game for preschoolers, objects in the bag may teach qualitative differences and similarities. For example: "Describe the shape or texture of the objects and guess what each might be" . . . etc.

THE SHOPPING GAME

Ages: **7 and older.**

Number of players: **2 or more.**

Place: **Indoors** or **outdoors.**

The first player, and each in turn, tells the next: "I am a . . . ," and chooses the name of a storekeeper (or craftsman or professional), and then adds: ". . . and I sell . . . ," naming any letter of the alphabet. Example: "I am a baker and I sell [or make] C. . . ." The next player must then guess all the things he makes, sells, or does, that begin with that letter. Possibilities for "C" include: Cakes, Cookies, Chocolate icing, Candy apples, Cheesecake, Cinnamon Danish pastry, Coffee ring, and Cream puffs.

The second player—when he is unable to think of more such products that begin with the named letter, or when he makes a mistake by naming something that is not sold or made by a baker (or whatever merchant is named), or at the end of an agreed-to time—scores himself according to the number of correct things he has named. He then continues, like the first player, saying to the next: "I am a . . . , and I make [or sell or do] G . . . [or any other letter of the alphabet that he cares to name]." The game continues until all players have had their turns. The player with the highest score wins.

Variation 1: This game may be played as a geography game, with one player saying: "I am from Africa [or any other continent, country or city] and I have B . . . [or any other letter of the alphabet]," and the next player then naming all the things he can think of that live, grow, or are found in that continent, country, or place that begin with the named letter. The game is played as before.

Variation 2: This game can be played as a transportation game. Each player in turn says: "I am going to England [or any other country or town], and I am going by C . . . [or any other letter of the alphabet]." The game is played as before. But the manner of transportation named by the next player must be possible under the circumstances. In the given example, it would have to be "Cargo plane," "Catboat," "Clipper ship," "Canoe," or any other mode of transportation beginning with the letter "C" that allows the player to cross the ocean. "Car" would not be allowed.

Note: In any of these games, other players may challenge the player who names the letter to be used. If that player is unable to cite at least one example, he loses his turn.

PANTOMIMES

Ages: **7 and older.**

Number of players: **3 or more.**

Place: **Indoors** or **outdoors.**

Pantomimes are direct descendants from the Mime Players of the Middle Ages, who enacted religious plays without words in Europe's cathedrals. These in turn were derived from pagan rituals that predate historical times. They have been popular, and still are, in all cultures. Traditional Chinese and Japanese dramas are still acted out in silence, or at least without speech on the part of the players. There are, of course, any number of variations of pantomime games for individual children or groups. It would be futile to try to enumerate all of them.

As a teaching and learning device, and for party fun at home and in school, pantomimes allow children to act out what they know, to recall gestures, actions, detail, and processes, to help them move gracefully, and to recreate dramatically the sum of their experience.

The first player is chosen by lot and stands before the rest, acting out by gesture and sound effect, but without speech, an animal, a mode of transportation, a trade, a profession, or, in the case of older players, a train of events. The other players must guess who he is, what he represents, or what story or event he is describing. The first player to guess what the pantomime represents becomes the next pantomime actor, and so on.

Variation: With children above the age of 8, several (3 or 4) players may be chosen to act out a pantomime for the rest. The players leave the room, agree to what they wish to represent, and try out their act out of sight of the rest. They then return to the room and enact their play without words. Sound effects are allowed. The first player who succeeds in guessing what the players represent may then choose 2 (or 3) others who have not yet had their turn as players, to create a new pantomime, as before. Play continues until all have had their turns.

FORBIDDEN WORDS

Ages: **7 and older.**

Number of players: **2 or more.**

Place: **Indoors** or **outdoors.**

One player is chosen to be "it" and leaves the room or stays out of earshot of the other players. The rest agree on a "forbidden word." When "it" is recalled, all others engage him in conversation and ask him questions designed to make him use the "forbidden word" as often as possible during an agreed-to time period. One player keeps score as to the number of times "it" uses the "forbidden word." But none let "it" know what word was chosen until the end of his turn.

The object of "it" is to try to discover the "forbidden word" and to avoid saying it. If he decides that he knows which word was chosen, and if he names the correct word during his turn, that turn ends and "it" joins the rest of the players for another round. Another player is then chosen, until all have had their turn to be "it."

Each mention of the "forbidden word" scores as 1 point against "it." But if "it" guesses the word before the end of his turn, his total score is erased. At the end of a complete round, those players who have no score are given additional turns until only one player remains who has no score. He wins that game.

Variation: Each player writes six words on six different pieces of paper, keeping each, face down, in front of himself on the table. Each player, in turn, then asks every other player one question at one turn (or six questions of his opponent in a game of 2 players).

The object of each player, in asking his questions, is to try to induce his opponents to use one of the "forbidden words" he wrote down on his slips of paper. Whenever an opponent uses a "forbidden word" in answering, the questioning player turns up the slip on which that word is written and keeps it in full view on the table. That player wins who first turns up all six slips of paper.

DEFINITION

Ages: **7 and older.**

Number of players: **2 or more.**

Place: **Indoors or outdoors.**

The first player, chosen by lot, names any one object, place, animal, or shape, or anything else that occurs to him. The next player then must give a definition of the named object. For example, if the first player says, "Cow," the next must identify it in an appropriate manner, e.g., "A domestic animal," "Bovine," "Cloven-hooved." It is useful to have a dictionary or an encyclopedia at hand while playing this game.

Any player who fails to give a proper definition loses his turn to name an object for the next player.

THE UNFINISHED STORY GAME

Ages: **7 and older.**

Number of players: **2 or more.**

Place: **Indoors or outdoors.**

The first player tells a story involving a critical situation—a house is on fire, a car crashes, or two people climb a mountain and one falls into a ravine and is injured. The next player, and all others in turn, are required to provide a plausible ending to the story.

RUMOR

Ages: **7 and older.**

Number of players: **6 or more.**

Place: **Indoors or outdoors.**

Players are seated in a circle. The first, chosen by lot, whispers a short sentence in the ear of the second. The second player repeats what he heard, or what he thinks he heard, by whispering this into the ear of the third, and so on, until the message reaches the last player. He then repeats the message as he received it and compares it to the sentence that the first player announces as the one that he whispered to the second player.

WHICH ANT?

Ages: **7 and older.**

Number of players: **2 or more.**

Place: **Indoors or outdoors.**

Players decide on a syllable or word ending, like "-*ant*," that is common for many different nouns. Others are suggested below. The first player then asks the second a question that provides a clue as to what he is talking about. *Example*: *Q*: "Which 'ant' has a long nose and big, floppy ears?" *A*: "An eleph-*ant*." *Q*: "Which 'ant' has leaves?" *A*: "A pl-*ant*."

In a game of 2 players, the first questions the second until he is stumped and cannot answer. It is then his turn to question the first, using the same syllable. In a game of more than 2 players, each asks the next one question in turn. That player wins who has given the largest number of correct answers at the end of a given number of turns.

Other syllables and word endings that can be used to play this game include *-ist-*, *-are-*, *-rat-*, and *-cat-*.

ABC ADJECTIVES

Ages: **7 and older.**

Number of players: **2 or more.**

Place: **Indoors** or **outdoors.**

The first player makes up a sentence that contains one adjective that begins with the letter "A." The next player, and each following player in turn, must substitute an appropriate adjective that begins with the following letter of the alphabet. *Example*: The first player says: "This is an *a*wful car." The second player says: "It is a *b*attered car." The third player says: "It is a *c*rashed car." The fourth player says: "It is a *dis*gusting car," and so on.

Any player who cannot continue the game by naming an appropriate adjective at his turn, drops out of the game for that round. Once 2 players have dropped out of the game, they start their own game among themselves, including others as they drop out. The game continues until all but a single player have dropped out of the first game. He is that game's winner and joins the second group, and so on.

Variation: The first player states a simple declarative sentence that does not include any adjective. The noun of that sentence must begin with the letter "A." The second player then repeats this same sentence and adds a phrase, including a noun that begins with the letter "B," and so on. *Example*: The first player says: "I have an *a*pple." The second player says: "I have an apple in a *b*asket." The third player says: "I have an apple in a basket for the *c*ook," and so on, right through the alphabet. All other rules remain as in the first game.

In any alphabet game involving younger age groups it is wise to exclude the letters from "U" to "Z." Allow children to use a dictionary or an encyclopedia to look up words and to enlarge their vocabularies, even while they are playing the game.

SILLY WILLY

Ages: **7 and older.**

Number of players: **2 or more.**

Place: **Indoors or outdoors.**

Any one version of this game can only be played once. But different versions can be improvised for succeeding rounds.

The first player, and one who is familiar with the game and with the principle involved, asks the second: "Silly

Willy likes butter, but he doesn't like milk. What does Silly Willy like?" If the second player fails to be able to tell what Silly Willy likes, the first asks the third: "Silly Willy likes boots, but he doesn't like shoes. What does Silly Willy like?" The game continues in this manner. Players who answer the first player with a sentence employing different nouns that describe what Silly Willy likes correctly, drop out of the game for that series of turns. The last player to be unable to guess what Silly Willy likes is the loser. In this instance Silly Willy likes anything that contains a double letter.

Other versions of this same game can deal with particular letters or qualities. *Example*: "Silly Willy likes peas, but he doesn't like sugar." He only likes things that start with the letter "P." "Silly Willy likes airplanes, but he doesn't like sleds." He only likes things that have wheels, and so on.

WORD ASSOCIATIONS

Ages: **8 and older.**

Number of players: **2 or more.**

Place: **Indoors** or **outdoors.**

The first player names any noun. The second player must answer with another with which the first can be associated. *Example*: The first player says "Lion." The second player says "Meat." But if the second player gives a less obvious answer, any player may challenge him to defend it. *Example*: If, in the above cited instance, the second player says "Fish," he may, but need not, be challenged. If he answers that a lion keeper did not know that lions don't eat fish, and that he therefore threw one into the lion's cage, he may be considered to have defended his association successfully. A successful challenger gains and an unsuccessful defender loses 2 points. If a response goes unchallenged, or if a challenge is defended successfully, the challenger loses and the second player gains 2 points. The second player then names a different noun for the next, and the game continues as at first.

An adult referee should arbitrate all disputes arising from this game among younger players. But when played by older age groups, the admissibility of a challenged player's defense may be decided by a majority vote among all players. Encourage discussion and give wide latitude to players who defend their associations.

VOCABULARY

Ages: **8 and older.**

Number of players: **2 or more.**

Equipment: **Thesaurus.**

Place: **Indoors.**

The first player names an adjective. The second player must then name as many words as he can think of that mean more or less the same thing. *Example:* The first player says "Big." The second player says "Large, great, huge, immense, enormous, vast, monstrous," and so on. The second player scores according to the number of admissible words that he has named. Any player may challenge him. The thesaurus decides admissibility of any word. At the end of each turn, that player names another adjective for the next player, and play continues as at first.

When challenged successfully, a player loses 2 points and the challenger gains 5 points. If the challenge is unsuccessful, the challenger loses 5 points and the player gains 5 points. That player wins who has the highest score when all players have had an equal number of turns in successive rounds.

SCRAMBLED LETTERS

Ages: **8 and older.**

Number of players: **2 or more.**

Equipment: **26 (or more) small squares or slips of paper, about 1" x 1"**
each. Write one letter of the alphabet on each. Prepare several sets for older age groups.

Place: **Indoors.**

All letters are shuffled and turned face down in the center of the table. The first player, chosen by lot, takes three slips of paper from the center and turns them face up. If possible, he makes a word out of two or more of the letters. Each following player then continues and plays in the same manner as the first, until all have had one turn. Thereafter, each player continues to draw one letter in turn, using it for different words in combination with other letters or words he already has placed in front of himself on the table.

At his turn, each player may demand from any other player either whole words or individual letters that another has in front of him on the table, which he can use to enlarge a word he has already placed or to make a new word, using one or more of his own letters. That player wins who, after all letters in the center have been drawn, has used the largest number of letters for completed words, placed on the table in front of himself, after he has deducted all unused letters that he drew and was not able to use to make words. A player, at his turn, may not demand individual letters that form part of a completed word from another player.

Challenges may be made and scored as in the previous game (see Vocabulary).

BLACKBOARD RELAY

Ages: **8 and older.**

Number of players: **Two teams of 6 or more players each.**

Equipment: **Schoolroom blackboard and chalk (or large sheet of wrapping paper, tacked to a wall, and 1 black felt-pen or crayon, if game is played in a room other than a classroom) for each team.**

Place: **Indoors.**

Players are divided into two teams. A line is drawn down the middle of the blackboard. Or, if played elsewhere than in a schoolroom, two sheets of large wrapping paper should be hung at shoulder height at an equal distance from both teams; one for each.

All players sit down. Each team decides on an order in which players are to run. At the command from the teacher or referee, the first member of each team races to the blackboard (or paper), picks up the chalk (or felt-pen), and writes the first word of a sentence that he thinks of on the blackboard or paper. He then runs back to his own team and hands the chalk or pen to the next player, who writes a second word next to the first, and so on.

That team wins whose last player is first to return to his seat or place among his teammates, provided his team has completed a full sentence and that all words are spelled correctly. If a team ends with an incomplete sentence, the first team member may run again, and so on, until that sentence is complete. Succeeding runners may correct the mistakes of any previous teammate while they are at the blackboard.

COLLAGE

Ages: **8 and older.**

Number of players: **1 or more.**

Equipment: **Newspapers, blunt scissors, paste, and notepaper for each player.**

Place: **Indoors.**

Each player cuts out words and sentences from his newspaper pages and combines them to make up his own story. In a game of several players, a theme may be decided on beforehand, or each player may make up whatever story occurs to him as he goes along, depending on what he finds.

HEADWORD

Ages: **8 and older.**

Number of players: **2 or more.**

Equipment: **1 blackboard; pencil and paper for each player.**

Place: **Indoors** or **outdoors.**

The teacher, or the first player, chosen by lot, writes any word on the blackboard. All players, including the one who writes the word on the blackboard, then try to make as many other words as they can think of out of the letters that make up the Headword. Players do not need to use all or any given number of the letters of the Headword, but they are limited to those that appear. They cannot use any letter in a new word they make more often than it appears in the Headword. That player wins who is able to find the largest number of words he can make.

Sample headword
Bridge. Some words that can be made: **Bed, Beg, Bid, Big, Bird, Bred, Die, Dig, Dire, Dirge, Erg, Gird, Grid, Id, Ire, Red, Rid, Ride, Ridge, Rig.**

This is an excellent game for building vocabulary. Players should be encouraged to look up in a dictionary any words they can't define. Such words should be discussed at the end of each round. Each round may be played for a given time period agreed to before the start of the game.

MISSING LETTERS

Ages: **8 and older.**

Number of players: **3 or more.**

Equipment: **Blackboard and chalk (or large piece of paper); pencils (or pens) for each player.**

Place: **Indoors or outdoors.**

The teacher or a player writes the first and last letter of a 4- or 5- (or more) letter word on a blackboard or large piece of paper. He marks an "x" between the first and last letter of the word for each of the missing letters —e.g., *B x x d* for *Bird*. The rest of the players in turn must try to guess the missing letters. The player who guesses the word writes a new word in the same manner for all others to guess. It is important to limit the game to words of a specified number of letters, or to establish a minimum and maximum number of letters, depending on the ages and abilities of the players.

Variation: Each player is given his own piece of paper and pencil and writes his own name on it. Below his name he writes the first and last letter of a noun as before, and then passes the paper to the next player to his right. Each player who correctly guesses the word given him scores 10 points. The winner is the player who has the highest score at the end of a given number of rounds.

BURIED WORDS

Ages: **8 and older.**

Number of players: **3 or more.**

Equipment: **Blackboard and chalk (or paper and pencil for each player).**

Place: **Indoors** or **outdoors.**

Each player in turn writes down a sentence in which a noun (name of a city, country, animal, person, fruit, or any other) is buried, because portions of the noun are split up between several words that mean something else entirely.

Examples:
I am**aze Brazi**lians with tricks.
Jane **came** last.
Carpenter**s nail** boards.

Each player passes his paper to the next and tries to find the buried word in the sentence that is passed to him in turn.

Variation: The teacher, or the first player chosen by lot, composes one sentence, like those described and shown above, and writes it on the blackboard. The first player to guess the hidden word may then make up a new sentence to be written on the blackboard and guessed by the rest, and so on.

ANAGRAMS

Ages: **8 and older.**

Number of players: **2 or more.**

Equipment: **Paper and pencil for each player.**

Place: **Indoors or outdoors.**

Each player is required to think of a 5-letter noun (limited, if desired, to animals, place names, or any other category). He then writes down the letters of the word so that they are totally scrambled, and passes his jumbled word to the next player to his right. The player wins who first unscrambles the letters and forms either the original word or any other word, using all the letters given him by his neighbor to the left. Of course, words of more than 5 letters may be used if the players so decide in advance.

Variation: Before he passes his paper to the next player, each player scrambles a list of 3 or more nouns, or a short sentence of 5 words in which each word, though scrambled, is written separately.

EARTH, WATER, OR AIR

Ages: **8 and older.**

Number of players: **2 or more.**

Place: **Indoors or outdoors.**

Players sit in a circle or decide on a sequence in which play passes from one to the next. The first player, chosen by lot, calls out either "Earth," "Water," or "Air." The next player in turn must name an animal that lives in whichever element is named. If he fails to do so, he loses his turn and 1 point. If he names an appropriate animal, he then has the right to name one of the elements for the next player, and so on. This game continues until one player has lost 10 points, or for a predetermined time period. The player with the lowest score is the winner.

LETTER LADDER

Ages: **9 and older.**

Number of players: **2 to 4.**

Place: **Indoors** or **outdoors.**

The first player thinks of any word and names its first letter only—e.g., "P" for pump. The second player thinks of any word beginning with the named letter and names its second letter—e.g., "A" for pancake. Play continues thus in turn until any player completes a word to which a following player cannot add another letter to change it or to make it longer. A player who at his turn fails to do so scores 1 point and begins another word as at first. That player wins, after each has had the same number of turns, who has the lowest score.

It is best to keep the number of players small, especially with younger age groups. If many players wish to play the same game, divide them into groups of three or four, each group playing the game among its own members.

Variation: All the same rules apply, except that specific categories are agreed to before the start of the game, e.g., foods, furniture, vehicles, boys' or girls' names.

PUZZLE WORD

Ages: **9 and older.**

Number of players: **2 or more.**

Equipment: **Pencil and sheet of paper for each player.**

Place: **Indoors.**

Each player draws a square, about 3″ x 3″, on his own sheet of paper and divides it into 9 smaller squares (see diagram). He then decides on a 9-letter word and writes that word into his square, 1 letter per space. The letters must be arranged so that, starting with the first, each following letter is placed into an adjacent square that has a common side with the previous one.

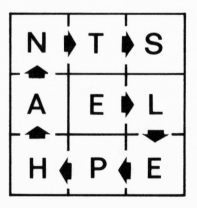

The example, using the word "elephants," shown below, demonstrates one way in which the letters must be written down so that, starting with the letter "E" a pencil line can connect all the letters in their proper order, going from one square to the next, without doubling back across any square or letter.

Once every player has made his own puzzle out of sight of all others, each passes his paper to the next player to his right, who then tries to solve it. That player wins who solves his puzzle first.

MOSAIC

Ages: **9 and older.**

Number of players: **3 or more.**

Equipment: **Blackboard and chalk; 2 pieces of paper and 1 pencil for each player.**

Place: **Indoors.**

Each player in turn writes any noun he chooses on the blackboard or on a large sheet of paper that all can see. All players are then required to write a story, using all the nouns listed. Each may use the nouns in any order he chooses.

THE MEMORY GAME

Ages: **9 and older.**

Number of players: **8 or more.**

Place: **Indoors or outdoors.**

Players sit in a circle or decide on the order of play. The first player, chosen by lot, declares what he has for sale. *Example*: "I sell apples." The next player, and each in turn, also declares what he has for sale. After all players have declared themselves, the first player announces: "My neighbor has . . . for sale," naming whatever the second player declared previously. Each player continues to announce his next neighbor's goods until all have spoken. Any player who fails to remember what his neighbor has for sale is out of the game.

At the end of that round, the first player announces what the next two players have for sale, and so on. The object is to see who can remember, in subsequent rounds, the goods first declared for sale by each, for an increasingly large number of players. The problem is made more difficult when players drop out of the game. But if each player pays attention, he is reminded by the players who follow him in the present round of what remains for sale in the next one.

Variation 1: One player is chosen as first speaker. He says: "I live in a city." The next player must repeat that sentence and add one of his own. *Example*: "I live in a city. In that city there is a street." Each player thereafter in turn must repeat all previously spoken sentences and add one of his own that is related and makes sense.

Any player who fails to repeat the previous part of the story is out of the game. The story goes around until all but one player are out. He is the winner.

Variation 2: Once players have caught on to the principle of this game, they can begin each new round with any sentence of the first player's choice.

CABLEGRAM

Ages: **9 and older.**

Number of players: **2 or more.**

Equipment: **Pencil and paper for each player.**

Place: **Indoors.**

Each player in turn calls out one letter (or more if less than 3 players are in the game) of the alphabet. Each writes down every letter as it is named. The object is for each player to compose a cable message, using the letters in the given order as the first letters for each succeeding word. The messages must make sense.

Example:

W P F B W I Y C H S

Will Pay For Broken Window If You Come Home Soon

OR

Willy Please Forgive Betty Where Is Your Cousin Henry Staying

Variation: The first player, chosen by lot, gives his first or last name. The letters that make up this name then become the initials for each of the words to be used for the Cablegram.

HANGMAN

Ages: **9 and older.**

Number of players: **2 or more.**

Equipment: **Blackboard (or pencils and paper for each player).**

Place: **Indoors.**

The teacher, or a player chosen by lot, decides on the first line of a nursery rhyme or other short sentence that is well known to all players. He then draws a series of dots on the blackboard or paper, each representing one letter of the sentence, with each group of dots representing one word separated from the next. *Example*: "I am silly," would be shown as:

●   ● ●   ● ● ● ● ●

Each player in turn may then guess any letter of the alphabet. When he guesses a letter that is part of the sentence and that has not yet been entered, then the first player or teacher must write it in over the proper dot. In case of a double-letter word, or whenever the same letter appears more than once in a sentence, the first player has the choice of placing a properly guessed letter wherever it fits. But the second identical letter is not put down until another player guesses it again.

If a player fails to guess a letter that can be written over a dot, he draws a circle for the first error, a line each for the body, legs, and arms of a stick man for each of the following errors, one line of a gallows for each of the following errors, a rope and finally a noose around the stick man's head for the rest, one line for each error (see illustration). When a player completes his drawing, he is out of the game. The player wins who either names the last remaining open letter or who guesses the whole sentence even before all the letters are named. Any player who tries to guess the whole sentence, but fails, must add two strokes to his hanged man at that turn.

GEOGRAPHY

Ages: **9 and older.**

Number of players: **2 or more.**

Place: **Indoors** or **outdoors.**

The first player names a city, state, or country. The next player must name another one of these that begins with the same letter as the last letter of that named by the first player. Each following player continues, and so on, always using the last letter of the city, state, or country named by the preceding player as the first letter for that which he names. Any player who is unable to name another city, state, or country according to these rules, is out of the game. That player wins who is the last remaining in the game.

Example:

First player: Boston; Second player: New York; Third player: Kingston . . . and so on.

Variation: The same game can be played with less experienced players, using animal names.

ALPHABET TRAVELS

Ages: **9 and older.**

Number of players: **3 or more.**

Place: **Indoors** or **outdoors.**

Each player in turn, starting with the first, who is chosen by lot, must make up a sentence, the principal words (nouns, adjectives, and verbs) of which begin with the letter of the alphabet that applies to his turn. The first player uses all "A's," the second all "B's," and so on. Each player must start with "I am going to . . ." and then name a place that begins with the letter to be used at his turn. The letter "X" is eliminated.

Example:

First player: "I am going to Africa, to ask an Ashanti for apricots."
Second player: "I am going to Boston to buy baked beans."
Third player: "I am going to California to collect cheap crops."
Fourth player: "I am going to Denmark to dunk delicious doughnuts."

A player is out of the game if he fails to construct the suitable sentence within the time allowed by common agreement before the start of the game. The last remaining player is the winner.

Variation 1: When the game is played in school, the players may be asked to write their sentences on a blackboard in turn. Or each may be required to write out, on his own sheet of paper, 22 such sentences (eliminating "V," "X," "Y," "Z"), using the letters of the alphabet. The player who first completes all 22 sentences is the winner. Or each player may be required to begin his sentence with "In my Zoo, I have a . . . " The name of each mammal, fish, or any other animal must begin with the first, second, and so on letter of the alphabet in turn. Any number of other variations can be improvised, depending on the players' ages, knowledge, or the information to be dramatized.

Variation 2: For ages 12 and above. Each player is given paper and pencil or pen and required to write, within a given time period, a short story of 50 (or more, or less) words, in which each noun, adjective, and verb must begin with a letter of the alphabet specially assigned to him. Anyone who fails to complete his story is out of the game. Those players who complete their stories at the end of the agreed-to time period, read them aloud to the rest.

TWENTY QUESTIONS

Ages: **9 and older.**

Number of players: **2 or more.**

Place: **Indoors or outdoors.**

One player is chosen by lot to be "it." He decides, silently to himself, on any object, person, animal, or plant. Having made his decision, he provides a clue to the rest of the players by announcing whether it is *animal, vegetable,* or *mineral.* It must be one of these, but may not be a combination of two or more. For example, a "car" is made of materials that belong to at least two of the three; e.g., rubber tires (vegetable) and a metal frame, body, and engine (mineral).

Each other player at his turn may then ask a single question that must be answerable by "it" with either Yes or No. If the others are unable to guess what "it" thought of by the twentieth question, he wins and thinks of another object, person, animal, or plant, and the game continues as before. If any player guesses what "it" is thinking of by or before the twentieth question, "it" has lost and the player who guessed the answer becomes "it" in turn.

Players who are new at the game should be told to ask the most general questions first, in order to reduce the number of possibilities by a process of elimination. For example, if the clue is "animal," the first question might be: "Is it human?" If the answer is No, the next question might be: "Does it live on land?" If the answer is Yes, the next question might be: "Is it a domestic animal?" ... and so on.

Variation 1: A form of Twenty Questions in which each player in turn asks one question of the "it" player, trying to find out his occupation. "It" decides on a profession before the start of the game. He gives players no clues whatsoever. All other rules remain the same. If players are familiar with different classifications of work, "it" may be required to state whether he is in a profession, trade, service, or craft, before the start of the game.

BOUTES-RIMES (Rhymed Ends)

Ages: **10 and older.**

Number of players: **3 or more.**

Equipment: **blackboard and chalk (or paper and pencil for each player).**

Place: **Indoors or outdoors.**

This game was first played in France in 1648, and invented by the poet Dulos. It became fashionable across all of Europe, and a favorite parlor game among adults.

Each player in turn writes down 4 words on the right-hand margin of his paper. The first and third, and the second and fourth words must rhyme.

Example:
If you were a **fish**
that swam in the **sea**
you'd make a good **dish**
and dinner for **me.**

Each player passes his paper to the next player to his right, who is then required to add a phrase so that each line ends with the given word to form a poem (see example above). Each round is played for a time period agreed to before the start of the game. Only completed poems score, each line counting 10 points for the player

who wrote it. That player wins who scores the greatest
number of points during a given number of rounds.

Variation: The teacher, or a player chosen by lot,
writes the 4 words on a blackboard. All other players
are required to compose a poem, as above, using the
same words. All poems are read aloud at the end of a
given time period. Players vote for the best poem after
each round.

DOUBLETS

Ages: **10 and older.**

Number of players: **1 or more.**

Equipment: **Paper and pencil for each player (or blackboard and chalk).**

Place: **Indoors or outdoors.**

Players agree on 2 words, each having the same number of letters. The object of each player is to transform
the first word into the second by changing one letter in
succeeding step words, until the letters spell the agreed-
upon second word. Each new step word must be a real
word. The player who reaches the second word in the
fewest steps is the winner. *Example*: How to change
head into *feet*:

head into **feet**:   Head
                   Heed
                        = 2 steps
                   Feed
                   Feet

Note the changed letter in each step. Other typical transformations included how to change *rain* into *hail*, *boy* into *man*, *hand* into *legs*, *bite* into *nuts*, *flour* into *bread*. It is done as follows, in the least possible number of steps.

rain	boy	hand	bite	flour
into	into	into	into	into
hail	man	legs	nuts	bread
Rain	Boy	Hand	Bite	Flour
Rail	Bay	Land	Site	Floor
Hail	May	Lend	Sits	Flood
	Man	Lens	Sets	Blood
		Legs	Nets	Brood
			Nuts	Broad
				Bread

WRITING A NOVEL

Ages: **10 and older.**

Number of players: **2 or more.**

Equipment: **1 large sheet of paper and 1 pencil.**

Place: **Indoors** or **outdoors.**

The first player, chosen by lot, writes a short, one-line sentence at the top of the paper. He then folds the paper over once, so that what he wrote is not visible to the next player. The next player writes down a second sentence, folds the paper over as before, and passes it to the next player, and so on. When every player has written his sentence, or when each player has com-

pleted the agreed-to number of turns, the paper is unfolded and the sentences read aloud by one player, as
if the whole were one continuous story.

The story can be made to seem more continuous if
every player after the first is required to begin his
sentence with: "And then . . ."; "After that . . .";
"Next . . ."; or "When . . ."

VII

Number Games

Coincidence is the mother of superstition. Many coincidences may occur when numbers are arranged in different ways. And for this reason, among others, people in the past have often attributed magic qualities to numbers. These superstitions were in part encouraged and sometimes firmly believed by the priesthood of early cultures. They were the official keepers of accounts and of the calendar, and were the surveyors of the land. They advanced number skills, kept them to themselves, and endowed them with ritual and mystical magic. The rest of the population regarded numbers with awe.

These early misconceptions about operations with numbers are with us still. They are treated in schools and
in classrooms as rituals, rather than as symbols of
language. Play with numbers desanctifies them, takes
away the dread with which many children regard them,
and brings them into the arena of use and usefulness.

Number concepts are a part of language. The ideas of
far and near, tall and short, many, few, and none at all
are less exact words than the same ideas expressed in
numbers. Besides, the possible combinations of letters
that make up vocabulary are really much more varied
and complex than almost any everyday number operation. For example, the 24 letters of the alphabet most
frequently used can be combined in 620,448,401,733,239,-
439,360,000 (six trillion trillion) ways. If possible word
combinations are added, even within rules of grammar
and syntax, the number of possible variations becomes
staggering. Despite their comparative simplicity and
economy, numbers give most children more trouble
than words do.

Most mathematical pastimes of the past and present
are exercises of logic, skill, or speed. It seems almost as
if the use of numbers in play were still considered a
solitary pastime, a reminder that at some former age
such activities were looked upon as heretical when ex-
ercised by any member of the tribe other than those
officially appointed by custom and by law.

There are countless solitaire number puzzles and paradoxes. These do not concern us here. Some, like Zeno's
puzzle, are insoluble. He suggested, and proved logi-

cally, that if you continue to halve the distance between two points, A B, starting from A, you'll never arrive at B. Theoretically, he was right of course. A recognition of the contradictions between everyday experience and symbology can teach students valuable lessons. It can make them aware that numbers, like letters, are an imperfect means of communication, and that unless they are expressed in terms of human need and experience, they can be meaningless and even misleading.

The number games I have adapted, with one or two exceptions, do not go back as far in history as most other games. They are far fewer in number than any other category of games, probably for all the reasons given above.

But all games have a mathematical basis. Any strategy can be calculated in advance and expressed numerically or algebraically, including chance, when the number of possible moves, players, and other given factors are known. Even the winning strategy for games like Tic-Tac-Toe can be stated in mathematical terms.

I have left out of this text any of the formulas or the explanations of mathematical principles on which these games are based. Instead, I hope that players will be encouraged to discover some of the patterns themselves through manipulation of numbers in play. As in all learning, pattern recognition is the dawning of understanding. Using objects and symbols as sets, and viewing mathematical operations as language tools, should help to free children from considering the quantification of qualities and events a dull schoolroom chore.

ODDS AND EVENS

Ages: **5 and older.**

Number of players: **2 or more.**

Equipment: **Small pebbles (or coins or beans).**

Place: **Indoors or outdoors.**

The first player chosen by lot to be "it" holds the pebbles in his hands behind his back, counting out whatever number he chooses into his right hand. Next he holds both hands out in front of him. Each of the other players in turn must guess whether the number of pebbles in his right hand is an "odd" or an "even" number. When all players have made their guesses, "it" announces whether the number of pebbles in his right hand is odd or even. The pebbles in the "it" player's right hand are then counted, and if "it" identified that number correctly, each player is scored a "winner" or "loser" accordingly. That player who guesses correctly three times on succeeding turns changes places with "it." If "it" identifies the number he holds in his right hand incorrectly, he changes places at once with the player who first called the right answer at that turn. All players start without score whenever a new "it" takes his place.

HOW MANY FINGERS?

Ages: **6 and older.**

Number of players: **3 or more.**

Place: **Indoors or outdoors.**

Egyptians of 4,000 years ago played this game. It is still known to all children in southern Europe as the game of Morra. And in England, children shout, "Buck, buck, how many horns do I hold up?" as they play this game.

The first "it" is chosen by lot. All others face away from him. "It" holds up as many fingers of one hand (or of both hands) as he chooses. The rest must guess the number of fingers he holds up. As soon as each player has made his guess, he turns around and faces "it." But he may not give any clue to others who have yet to guess. The first player to guess the right number becomes "it." The game continues as at first.

Variation: One player is selected as referee. All the others, on command, hold up as many fingers of one hand as they wish, and at the same time shout out what they believe is the sum of the fingers held up by all players at that turn. Anyone who guesses the right number scores 1 point. Each player keeps his own score with his free hand. As soon as one player receives 5 points, that round ends and the winner becomes the referee. The game continues as before.

DOT TIC-TAC-TOE

Ages: **6 and older.**

Number of players: **2 or more.**

Equipment: **Blackboard and chalk (or paper and pencil).**

Place: **Indoors** or **outdoors.**

Ten (or 20, or any number that is a multiple of 10) dots are marked on a piece of paper, either at random or arranged in lines. Each player at his turn crosses out one, two, or three dots. A player may cross out the same or any different number of dots at succeeding turns. The player who crosses out the last dot is the winner.

Variation 1: Players may be required to name the number of dots they cross out and the sum of the remaining dots at the end of each turn. They should be encouraged to try to calculate their strategies, rather than to cross out dots at random.

Variation 2: Dots are drawn according to the following diagram. If more than two persons play, two lines of dots, each two dots longer than the last, are marked for each additional player. Each player may erase or cross out from one to two dots (no less than one, but no more than two) from any single row at his turn. The loser is the player who, at his turn, must erase or cross out the last dot.

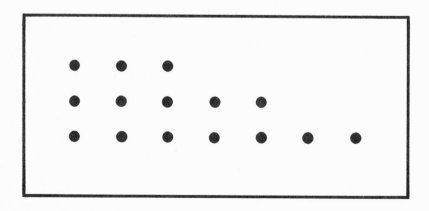

THE WHEEL OF FORTUNE

Ages: **6 or older.**

Number of players: **2 or more.**

Equipment: **Draw a large, spoked wheel, 24" or larger in diameter, on a blackboard or on a large sheet of wrapping paper. Write any number in between each spoke of the wheel (see diagram).**

Place: **Indoors.**

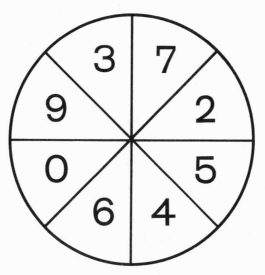

Each player in turn is blindfolded and led up to the blackboard. With chalk or crayon each player at his turn makes a mark in a place at which he hopes to find the highest number. If his mark lands inside any space between spokes, he wins that number and may mark it down on a piece of paper. If his mark lands on a spoke, on the rim of, or outside the wheel, he does not score at that turn. When each player has had three or more equal turns, that player wins who has the highest score, provided he has added the numbers he won correctly.

NUMBER GUESSING

Ages: **7 and older.**

Number of players: **2 or more.**

Equipment: **A heap of pebbles (or marbles, beans, jelly beans, or gum balls); a jar.**

Place: **Indoors.**

One player is selected as first referee, and fills the jar. Each player in turn tries to guess the number of objects in the jar. They are then counted, and that player who comes closest receives 50 points. Those who lose receive a minus score based on the difference between their guesses and the actual number in the jar. After each turn, the referee or teacher subtracts from or adds to the objects in the jar, and the game continues as before. After a given number of rounds, the player with the highest score wins. He then becomes the referee, and so on.

Variation: This game can also be played with random numbers of dots made on a piece of paper that is passed rapidly from player to player. Each writes down his guess immediately after he has inspected the paper. Each player is allowed only three seconds per turn to inspect the paper.

ODD MAN WINS

Ages: **7 and older.**

Number of players: **2.**

Equipment: **An odd number of pebbles (or counters or marbles)—15, 17, 19, etc.**

Place: **Indoors or outdoors.**

The counters are heaped or grouped on a table or on the ground. The first player is chosen by lot. Each player may, in turn, draw one, two, or three counters from the pile. After no counters are left in the center, the player wins who has drawn an odd-numbered sum of counters.

Variation: The same game can be played with an even pile of counters, in which that player wins who has drawn an even sum of counters.

BUZZ

Ages: **7 and older.**

Number of players: **2 or more.**

Place: **Indoors** or **outdoors.**

Players sit in a circle. Beginning with the first player, chosen by lot, all players count off by ones—the first player saying "One," the second, "Two," and so on. The player at whose turn the number 7 is reached, or a multiple of 7 (14, 21, 28, etc.), must say "Buzz" instead of naming the number. Any player who names 7 or a multiple of 7 is out of the game. The last player to remain in the game is the winner.

Variation 1: On reaching the number 70 (or any of its multiples), the player at whose turn it comes up must say "Buzz-Buzz." On reaching 77 (or any multiple), the player must say "Buzz-Buzz-Buzz." Any player who fails to do so is out of the game. The rest of the rules remain the same.

Variation 2: Any other number and its multiples may be chosen for the same game. Or, when children are able to manage to keep the number 7 and all its multiples in mind, another number (or any of its multiples) may be added (for example, the number 3), and the player at whose turn it comes up must say "Fizz." When a number is reached that is a multiple of both 7 and 3, that player must say "Buzz-Fizz."

On the addition of a third number (for example, 5 and its multiples), the substitute word is "Quack." And on addition of a fourth number (for example, 11 and its multiples), the substitute word is "Cock-a-doodle-doo." Thus, the player at whose turn 15 comes up is required to say "Fizz-Quack." The number 77 becomes "Buzz-Cock-a-doodle-doo," and 105 becomes "Buzz-Quack-Fizz."

Any other numbers may, of course, be substituted, to give the game greater variety in succeeding rounds.

CENTURY GAME

Ages: **8 and older.**

Number of players: **2 or more.**

Equipment: **Blackboard and chalk (or pencil and paper for all players).**

Place: **Indoors or outdoors.**

The first player, chosen by lot, writes down any number between 1 and 10. Each player in turn adds a similar number and writes the resulting sum. Play continues in turn. That player wins whose final addition brings the sum to exactly 100, but no more. Depending on the number of players, this game requires a good deal of strategy once the sum of the numbers exceeds about 70.

Variation 1: Each player may add a number no greater than 15, 20, or 25, but no less than 10 (or 9 or less). This game can also be played to a winning score greater than 100, depending on the players' ages, by common agreement before the start of the game.

Variation 2: This game may also be played in reverse. Players start with the sum of 100 (or more). Each in turn then subtracts a number no greater than 10 (or whatever number is chosen) and no less than 1. That player wins at whose turn the number 1 is reached.

Variation 3: Any of these games may be played so that a player loses the game if 100 (or more) is reached by addition, or 1 is reached by subtraction, at his turn. All the other rules or their variations remain the same.

MAGIC SQUARES

Ages: **9 and older.**

Number of players: **2 or more.**

Equipment: **Blackboard and chalk (or pencil and paper for each player).**

Place: **Indoors or outdoors.**

Each player divides a large square into 9 smaller ones (see diagram). Each player is required to place one each of the numbers from 1 through 9 into the squares, so that the sum of any three numbers placed in a straight line (vertically, horizontally, and diagonally) adds up to 15 in every case. The player who first solves this problem is the winner.

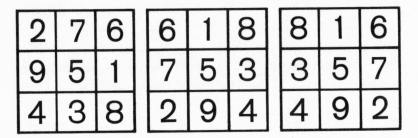

Variation 1: Using a similar square, divided into nine equal, smaller ones, and the numbers 1, 2, 3, 10, 11, 12, 19, 20, and 21, each player must place one per square so that any 3 numbers in a straight line in any direction add up to 33.

20	1	12
3	11	19
10	21	2

Variation 2: Each player draws a diagram like that shown below, and places the numbers 1 through 11 into all the circles of the wheel (see diagram) so that the sum of any three numbers in circles connected by lines adds up to the same amount as all other sets of three circles. That player wins who first solves this puzzle.

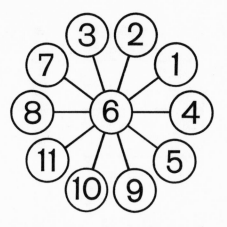

Variation 3: Each player places the numbers 1 through 7 into the seven circles shown below (see diagram) so that the sum of the numbers of any three circles connected by lines adds up to 12. A slightly more difficult version of this game is that in which the sum of the numbers inside the circles A and B, C and D, etc., must also add up to 12 each.

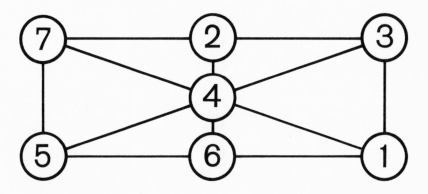

Variation 4: Each player draws and divides a large square into 16 equal smaller ones (see diagram). He then arranges the numbers 1 through 16, one per square, so that the sum of any four squares in each row (horizontal, vertical, and diagonal) adds up to 34.

1	15	14	4
12	6	7	9
8	10	11	5
13	3	2	16

NUMBER TIC-TAC-TOE

Ages: **9 and older.**

Number of players: **2.**

Equipment: **Blackboard and chalk (or pencil and paper).**

Place: **Indoors** or **outdoors.**

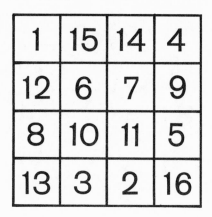

Draw a nine-square Tic-Tac-Toe diagram (see diagram). One player uses the even numbers between 1 and 10 (2, 4, 6, 8); the other player uses only the odd numbers (1, 3, 5, 7, 9). The odd-number player has one extra number and goes first, placing one of his numbers into any square. The second player follows in turn, and so on. Each player may use each of his numbers only once. The object is for each player to make a row of three numbers in any direction (vertically, horizontally, or diagonally), the sum of which is 15. That player wins who first succeeds in doing so.

Players change from even to odd numbers in alternate rounds.

VIII
Party Games

The children of India and Japan enjoy special holidays devoted to them, each with its particular toys, games, and sometimes parties held in their honor. Few cultures cherish children or celebrate childhood in this public a manner. Only Christmas and birthdays remain occasions on which our children are favored in such a fashion.

This is no coincidence, since we do not treat childhood as an especially worthwhile time of life. Our interest in children is largely concerned with making them suffer rather than helping them to enjoy this transient state.

As Philippe Ariès[1] points out, Western culture has extended the period of immaturity during the past four
hundred years. But at the same time it has certainly
treated childhood as a handicapped period, which
authoritarian education has simultaneously sought to
overcome and managed to prolong. This contradiction
may be one cause of the disorientation of many of our
young.

I do not suggest that game-playing will solve this problem. But it can allow children to savor some of the
exuberance that is their exclusive property and to get
a foretaste of independence and self-government. It is
one of the few, if often misdirected, privileges we still
allow them. A party is a good time to encourage and to
stimulate children's games.

Children's parties do not happen. They need planning
and supervision. Food and drink, if they are served,
and unobtrusive management by adults, are quite as
important as favors, decorations, presents, or even
games. Adults generally reveal their true concerns
about children when they attend and supervise a children's party.

FOOD. Finger foods are best for any kind of children's party. Hamburgers or frankfurters, potato chips, raw carrots, and small tomatoes, cake, ice cream, and a fruit punch are probably the most successful menu. It can be prepared beforehand. These foods can be easily served, eaten, and drunk from paper plates and cups. This kind of forethought makes a children's party enjoyable for adults and for children.

ADULTS. For preschool children, indoor parties at home should be kept small—four to six children at the most. You should have one adult solely concerned with food preparation and serving, plus two others to supervise the children. The ratio of children to adults can be increased at parties for older children who need less supervision. Still, at least one adult should be in attendance at parties for children up to the age of puberty. And even after adolescence, it's a good idea if children know that an adult is somewhere in evidence, if only as a symbol of restraint. Ban from the premises all adults other than those who are actively helping to make the party a success.

PLANNING. Just as the menu should be thought out and food bought in advance, so should the sequence of events—when games will be played, when food will be served, when the party will begin and end—be planned ahead. Choose the games you think the children might enjoy. Assemble required materials if any are needed. Select alternate games, in case children don't enjoy some of those you choose. Allow children to help in your plans. If you offer favors, have one prize for each child —and make sure each gets or wins one in time.

Once you have made these preparations, and depending on the ages of the invited children, allow them to manage as much on their own as they can. Step in only when you are needed to settle disputes or to help when they have accidents.

Finally, remember that this is their party—not yours. Provide room for them to eat, romp, and play. If the party is indoors, remove your valuables and breakables from the scene of the party beforehand. Close, lock, or prohibit the use of rooms that you wish to keep secure from invasion. Roll up the rug in the room in which the party is to be held. Fence off dangerous outdoor areas if the party is held in the open. Ask small children frequently whether they need to use the bathroom. These and similar considerations will make the party fun for the children and eliminate foreseeable disasters for you and for them.

Don't ask your child to help clean up the mess caused by his birthday party. It's given in his honor. But his brothers and sisters can and should help you put your home back in order after such a party, if they are old enough. It won't be such a big job, if you follow the above recommendations.

You may wish to give an informal party for your child and his friends on other occasions, without going to all this trouble. But whether you make a big or a small party for children, at home or in school, indoors or out, the games you suggest and help them to play will to a large extent determine the party's success.

HOT OR COLD

Ages: **4 and older.**

Number of players: **2 or more.**

Equipment: **Any small object or cloth.**

Place: **Indoors or outdoors.**

This game is especially useful for teaching children to get used to following and to giving directions accurately. The object is hidden while one player, chosen to be "it" is not in the room. He is then brought back and asked to find it. Other players tell him when he is "hot" or "cold," depending on whether he is approaching or going away from the place where the object is hidden. When the player has found the object, he then takes his turn at hiding it and joins the rest in directing the next player.

Variation: Once the child has learned to follow and give these simple instructions, this game may be played using "right" and "left," or "forward" and "backward" as the guiding words.

MATCHING GRASSES

Ages: **4 and older.**

Number of players: **2 or more.**

Place: **Outdoors.**

Each player picks a blade of grass. The first makes a loop out of his blade, holding the ends between thumb and index finger of one hand. The second pushes his blade of grass through the loop made by the first, and then makes a loop of his blade in the same manner as the first. Both players now pull against each other's blades. That player wins whose blade of grass remains intact. The winner receives his opponent's broken pieces, and both score according to the number of pieces they have collected at the end of successive turns.

BUTTON, BUTTON

Ages: **4 and older.**

Number of players: **6 or more.**

Equipment: **A button (or pebble or coin).**

Place: **Indoors** or **outdoors.**

One player is chosen by lot to be "it." The rest sit in a circle. "It" stands in the center. The players who sit in the circle pass a button or pretend to pass it from one to the next. Players may "pretend" to pass the button in any direction, while others actually hand it on, to prevent "it" from discovering who has it. After a given period of time, or after "it" has counted to an agreed-upon number, or when he calls, "Stop," the players in the circle must stop passing the button or pretending to pass it. "It" must then try to guess who has the button. He is allowed three guesses, or as many as one-third of the number of players, whichever is more.

If "it" fails to identify the player who has the button after he has exhausted the number of tries allowed, the game resumes as before. If he guesses who has the button, he changes places with the player who holds it. Play continues as before.

Variation 1: The button is strung on a thread or string, large enough so that it stretches all around the circle of seated players. Each holds the string, and the button is passed along it from one player to the next. All other rules remain the same, and the game is played as before.

Variation 2: Players may sit around a large table and pass the object, or pretend to pass it, under the table from one to the next.

GRIN OR BEAR IT

Ages: **4 and older.**

Number of players: **4 or more.**

Place: **Indoors** or **outdoors.**

One player is chosen to be "it" for the first turn. The rest line up, facing him. The object of "it" is to make any other player grin or laugh. The lined-up players try to keep their faces completely immobile and serious. The first player to smile or laugh at "it's" antics becomes "it" in turn, and changes places with him. Play continues until players tire of the game.

BOB APPLE

Ages: **4 and older.**

Number of players: **4 or more.**

Equipment: **Large pan or bucket filled with water; apples.**

Place: **Indoors** or **outdoors.**

This, originally, was a Hallowe'en game, recorded in England as early as the fourteenth century. The order of players is determined by lot. The first player, and each in turn after him, kneels next to the bucket with his arms held or tied behind his back, and attempts to pick one apple out of the bucket with his mouth or teeth.

Variation: This game can also be played with cherries. Either apples or cherries are tied at their stems with string, and are hung from the ceiling, above the heads of the players. Each player in turn tries to pull down one apple or cherry by jumping up and biting into whichever is provided. This feat is more difficult for players if their hands are tied behind their backs with a cloth.

PIN THE TAIL ON THE DONKEY

Ages: **4 and older.**

Number of players: **2 or more.**

Equipment: **This game can be bought ready-made in toy stores, or the required materials can be easily assembled at home. Draw a large (3 feet long) animal (donkey, tiger, cat, or any other animal that has a tail) on a piece of board, cloth, or wrapping paper, leaving the tail off the drawing. Then draw and cut out a tail, using similar material. If cloth is used for both, sew the female side of snap fasteners to the large drawing and the male side to the tail. Other methods include sewing regular buttons on the large drawing and making a buttonhole in the tail. The easiest and fastest method, which works especially well when both tail and donkey are made of paper, is to take a piece of cellophane or masking tape about 3 inches long and to fold it, sticky side out, several times in on itself. Stick it to the top of the tail. It will adhere to the body of the animal often enough and long enough to last out the game.**

Place: **Indoors.**

Place the drawing of the animal on a wall at players' eye level. Blindfold each player in turn and give him the animal's tail. He must try to find the animal and attempt to attach the tail where he thinks it belongs. Other players call "Stop," if the blindfolded player appears to approach any part of the room or furnishings where he might hurt himself. Once the player has fastened the tail, he removes his blindfold to see the result. If prizes or favors are given out, let each child receive his for trying, rather than for succeeding in putting the tail where it belongs.

Variation: When played by older children, each player may be turned around several times after being blindfolded and before starting out, so that his sense of direction is confused. Other players may also, by agreement before the start of the game, give directions similar to those described in Hot or Cold (see p. 224).

SEEK—DON'T SPEAK

Ages: **5 and older.**

Number of players: **4 or more.**

Place: **Indoors.**

All players but one leave the room. The remaining player hides an object that was previously agreed on by all players, anywhere in the room. He then recalls all other players. Each player who sees the hidden object sits down on the floor without telling where he found it. When all players have found the hidden object, that player who first sat down must tell where he found the hidden object, and if he identifies the place accurately, hides the same or another object for the next round of the game.

PAPER-CLIP FISHING

Ages: **5 and older.**

Number of players: **2 or more.**

Equipment: **A corrugated or other cardboard box with high sides—high enough so that seated players cannot see the bottom. Empty a package of paper clips into the box. Provide a magnet on a string or one hung by a string from a pole.**

Place: **Indoors.**

All players are seated around a table on which the box is placed. The first player, chosen by lot, is given the magnet and dangles it inside the box. He may trawl as far as he can reach, without standing up or looking inside the box. He scores according to the number of paper-clip "fish" that are attached to the magnet when he pulls it out. Only those "fish" count that are attached to the magnet when it is clear of the box. Those that fall back into the box do not count. The next player to his right then fishes in turn. That player wins, at the end of an equal number of rounds for all players, who has caught the largest number of "fish."

BLOW-BALL

Ages: **5 and older.**

Number of players: **Two equal teams of 3 or more players each.**

Equipment: **A large table, divided in half by a chalk line; Ping-Pong ball.**

Place: **Indoors.**

Each team of players lines up on opposite sides of the table. The ball is placed in the center. On command of the referee, or one player on alternate sides in succeeding innings, players start blowing vigorously at the ball. The object of each team is to blow the ball off the opposite end of the table. Whenever one team succeeds in blowing the ball off the opposite end of the table, this counts as 1 goal point for that side. No player may touch the ball with his hands or body in order to score or to prevent a score for the opposing side. Each team's table-end may be protected only by blowing. That team wins which scores the largest number of goals at the end of a predetermined number of innings, or after a given period of time. Each goal scored for either side counts as an inning.

A ball which is blown off the sides of the table does not count. But whenever this occurs, the ball is placed once more in the center, and the game continues as at first. Each team may place one or more members on the sides of the table, but not beyond the halfway line marking its own side of the table.

Variation: This game may also be played with a feather, or with a Ping-Pong ball on a court marked on the floor.

SOAP BUBBLE BATTLE

Ages: **5 and older.**

Number of players: **2 or more.**

Equipment: **Soap bubble pipe and soapy water. Home-made soap mixtures produce stronger bubbles than commercial ones. Mark 3 parallel lines, across the width of the room, 3 feet apart (see diagram).**

Place: **Indoors or outdoors.**

Divide players into even teams and line them up on each side of the center line. Each team blows one bubble in alternate turns. Once a bubble is formed, members of opposing teams try to blow the bubble past the line marking the far end of the opponents' side. Players may cross into each other's field. Each "goal" scores as one point. The bubble must be intact while crossing the end of a team's zone.

Variation: Stretch a rope across the room 3 feet above floor level. The game is played by the same rules as above, except that each team must remain on its own side of and two feet away from the rope. The object is to blow the bubble onto the opponent's side of the rope.

CARD TOSS

Ages: **5 and older.**

Number of players: **2 or more.**

Equipment: **2 decks of playing cards with different colored backs, and a bowl or wastebasket.**

Place: **Indoors.**

Players divide into equal teams. Both teams sit in semicircles on the floor, equidistant from the bowl placed in the center. The playing cards are divided equally, one color per team.

One member of each team alternately tries to toss one card into the bowl. Cards score only if they land inside the bowl. That team wins which, after all cards have been played, has landed the largest number of cards in the bowl.

THE SWINGING GAME

Ages: **5 and older.**

Number of players: **2 or more.**

Equipment: **A swing.**

Place: **Indoors** or **outdoors.**

The swing, because of its symbolic reaching toward the sky, has long been a part of ritual festivals, as it is in India, for instance. Here, intricately carved and decorated swings are a part of religious ceremonies and customs. And as late as 1895 it was still a feature of the All Souls' Day celebration in Bolivia, at which time "old and young swing all day long, in the hope that while they swing they may approach the spirits of their departed friends as they fly from Purgatory to Paradise." This tradition seems likely to have been a remaining fragment of pre-Columbian Indian culture.

A swing can serve as the vehicle for an amusing contest. An apple or a lollipop is suspended or held by an adult before an indoor or outdoor swing, while the player, starting from a standstill position, pumps himself high enough so that he can catch it either in one hand or with his teeth. That player wins who is able to do so with the fewest number of back-and-forth swings.

Variation: A balloon is suspended ahead of the swing. Each player is given a thumbtack, and tries at his turn to burst the balloon in four back-and-forth swings, starting from a standstill position.

TUG OF WAR

Ages: **5 and older.**

Number of players: **4 or more for each of two teams.**

Equipment: **Chalk or ribbon.**

Place: **Gym** or **outdoors.**

Mark a line with chalk or ribbon across the center of the floor or playground. Each team lines up, one player behind the other, each grasping the next member of his own side round the waist from behind, using both arms. The first players in line on both teams face each other across the dividing line, grasping each other's arms or hands. Each team pulls against the other on the word "Start" from the referee. That side loses whose first player touches or crosses the center line with his foot.

Variation 1: This game can be played with a rope by which opposing teams try to pull one another across the center line.

Variation 2: Players divide into two equal teams. Each individual team member then tries to tag an opponent.

When he succeeds in doing so, he and the tagged player join hands and attempt to force one another across the marked line from either side. That player who touches or puts his foot onto or across the line is out of the game. That team wins which forces the larger number of the opposing side across the line.

Note: Do not play this game near trees, walls, or rocks. One team or individual team members may fall backward when opponents suddenly give way.

SHOVE HA'PENNY

Ages: **6 and older.**

Number of players: **2 or more.**

Equipment: **Large tabletop (wood, plastic, formica, or glass-topped), on one side of which a long rectangle, divided into 9 equal spaces, is drawn with chalk or marked with tape (see diagram). The spaces are numbered 1 through 9. One equal-sized button or coin for each player.**

Place: **Indoors.**

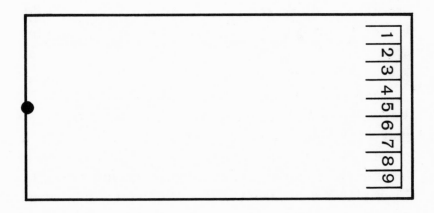

This game is very old and is probably the ancestor of shuffleboard, the perennial shipboard game. Each player in turn takes his place on the side of the table furthest from the rectangle drawn on it. He places his coin or button on the table so that a part of it overlaps the edge. Using the flat of his hand, he slaps as hard as necessary against the edge of the coin, aiming for the rectangle drawn on the table.

If the coin goes beyond the rectangle, stops short of it, or touches any of the lines, that player's turn is voided and play passes to the next. Each player whose coin rests in any of the spaces of the rectangle scores the number value of that space, adding it to previously won points. That player wins who first scores exactly 31 points. Any player who exceeds that score may, at any succeeding turn, aim for the number 9 space. If he succeeds in landing in that space, he wins the game, provided no other player has managed to do so before him.

Variation 1: The rectangle drawn for the game may be extended to include 10 spaces. Also, when a player exceeds the winning score of 31 (or any other), he may, by agreement before the game, attempt to reverse his score by subtracting points he wins at subsequent turns until he reaches that exact score of 31.

Variation 2: Players may also "shoot" coins by snapping one against another, as in "Tiddlywinks." Each player's coin stays in place after every turn, unless it lands exactly in a numbered space of the rectangle. Each player continues to "shoot" on succeeding turns from the position his coin occupied at the end of the previous turn.

CLOTHESPIN RELAY

Ages: **6 and older.**

Number of players: **Two or more teams of 4 or more players each.**

Equipment: **4 clothespins for each team.**

Place: **Indoors** or **outdoors.**

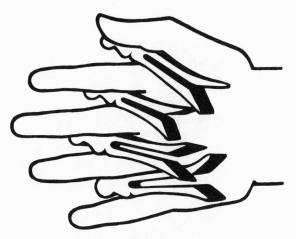

All teams are seated on the floor or ground in straight, parallel lines. The players of each team are seated one behind the other, each an arm's length apart. The first player of each team takes the 4 clothespins and places each between two fingers of the same hand. On the word "Start" from a referee, he passes the clothespins to the team member behind him, who must take them from him in either hand, in exactly the same manner in which they were handed to him—one between each two fingers. He then passes the clothespins back to the next team member, and so on, until the last team member in line holds them in hand. Whenever a clothespin is dropped, or when a team member grasps it in any other than the prescribed manner, all clothespins of that team must be handed back to the first player in line and the game resumes as before. That team wins whose last player first receives the clothespins without fumbling.

PARTY DOTS

Ages: **6 and older.**

Number of players: **3 or more.**

Equipment: **1 pencil (or crayon) and 1 piece of paper for each player.**

Place: **Indoors.**

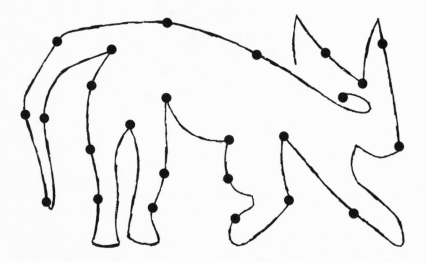

Each player makes 25 dots on his paper with his pencil or crayon. Each then passes the paper on to the player to his right. Each player then tries to draw a picture of a person, animal, or object, connecting all the dots on the page given to him, in any manner he chooses.

HEADS, BODIES, AND LEGS

Ages: **6 and older.**

Number of players: **Groups of 3 players.**

Equipment: **1 pencil (or crayon) and 1 piece of paper, folded into 3 equal parts, for each group.**

Place: **Indoors.**

The first player of each group receives the folded paper and pencil. He draws a face of a person or of an animal on the top third of the paper, carrying the lines of the neck a little past the first fold. He then folds back that third of the sheet on which he has drawn, so that it cannot be seen by the next player. He passes his paper to the player on his right in his group.

The next player, without looking at the head drawn by the previous player, adds torso and arms of any person or animal he chooses, using the neck lines indicated by the first player as guides. He stops a little below the next fold, folds the paper again, so that neither the head nor the torso can be seen, and passes it on to the third player.

The last member of each group, starting from the lines he sees at the fold, draws the legs of any person or animal he wishes. When all players in a group have finished their drawings, the sheet is unfolded and the creature invented by all three is revealed.

JACKS

Ages: **6 and older.**

Number of players: **2 or more.**

Equipment: **5 jacks or small pebbles.**

Place: **Outdoors.**

In the Orient, as in ancient Greece, the game of jacks was considered a girls' game. Elsewhere it is played by both boys and girls. Though jacks can still be bought in most toy stores, many children no longer know how to play this game. It can also be played with marbles and with pebbles.

Place 4 of the 5 jacks on the ground. The first player throws 1 jack into the air and must pick up a second with the same hand with which he threw the first, before catching it. If successful, he places the caught jack aside, throws again, and picks up the third. His turn continues until he fails to catch or pick up the required jack, or until he has thrown and picked up all 4 jacks in turn. On completion, he throws a jack up in the air once more and picks up all 4 jacks on the ground at the same time, before catching the thrown jack. If he succeeds he has won one round and the next player takes his turn.

Variation 1: Each player in turn, after throwing 1 jack up in the air and picking up the next from the ground, must catch the first, and all succeeding thrown jacks, on the back of his hand.

Variation 2: After picking up the second jack from the ground and catching the first, a player picks up 2 at a time, 3 on the next throw, and 4 on the third.

Variation 3: All jacks are held in hand—the same that throws the first jack—and the player puts down 1 on the ground before each thrown jack is caught, until all 4 jacks have been put down.

Variation 4: The 4 jacks are placed on the ground in a line. The first and third and the second and fourth must be picked up at each succeeding throw, 1 each, in that order.

Variation 5: A square is scratched into or drawn on the ground. The 4 jacks are placed in a heap in the center. One must be picked up at each throw and placed into one of the four corners of the square before the thrown jack is caught.

OUTLINES

Ages: **6 and older.**

Number of players: **2 or more.**

Equipment: **1 black and 1 colored pencil (or crayon) and 1 piece of paper for each player.**

Place: **Indoors.**

Each player draws a single curved line or squiggle with his black pencil, without lifting the pencil off the page. He then passes his paper to the player on his right. It is then the object of each player, using his colored pencil, and not lifting it off the page once he starts, to make a drawing of a face, a person, an animal, or an object, by continuing the line drawn by his neighbor, and incorporating it into his drawing. Emphasis should be on whimsy and humor.

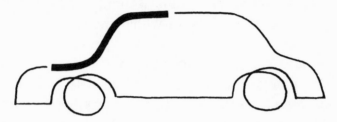

STONE, SCISSORS, AND PAPER

Ages: **6 and older.**

Number of players: **2 or more.**

Place: **Indoors** or **outdoors.**

Fingers are the first playthings of every baby and so baby finger games are popular everywhere. "This little piggy went to market" and "Here's the church and here's the steeple" are representative of a large family of games that, like Cat's Cradle, require separate volumes to do them justice.

Stewart Culin collected the games of the Orient at the end of the nineteenth century.[11] He described, among others, the many hand-clapping games that were then played by the children of China, Japan, and Korea. The Japanese game of *Janken*, in which the closed fist is a stone (*ishi*), two extended fingers represent a pair of scissors (*hasami*), and an open palm is a piece of paper (*kami*), is identical to the Italian game. It is futile to speculate about whether this game developed spontaneously on opposite sides of the globe or whether an early traveler, like Marco Polo, transported it East or West. The Japanese version of the game often decides who shall perform some small task. The Korean one formerly led to public contests to which admission was charged and in which champions participated who had been formally instructed in special classes.

The three positions of the hand and fingers are described above. Each player shakes his fist, simultaneously with all the others, counting out loud up to the number three in unison. On the count of three, each player makes whichever of the three gestures he decides on—stone, scissors, or paper.

In a game of 2 players, when both make the identical gesture, it is a draw. But if the gestures differ, they score in the following manner:

Scissors wins over paper because it can cut it.

Paper wins over stone because it can wrap it.

Stone wins over scissors because it can hone it.

In a game of more than 2 players, each scores according to his standing vis-à-vis each of the other players, scoring or not scoring points, in accordance with the above-stated method of winning or losing.

Play continues in sets of 3 turns or for a given number of rounds. That player wins the game who scores the largest number of sets or points.

TANGRAM

Ages: **7 and older.**

Number of players: **2 or more.**

Equipment: **A 3-inch square, or a 2-inch by 3-inch rectangular piece of paper or shirt-board for each player (all must be of equal size); a pair of scissors for each player.**

Place: **Indoors.**

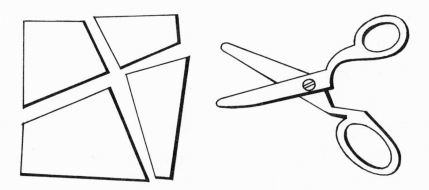

Each player is given his own square or rectangle and a pair of scissors. Each then cuts his paper or board apart with two (or, by common agreement, three) straight cuts of his scissors (see illustration). When each has cut apart his own paper or board, he mixes his cut-up pieces and passes them to the player on his right. Each player has five (or more) minutes to arrange the pieces so that they form the original square or rectangle. The player who first completes his puzzle scores 10 points.

Once a player has scored, each again shuffles the pieces in front of him and passes his puzzle on to the next player to his right. Play continues as before. The game ends when each player has had the opportunity to work all puzzles but his own. The player with the highest score wins.

Variation: Other geometric figures—triangles, circles, hexagons, parallelograms, etc.—can be used for this game in succeeding sessions. Aside from being a challenging game, this helps to familiarize players with the names and the configurations of various basic shapes.

MUMBLEDYPEG

Ages: **8 and older.**

Number of players: **2 or more.**

Equipment: **1 pointed stick (or peg) for each player.**

Place: **Outdoors on soft ground.**

A starting line is marked. The first player, and each following player in turn, tries to toss his peg in such a manner that it sticks in the ground. Any peg is considered "safe" if another peg can be passed under it, no matter how far it leans to one side. Any player may knock down any peg thrown by previous players, while still getting his own peg to stick in a safe manner in the ground. That player wins who throws his peg farthest, getting it into the ground safely.

Variation: Instead of throwing his peg farthest, each player tries to knock down pegs of any previous player, while still getting his peg safely into the ground. Any player whose peg is not safe when thrown, or whose peg has been knocked down, is out of the game. Players with safe pegs may pull them out of the ground at their turn in succeeding rounds, and may throw again for as long as they remain in the game. The last player with his peg in a safe position wins the game.

IX

Strategic Games

Only relatively few truly different kinds of strategic games have evolved throughout history. The same or similar games crop up in many parts of the world. In some instances, this is clearly due to the migration of people. But in others, the same game seems to have been developed spontaneously in distant places.

The games in this chapter include most known variations, except those that are esoteric, and modern race games that have their origin in the Royal Game of Goose. The latter depend on their topicality rather than on strategy, and for this reason alone cannot be improvised. Chess is excluded because it is too complicated, and requires too many and too varied and formal playing pieces to be adaptable to the scope of this book and to the age groups to which it addresses itself.

All the game diagrams and playing fields shown in this chapter can be scratched into the ground or drawn on paper, floor, or pavement. Buttons, coins, or pebbles can be used as play money, playing pieces, or counters. Some of these games can be bought in expensive game-board sets. A collection as complete as this would cost a small fortune. But as they are described here, the equipment necessary for them is within the reach of anyone.

Strategic games are battles in fun and make-believe. They are nonetheless real. The limitations of rigidly enforced rules and evened-out odds make them aggressive rather than hostile pursuits. The consequences of winning or losing are harmless. And therein lies the difference between violence and permissible, survival-assuring aggression.

All the races of man, except the Eskimo and the Australian Aborigine, play strategic games like those represented in this book. Included are contests that were old in the days of the Pharaohs of Egypt. Here are games that have been played in African villages, in desert tents, in medieval castles, and in the hide shelters of the American Indian.

Each of these games has its own history and tells its own story. All represent real struggles of people against each other and with nature. Here are contests among knights in armor, pitched battles between whole armies, the chase of hound and hare and fox and geese. The wily leopard stalks the cattle of the Indian herdsman, and rebellious Chinese soldiers chase their corrupt warlord out of their encampment.

As the Dutch historian Johan Huizinga states, men at all times have hidden in games those struggles that were most serious to them. They used games, as we still do in industry and in preparation for war, to attempt to meet and influence the outcome of life's contests. The underlying strategy of games mirrors that of real life. The mathematician J. Von Neumann's "theory of games" is the mathematical principle on which much of our computer technology is based.

Both games and life require foresight, the planning of moves, and the consideration of the opponent's possible countermoves. Strategic games help to teach these skills. But the probable outcome of games and of real-life contests cannot be predicted without taking luck into account. Chance may help or hinder success in battle, of the hunt, of planting and reaping, or of a journey. Early man hoped to appease and thereby influence what to him were inexplicable forces of nature.[3] In most instances, this took the form of ritual games, some of which are described here.

No ages are indicated for any of these games. Generally, children below school age are not prepared to play any except Tic-Tac-Toe or Three- to Nine-Men Morris. A child of seven or eight should be able to play checkers and a few of its variations, and some of the games in the Alquerque family, with reasonable success. But this, of course, depends in large measure on the child's individual development, on his home and school stimulation and experiences. As with all games, it is best to start out with those that are simple, increasing the complexity of those that are played as the child's experience increases.

Many strategic games have certain rules, moves, jumps, and captures in common. They are explained and illustrated below, in order to avoid duplicating them for each game.

Players. The number of players that may join each game is given in each set of rules.

Counters. Playing pieces are called counters throughout this chapter. In all strategic games, opposing players use counters of different colors. The number of counters to be used by each player is given in the rules to every game. Any of these games can be played using checker counters, poker chips, pieces of colored paper or cardboard, matchsticks, buttons, coins, or pebbles that are marked differently for each player.

Dice. Some of the games in this chapter require the use of dice. You may either use regular dice or make your own out of sugar cubes, marking point values on each of the six sides with a soft pencil, or coloring them red on three sides each with a crayon or felt marker, depending on the requirements for each game. Flat pebbles, marked on one side only, can also be used. Mark four pebbles with 1, 2, 3, and 6 respectively, and throw all of them at one turn. Only numbered sides upper-most score.

Forfeits. Play money, matchsticks, paper clips, poker chips, or sugar cubes can be used in games that call for payment or fines. At the beginning of each such game, every player receives the same amount. These are paid out during the game as the rules require.

First Move. In some strategic games, players place their counters on *Start*, and then move in turn. In others, players begin by placing their counters on specified points on the diagram. But in all games, the first move is decided by the throw of dice, by bucking up, by a flip of a coin, or by counting out. Players alternate in taking first turn in succeeding games.

Home Base. In some games—as in checkers—each player starts his counters from one side of the game diagram. The places or squares from which play begins are called home base.

Moves. The following words are used to describe moves in the rules for many of the games in this chapter:

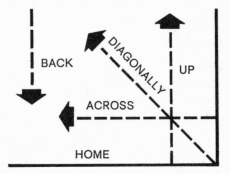

Up	away from home base
Back	back toward a player's own home base
Across	from side to side of the game board
Diagonally	from corner to corner of the game board, or from corner to corner of one square to the next

Captures. In all games, there are many ways to win—
and to lose. In some games, players try to trap, capture,
or block each other's counters in ways that are described by the following terms, used throughout this
chapter to name such moves.

Block	to hem in one or more of an opponent's counters so that they cannot move.

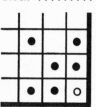

Capture	to land on the same space as that occupied by an opponent's counter, and remove the latter from the game.

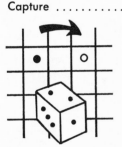

Approach	to capture by moving a counter next to one or more of the opponent's counters standing in one line.

Withdraw . . . . to capture by moving **away** from one or more of the opponent's counters standing in one unbroken line.

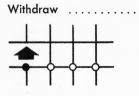

Trap . . . . to capture by moving two counters, one on each side, in line with an opponent's counter.

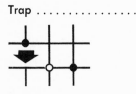

Intervene . . . . to capture two counters by moving one counter between those of an opponent, all three being in line.

Short Jump . . . . to capture an opponent's counter by jumping in a straight line from a point immediately next to it, to an empty point immediately beyond.

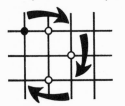

Multiple Short Jump . . . . . . to capture by the short jump, repeated several times, in as many different directions, as far and for as long as the jumping counter can land on an empty space or point directly beyond each counter that it jumps.

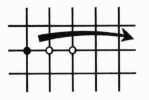

Long Jump . . . . to capture an opponent's counter by jumping in a straight line from a space or point immediately next to him, to any one of several spaces or empty points beyond.

Line Jump . . . . to capture by jumping over any **odd** number of an opponent's counters in a straight line, from a space or point immediately next to the first in line, to an empty space or point immediately beyond the last.

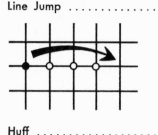

Huff . . . . to remove the counter of a player who has failed to jump at his turn. (In some games, players may capture and jump or not as they please. In others, jumps must be made whenever possible. In the latter case, an opponent may huff, i.e., remove the counter of a player who fails to jump. However, if a player does jump with one of his counters at his turn, his opponent may not at the following turn remove any other counter that might have jumped.)

Removal . . . . to remove from the game board all counters that are trapped, jumped, intervened, or huffed. (They remain off the board for the rest of that game.)

Crown . . . . to place a counter, of the same color, on a counter that has arrived at the opponent's home base. (Crowned counters are then moved as the rules for the particular game require.)

GAME 1: ALQUERQUE

This game was played by ancient Egyptians over two thousands years ago. The earliest rules that have been discovered were written in Arabic about A.D. 950. The game was then called *El-quirkat*. It was brought to Spain by Moorish invaders. The Spaniards in turn taught it to the Indians when they discovered Central America.

Rules:

1. A game for 2 players; each player uses 12 counters.
2. Counters are arranged on game field as shown (see diagram).

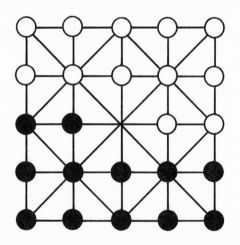

3. Each player in turn moves 1 counter to any empty space immediately next to it—up, across, or diagonally—but never backward.
4. Players must capture when possible, by the short

jump or by the multiple short jump in any direction, except backward. If a player fails to jump at his turn, his counter is huffed.

5. Any counter reaching an opponent's home base may not move away from it unless it can jump 1 or more of the opponent's counters. It may then move as before.

6. A player wins when he has captured all of his opponent's counters or has blocked them on his last move so that they cannot move—even if the opponent has more counters on the field.

7. The game is a draw if an equal number of counters of both players have reached the opponent's home base, or if they block each other so that neither can move. It is possible to avoid draws through clever strategy.

GAME 2: COYOTE AND CHICKEN

The Spaniards call this game *De cercar la liebre,* or Catch the Hare. Arizona Indians play the same game and call it *Pon chochotl,* or Coyote and Chicken. The Japanese call it *Yasasukari musashi,* or the Soldiers' Eight-way Hunt. But no matter how played or where, this game clearly shows that you just can't hunt with the hounds and run with the hare.

Rules:

1. A game for 2 players. The Chicken player uses 1 counter; the Coyote player uses 12.

2. Counters are arranged on a field as shown (see diagram).

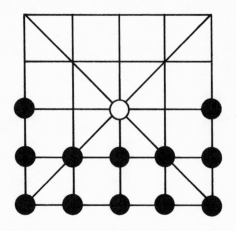

3. The Chicken player moves his counter to any next empty space at his turn, and may capture by the short jump and the multiple short jump, up, back, across, or diagonally.

4. The Coyote player may move 1 of his counters in any direction also, 1 space per turn, but he may not jump or capture.

5. The Chicken wins by capturing so many Coyotes that they cannot block him. The Coyotes win if they block the Chicken so that he can no longer move. Players take turns being Coyotes and Chicken.

GAME 3: KONO

Played in Korea, and elsewhere in the Orient, this game is one of maneuver, hide-and-seek, and deception.

Rules:

1. A game for 2 players. Each player uses 7 counters.

2. Counters are arranged on the field as shown (see diagram).

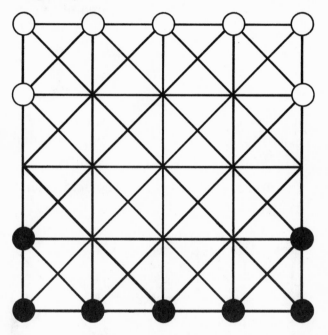

3. Each player at his turn moves 1 counter to any next empty space in any direction, up, back, across, or diagonally. He may also jump his own or his opponent's counters by the short jump or by the multiple short jump. But no counters are captured or removed from the field at any time.

4. The object of this game is to be the first to occupy the opponent's home base with all counters —in a reversal of the starting position of the game.

GAME 4: WARLORD

For centuries, both China and Japan were ruled by warlords, tyrants who roamed the countryside with their armies, robbing and destroying each other and the villagers. Now and again solders would rebel, kill, or chase away their warlord and appoint one of themselves in his stead. This game acts out a part of history that in real life was a question of life and death.

Rules:

1. A game for 2 players. One player (the Soldier) uses 16 small Soldier counters; the other player (the Warlord) uses 1 large counter.

2. Counters are arranged on the field as shown (see diagram).

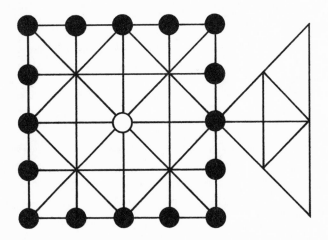

3. Rules are the same as in Game 2, except that only the Warlord may enter the triangle. He loses if he is blocked by the Soldiers and cannot

escape from the triangle by the short jump or the multiple short jump.

GAME 5: TIGER

In the jungles of Malaya, tigers (*rimau-rimau*) sometimes attack man (*orang-orang*), and the men in turn try to catch the tigers. This deadly hunt is played as a game on boards made of cloth or wood, or sometimes drawn on the ground. Pebbles or sticks are used as counters, and even coins—winner take all.

Rules:

1. A game for 2 players; 24 Men counters for one, 1 Tiger counter for the other.
2. Nine Men counters are arranged on the field as shown (see diagram).
3. The Tiger always goes first. On his first move he removes any 3 Men from the board and places his counter on any empty space on the board.

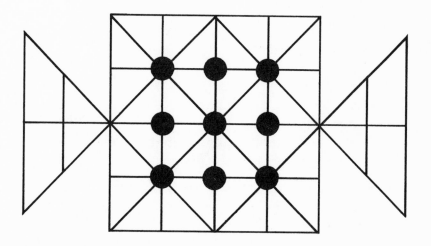

4. The Men player enters 1 more counter at each following turn on any empty space of his choice.

5. The Tiger at his next turn moves 1 space in any direction, or may—but need not—jump and capture by the line jump (over one or any odd number of Men in one line).

6. The Men may not move until all Men counters have been entered, 1 per turn. One Man may then move 1 space per turn, but may not jump or capture.

7. The Men win if they block the Tiger so that he cannot move or jump. The Tiger wins if he captures more than 14 Men.

GAME 6: TWO ARMIES

This is a war game played in India. It is called *Mogol Putt'han*, or Sixteen Soldiers. It differs from the Chinese and Japanese Sixteen-Soldier games in that here two armies battle each other.

Rules:

1. A game for 2 players. Each uses 16 counters.

2. Counters are arranged on the field as shown (see diagram).

3. All rules of Game 1 are followed, except that counters may move and capture in all directions, including backward.

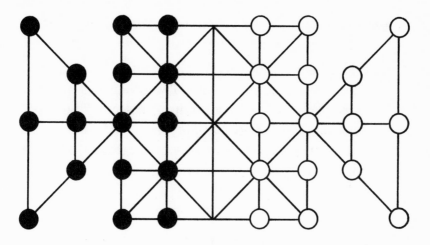

4. The object of this game is to capture all of the opponent's counters, or to block them so that he cannot move.

GAME 7: COWS AND LEOPARDS

Leopards creep silently out of the forests of Ceylon and pounce on unwary cattle. Played as a game, *Kotiyo saha harak*, or Cows and Leopards, requires great skill on the parts of both hunters and leopards. And sometimes, the cows surround and hem in the leopards, who then must flee into the night, defeated.

Rules:

1. A game for 2 players. The Cow player uses 24 counters; the Leopard player uses 2 counters. (Use field shown in diagram.)

2. Players take turns being Leopards and Cows in alternate games.

3. The Leopard begins by placing 1 of his counters anywhere on the board. The other player then enters 1 Cow at any point. The second Leopard is then entered on that player's turn, after which the Cow player enters 1 Cow per turn until he has placed all of them on the board.

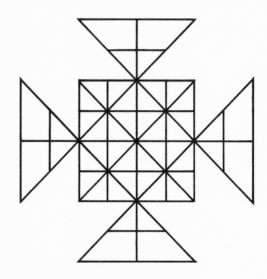

4. On the Leopard player's third turn, after he has entered both his counters, he may move either of them 1 space in any direction; or he may jump and capture—if he wishes—by the short jump or by the multiple short jump. The same rule applies to all subsequent turns.

5. The Cows may not move until all have been entered. The Cow player may then move 1 Cow per turn, 1 space in any direction. But no Cow may jump or capture.

6. The Leopards win if they capture 8 or more Cows, since it is almost impossible for less than 16 Cows to win. The Cows win by trapping both Leopards so that they can no longer move.

GAME 8: WAR CAMP

The people of Ceylon play the game of *Perali kotuma,* meaning "war enclosure." It is very similar to the Arab game of *El-quirkat.*

Rules:

1. A game for 2 players; each uses 23 counters.
2. Counters are arranged on the game board as shown (see diagram).

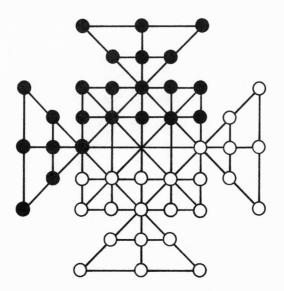

3. All rules are the same as in Game 1. They apply also to all moves inside the triangles of this game board.

4. The object of this game is to capture or block the opponent's counters.

GAME 9: TERCHUCHU

This is an East Indian game played on an enlarged Alquerque board. The greater the choice of moves, the more difficult the game and the more foresight required of both players.

Rules:

1. A game for 2 players. Each uses 9 counters.
2. Counters are arranged on the field as shown (see diagram).

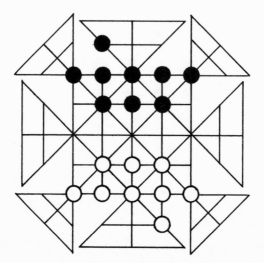

3. Counters may move and capture in all directions, including backward.

4. All other rules are the same as in Game 1, except:

   a) Counters may move 2 spaces at 1 turn inside the triangles.

   b) A player loses if all his counters are blocked inside the triangles.

GAME 10: SENAT

One of the most ancient games, Senat was played in Egypt over three thousand years ago. It was more recently played by Egyptians and African tribes as the game of Seega. Only pictures of the earlier game survive. But the placement of counters and a comparison of the moves pictured with those of the game that was still played one hundred and fifty years ago have enabled anthropologists to reconstruct the old rules.

Rules:

1. A game for 2 players. Each uses 12 counters (see diagram).

2. Each player in turn places 2 counters on any squares of the field except the center square, and continues in turn to do so until all counters have been placed.

3. The player who placed the last 2 counters makes

the first move. Players move 1 counter per turn, 1 square in any direction except diagonally.

4. If the first player cannot move on his first turn, he may remove 1 of his opponent's counters to enable him to do so.

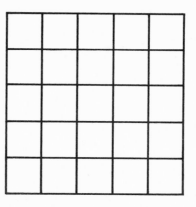

5. Captures are made by trapping—but only after all counters have been placed and moves have begun. After making a capture, a counter may continue to move, if in so doing it can capture more of the opponent's counters. A player's counter may safely move between 2 of his opponent's counters without being taken.

6. The object of the game is to trap or block all the opponent's counters. If, after play has begun (see Rule 4), neither side can move, the player with the most counters on the board wins.

GAME 11: SEVEN SQUARES

This and the next game follow all the rules of Senat—

Game 10. However, they are played on larger fields with more counters, and therefore they are more difficult and require greater foresight.

1. A game for 2 players. Each uses 24 counters (see diagram).

2. Follow all rules of Game 10.

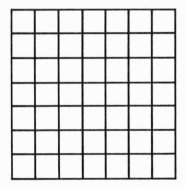

GAME 12: NINE SQUARES

1. A game for 2 players. Each uses 40 counters (see diagram).

2. Follow all rules of Game 10.

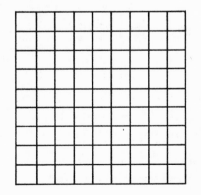

GAME 13: BLOCK OR JUMP

Board games change in time. As they are handed on
from generation to generation, from country to country,
their rules and diagrams take on new forms. When the
same game has been played again and again, it becomes
less of a challenge. Players try different ways to keep
the game interesting. This form of Senat is still played
in Africa.

Rules:

1. A game for 2 players. Each uses 12 counters.

2. Counters are arranged on the field as shown (see
    diagram).

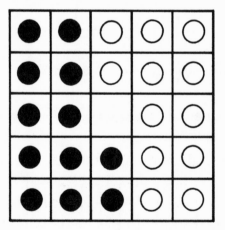

3. Players move 1 square with 1 counter per turn,
    in any direction except diagonally. A player may
    —but need not—capture by the short jump or
    by the multiple short jump.

4. The object of the game is to capture or block
    all of the opponent's counters.

GAME 14: DERRAH

This game may be the ancestor of Tic-Tac-Toe. It requires more skill and is therefore more fun. Adults and children of North Africa and Nigeria play this game.

Rules:

1. A game for 2 players. Each uses 12 counters (see diagram).

2. Each player in turn places one counter on any square of the field, until all counters have been placed.

3. First move is made by the player who placed the first counter. After all counters are placed, each player moves 1 counter, 1 square per turn, in any direction except diagonally.

4. The object of the game is for each player to move so as to form rows of 3—and only 3—of his own counters in any direction except diagonally. Each time a player completes such a row of three, he takes 1 of his opponent's counters and

removes it from the field. The game ends when one of the players can no longer form a row of 3 of his own counters—and the other player is the winner.

5. *Note:* Rows of 4 counters do not count. Rows of 3 arranged during the placement part of the game—before counters may move—also do not count.

GAME 15: HASAMI SHOGI

Winning by moving a given number of counters to form a row is a challenge common to a whole family of board games. The most difficult of these is the Chinese game of Wei-Ch'i (see Game 33). It would take a small book to give all the rules and variations of this game. The rules given below for one of these games are not so difficult. They are those used by the children of Japan.

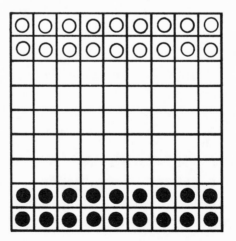

Strategic Games

1. A game for 2 players. Each player uses 18 counters.

2. Counters are arranged on the field as shown (see diagram).

3. Each player moves 1 counter per turn, 1 square in any direction.

4. The object of the game is for a player to complete a row of 5 of his own counters, in any direction, on any of the squares of the board, except on those of his own home base. The first player to do so wins.

5. An opponent's counters may be captured by trapping in any direction. But a player's counter may safely move between 2 of the opponent's without being captured.

6. A player may jump his own and his opponent's counters by the short jump or the multiple short jump in any direction, but no captures are made by jumping.

GAME 16: SHOGI

This is another version of Hasami Shogi. The object is to win by trapping the opponent's counters.

Rules:

1. A game for 2 players. Each uses 9 counters.

arranged on the field as shown (see

273

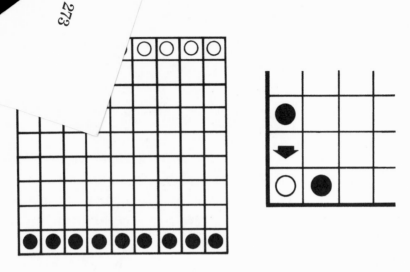

3. Follow all rules of Game 15, except Rule 4.

4. In this game, counters may be trapped in the corners of the game board as shown (see diagram).

GAME 17: CHECKERS

This game is related to both Chess and Alquerque (see Game 1). It was probably invented in southern France in the twelfth century A.D. In France it was called Dames, and later, in England, Draughts. The Pilgrim Fathers brought this game with them when they landed at Plymouth, and they gave it the name of Checkers.

Rules:

1. A game for 2 players. Each uses 12 counters.

Rules:

1. A game for 2 players. Each player uses 18 counters.

2. Counters are arranged on the field as shown (see diagram).

3. Each player moves 1 counter per turn, 1 square in any direction.

4. The object of the game is for a player to complete a row of 5 of his own counters, in any direction, on any of the squares of the board, except on those of his own home base. The first player to do so wins.

5. An opponent's counters may be captured by trapping in any direction. But a player's counter may safely move between 2 of the opponent's without being captured.

6. A player may jump his own and his opponent's counters by the short jump or the multiple short jump in any direction, but no captures are made by jumping.

GAME 16: SHOGI

This is another version of Hasami Shogi. The object is to win by trapping the opponent's counters.

Rules:

1. A game for 2 players. Each uses 9 counters.

2. Counters are arranged on the field as shown (see diagram).

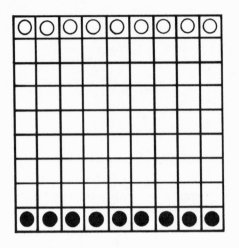
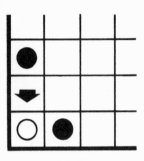

3. Follow all rules of Game 15, except Rule 4.

4. In this game, counters may be trapped in the corners of the game board as shown (see diagram).

GAME 17: CHECKERS

This game is related to both Chess and Alquerque (see Game 1). It was probably invented in southern France in the twelfth century A.D. In France it was called Dames, and later, in England, Draughts. The Pilgrim Fathers brought this game with them when they landed at Plymouth, and they gave it the name of Checkers.

Rules:

1. A game for 2 players. Each uses 12 counters.

2. Counters are arranged on the field as shown (see diagram).

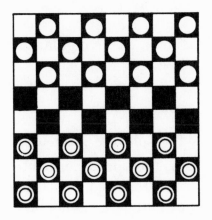

3. Players in turn move 1 counter, to any unoccupied, adjacent black square, in a forward, diagonal direction only. Captures must be made, in the same direction by the short jump and by the multiple short jump. Counters that fail to capture on their turns are huffed.

4. Counters reaching an opponent's home base are crowned Kings. Kings move and capture by the short jump and multiple short jump, both backward and forward diagonally, always staying on the black squares. Kings must capture Kings and ordinary counters, and are captured by either when possible. A King that fails to capture at his turn is huffed.

5. The object of the game is to capture or block all the opponent's counters. If neither player can capture or block the opponent's remaining counter or counters, the game is a draw.

GAME 18: LOSER

In this game, the player who wins loses and the loser wins. It is played in England, France, Germany, and Russia as a variation of the regular game of Checkers. See if you can lose.

Rules:

1. A game for 2 players. Each uses 12 counters.
2. The field is the same, the counters are arranged and the rules followed, as in Game 17, except that instead of huffing a counter that fails to jump, an opposing player insists that the jump be made. If a player has the choice of two jumps at his turn, his opponent may also insist that he choose that jump which will account for the capture of the greater number of counters.
3. The player who loses all his counters first is the winner.

GAME 19: DIAGONAL CHECKERS

Only very rarely is a new game principle invented. Such invention is limited by mathematical possibilities. But the variations of rules and play, once such a board has been developed, seem infinite.

Rules:

1. All rules of Game 17 apply, except that:

can capture opposing counters by jumping over them to any unoccupied space beyond in any direction.

GAME 22: ENGLISH CHECKERS

Rules:

1. A game for 2 players. Each uses 12 counters.
2. Field and counters are arranged as in Game 17, except that Kings may move not only diagonally, but also back, forward, and sideways as shown (see diagram).

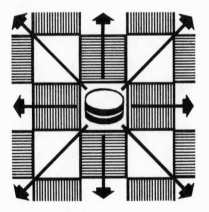

GAME 23: COPS AND ROBBERS

Rules:

1. A game for 2 players. Each uses 12 counters.
2. Field and counters are arranged as in Game 17.

3. Players move 1 counter per turn as in Game 17
—diagonally forward, back, or by the short
jump or multiple short jump in either direction.
No Kings are crowned. No captures are made.

4. The object of the game is to be the first to occupy the opponent's home base with all counters,
or to block him so that he cannot move.

GAME 24: POLISH CHECKERS

After inventing Checkers, the French developed a new
version that became popular in 1727.

Rules:

1. A game for 2 players. Each uses 20 counters.

2. Counters are arranged on the field as shown
(see diagram).

3. Each player in turn moves 1 counter as in Game
17. Captures are made forward and back by the
short jump and the multiple short jump. Captures must be made. If there is a choice of jumps,
the one which will capture more of the opponent's counters must be chosen.

4. Captured counters may be removed only after a
multiple short jump has been completed. Once
jumped at one turn, a counter may not be
jumped again at that turn.

5. Kings are crowned as in Game 17. On arrival at
the opponent's home base, a counter may not be

crowned if, at that turn, it can continue to jump. It must advance again until it can rest at the opponent's home base, and may then be crowned.

6. Kings move as in Game 17. But they may move any number of squares diagonally, either forward or back at 1 turn in 1 line. They may capture one or more of the opponent's counters several squares away at 1 turn, provided none of his own side's counters stand between and an empty square lies immediately beyond the captured counters. A King may also continue to jump in a different direction after a capture has been made, and may capture in that direction also.

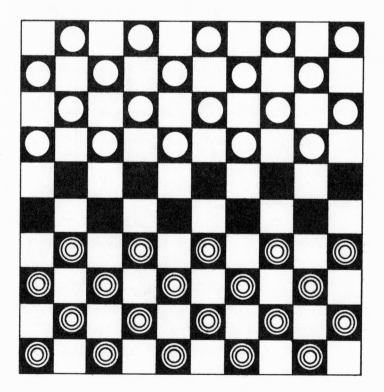

GAME 25: REVERSI

Rules:

1. A game for 2 players. Each uses 32 counters.

2. Counters are marked X on one side and O on the other. One player places counters X side up, the other uses the O side. Or counters marked with different colors on each side may be used, each player using one color.

3. The first player places 1 counter on any one of the central four squares of the field (see diagram).

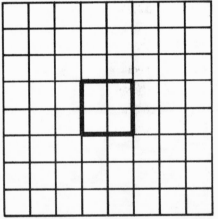

4. The second player then places 1 counter on any other of the four central squares of the field.

5. Play continues thus in turn, until the 4 central squares have been filled. Thereafter, each player in turn places one of his counters on any square on the field, provided that such a square touches a square occupied by one of the opponent's counters.

6. Any intervened counter (see "Captures," pp. 253 and 254) is turned over and remains on the field. It then becomes the property of the player making the capture. A counter may thus change sides many times during the game.

7. At the end of the game—when all squares have been filled—the player with the greatest number of counters on the field is the winner.

GAME 26: QUADRUPLE ALQUERQUE

An enlarged and more intriguing version of Game 1. It shows how the Alquerque games are related to Checkers.

Rules:

1. A game for 2 players. Each uses 40 counters.

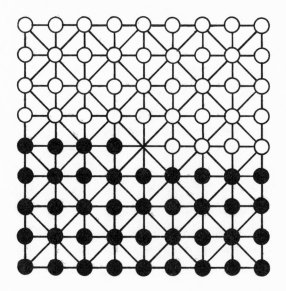

2. Counters are arranged on the field as shown (see diagram).

3. All rules of Game 1 apply, except that counters must jump or be huffed.

Note: Moves and jumps in this game are made from point to point, along the black and white lines shown, not from square to square.

GAME 27: FANORAMA

The island of Madagascar (now Malagasy Republic) lies off the eastern coast of Africa. The game of Alquerque found its way even to these distant shores. By the seventeenth century, the Madagascans were playing a new version as a part of their religious rites. They believed that in playing this game, they could influence and foretell the outcome of battles. I imagine that it was quite an accurate fortuneteller. Whenever the game predicted victory, tribal warriors would take up spears and shields, armed with courage and a will to win. But if the game told of a coming rout, these soldiers would enter battle in fear, and be defeated by their own lack of confidence and courage.

This is the secret of the force of magic. Those who believe in it bring about by their own efforts the success or failure that has been foretold, as do children today who trust in the magic of not stepping on the cracks of concrete pavements. Many believe that they'll pass (or fail) a school test, depending on whether or not they step on the lines on their way to class.

Rules:

1. A game for 2 players. Each uses 22 counters.
2. Arrange counters on the field as shown (see diagram).

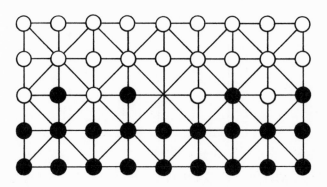

3. Each player in turn moves 1 counter in any direction to an adjacent unoccupied point.
4. Captures are made by approach and withdrawal (see "Captures," pp. 253 and 254). On making a capture, a player gets another move at that turn with any other counter, for as long as he can continue to make more captures. Captures must be made. In moving to a point at which opponent's counters are found on both sides, only those on one side or the other may be taken.
5. Each approach or withdrawal at the same or successive turns must be made along different paths. That player wins who captures all of his opponent's counters.

GAME 28: LEAPFROG

Rules:

1. A game for 2 players. Each player uses 50 counters (see diagram).

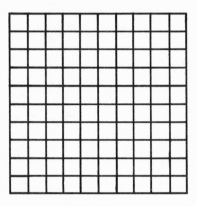

2. Each player in turn places 1 counter on any square of the field, until all squares are filled with counters.

3. When all the squares have been filled, each player at his turn removes 1 of his own counters, anywhere from the field.

4. At following turns, each player captures as many of the opponent's counters as he can, by the short jump and by the multiple short jump in any direction. A player's turn does not end until he has made all possible captures with any of his counters on the field. This means that a player may capture and jump with more than 1 counter per turn if he is able.

5. If a player at his turn cannot jump and capture,

the game ends. The player who has captured the greatest number of his opponent's counters wins.

Note: The initial placement of counters will to a large extent determine the outcome of this game.

GAME 29: WARRIORS

This is an old Indian game of the Southwest and Mexico. Imagine Zuni braves in the setting sun, squatting on the clay roofs of their huts, concentrating, arguing, watching, as players made their moves. The board diagram for this game was often permanently scratched into the clay roof of an Indian dwelling. It is possible that this game may have stemmed from the Spanish Alquerque, or it may have been invented in the Americas quite independently. No one knows.

Rules:

1. A game for 2 or 4 players. Each uses 6 counters and 1 King. The King is called "the Priest of the Bow." When 4 play, they divide into teams of two, and each team sits across the field from the other.

2. Counters are arranged on the field as shown (see diagram).

3. Counters move from point to point (intersection to intersection) diagonally, forward only, along the lines of the board. No backward moves are permitted. Kings, however, may move diagonally, both forward and across, but never back, along the lines of the field from point to point.

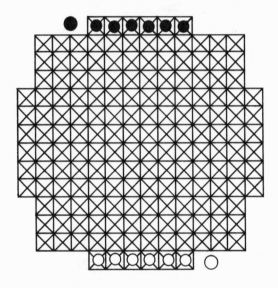

Both counters and Kings may move only from one point to the very next at each turn. *Note:* According to Indian lore, there is a reason why Kings may move in more directions than ordinary Men. This game acts out a chase across the canyons of the Southwest. The Men must walk along the hills. But the Kings, with the power of magic, can fly across the canyons with ease.

4. Kings are kept off the field at the start of the game. A player may place his King only in the position of the first counter which he loses.

5. Captures are made by trapping. But a counter

(or King) may move between 2 counters of an opponent without being captured.

6. The object of the game is to occupy the opponent's home base and to capture as many of the opponent's counters as possible on the way. The player or team that occupies the opponent's home base with the most counters is the winner.

GAME 30: HALMA

This is a comparatively recent game. It was probably first played in Europe, and invented sometime during the last century.

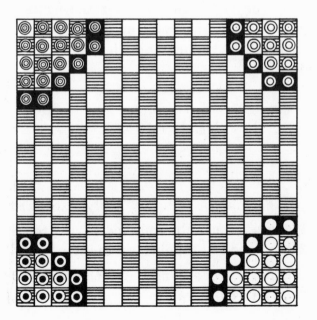

Rules:

1. A game for 2 or 4 players. If 2 play, each uses 19 counters; if 4 play, each uses 13.
2. Counters are arranged on the field as shown (see diagram).
3. Each player in turn moves 1 counter to a diagonally adjacent square of the same color in any direction. Or he may jump, according to the rules (see diagram). That player wins who first occupies the opponent's home base with all of his counters.
4. Jumps: a counter may jump by the short jump or by the multiple short jump, diagonally in any direction, over his own and/or over his opponent's counters. No captures are made.
5. Note that on any move or jump, each counter stays on either the black or the white squares of the board, depending on which color it started from at the beginning of the game.

GAME 31: BY THE NUMBERS

Rules:

1. All the rules of Game 30 apply, except that:
2. Players use counters numbered 1 through 19 if 2 play, and 1 through 13 if 4 play.
3. Counters are arranged on the game field as shown (see diagram).

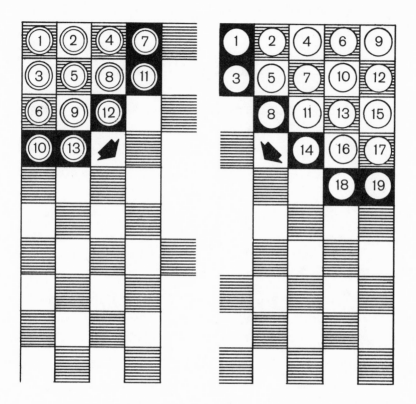

4. Each player, moving one counter at each turn, and jumping as in Game 30, attempts to be first to occupy his opponent's home base, but with all numbered counters in the order of their starting position.

GAME 32: TABLE

This game was played in Scandinavia at least as long ago as the fifth century A.D. It was brought to the Brit-

ish Isles by Norse invaders and became the only strategic game (so far as we know today) played by the
Saxons. It disappeared completely for many centuries
after the advent of Chess, and was eventually recon-
structed from manuscripts. This, like many ancient
games, may well have been a religious game by which
the King was ritually deposed once each year.

Rules:

1. A game for 2 players. One player has 24 Noble
   counters and 1 King; the other player has 48
   Soldier counters. Players change counters for
   succeeding games.

2. Counters are arranged on the game field as
   shown (see diagram).

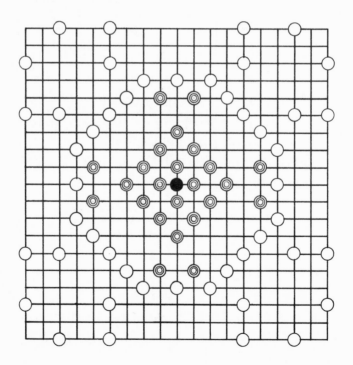

3. The King's Nobles move first. Each player in turn moves 1 counter forward, back, or sideways as many spaces as he wishes, without changing direction at that move. But counters never move diagonally.

4. Captures are made by trapping in either forward, backward, or sideways directions, but never diagonally. A player's counter may safely move between 2 counters of the opponent without being captured.

5. The King may be captured only if he is completely surrounded by 4 attackers (see diagram).

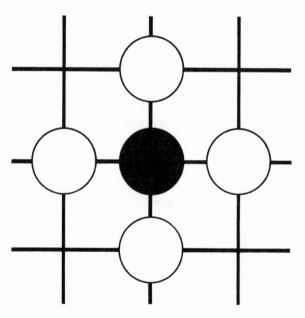

6. The King wins if he is able to reach any square on the outer edge of the playing board.

7. The Attackers win if they trap the King.

GAME 33: WEI CH'I (or GO)

First mentioned in Chinese writings in the seventh century B.C., this game eventually found its way to Korea and Japan. As recently as the last century, being a really first-rate player was equivalent to holding a university degree. In Japan, where it is known as the game of Go, classes were given, instructing students in the intricacies of the game, and diplomas were awarded to successful graduates. The Chinese philosopher Confucius advised the rich and idle to play Wei Ch'i to occupy their minds and to keep active and alert. This game is called *Pa-Tok* in Korea. Korean boards are made of hollow tables within which wires are strung, so that when counters are placed on the board, it makes a musical sound.

This game depends entirely on the skill and foresight of the players. For beginners, it is an easy game in its simplest form. For those who play it often, many more complicated moves become apparent. Thus, it can be played either as a very simple game, or as a very difficult one. It all depends on the players. The few rules are the same in either case. In the Orient, players use polished, oval stones as counters, black for one player and white for the other. The Japanese name for this game means the "enclosing game."

1. A game for 2 players. Each uses 181 counters, black counters for one, white for the other, or marked in any other way so that each player's counters can be easily distinguished from those belonging to his opponent.

2. Each player piles his counters next to him off the field.

3. Counters are placed by each player—1 per turn —on the intersections of lines, not on the squares (see diagram). Once placed, the counters are not moved.

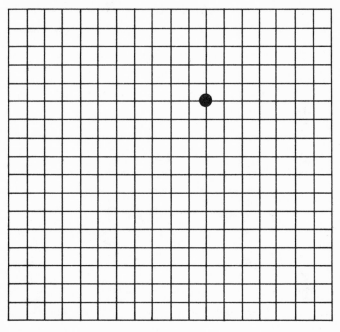

4. Object of the game: Each player tries, through strategic placement of his counters, to enclose the largest possible territory on the field. Players continue to place their counters in turn, enclosing different portions of the board until no further territory remains to be enclosed.

5. Captures: Any counter or group of counters completely surrounded by the opponent's counters is captured and removed at once from the board (see diagram).

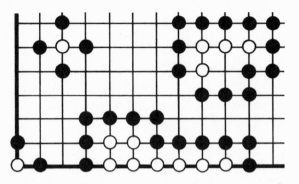

6. Any group of counters that is completely enclosed by the opponent, but in a territory
within which there are 2 empty intersections,
may not be captured. Both players abandon
that portion of the board and continue to play
on other parts (see diagram).

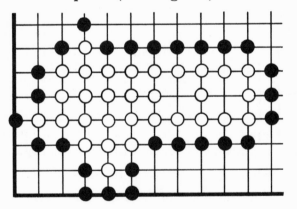

7. Another grouping of opposing counters that is
abandoned by both players is called, in Japanese, *seki*, meaning "impasse" (see diagram).
It consists of an empty intersection that is partially or wholly enclosed so that any counter
entered by either player would cause the entering player's territory to be captured by his
opponent on his next move.

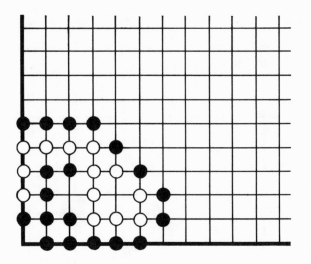

8. The game is over when 2 completely enclosed territories, each belonging to an opposing player, are in contact with each other, or when both players agree that no further territory remains to be enclosed. Those counters of either player that would be captured if the game were to be played until all counters are placed are then removed from the board. Each player then places his counters in those territories that he has or would have captured, filling all empty intersections.

9. The player who has enclosed the largest territory is the winner.

10. *Exception*: In the event that an arrangement of counters as shown in the diagram below takes place, and it is "white's" turn to place a counter, he may capture the black counter marked "a." But "black," at his turn, may not place a counter at "a," in order to capture

white counter "s." He may do so only *after* "white's" next move, making another placement elsewhere on the field in the meantime.

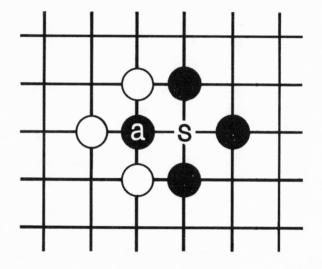

GAME 34: PACHISI

Emperors and maharajahs played this ancient national game of India. Their game boards were palace courtyards inlaid with marble. Slaves served as counters. The royal players relaxed between turns and were entertained by music and dancers. Food and drink was served to them as they pondered each move. In 1896, this game was introduced to England under the name Ludo, and it has since become a favorite throughout the world.

Rules:

   1. A game for 2 or 4 players. Each uses 4 counters; 6 dice are used (see diagram).

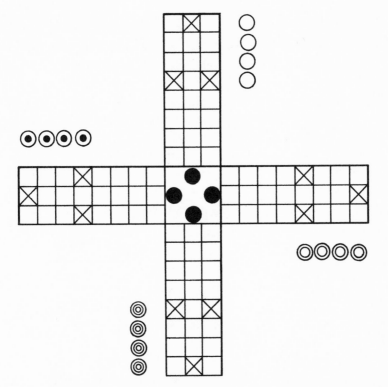

2. Each player faces one arm of the cross of this game field. He places his 4 counters on the home circle in the center castle nearest him. When 2 players play, each places 4 more counters of a different color on the circle opposite his own, playing them in turn as partners to his own counters, as if 4 players were in the game. In a game of 4 different players, counters on opposite sides of the field are partners, and do not capture one another. They help each other by blocking the opponent's counters when possible. Partners win and lose together.

3. Each player moves his counters from the home circle down the middle path of the arm of the

cross facing him. Counters then move to the *right* on the outside path, all around the board, back up the middle path of the arm facing the player, to the same circle in the center castle, according to the rules. The first two partners who return all their counters to their circles in the center castle are the winners.

4. Counters are moved by the throw of 6 dice, on which three sides are white and three sides colored. Colored and white sides shown uppermost, *not* spots on the dice, are used to determine moves:

2 colored sides up	move 2 squares and turn ends
3 colored sides up	move 3 squares and turn ends
4 colored sides up	move 4 squares and turn ends
5 colored sides up	move 5 squares and turn ends
6 colored sides up	move 6 squares and throw again
1 colored side up	move 10 squares and throw again
0 colored sides up	move 25 squares and throw again

Note: If players prefer, 6 coins instead of dice may be used for this game. Score 2, 3, 4, 5, 6, 1 and 0 *Heads Up* instead of colored sides.

The score of any roll of the dice may *not* be split among several counters. But a second or third throw may be used for any counter, either to enter or to move in play. A player's first counter to leave the circle may enter the game on the throw of any number. But the next three counters and all those returned by capture may leave the home castle only on the throw of 6, 1, or 0 colored sides up.

5. Captures are made by a counter's landing on the same space as that occupied by an opponent. Captured counters are sent back to their home circle and must start again (see Rule 4). More than one counter of one player, and any belonging to a partner, may safely occupy the same square. These may be captured only by the same number or more of the opponent's counters landing on that square in one turn.

   Note: A player need not move his counters until the end of his turn to throw the dice, making such multiple capture possible.

6. Marked squares are *safe*. No captures may be made on them. More than one counter belonging to one player and his partner may share a safe space at one time. But *safe* spaces may not be shared by opponents.

7. *Blockade*: opposing counters may not pass each other on the board. They must either capture or wait until the blocking counter has moved. A blocked counter may move as close as possible at its turn with a dice score that will bring it to the square before the blockade, but unless it can do so, it must pass up that score or turn. A player may not use a part of a throw to move. Players may refuse a throw or turn, and wait for future turns to move.

8. If a counter that has already completed the course reaches a safe space at the base of the arm of the cross, and that player decides that his partner needs help, he may, if he wishes, move that counter around once again.

MERELLES

The following four games are among the oldest known. They are all in-a-row games, the object being to line up three or more counters to win. Designs for such game boards have been found inscribed in Egyptian temples and in Greek, Roman, and Cretan pavements. The names given to games in each country show how they travel from country to country. In the case of these games, all sound like the Latin word *merellus*, meaning "coin" or "token": *Merelles* in France; Merrymen, Merryholes, and Nine-Men Morris in England; *Mühle* in Germany; *Mlyn* in Czechoslovakia; and *Melnitsa* in Russia. The Vikings played these games, as can be seen by designs they carved into the decks of their ships. English shepherds in the time of Queen Elizabeth cut their game diagrams into village greens. William Shakespeare mentions them:

> The nine-men's morris is filled up with mud;
> And the quaint mazes in the wanton green,
> For lack of tread, are undistinguishable.
>
> *A Midsummer Night's Dream,*
> Act II, Scene I

GAME 35: THREE-MEN MORRIS

Rules:

1. A game for 2 players. Each uses 3 counters (see diagram).

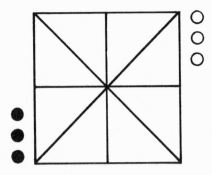

2. Each player enters his counters, 1 per turn, on any 3 points of the game board. When all have been entered, each player moves 1 counter per turn to any next point along the lines of the board. No points may be passed in making moves. That player wins who first completes a line of 3 of his counters on any straight line of the board, up and down, sideways, or diagonally.

GAME 36: SIX-MEN MORRIS

Rules:

1. A game for 2 players. Each uses 6 counters.

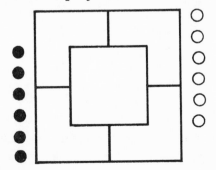

2. All rules are the same as in Game 35, except that:

3. Whenever a player has formed a row of 3 of his counters on any side of either of the 2 squares, he may remove one of his opponent's counters. He may do so both during the placement part of the game and after the counters are being moved from point to point. A player wins when he either blocks his opponent so that he cannot move or captures 4 of his counters.

GAME 37: NINE-MEN MORRIS

Rules:

1. A game for 2 players. Each uses 9 counters (see diagram).

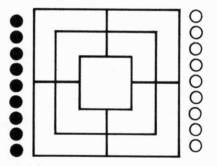

2. All rules are the same as in Games 35 and 36, except that:

3. Rows of 3 may also be made on the lines that intersect the squares. A player wins when he either blocks his opponent so that he cannot move or captures 7 of his counters.

GAME 38: TIC-TAC-TOE

Rules:

1. A game for 2 players. Each uses 5 counters (see diagram).

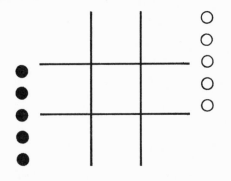

2. Each player in turn places 1 counter on any square of the board until all 5 counters have been played. The object of the game is to see which player is able to complete a row of 3 of his counters, up and down, sideways, or diagonally.

BACKGAMMON

This is one of the basic playing fields on which many different kinds of games have been played since Egyptian days. Certainly the Romans knew this game and carried it to the outposts of their empire. Many of their game diagrams have been unearthed. Some of the games played on them were described by writers of that time. The game boards used for Alea, Tabula, and Ludus Latrunculus were early variations of the game that in our day is known as Backgammon. Romans and early Christians played these games passionately, sometimes as gambling games. From time to time, both church and state attempted to outlaw them—with little success. Even today some countries forbid certain games; for instance, playing Monopoly is prohibited behind the Iron Curtain.

Backgammon has a vocabulary all its own. To simplify the rules, here is a glossary of terms:

INNER TABLE: that section of the field to the left of player (**A**) and to the right of player (**B**) (see diagram).

OUTER TABLE: that section of the field to the right of player (**A**) and to the left of player (**B**) (see diagram).

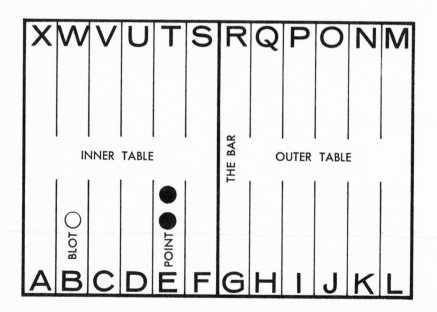

THE BAR:	the line on the game field that separates the inner table from the outer table.
A POINT:	any space on the field occupied by two or more of one player's counters. A player may not land on a point held by his opponent.
A BLOT:	any space on the field occupied by a counter.
BEARING OFF:	removing a player's own counters from the playing field.
GATE OR SPACE:	any space (marked from A to X) on the board.

GAME 39: ALEA

Ancient writers did not always describe in detail the rules of the games of their time. Many rules given in this book are based on these early writings. Hence, in playing these games and testing the rules, it was often found necessary to change or enlarge upon some of the rules so that the games could be played successfully. The following rules are more or less those that the Romans might have used.

Rules:

1. A game for 2 players; each player uses 15 counters; 3 dice are used (see diagram, p. 306).

2. This is a race game. Each player in turn enters his counters at gate A and moves them all around the field to and past gate X, off the board, according to the rules below. That player wins who first removes all of his 15 counters.

3. Each player in turn throws the dice, enters and

moves his counters according to his dice score. Counters may be entered on the throw of any number.

4. Dice Score: The sum of the points shown uppermost on all 3 dice may be used to move 1 counter per turn as many gates as points shown; *or* the player may use the sum of 2 dice to move 1 counter, and the points shown on the third die to move another counter; *or* 3 counters may be moved at 1 turn, moving 1 counter the number of points shown on 1 die, a second counter the number of points on a second die and a third counter the number of points on the third die. *The score of the 3 dice may not be divided in any other way.*

5. If 2 or more counters of 1 player are at 1 gate, the opponent's counter may not land on that gate.

6. If a player's counter lands on a gate occupied by 1 of the opponent's counters, he captures it and sends it off the board. The opponent must then enter that counter again in the usual manner before moving any of his counters on the field at his next turn.

7. A player may not move any counter past gate L until all of his counters have been entered on the board once.

8. None of a player's counters may be moved off the field past gate X until all of his counters have passed gate R.

9. A player must, if possible, use all of his dice

score at his turn. However, if he cannot use all or part of his throw at that turn—perhaps because his counters are blocked by the opponent —that part of the score is lost. At no time may a part of the score of a die be used to move a counter.

GAME 40: CHASING THE GIRLS

A game of tag on a board. This game could as easily be called Chasing the Boys. It all depends on who is chasing whom.

Rules:

1. A game for 2 players; 6 counters each; 2 dice.
2. Counters are arranged on the game field as shown (see diagram).

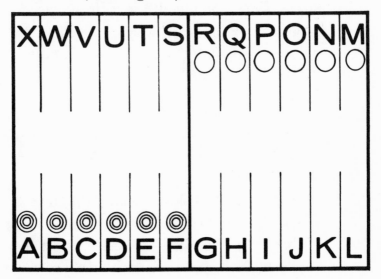

3. Players move their counters around the field from left to right, according to the rules below. They continue their chase, around and around, until one player has captured all the counters of his opponent.

4. Dice Score: Counters are moved *only* on the throw of 6, 1, or doubles. No other scores count. On the throw of a 1 and any number other than 6 or 1: move 1 counter 1 space, and turn ends.

On the throw of a 6 and any number other than 6 or 1: move 1 counter 6 spaces, and turn ends.

On the throw of a 6 *and* 1: *either* move 1 counter 7 spaces, *or* move 2 counters, one 6 spaces, the other 1 space, and turn ends.

On the throw of a 6 *and* 6: move 4 counters 6 spaces each, and throw dice again.

On the throw of *any other* double: *either* move 1 counter as many spaces as the sum of the score, *or* move 2 counters, each the number of spaces shown on one die, and throw dice again.

5. If a counter lands on a space occupied by the opponent's counter, that player captures the opponent's counter and removes it from the board for the rest of the game.

6. If one player's counter lands on a space occupied by one of his own, he *must*, at that move, continue it to the next unoccupied space on the board.

7. When a player has lost all but 1 counter:

   a. He moves the counter at once—without throwing the dice—to the nearest corner space: A, F, L, M, R, or X. His last counter may occupy *only* these spaces, for the rest of the game.

b. At each succeeding turn: on the throw of 1 and any number other than 1 or 6, that counter moves to the next of the corner spaces. On the throw of 6 and any number other than 1 or 6, the counter moves 2 corner spaces. On the throw of 1 *and* 6, the counter moves 3 corner spaces. On the throw of *double* 1, the counter moves 2 spaces *and that player throws again*. On the throw of *double* 6, he moves his counter 4 corner spaces *and throws again*. The player who has lost all but 1 counter may throw again if he throws *any* double, even if it is not a double that allows him to move.

c. The single counter may capture or be captured only on those 6 gates listed above. However, it may not be captured, even at these points, if it is surrounded by the opponent's counters, one on each of the 2 spaces immediately adjacent to the space it occupies.

d. If both players are reduced to 1 single counter each, Rule 7 applies to both.

8. The player who captures all of his opponent's counters is the winner.

GAME 41: TOURNE CASE

Rules:

1. A game for 2 players; 3 counters each; 2 dice.
2. Counters are arranged on the game field as shown (see diagram).

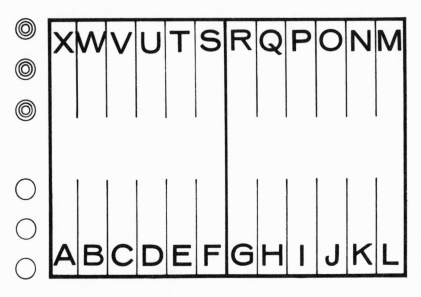

3. One player races the course from A to L, the other from X to M, according to the rules below. That player wins who first reaches his goal with his 3 counters.

4. Each player in turn throws both dice and moves 1 counter only, as many spaces as the sum of both dice, or moves 2 counters, one the number of spaces shown on one die, the other the number of spaces shown on the other die. The sum of the score may *not* be divided in any other way. Doubles score only *half* the sum of the

score thrown, and only 1 counter may be moved on the throw of doubles.

5. A player's own counters may not pass each other.

6. If one player's counter lands on a space opposite a space occupied by one of the opponent's counters, the latter is captured and sent off the board. It must be entered again at A or X, depending on the side to which it belongs.

7. No more than 1 counter may occupy the same space at one time. If no other move is possible, then that part of the throw at that turn is lost.

GAME 42: SIX ACE

Rules:

1. A game for 2 or 4 players; 12 counters each; 2 dice.

2. If 2 play, 6 counters for each are arranged on the game field as shown (see diagram). If 4 play, counters are arranged as shown. The remaining 6 counters of each player are kept in reserve for use during play.

3. The 6 spaces occupied by each player's 6 counters are his *home*. The 6 counters kept off the field at the beginning of play are the *reserve*. The spaces in the center of the field (see diagram) are the *pool*.

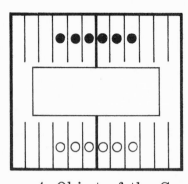 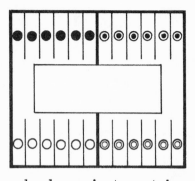

4. Object of the Game: each player in turn tries to eliminate all of his counters on his home, adding them, according to the rules, to his opponent's home, his own reserve, or the pool. That player wins who first eliminates all counters from his home, and then is the first to throw a 6 with either of the dice at his turn.

5. Each player throws the dice in turn. Each die is scored separately as follows:

Throw a 1: add 1 counter from your reserve to opponent's home.

Throw a 5: add 1 counter from your reserve to the pool.

Throw a 2: take 1 counter (if any are in the pool) from the pool and add it to your home.

Throw a 6: take 1 counter from your home and add it to your reserve.

Throw a 3 or a 4: no score—no move is made.

Throw double 2: take 2 counters from pool and add them to your home (or up to 2, or none, depending on number of counters in pool).

Throw any other double: move for each die as above, **and throw again.**

6. In a game of 4 players, all above rules apply. Turns are taken from left to right. Each player adds to or takes from the home of the player on his left at each turn.

GAME 43: FAYLES

Rules:

1. A game for 2 players; 15 counters each, black for one player, white for the other, or marked so that opponents' counters are easily distinguished; 3 dice.

2. Counters are arranged on the game field as shown (see diagram).

3. The player of the white counters moves *counterclockwise*, according to the rules. The player of black moves *clockwise*. L is the exit gate for white; M is the exit gate for black (see diagram).

4. Each player at his turn throws the dice and moves any 3 counters. Each counter may move as many gates as the points shown on one of the

3 dice. *Or* a player may move 1 counter as many gates as the sum of all 3 dice. The score may not be divided in any other way.

5. Each player completes the course indicated in Rule 3. The player wins who first moves all of his counters off the field through his exit gate.

6. A counter may not pass or land on a gate occupied by 2 of the opponent's counters.

7. If a counter lands on a gate occupied by 1 of the opponent's counters, the latter is sent off the field and must be entered again at gate L or M, depending on whether it is black or white.

8. If a player at his turn cannot use *all* of his throw of the dice, *he loses the game.*

GAME 44: MODERN BACKGAMMON

Rules:

1. A game for 2 players; 15 counters each; 2 dice.

2. Counters are arranged on the game field as shown (see diagram). Dice are thrown for first move.

3. Each player moves 1 counter per turn as many spaces as points shown uppermost on the dice. A player moves his counters from their starting position in the following direction: from his opponent's inner table to his opponent's outer table, to his own outer table, to his own inner

table, according to the rules. Each player thus moves in an opposite direction, starting any of his counters from any position at the beginning of the game. That player wins who first bears-off all his counters from his own inner table, according to the rules.

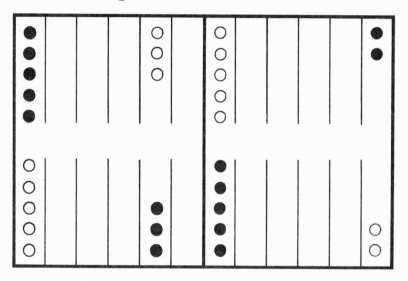

4. Dice Throws: counters are moved according to the throw of both dice:

   a. The sum of the points shown on both dice at one turn may be used to move 1 counter as many spaces, *or*

   b. The score of each die may be used to move 2 counters at one turn, each as many spaces as the points shown on one or the other of the dice. The dice score may not be divided in any other way.

   c. On the throw of a *double*, the score is doubled at that turn. One counter can be moved 4 times as many spaces as the points shown on one die, *or* the score may be divided among 2, 3, or 4 counters, moving each as many spaces as shown on 1 die or multiples thereof. The score may not be otherwise divided.

d. If a player can make use of the points shown on only 1 die, he must use the *higher-scoring* die if possible. He loses the rest of the score.

5. When a counter lands on a blot held by the opponent's counter, the latter is captured, removed from the board, and placed on the bar. The opponent *must* at his next turn enter captured counters on the first space of the other player's inner table. None of a player's counters on the field may be moved until *all* captured counters are again entered in the game.

6. A player's counter may not land on a point held by his opponent. If no other move is possible, he loses that turn or part of the score.

7. Captures are not mandatory. A player may capture with 2 counters at one turn if the dice allow.

8. *Bearing-off*: A player may not bear-off until:

a. *All* of his counters have entered his own inner table *and*

b. Any captured counter—even after bearing-off has started—has completed the track and returned to his inner table. Even after all counters are on the player's own inner table, he may not bear-off if his dice score permits a move, bringing any counter or counters closer to the edge of his inner table. More than 1 counter may be borne-off at a turn if the dice score allows.

9. *Victories*: The first player to bear-off all his counters wins the game. Victories are scored as follows:

  a. If the loser has already borne-off 1 or more counters, a *single victory* is scored.

  b. If the loser has not yet borne-off any counter, a *double victory* or *Gammon* is scored.

  c. If the loser has not yet borne-off any counter *and* has one or more captured counters on the bar, a *triple victory* or *Backgammon* is scored.

GAME 45: PUFF

Another version of Backgammon, played in England and Germany.

Rules:

1. A game for 2 players; 15 counters each; 2 dice.

2. Both players enter their counters from outside the field at A, according to the throw of the dice at each turn, going in a counterclockwise direction and bearing-off at X (see diagram, p. 306).

3. The player who first bears-off all of his counters at X, according to the rules, is the winner.

4. All counters belonging to one player must be en-

tered before any of that player's counters already on the field may be moved. Captured counters must be re-entered at A before any other move is made.

5. Dice Score: The score of each die is used to move each of 2 counters of every turn. The sum of the throw may *not* be used to move 1 counter. The score of the lower-scoring die must be used first at each turn, before the higher-scoring die is used. If the lower-scoring die cannot be used to move any counter, then the whole of that turn is lost.

6. Doubles: The points shown uppermost, as well as those *underneath*, each of the 2 dice, are used to move 4 counters (Rule 5 applies here also). After a player has thrown his *first double* in any game, he gets a second throw at each turn at which he throws another double.

7. For blots, points, and captures, Rules 5, 6, and 7 of Game 44 are followed, except that no more than 2 counters may occupy a point.

8. Counters may be borne-off at any time and from any point or blot on the board, whenever the throw of the dice permits, provided that all player's counters are entered on the board at that time.

GAME 46: TRIC-TRAC

Though played on a Backgammon board, this is not a race game, but one that is won by scoring points. Points

are won by landing on particular spaces on the field
and on blots held by the opponent. Each player must be
careful to divide his dice score in the most advantageous manner, because if he fails to take advantage
of his score, his opponent may lay claim to the points
he might have won had he used his score properly. Tric-
Trac was invented in France in the sixteenth century,
and is the ancestor of numerous variations still popular
in many parts of Europe. Players should rule off a
score card and have pencils handy before the game
begins.

Rules:

1. A game for 2 players; 15 counters each; 2 dice
   (see diagram, p. 306).

2. One player at his turn, enters his counters at L;
   the other enters his at M, each moving his counters around the field counterclockwise, according
   to the throw of the dice, as in Game 44.

3. In this game, no captures are made, and no
   counters are borne-off. Players continue to move
   their counters around the field until one player
   has reached a score of 25.

4. Scoring:

   a. For the player who enters at *L*:

   2 **points** for landing with 2 counters on **L**
   2 **points** for landing with 2 counters **each** on **A** and **F**
   1 **point** for landing on a blot held by the opponent

b. For the player who enters at M:

2 **points** for landing with 2 counters on **M**
2 **points** for landing with two counters **each** on **S** and **X**
1 **point** for landing on a blot held by the opponent

5. After a player has thrown the dice at his turn, he first decides *how* and *which* counters to move. He then marks down his point score, if any. Finally, he actually moves his counters. If he has failed to use his dice score to score points, and his opponent is able to see how this might have been done, the opponent may then, *after the counters have been moved*, claim the points that would have been won by that player, had he planned his moves properly. The opponent then adds these points to his own score.

GAME 47: PAUMECARY

The paying of forfeits and fines, and the right to claim favors from the loser, are ancient rights of winners. Here is a fourteenth-century British version of the game of Tabula in which the winner may slap the loser. It is of course permissible to demand other punishment, forfeits, or favors.

Rules:

1. A game for 2 players; 15 counters; 2 dice.

2. Only half of the Backgammon board is used (see diagram). Players enter their counters at A, going around A, F, S and bearing off at X.

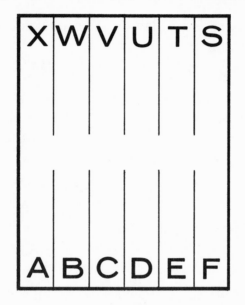

3. Counters are entered and moved on the throw of the dice at each turn (see Game 45, Rules 5 and 6). Blots can be taken and points piled with as many counters of one player as that player chooses. Opposing players may not share a point.

4. When a player has entered *all* his counters, he may then begin to bear-off at X.

   a. When one player has borne-off all his counters, he continues to throw the dice at his turn, to help the losing player enter and move his counters, and to bear them off the board.

   b. For every counter of the opponent borne-off by the winner at his turn, the winner slaps the hand of the loser.

GAME 48: RAVA

Rules:

1. A game for 2 players; 15 counters each; 2 dice; Backgammon field.
2. All rules for Backgammon apply, in addition to the following:
   a. Each player heaps his 15 counters at A and X respectively at the beginning of the game.
   b. On the throw of a *double*, both top and bottom points of the dice are scored; the move is made, and the dice are thrown again.
   c. Neither player may heap his counters on points on his own side of the board, except on the last space of his own side.
   d. Blots may be taken as in Backgammon, and no counter on a side may be moved until all counters are in play.
   e. Before any counters may be borne off, all of a player's 15 counters must be on the opponent's inner table.
   f. The first player to bear off his counters on the exact throw of the dice wins the game.

GAME 49: EMPERADOR

Rules:

1. A game for 2 players; 15 counters each; 3 dice; Backgammon field.

2. Rules 2, 4, 5, and 6 of Game 44 apply, except that:

3. On re-entry of a captured counter, it may not enter if with that score it must land on a point.

4. Points may be made only on the opponent's side of the board.

5. That player wins who manages to place 2 of his counters on any 6 consecutive spaces on the board (see diagram).

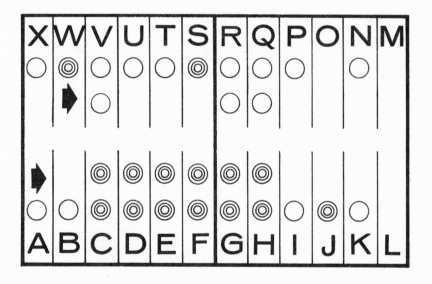

AGE, PLACE, AND MATERIALS INDEX OF GAMES

Chapter I

Ball, Bowling, Beanbag,

Name of Game	Number of Variations	Lowest Age Group	Minimum Number of Players
Pitch Ball	1	4	2
Bell Ball		5	1
Patsy Ball	1	6	1
Sevens		6	1
Pass the Ball	2	6	6
Call Ball	2	6	5
Tag Ball	2	6	3
Dodge Ball	1	6	12
School Ball	7	6	12
Catch the Ball	1	7	12
Odd Ball	1	7	12
Throw and Go	1	7	5
Chase Ball		8	4
Center Ball		8	10
Piggyback Ball		10	12
Highball		12	12

Bowling

Name of Game	Number of Variations	Lowest Age Group	Minimum Number of Players
Stake Ball	1	7	6
Ball Bowling		7	1
Battle Ball	1	8	10
Ricochet		8	1

NOTE: This index allows you to find the games and all their variations, listing the lowest age group at which an average child is likely to be able to play and enjoy them; the minimum number of players required to play each game; where each is best played, indoors and out of doors, at home, in school, or in a car; and whether or not special materials, such as a ball, a blackboard, or pencil and paper are required.

and Balloon Games

In Class or at Home	Gym	Hard Surface	Soft Surface	Page Number
X		X	X	29
		X		30
	X	X		30
X	X	X	X	31
	X	X	X	33
	X	X	X	35
	X	X	X	37
X	X	X	X	38
	X	X	X	39
	X	X	X	42
X			X	42
	X	X	X	43
	X	X	X	45
			X	45
			X	46
	X	X	X	48

Games

In Class or at Home	Gym	Hard Surface	Soft Surface	Page Number
X		X	X	52
X	X	X		54
	X	X		55
X	X	X		56

Name of Game	Number of Variations	Lowest Age Group	Minimum Number of Players
Trap Ball	2	9	2
Hand Tennis		12	2

Balloon Ball	2	6	12
Roll Ball		7	6
Hole Ball		7	1
Relay Ball	1	8	24
Corner Goal Ball	1	9	12
Rounders	1	9	18

Chapter II   Marble

Bounce Eye		5	2
Marble Shoot	5	6	2
Target		6	2
Ring Game		6	2
Shoot Out		7	2
Marble Bocche	3	7	2
Nine Holes		7	2
Marble Bridge	1	7	2
Picking the Plums	1	7	2

Chapter III   Button

Button-Stringing Contest		4	2
Knock 'Em Down		6	1
Snip-Snap	1	6	2
Snap Pebble		6	2
London		7	2
Toss-up		8	2

Sticks, Bats, Mallets, and Rackets

| Indoors | | Outdoors | | |
In Class or at Home	Gym	Hard Surface	Soft Surface	Page Number
		X	X	60
	X	X		62

Courts or Playing Fields

In Class or at Home	Gym	Hard Surface	Soft Surface	Page Number
X	X			64
			X	67
			X	68
	X	X •	X	69
	X	X	X	70
			X	72

Games

In Class or at Home	Gym	Hard Surface	Soft Surface	Page Number
X		X	X	80
X		X	X	81
X		X	X	83
X		X	X	83
X		X	X	85
X		X	X	86
			X	87
X		X		89
X		X	X	90

Games

In Class or at Home	Gym	Hard Surface	Soft Surface	Page Number
			X	93
X				94
X		X		95
X		X	X	96
X		X		97
		X		99

Name of Game	Number of Variations	Lowest Age Group	Minimum Number of Players
Hopscotch	3	5	1
Rope-Skipping	7	6	1
Cock-Fighting	4	6	2
Leapfrog	1	6	2
Hopping Bases	4	6	13
Obstacle Hop		7	2
Jump Up		7	2

Foot Races	2	4	2
Stoop Tag		4	8
Musical Chairs		4	8
Follow the Leader	1	5	6
Hoop Games	2	5	1
Tag	7	5	3
Fox and Rabbit		5	10
Potato Race	1	5	2
Pair Race		5	13
Cat and Mouse		5	12
Butterfly Hunt		6	24
Lion and Gazelles		6	8
Blind Man's Buff		6	8
Race for the Empty Space		6	12
Hand-Hold Tag		6	6
Handkerchief Tag		6	10
Counting Out Catch	1	6	10
Man in the Middle	2	6	10
Three's a Crowd	2	6	24
Number	1	6	11
Count to Ten		6	4
I Spy	1	7	6

and Jump

| | Indoors | | Outdoors | | |
In Class or at Home	Gym	Hard Surface	Soft Surface	Page Number
		X	X	102
		X	X	106
		X	X	109
	X	X	X	110
		X	X	112
			X	114
		X	X	115

Catch Games

| | Indoors | | Outdoors | | |
In Class or at Home	Gym	Hard Surface	Soft Surface	Page Number
X	X	X	X	118
X	X	X	X	119
X				120
X	X	X	X	121
		X	X	122
	X	X	X	123
X	X	X	X	126
X	X	X	X	127
X	X	X	X	128
	X	X	X	129
	X	X	X	129
		X	X	130
X	X	X	X	130
	X	X	X	131
	X	X	X	132
	X	X	X	132
	X	X	X	133
	X	X	X	134
	X	X	X	136
X				137
X	X	X	X	138
		X	X	139

Name of Game	Number of Variations	Lowest Age Group	Minimum Number of Players
Hand It Over		7	24
Relay Races	8	7	12
Green and Blue		7	12
Slap Tag		7	12
Send-Off		7	12
Prisoners' Base	1	7	10
Poison	2	7	12
About Face	1	7	11
Indoor Tag		7	8
Hunt the Fox		7	10
Circle-Go-Round	1	7	12
Wheelbarrow Race		7	4
Hare and Hounds		9	6

Chapter VI
Word Games

Name of Game	Number of Variations	Lowest Age Group	Minimum Number of Players
Who Am I?	1	4	6
Cooperative Tale		4	2
Nursery Rhyme Bee		5	2
Bird, Insect, or Fish	3	5	2
Because		5	2
The ABC Game	4	5	2
Simon Says	1	5	3
All Birds Fly	1	6	6
How Many Words		6	6
The Eating and Drinking Game	3	6	2
What Is My Job?	1	6	2
Take a Trip		7	2
Alphabet Questions		7	2
Question and Answer		7	2
Observation	1	7	2
The Shopping Game	2	7	2
Pantomimes	1	7	3
Forbidden Words	1	7	2

In Class or at Home	Gym	Hard Surface	Soft Surface	Page Number
		Indoors	Outdoors	
	X	X	X	140
	X	X	X	141
	X	X	X	143
	X	X	X	144
	X	X	X	145
	X	X	X	146
	X	X	X	148
X	X	X	X	149
X	X			150
	X	X	X	152
	X	X	X	153
X	X		X	154
		X	X	154

Use a Black-board	Use Paper and Pencil	In Class or At Home	In the Car	Camping or on Beach	Page Number
		Indoors		Outdoors	
		X		X	159
		X	X	X	160
		X	X	X	160
		X	X	X	161
		X	X	X	162
		X	X	X	163
		X	X	X	164
		X	X	X	165
		X		X	166
		X	X	X	167
		X	X	X	168
X	X	X			169
		X	X	X	170
		X	X	X	171
	X	X			172
		X	X	X	173
		X		X	175
		X		X	176

Name of Game	Number of Variations	Lowest Age Group	Minimum Number of Players
Definitions		7	2
The Unfinished Story Game		7	2
Rumor		7	6
Which Ant?		7	2
ABC Adjectives	1	7	2
Silly Willy		7	2
Word Associations		8	2
Vocabulary		8	2
Scrambled Letters		8	2
Blackboard Relay		8	12
Collage		8	1
Headword		8	2
Missing Letters	1	8	3
Buried Words	1	8	3
Anagrams	1	8	2
Earth, Water, or Air		8	2
Letter Ladder	1	9	2
Puzzle Word		9	2
Mosaic		9	3
The Memory Game	2	9	8
Cablegram	1	9	2
Hangman		9	2
Geography	1	9	2
Alphabet Travels	2	9	3
Twenty Questions	1	9	2
Boutes-Rimes	1	10	3
Doublets		10	1
Writing a Novel		10	2

Chapter VII   Number

Odds and Evens		5	2
How Many Fingers?	1	6	3

		Indoors		Outdoors	
Use a Black- Board	Use Paper and Pencil	In Class or At Home	In the Car	Camping or on Beach	Page Number
		X	X	X	178
		X	X	X	178
		X		X	179
		X	X	X	179
		X	X	X	180
		X	X	X	181
		X	X	X	182
		X			183
	X	X			184
X	X	X			185
	X	X			186
X	X	X		X	187
X	X	X		X	188
X	X	X		X	189
	X	X		X	190
		X	X	X	190
		X	X	X	191
	X	X		X	192
X	X	X			193
		X	X	X	193
X	X	X		X	195
X	X	X		X	196
		X	X	X	197
		X	X	X	198
		X	X	X	199
X	X	X		X	201
X	X	X		X	202
	X	X		X	203

Games

		X	X	X	208
		X		X	208

Name of Game	Number of Variations	Lowest Age Group	Minimum Number of Players
Dot Tic-Tac-Toe	2	6	2
The Wheel of Fortune		6	2
Number Guessing	1	7	2
Odd Man Wins	1	7	2
Buzz	2	7	2
Century Game	3	8	2
Magic Squares	4	9	2
Number Tic-Tac-Toe		9	2

Chapter VIII   Party

Hot or Cold	1	4	2
Matching Grasses		4	2
Button, Button	2	4	6
Grin or Bear It		4	4
Bob Apple	1	4	4
Pin the Tail on the Donkey	1	4	2
Seek—Don't Speak		5	4
Paper-Clip Fishing		5	2
Blow-Ball	1	5	6
Soap Bubble Battle	1	5	2
Card Toss		5	2
The Swinging Game	1	5	2
Tug of War	2	5	8
Shove Ha'penny	2	6	2
Clothespin Relay		6	8
Party Dots		6	3
Heads, Bodies, and Legs		6	3
Jacks	5	6	2
Outlines		6	2
Stone, Scissors, and Paper		6	2
Tangram	1	7	2
Mumbledypeg	1	8	2

Use a Black-Board	Use Paper and Pencil	Indoors In Class or At Home	Outdoors In the Car	Camping or on Beach	Page Number
X	X	X		X	209
X	X	X			211
		X		X	212
		X		X	212
		X	X	X	213
X	X	X		X	214
X	X	X		X	215
X	X	X		X	218

Games

Use a Black-Board	Use Paper and Pencil	Indoors In Class or At Home	Outdoors In the Car	Camping or on Beach	Page Number
		X		X	224
				X	224
		X		X	225
		X		X	226
		X		X	226
		X			228
		X			229
		X			229
		X			230
		X			231
		X			232
		X		X	233
				X	234
		X			235
		X		X	237
	X	X			238
	X	X			239
				X	240
	X	X			242
		X		X	243
	X	X			245
				X	246

Chapter IX
Strategic Games

Game Number	Name of Game	Number of Players	Page
34	Pachisi	2 to 4	298
35	Three-Men-Morris	2	302
36	Six-Men-Morris	2	303
37	Nine-Men-Morris	2	304
38	Tic-Tac-Toe	2	305
39	Alea	2	307
40	Chasing the Girls	2	309
41	Tourne Case	2	312
42	Six Ace	2 to 4	313
43	Fayles	2	315
44	Modern Backgammon	2	316
45	Puff	2	319
46	Tric-Trac	2	320
47	Paumecary	2	322
48	Rava	2	324
49	Emperador	2	324

BIBLIOGRAPHY

1. Ariès, P. **Centuries of Childhood.** New York: Vintage, 1962.

2. Arnold, A. **Teaching Your Child to Learn from Birth to School Age.** Englewood Cliffs: Prentice-Hall, 1971.

3. Arnold, A. **Your Child's Play.** New York: Essandess Division of Simon and Schuster, 1968.

4. Arnold, A. **The Yes and No Book.** Chicago: Reilly and Lee, 1970.

5. Bancroft, J. H. **Games for the Playground, Home, School and Gymnasium.** New York: Macmillan, 1909.

6. Béart, C. **Jeux et Jouets de L'Ouest Africain.** 2 vols. Dakar: IFAN, 1955.

7. Bell, R. C. **Board and Table Games from Many Civilizations.** London: Oxford University Press, 1960.

8. Caillois, R. **Man, Play and Games.** Glencoe, Ill.: The Free Press, 1961.

9. Champlin, J. D., and Bostwick, A. E. **The Young Folks' Cyclopedia of Games and Sports.** New York: Henry Holt and Co., 1899.

10. Coudeyre, M., and Mathieu, G. A. **Paris Review.** Paris: U.S. Lines, 1956.

11. Culin, S. **Games of the Orient.** Tokyo: Charles Tuttle Co., 1958 (orig. ed., 1895).

12. D'Allemagne, H. R. **Histoire des Jouets.** Paris: Hachette, ca. 1902.

13. D'Allemagne, H. R. **Récréations et Passe-Temps.** Paris: Hachette, ca. 1903.

14. D'Allemagne, H. R. **Sports et Jeux D'Adresse.** Paris: Hachette, ca. 1904.

15. Evans, P. **Hopscotch.** San Francisco: The Porpoise Bookshop, 1955.

16. **Every Boy's Book.** London: George Routledge and Co., 1860.

17. **Every Little Boy's Book.** London: George Routledge and Co., ca. 1880.

18. Falkener, E. **Games Ancient and Oriental and How to Play Them.** New York: Dover, 1961 (orig. ed., 1892).

19. Furness, J. C. **String Figures and How to Make Them.** New York: Dover, 1962 (orig. ed., 1906).

20. Goldstein, K. S. "Strategy in Counting Out, an ethnographic folklore field study." Toronto: American Folklore Society, 1967 (unpublished).

21. Gomme, A. B. **The Traditional Games of England, Scotland and Ireland.** 2 vols. New York: Dover, 1964 (orig. ed., 1894 and 1898).

22. Haddon, K. **Cat's Cradles from Many Lands.** London: Longman's Green and Co., 1911.

23. Huizinga, J. **Homo Ludens.** Boston: Beacon Press, 1955.

24. Leslie, Miss. **American Girl's Book.** Boston: Munroe and Francis, 1851.

25. Loyd, S. **Cyclopedia of Puzzles.** New York: Franklin Bigelow Corp., 1914.

26. Murray, H. J. R. **A History of Board Games.** London: Oxford, 1952.

27. Newell, W. W. **Games and Songs of American Children.** New York: Dover, 1963 (orig. ed., 1883).

28. Opie, I., and Opie P. **Children's Games in Street and Playground.** New York: Oxford, 1969.

29. Pick, J. B. **The Phonenix Dictionary of Games.** London: J. M. Dent, 1963.

30. **Simulation Games for the Social Studies Classroom.** New Dimensions. Foreign Policy Association. 1969, 1:1.

31. Smith, C. F. **Games and Game Leadership.** New York: Dodd, Mead, 1932.

32. Strutt, J. **The Sports and Pastimes of the People of England.** Thomas Tegg and Sons, 1801.

33. **The Boy's Treasury of Sports, Pastimes and Recreations.** New York: Austin and Co., 1850.

34. Wagner, H. **Illustriertes Neues Spielbuch.** Leipzig Otto Spamer, 1886.

PICTURE SOURCES

Half title: Sargent, E., **Sargent's Standard First Reader,** Boston: L. Shorey, 1866, p. 20.

Dedication page: Wagner, H., **Illustriertes Neues Spielbuch,** Leipzig: Otto Spamer, 1886, p. 41.

Title page: Moulidars, T. de, **Un Million de Jeux et de Plaisirs,** Paris: Librairie Contemporaine, ca. 1880, p. 315.

Contents page: The Boy's Treasury of Sports, Pastimes and Recreations, New York: Austin and Company, 1850, p. 58.

1. D'Allemagne, H. R., **Sports et Jeux D'Adresse,** Paris: Hachette, ca. 1904, p. 59.

2. **The Girl's Own Book,** Boston: American Stationer's Company, 1837, p. 40.

5. Cf. page 1; p. 197.

6. Cf. contents page; p. 59.

8. Wood, J. G., **The Boy's Modern Playmate,** London: F. Warne and Company, ca. 1890, p. 14.

11. Dilaye, F., **Les Jeux de la Jeunesse,** Paris: Hachette, 1885, p. 302.

12. Cf. dedication page; p. 123.

17. Cf. page 7; p. 43.

18. **Juvenile Games for the Seasons,** Edinborough: Oliver and Boyd, 1823, p. 43.

21. Cf. page 1; p. 119.

22. Cf. dedication page; p. 61.

23. Cf. page 6; p. 40.

24. Champlin, J. D., and Bostwick, A. E., **The Young Folks' Cyclopedia of Games and Sports,** New York: Henry Holt and Company, 1899, p. 51.

25. Ibid: p. 25.

27. Strutt, J., **The Sports and Pastimes of the People of England,** Thomas Tegg and Sons, 1801, p. 96.

28. **Every Boy's Book,** London: Routledge and Company, 1860, p. 36.

47. Cf. dedication page; p. 36.

49. Cf. page 27; p. 267.

50. **(top).** Ibid: p. 271.

50. **(bot.).** Cf. page 1; p. 279.

51. D'Allemagne, H. R., **Récréations et Passe-Temps,** Paris: Hachette, ca. 1903, p. 63.

52. Cf. dedication page; p. 148.

57. **(bot.).** Ibid: p. 148.

58. Cf. page 27; p. 105.

59. **(top).** Cf. contents page; p. 25.

59. **(bot.).** Cf. page 1; p. 171.

60. Cf. half title; p. 65.

61. Cf. dedication page; p. 28.

62. **Cassell's Book of Sports and Pastimes,** London: Cassell, Peter, Galpin and Company, ca. 1880, p. 227.

74. Cf. page 27; p. 96.

75. Cf. page 1; p. 315.

76. (top). Harper's Young People, New York: Harper and Brothers, 1883, p. 380.

76. (bot.). The Nursery Magazine, Boston: L. Shorey, III: 18, June 1868, p. 175.

77. Cf. page 18; p. 122.

78. Cf. page 62; p. 244.

79. (top). Cf. dedication page; p. 149.

79. (bot.). Cf. page 28; p. 17.

80. Cf. dedication page; p. 149.

82. (bot.). Cf. page 62; p. 249.

89. Ibid: p. 245.

91. Cf. page 18; p. 85.

92. Cf. page 1; p. 140.

93. Cf. page 8; p. 177.

100. Cf. page 18; p. 34.

101. Cf. page 8; p. 15.

106. Cf. page 18; p. 124.

108. Cf. dedication page; p. 111.

111. Cf. contents page; p. 65.

116. Cf. dedication page; p. 109.

117. Cf. page 28; p. 5.

119. Cf. page 1; p. 62.

120. Cf. contents page; p. 49.

122. Cf. page 28; p. 28.

124. Cf. dedication page; p. 83.

131. Ibid: p. 123.

136. Ibid: p. 41.

155. **Social Amusements, or Holidays at Aunt Adela's Cottage,** Boston: William Crosby and Company, 1839.

156. Cf. page 76 (bot.); VI, 1869, p. 109.

158. Cf. page 8; p. 189.

204. Cf. page 76 (bot.); IX: 49, 1871, p. 5.

205. Cf. dedication page; p. 123.

219. **The Holiday ABC Book,** no publ., ca. 1850.

220. Cf. page 76 (bot.); XVIII: 3, p. 81.

221. Cf. dedication page; p. 41.

227. Cf. page 26; p. 391.

234. Cf. page 8; p. 14.

240. Cf. page 24; p. 443.

241. Ibid: p. 444.

242. Ibid.

243. Cf. page 51; p. 151.

247. Cf. dedication page; p. 87.

248. Miss Leslie, **American Girl's Book,** Boston: Monroe and Francis, 1851, p. 142.

339. Ibid: p. 320.

340. Cf. contents page; p. viii.

342. **Cabinet des Etampes,** Paris: Bibliothèque Nationale.

343. Cf. p. 27.

NOTE: All other diagrams and illustrations designed by the author.